Mountain Biking Colorado

Help Us Keep This Guide Up to Date

Every effort has been made by the author and editors to make this guide as accurate and use-ful as possible. However, many things can change after a guide is published—trails are rerouted, regulations change, techniques evolve, facilities come under new management, etc.

We would love to hear from you concerning your experiences with this guide and how you feel it could be improved and kept up to date. While we may not be able to respond to all comments and suggestions, we'll take them to heart and we'll also make certain to share them with the author. Please send your comments and suggestions to the following address:

The Globe Pequot Press
Reader Response/Editorial Department
P.O. Box 480
Guilford, CT 06437

Or you may e-mail us at:

editorial@GlobePequot.com

Thanks for your input, and happy trails!

Mountain Biking Colorado

Second Edition

Stephen Hlawaty

FALCON®

GUILFORD, CONNECTICUT
HELENA, MONTANA

AN IMPRINT OF THE GLOBE PEQUOT PRESS

A FALCON GUIDE ®

Photographers: Stephen Hlawaty, Amanda Hlawaty, John
Gray, Jeremy Moore, Peter Boniface

ISBN 0-7627-1225-2

Manufactured in the United States of America
Second Edition/First Printing

Contents

Preface ix

Acknowledgments xiii

Introduction xv

    Getting Around Colorado xvi

    How to Use This Book xviii

    How to Use These Maps xix

The Rides
Northwest 1

   1. Three Forks Trail 3

   2. Chutes and Ladders 9

   3. Troy Built Loop 14

   4. Crag Crest Trail 19

     Honorable Mentions—Northwest

     A. Dinosaur National Monument 25

     B. Tall Pines Trail 26

Southwest 27

   5. Aspen to Buck Trail 29

   6. Deep Creek Trail 35

   7. Wasatch Trail 40

   8. Hermosa Creek Trail 46

   9. Log Chutes Trail 52

 10. Sand Canyon Trail 58

     Honorable Mentions—Southwest

     C. Portland Creek Trail 64

     D. Ute Mountain Ute Tribal Park 64

North Central Mountains 67

 11. Nipple Peak Loop 69

 12. Lower Bear Trail 74

 13. Bockman Campground Loop 80

 14. Hot Springs to Mad Creek to Red Dirt Trail Loop 85

 15. Howelsen Hill Loop 6 91

 16. Arapaho Ridge Trail 97

 17. Base Camp to Mountain View Trail 102

 18. Muddy Slide and Morrison Divide Trails 108

 19. Tipperary Creek Loop 114

     In Addition: Extreme Snow Bikes—Alpine Snow Bicycle Association 120

 20. Grand Traverse and Cougar Ridge Trail 122

     In Addition: The Tenth Mountain Division 128

21. Searle Pass and Kokomo Pass Trail 130

22. Wise Mountain and the Colorado Trail 135

    Honorable Mention—North Central Mountains

    E. Baker's Tank Loop 140

South Central Mountains 141

23. Deer Creek Trail 143

24. Deadman Gulch 149

25. Dyke Trail 155

26. Mount Princeton to Raspberry Gulch 161

27. Bear Creek to Methodist Mountain 167

28. Hartman Rocks 173

29. Monarch Crest Trail 180

30. Wheeler Monument 186

31. Trout Creek Trail 192

32. Zapata Falls 198

33. Cat Creek Trail 203

    In Addition: Colorado's Off-Road Wheelchair Racing 208

    Honorable Mentions—South Central Mountains

    F. Old Midland Railroad Grade 211

    G. Reservoir Hill 212

Front Range 213
   34. Hewlett Gulch 215
   35. Young Gulch 220
   36. Mill Creek Trail 224
   37. House Rock to Pierson Park 230
   38. Sourdough Trail 235
      In Addition: The RTD's Bike-n-Ride Program 240
   39. Walker Ranch Loop 242
   40. White Ranch 247
      In Addition: Mountain Lions 252
   41. The Hogback: Dakota Ridge and Red Rocks Trail 254
   42. Waterton Canyon 259
   43. Kenosha Pass to Georgia Pass 265
   44. Baldy Trail to Gashouse Gulch Trail 270
   45. Jackson Creek Loop 274
   46. Rampart Reservoir Shoreline Loop 279
      In Addition: Huckleberry Bread Pudding 284
   47. Waldo Canyon 285
      In Addition: Composition of "America the Beautiful" 290
   48. Shelf Road 292
      Honorable Mentions—Front Range
      H. Crosier Mountain Loop 297
      I. Deer Haven Ranch 297

Eastern Plains 299
   49. Picketwire Canyonlands 301
      Honorable Mention—Eastern Plains
      J. Pawnee National Grasslands 307

The Great Escape 309
   50. Telluride to Moab: Hut to Hut 310
      Day 1: Telluride to Last Dollar Hut 317
      Day 2: Last Dollar Hut to Spring Creek Hut 321
      Day 3: Spring Creek Hut to Columbine Hut 326
      Day 4: Columbine Hut to Big Creek Cabin 331
      Day 5: Big Creek Cabin to Gateway Hut 336
      Day 6: Gateway Hut to La Sal Hut 341
      Day 7: La Sal Hut to Moab 346

The Art of Mountain Biking
      Mountain Bike Beginnings 353
      Mountain Biking into Shape 354

Be Safe–Know the Law 355
The Mountain Bike Controversy 356
Etiquette of Mountain Biking 357
Trail Maintenance 358
On-the-Spot Quick Fix 359
Rules of the Trail 360
The Necessities of Cycling 361
Be Prepared or Die 361
Be Safe–Wear Your Armor 362
First-Aid Kit 363
Oh, Those Cold Colorado Days 364
To Have or Not to Have—Other Very Useful Items 364
Types of Off-Road Terrain 366
Techniques to Sharpen Your Skills 366
Going Uphill–Climbing Those Treacherous Hills 367
Going Downhill–The Real Reason We Get Up in the Morning ... 368
Watch Out! 368
Last-Minute Check 369

Repair and Maintenance

Fixing a Flat 371
Lubrication Prevents Deterioration 373

Appendix

Bicycle Clubs and Organizations 375
Colorado Festivals 378
Rocky Mountain Colorado Campgrounds 381
Further Reading 389
About the Author 391

Preface

Growing up in New York City, my friends and I took to the streets, the cemeteries, and the railroad tracks with our three- and five-speed Ross, Schwinn, and Huffy bicycles. We'd set up ramps of brick and plywood before "trains" of old metal garbage cans and clear as many of those rusted "cars" as we could. In hindsight, those cemeteries were anything but eternal resting places, and train tracks nothing more than modified singletrack. One thing was certain, we had inherited the earth, albeit of stone and steel, and knew enough to enjoy what had been given to us.

That single truth remained steadfast throughout my years growing up: through weekends camping as a Boy Scout in the cold rain and snow of the Middle Atlantic states, through timeless hours spent chopping wood for the clubhouse in Hawley, Pennsylvania, through many a star-filled night, staring aimlessly into campfires ablaze with the hope and the understanding of my many years to come and of the few that had passed already. And as the flames of my childhood forged the frame of my life, my inheritance took shape and began to grow in the embers of my eyes.

It wasn't until moving to Colorado that I realized the sheer magnitude of this inheritance. Standing in awe before the Rocky Mountains, absorbed in the cool darkness of a 14,000-foot mountain shadow (one of fifty-four), I welcomed Colorado as my new home. And Colorado, for its part, had welcomed me as its newest inheritor, offering me verdant forests larger than the entire state of Maine, 300 miles of Rocky Mountain highs, champagne powder, crashing rivers, lonesome deserts, sprawling grasslands, and the sweetest cantaloupes in the world. But what's always to be remembered, is that this is a shared inheritance. And due courtesy should be given to those who have come before us.

As mountain bikers, we owe much to the original "clunkers" who in 1974 took their modified Schwinn Excelsiors to the top of Mount Tamalpias in Marin County, California, and descended with news of the next great and future king in the way of outdoor recreation. Mountain biking had been born. But although mountain biking was born in California, its soul lives in Colorado. That's not to say, however, that mountain biking is dead. Far from it. Mountain biking has only found itself a heaven on earth in which to lay its tracks.

And nowhere in Colorado do these tracks sink deeper than in the hallowed hills of Crested Butte. As local lore has it, after the summer's forest fire season had ended, local firefighters would return from their mountain posts via their town bicycles, careening down mountain dirt roads at breakneck speeds. One such road led to the top of 12,705-foot Pearl Pass. In the summer of 1976, a crew of motorcyclists from Aspen roared over Pearl Pass and descended upon Crested Butte, commencing to boast about their achievement. Viewing the incident as a cultural invasion and a challenge to their bravado, the firefighters decided to do their Aspen neighbors one better. On a cold September morning, about fifteen of Crested Butte's finest smoke

Returning from an overlook of Wilson Peak along Last Dollar Road.

eaters began their climb of Pearl Pass to Aspen on their town bikes. The tour ended at Aspen's Hotel Jerome, and Colorado mountain biking had been born. Interestingly enough, the same spirit that sparked the birth of mountain biking in Colorado also fueled the flames of the birth of the state.

"Gold! Gold!! Gold!!! Gold!!!! Hard to Get and Heavy to Hold!" read the headlines in 1858 when the valuable metal was discovered along the Platte River at the base of the Rocky Mountains. Within a year, 50,000 emigrants had forced settlers old and new to consider establishing an organized government on the Colorado frontier. "Government of some kind we must have," hailed one new Coloradan, "and the question narrows itself down to this point: Shall it be the government of the knife and the revolver, or shall we unite in forming here in our golden country . . . a new and independent state?"

It is this spirit of independence and, at the same time, a willingness to get along with each other that define the character of the Colorado people. From Colorado's most recent mountain bikers to its earliest settlers, the people of Colorado have learned to adopt and adapt to their changing environments, reinventing what it means to be a Coloradan. It is this spirit that connects Colorado mountain biking irrevocably to the history of this land. And it is this land that invites mountain bikers to share the spirit and accept their inheritance.

Since coming to Colorado, I've past through many centuries, collecting the inheritances of the ages along the way. I've journeyed through a single dinosaur print, one step in North America's longest recorded set of Precambrian dinosaur tracks impressed upon the desert sands of Picketwire Canyon. I've marveled at the thousands-of-years-old ancient Anasazi cliff dwellings carved meticulously within the walls of Sand Canyon. I've passed pioneering homesteads of sod and timber in the dusty, rocky foothills of the Front Range, conscious of why these sod house doors all open inward. I've sat entranced at a farmer's kitchen table, listening to stories of Colorado's strange and sometimes macabre beginnings. I've stopped to spy a bull moose taking his drink from the cool waters of a glacial runoff, and I've bathed nude in the healing hot waters of a natural thermal spring on the Western Slope.

And now, having accepted my rightful place among the riches of our world, I hope to pass this inheritance on to you, making mountain biking the portal through which to feel the power, admire the beauty, and revere the majesty that is Colorado.

Nil Sine Numine ("Nothing Without Providence"—Colorado state motto)

Acknowledgments

As with any creation, this book is born of the workings of many hands, and I remain forever grateful.

Papa, you're a proud, hard-working cabinetmaker and father, and a craftsman of both. "I'm better than most and just as good as some," you'd say—an understatement that has always inspired me to do my best. When book deadlines were freaking me out, you volunteered to relocate from New York City to Colorado to chauffeur me from ride to ride, just to ease the burden of constant driving and then riding. Mama, you're the epitome of good-heartedness. Your support and kindness is forever expressed in your gleaming eyes and loving smile, a vision that will forever brighten my dimmest days. So to my parents, know that any successes I may achieve remain uniquely your own, as is the love with which you've raised me. Thank you.

To Roland and Ingrid, your lifelong achievements have always challenged me. This book testifies to the good that occurs when one is flanked on either side by the greatness that is my older brother and younger sister.

I may never have had the opportunity to write this book had it not been for my mountain biking mentor and good friend John Gray. Always the defender of the struggling artist, John sent me the classified ad for this assignment, enabling my lifelong dream to be realized. Rave on John Gray.

Amber Beyer, you opened your home to me when I was on the road and opened my eyes to the benefits of rice milk and whole grains. Thanks for the meals: They were all nutritious, delicious, and they made me feel so ambitious.

A special thank-you goes to Dave Herz, my boss when I worked as a hod for his stucco crew, for understanding when I had to quit midseason to pursue this project full bore. Facing five inches from the wall, you'll never know the world you've shown me.

Many thanks go out to the city-slicker boys back home—Mark Reinstadler, Paul Iovane, and Michael Iovane—who came to visit me with sea-level lungs, but hung tough on some grueling Rocky Mountain rides.

John Barnes, Curtis Church, Jeremy Moore, Jules Farmer, and Peter Boniface, you guys are tough stuff. Thanks for all the good vibes through a lot of these rides. Pete, after your bout with the La Sals on the hut trip, I really do believe you can take on a bolt of lightning. Thanks also go to Kelly Keim. How 'bout them BV bears?

During the course of my research, I've met many unique individuals who've dedicated themselves to their passions. Thank you Michael Whiting of Wildernet and Team Phoenix for opening my eyes to the bigger picture. Thank you Richard Fischer of Extreme Snow Bikes and the Alpine Snow Bicycle Association for that windy snow ride atop Berthoud Pass. Tim Blumenthal of IMBA, thank you for all your help and insights into the future of Colorado mountain biking. Thank you

Grant Lamont, race-coordinator extraordinaire, for helping me out with the Howelsen Hill map.

I'd like to thank all the strangers that I've met on the trails who, offering to pose for the camera and wait while I diligently took notes, reminded me that a good time shared makes friends of us all.

Thanks to all at Sore Saddle Cyclery in Steamboat Springs who kept my bicycle in great shape.

A respectful bow goes to my old Stumpy—steel is real.

Thank you Scott Adams and Ryan Croxton of Falcon Guides for polishing the blood, sweat, and tears I offered as a finished manuscript.

Of course, my life, and all that it may accomplish, has been forever blessed by the presence of my beautiful wife, Amanda Hlawaty. From the scorching desert sands of Picketwire Canyonlands to soaked sleeping bags in an early autumn snowstorm in Telluride, your confidence and patience during the harried summers of 1998 and 2002 were only equaled by your sense of humor. Thanks for the laughs; your smile will always offer my present unbridled promise for the future.

Lastly, thank you readers and riders for choosing *Mountain Biking Colorado*. I hope you find it to be as good as some and better than most.

Introduction

If variety is the spice of life and mountain biking one of life's appetizers, then Colorado is the cayenne to one of life's spiciest pleasures. Anyone with an appetite for mountain biking will find a feast fit for a king or queen among Colorado's more than 15 million acres of state and national public forestland. With roughly 36 percent of the entire state of Colorado open to public use, yours is left the enviable repast of fine riding.

With forty-four state parks, eight national parks, thirteen national forests and grasslands, and a smattering of national monuments, Colorado offers mountain bikers a veritable smorgasbord of mountain biking terrain, excluding roughly forty wilderness areas of course. But what really sets Colorado apart from other mountain biking venues isn't so much the size of available public lands but, rather, the quality and variety of that land.

Take, for instance, Colorado's Western Slope. To the north lie rolling, sage-filled meadows, high-desert plateaus and buttes, and thick mixed conifer forests. To the south lie the always dramatic and jagged San Juan Mountains, along with the blistering hot deserts near Colorado's Four Corners region. The riding here runs the gamut between high-alpine and high-desert terrain.

Central Colorado may well typify the Colorado mountain experience, since it includes most of the state's major ski resorts, many of which provide lift-accessed mountain biking terrain. Indeed, Winter Park and Crested Butte (birthplace of Colorado mountain biking and home to the Mountain Bike Hall of Fame and Museum) testify to this area's reigning mountain biking supremacy.

Colorado's Front Range includes a region where the mountains meet the Colorado plains. While the mountain bike trails along the Front Range may not be as long as those found in Colorado's interior mountains, they, nevertheless, hold their own unique characteristics. Here, you will find an abundance of steep, rocky, and sandy terrain. Given to the area's predominately exposed terrain, temperatures can well range into the high 90s. A vision-questing mountain biker's dream.

East of the Front Range lie Colorado's sprawling plains where you'll find the Pawnee National Grasslands and the Comanche National Grasslands. Nearly six million settlers traveled west across this onetime thoroughfare as part of the Homestead Act of 1862. The grasslands offer mountain bikers a relatively smooth ride compared to the terrain to the west. Here rides are complemented by the expansive feeling that accompanies seeing where the sky greets the land.

While Colorado provides the flatter, high-plateau mountain biking experience, most of us demand the mountains. In these circles, altitude is everything. And that's good, since Colorado's Rocky Mountains deliver. Fifty-four mountains reach altitudes in excess of 14,000 feet, 300 peaks exceed 13,000 feet, and there are more than 1,000 summits that are higher than 10,000 feet.

Underscoring the variety of rideable terrain is the fact that Colorado enjoys 300 days of annual sunshine. Although volumes can be written about what makes Colorado a great mountain biking venue, proof, as they say, is in the pudding. So enjoy yours.

Getting Around Colorado

Area Codes

Colorado currently has four area codes: The Denver/Boulder metro area uses **303** and **720**. The **719** area code services the greater southeastern part of the state, including Colorado Springs, Pueblo, Buena Vista, and Alamosa. The **970** area code services the northern Front Range and Eastern Plains, as well as the Western Slope, extending north from Steamboat Springs to Durango and Cortez.

Roads

For current information on statewide weather and road conditions and closures, contact the **Colorado Department of Transportation** (CDOT) at the toll free hotline, (877) 315–ROAD. Denver metro area and out-of-state callers can still access the hotline by calling (303) 639–1111. The same information can also be found by visiting CDOT's Web site at www.dot.state.co.us.

By Air

Denver International Airport (DIA) is 23 miles northeast of downtown Denver. Along with servicing the majority of flights into Colorado, Denver International also links flights throughout the global village. For more information, contact its Web site at www.flydenver.com.

Roughly 60 miles south of Denver lies the **Colorado Springs Airport** (COS), which serves the southern half of the Front Range and Eastern Plains. For more information, contact its Web site at www.flycos.com.

Servicing the northwestern towns of Steamboat Springs and Hayden, the **Yampa Valley Airport** (HDN) can be reached at (970) 276–3669.

The **Walker Field Airport** (GJT) in Grand Junction services Colorado and Eastern Utah. Walker Field Airport features commercial carrier service with more than twenty daily departures to Denver, Phoenix, and Salt Lake City and over 500 one-stop connections to cities in the United States, Canada, Europe, and Central America. For more information, check out its Web site at www.walkerfield.com.

The **Durango–La Plata County Airport** lies 14 miles southeast of Durango and is served by five airlines: United Express, from Denver; America West Express, with non-stop service to Phoenix; American Eagle, with flights to Dallas–Fort Worth; Continental Express, providing daily service to Houston; and Rio Grande Airlines in and out of Albuquerque. For more information, contact its Web site at co.laplata.co.us/airport.html.

To book reservations online, check out your favorite airline's Web site or search one of the following travel sites for the best price: www.cheaptickets.com, www.expedia.com, www.previewtravel.com, www.priceline.com, www.travel.yahoo.com, www.travelocity.com, www.trip.com, or www.orbitz.com—just to name a few.

Most major airlines will carry your bicycle for a fee that varies between $50.00 and $90.00.

By Rail

Amtrak has two routes that travel through Colorado daily. The **California Zephyr** travels between Chicago and Oakland via Fort Morgan, Denver, Winter Park, Granby, Glenwood Springs, and Grand Junction. The stations in Grand Junction, Glenwood Springs, and Denver have checked baggage service, and it costs $12.00 to carry a bike. The **Southwest Chief** travels between Chicago and Los Angeles via Lamar, La Junta, and Trinidad.

For more details, call (800) 872–7245 or visit www.amtrak.com for more information.

By Bus

Greyhound serves most cities in Colorado and the major ski resorts along Interstate 70 and U.S. Highway 40. Greyhound will carry boxed bikes for $15.00, and boxes are available at most major terminals for $10.00. Call Greyhound at (800) 231–2222 or visit www.greyhound.com for more information.

Roaring Fork Transit (RFTA) runs frequent service from Glenwood Springs to Aspen, making it a convenient connection with Amtrak and Greyhound. Each (RFTA) bus has a bike rack that carries four bikes; the cost is $2.00 per bike. For more information, check out the Web site at www.rfta.com.

Denver/Boulder Regional Transportation District (RTD) serves Boulder and Metro Denver from downtown and the airport. There is a free permit for light rail trains, and no permit required for buses. All buses carry bicycles. Bikes are allowed on off-peak light rail trains, but a permit is required. There are bike lockers located at more than thirty different locations. For more information contact Ken Epperson at (303) 299–2223. All RTD buses carry bicycles.

For more information, check out the Web site www.bikemap.com/transit/co.htm for links to local bus services that carry bikes.

Shuttles

From **Denver International Airport,** taxicabs, charters, and luxury limousines can deliver you to almost any Colorado location by prior arrangements. Check the Denver International Airport Web site at www.flydenver.com/z106.html for a detailed listing of all available shuttle options.

Visitor Information

For general information on Colorado, visit the official Web site of Colorado travel: www.colorado.com. The site contains a wealth of vacation information.

Visitors to Colorado can find vacation information, free state maps and brochures, and clean restrooms at **Colorado's Welcome Centers.** Colorado's Welcome Centers are located near most of the major highways entering Colorado. For more information, contact their Web site at www.state.co.us/data2/fs/welcome.htm.

How to Use This Book

Stuffed with plenty of useful Colorado-specific information, *Mountain Biking Colorado* features fifty mapped and cued rides and ten honorable mentions, as well as everything from advice on getting into shape to tips on mountain bike camping and getting the most out of cycling with your dog.

What You'll Find in This Guide

Each region begins with a Section Intro where you're given a sweeping look at the lay of the land. To aid in quick decision making, we then start each featured ride within each region with a Ride Summary. These short summaries give you a taste of the adventures that will be featured in the section. You'll learn about the trail terrain and what surprises each route has to offer. If your interest is piqued, look further into the ride and read more. If not, skip to the next ride in the region.

Now to the individual chapter. The ride specs are fairly self-explanatory. Here you'll find the quick, nitty-gritty details of the ride: where the trailhead is located, ride length, approximate riding time, difficulty rating, type of trail terrain, who to contact about the ride, when the ride is open, any fees or permits needed, maps you should take along, the nearest town, what other trail users you may encounter, and if dogs are permitted. Our Getting There section gives you dependable directions from a nearby city right down to where you'll want to park. The Ride Description is the meat of the chapter. Detailed and honest, it's the author's carefully researched impression of the trail. Although it's impossible to cover everything, you can rest assured that we won't miss what's important. In our Miles and Directions section we provide mileage cues to identify all turns and trail name changes, as well as points of interest. Between this and our Route Map, you simply can't get lost. The Ride Information box contains more useful information, including local sources of information, local events and attractions and restaurants in the area. We'll also tell you where to stay, what to eat, and what else to see while you're riding in the area.

The Honorable Mentions section details additional rides in each region that will inspire you to get out and explore.

How to Use These Maps

Regional Location Map

This map helps you find your way to the start of each ride from the nearest sizeable town or city. Coupled with the detailed directions at the beginning of the cue, this map should visually lead you to where you need to be for each ride.

Profile Map

This helpful profile gives you a cross-sectional look at the ride's ups and downs. Elevation is labeled on the left in feet, mileage is indicated on the top. Road and trail names are shown along the route, with towns and points of interest labeled in bold.

Route Map

This is your primary guide to each ride. It shows all of the accessible roads and trails, points of interest, water, towns, land-marks, and geographical features. It also distinguishes trails from roads, and paved roads from unpaved roads. The selected route is highlighted, and directional arrows point the way. Shaded topographic relief in the background gives you an accurate representation of the terrain and landscape in the ride area.

The Maps

We don't want anyone, by any means, to feel restricted to just the roads and trails that are mapped here. We hope you will have an adventurous spirit and use this guide as a platform to dive into Colorado's backcountry and discover new routes for yourself. One of the simplest ways to begin this is to just turn the map upside down and ride the course in reverse. The change in perspective is fantastic and the ride should feel quite different. With this in mind, it will be like getting two distinctly different rides on each map.

For your own purposes, you may wish to copy the directions for the course onto a small sheet to help you while riding, or photocopy the map and cue sheet to take with you. These pages can be folded into a bike bag or stuffed into a jersey pocket. Just remember to slow or even stop when you want to read the map.

Symbol	Name	Symbol	Name	Symbol	Name
5	Interstate Highway	Airfield		Golf Course	
8	U.S. Highway	Airport		Hiking Trail	
3	State Road	Bike Trail		Mine	
23	County Road	No Bikes		Overlook	
45	Forest Road	Boat Launch		Picnic	
	Paved Road	Bridge		Parking	
	Paved Bike Lane	Bus Stop		Quarry	
	Maintained Dirt Road	Campground		Radio Tower	
	Unmaintained Jeep Trail	Campsite		Rock Climbing	
	Singletrack Trail	Canoe Access		School	
	Highlighted Route	Cattle Guard		Shelter	
	Ntl Forest/County Boundaries	Cemetery		Spring	
	State Boundaries	Church		Swimming	
	Railroad Tracks	Covered Bridge		Train Station	
	Power Lines	Direction Arrows		Wildlife Refuge	
	Special Trail	Downhill Skiing		Vineyard	
	Rivers or Streams	Fire Tower		Most Difficult	
	Water and Lakes	Forest HQ		Difficult	
	Marsh	4WD Trail		Moderate	
		Gate		Easy	

Northwest

Colorado's northwest corner is distinguished by rolling, sage-filled ranchland, high-desert plateaus and buttes, river-carved gorges, sandy deserts, and green, mountainous forests. Since the northwest is Colorado's most remote region, it's no surprise that the area west of the town of Craig to the town of Dinosaur is home to some of the few remaining wild horse herds in the country. Here, the open, sage-filled meadows and rolling hills provide ample room to roam for horses and riders alike. Lying 3 miles east of the Colorado-Utah border, Dinosaur, Colorado, is gateway to Dinosaur National Monument. The monument's Dinosaur Quarry building, located 7 miles north of Jensen, Utah, allows you to observe real dinosaur bones extracted from a cliff face. The monument's 210,000 acres deliver spectacular canyon country views. The high-clearance, four-wheel-drive road (Echo Road), which leads to Echo Park, confluence of the Green and Yampa Rivers, is a must ride, offering stellar canyon scenery.

Lying to the southeast of Dinosaur National Monument, White River National Forest offers this region its only high-alpine relief. South of Glenwood Springs, home to the world's largest hot springs pool, the Tall Pines Trail travels from the town of Carbondale to the town of Redstone. These towns provide a down-to-earth atmosphere separate from the glitz and glitter of their neighboring town of Aspen. In the 1910s, Carbondale was a dominant producer of potatoes, whose legacy continues today in its annual Potato Festival, held each October. In the 1960s, Redstone's beehive-like brick ovens, once used to turn coal into coke, were used as living quarters for resident hippies.

As one travels west from Glenwood Springs along Interstate 70, one passes the little-known town of Rifle. Just north of Rifle, on Colorado Highway 325, lies the Rifle Gap State Recreation Area and White River National Forest. As well as the rugged Three Forks Trail, this area includes some of America's finest technical climbing routes. West of Rifle is the small town of Palisade. Here local farmers sell some of the world's sweetest peaches at roadside stands. Continuing west, mountains give way to mesas, buttes, and deserts.

The Grand Mesa, near Grand Junction, is one of the world's largest flat-topped mountains. In sharp contrast to the surrounding deserts below, the Grand Mesa boasts more than 200 lakes. To the north of Grand Junction, the town of Fruita delivers incredible singletrack along the moonscaped terrain of the Book Cliffs. John

Wesley Powell, the first successful Colorado River explorer, named these cliffs after he noticed that they looked like edges of bound books standing in a row. This geological library stretches over 150 miles to Price, Utah. While visiting Fruita, don't miss an opportunity to see the Colorado National Monument. This 20,000-acre landscape includes incredibly sculptured spires and crags that create a perfect backdrop to a day's bicycling tour on Rim Rock Drive. Rattlesnake Canyon, home to the world's second (to Moab) largest group of natural stone arches, is also a must see.

1 Three Forks Trail

Since this is a very remote and seldom used trail, wildlife and signs of wildlife are abundant. Mule deer, elk, black bear, and beavers are all present. The trail parallels the mellow Three Forks Creek—though that's not to say these waters haven't seen their fare share of activity. There are more than thirty beaver dams constructed along the creek. Enjoy excellent fishing, with brook trout averaging nine to eleven inches. Rainbow and brown trout can also be found. On your ride, you'll see aspen, sub-alpine fir, spruce, oak brush, serviceberry, and willows along the banks of the creek. The trail starts at 7,500 feet and rises to 9,257 feet.

Start: From the Three Forks Trail trailhead in White River National Forest.
Length: 11.2-mile out-and-back, with options to extend into a loop.
Approximate riding time: Advanced riders, 1.5 to 2 hours; intermediate riders, 2.5 to 3 hours.
Technical difficulty: Technically easy to moderate. Although most of this trail rolls over smooth singletrack, much of the singletrack, particularly as you near the top, is overgrown, making for a limited field of vision.
Physical difficulty: Physically moderate due to its elevation gain and steeper sections near the top.
Terrain: Singletrack. The trail rolls over hilly terrain, through dense conifer and aspen forests, and past many beaver ponds. The trail is remote and sees little traffic, owing primarily to its severely overgrown segments. With a variety of creeks in the area, there are a few muddy sections.

Trail contacts: City of Rifle Parks and Recreation Department, P.O. Box 1908 Rifle, 81650; (970) 625-2151.
White River National Forest Rifle Ranger District, 0094 County Road 244, Rifle, 81650; (970) 625-2371.
Blanco Ranger District, 317 East Market Street, Meeker, 81641; (970) 878-4039.
Schedule: Late June to October.
Fees and Permits: $4.00 for daily entrance fee into Rifle Mountain Park; $10.00 for overnight camping.
Maps: USGS maps: Triangle Park; *Trails Illustrated* map 125; White River National Forest Map.
Nearest town: Rifle.
Other trail users: Campers, hikers, anglers, hunters, and picnickers.
Canine compatibility: Dog friendly.

Getting There

From Glenwood Springs: Drive west on I-70 for 25 miles to exit 90. Bear right onto Colorado Highway 13, heading north. Drive through Rifle on CO 13 and continue out of Rifle for 0.75 mile before intersecting County Road 325. Bear right onto CR 325 and follow the signs for Rifle State Park. Pass Rifle Gap Park and Rifle Falls State Park on your way to Rifle Mountain Park. After passing a large trout hatchery, CR 325 turns to dirt and becomes CR 217. Cross a cattle guard and continue through the White River National Forest where CR 217 turns into Forest Road 832. Once in the forest, continue straight on FR 832 to its fork with FR 825. The right fork (FR 825) leads through a narrow canyon to Triangle Park. Bear left and drive for another 0.25 mile before parking your vehicle at the Three Forks Trailhead. *DeLorme: Colorado Atlas & Gazetteer: Page 34, B-4.*

The Ride

The town of Rifle received its name logically enough. In the mid-nineteenth century, a party of explorers traveled roughly 190 miles from Denver to Colorado's Western Slope. Upon reaching the junction of a small creek and the Colorado River (then called the Grand River), the party found an old rifle leaning against the trunk of a tree. The rest, as they say, is history. Located at the intersection of I–70 and Colorado Highway 13, Rifle has somehow staved off the endless hordes of Colorado summer vacationers. I–70 motorists, in their 80-miles-per-hour dash to get to either Grand Junction or Vail or beyond, often shoot right past the little town. What they don't know is that rivers run deep in Rifle, rivers whose undercurrents have attracted serious high-country players for some time.

Surrounded by the White River National Forest, Rifle is home to some first-class hunting (Rifle is home to the world's largest mule deer herd), fishing, spelunking, camping, rock climbing, and mountain biking. A fifteen-minute drive north of Rifle delivers you to the Rifle Gap Reservoir, where gold-medal fishing takes center stage.

One of the trail's more overgrown sections.

The Harvey Gap Reservoir, east of the Rifle Gap, is one of the West's premier wind-surfing destinations. Four miles north of the Rifle Gap is Rifle Falls State Park, which features a spectacular 60-foot triple waterfall. The falls' moss-covered lime-stone walls invite spelunkers to delve deep into the 90-foot cave behind its watery veil. But perhaps the most significant outdoor activity to emerge from Rifle in recent years is rock climbing.

Following County Road 325 east, past Rifle Falls State Park, you enter Rifle Mountain State Park, a 400-acre, 2.5-mile-long stretch of towering limestone canyon walls. Prior to 1991, Rifle Mountain Park was the locals' private stash. The park's riparian ecosystem provided cool relief from the summer temperatures of the Western Slope's lower elevations. Only a handful of climbers knew of the park's climbing potential. Rifle local Mark Tarrant and his Denver pal Richard Wright were among some of the first to climb the park's walls for sport. Together, Tarrant and Wright laid what many climbing faithfuls believe to be the first route in Rifle: "Rumor Has It . . . ." Rumor had it, indeed, and word spread fast throughout Colorado climbing circles that Rifle was the hot new ticket.

Owing to its easy access, proliferation of climbing routes, and classic limestone features, Rifle Mountain State Park has quickly become one of America's premier climbing destinations. Although most of the park's climbing routes are reserved for top-level athletes, there are a number of moderate and easy routes to be had, most of which are located above the park's ice caves. With access to these caves provided by the "Ice Age Trail," Rifle climbers, hikers, and mountain bikers are never too far from staying cool.

Like the ice caves, Colorado's mystique depends in large part on its secret stashes, those places that, for one reason or another, remain hidden from the rest of the world. These climbing routes, powder fields, and mountain bike trails may never get used, except by the few who know where the stashes are kept. Three Forks Trail is one such stash.

The hard-packed, smooth singletrack of Three Forks Trail quickly gives way to the rough-and-tumble ways of a secret stash that has yet to be smoothed over by the masses. Heading in a northwesterly direction, the trail snakes its way through mixed conifer forests, meadows, aspen groves, and creeks on its way to Forest Road 211. As the trail climbs steadily, you can't help but notice the disintegration of the singletrack. Nothing short of Jedi training could keep you from bonking once or twice on this severely overgrown trail. Once you arrive at the Three Forks and Tangle Gulch intersection, even the Force can't help you.

The remoteness of the trail is really made apparent after passing a variety of beaver ponds. These ponds mark the spot beyond which big game most likely fre-quent. Riding through a miniature berry bush forest, one recognizes the flattened vegetation of the forest. There seems to be no rhyme or reason as to why certain areas of the forest would be flattened, that is, until one realizes that these areas of forest are bedding for big game. Were it not for the trail's limited use, these big game animals would probably be more comfortable some distance from any trail, as opposed to directly beside it. After passing these beds of elk, mule deer, and bear, you begin your final push to the top through a magical stand of aspen. As you slowly crank through this stand, you should notice the "bear trees" among the aspen. "Bear trees" are those scarred by the teeth and claws of bears. These scars can be 8 to 10 feet high (as high as a bear can reach standing on its hind legs) on any tree.

Having climbed through these aspens unscathed, take in the views of the Flat Tops Wilderness Area to the north, home to Colorado's largest herd of elk. After riding through the meadow, you'll arrive at a grouping of twelve aspens on your left—one of which will have "Alijandro" carved into it—beside the trail marker for 2150. From here the trail descends through another little ravine to its connection with FR 211. From FR 211, either return the way you came or bear right onto FR 211 to Triangle Park, intercepting FR 825 back to your vehicle.

Should you want to ride this as an out-and-back, the return descent from the meadow is very fast, bumpy, and overgrown. Since the trail itself can barely be seen in spots, the descent can be tricky. Many little bumps and holes in the trail are difficult to detect at high speeds. One thing to be cautious of is the skewer to your front tire. Be sure that it's locked (folded) to the back of the bicycle, not toward the front, as thick vegetation, coupled with a speedy descent, may cause the skewer to open and release your front tire.

Once you intersect with the Coulter Lake/Guest Ranch Trail for the second time, you can either bear right onto the Coulter Lake/Guest Ranch Trail and include a mini loop in your out-and-back ride, or you can simply continue descending on Three Forks Trail back to your vehicle.

Miles and Directions

0.0 START at the Three Forks Trail 2150 Trailhead.

0.4 Bear right. Cross Three Forks Creek via a wooden footbridge, and Stump Gulch. Climb from the creek and continue riding through a dense pine forest, with the creek to your left.

1.4 The singletrack forks. Bear left and cross Garden Gulch.

1.7 The trail cuts sharply to the north (right), around a rocky section of trail. Bear right here, crossing GV Creek and Irish Gulch.

2.3 Three Forks Trail 2150 intersects with Coulter Lake/Guest Ranch Trail. Continue riding straight.

2.4 Cross Trappers Gulch and continue riding in a westerly direction, bushwhacking over severely overgrown trail.

3.3 After crossing a small creek, Three Forks Trail 2150 intersects with Tangle Gulch Trail. Bear right here, following signs for Three Forks Trail and Hoover Gulch. Ride in an easterly direction through tall stands of pine.

4.0 After passing the beaver ponds on your right and crossing a small creek, the trail forks again. The left fork is a game trail. Take the right fork, heading in an easterly direction. Climb steadily through the drainage and onto the crest of the mountain, Little Hill.

4.7 The trail tops out into a large meadow, surrounded on all sides by tall stands of aspen. Head in a northerly direction through this meadow. The Flat Tops Wilderness Area should come into view.

5.6 Three Forks Trail intersects with FR 211 (Bar HL Road). Turn around here and return the way you came. **Option:** For a longer loop, bear right onto FR 211 and head to Triangle Park. From Triangle Park, descend down the four-wheel-drive road of FR 825 to its intersection with the Three Forks. Note: The longer, looped version of this ride can be done in the opposite direction as well, starting your ride by climbing FR 825 to Triangle Park and FR 211 to the Three Forks Trail. This option will have you descending the singletrack of Three Forks Trail to your vehicle.

11.2 Arrive at your vehicle.

Ride Information

Local Information

Rifle Chamber of Commerce, P.O. Box 809, Rifle, 81650; (970) 625-2085 or (800) 842-2085.

City of Rifle, 202 Railroad Avenue, P.O. Box 1902, Rifle, 81650; (970) 625-2121.

Local Events and Attractions

Flat Tops Trail Scenic Byway, Meeker; (970) 879-4039.

The Roan Cliffs, Rifle; (970) 625-2085 or (800) 842-2085.

Rifle Gap State Park, Rifle; (970) 625-1607; www.dnr.state.co.us/parks.

Rifle Falls State Park, Rifle; (970) 625-1607; www.dnr.state.co.us/parks.

Glenwood Hot Springs, Glenwood Springs; (970) 945-7131.

Rifle Rendezvous, in May, Rifle; (970) 625-2085 or (800) 842-2085 (providing a taste of the Old West with an old-fashioned shoot out, tribal dancing, and other events).

Garfield County Fair, in August, Rifle; (970) 625-2085 or (800) 842-2085.

2 Chutes and Ladders

Chutes and Ladders is a long-time favorite of Fruita mountain bikers. Recalling the ups and downs of the old childhood board game, Chutes and Ladders offers a technically rolling romp over some of the best slickrock outside of Moab, Utah. The ride offers many short climbs and descents over slickrock and through sand. It delivers one of the smoothest and narrowest sections of singletrack in all of Colorado. After negotiating the rocky terrain of the Book Cliffs, the tireless rider is rewarded with a fast and straight singletrack shot through a cow pasture—smooth as butter.

Start: From the Chutes and Ladders Trailhead.
Length: 8.1-mile loop.
Approximate riding time: Advanced riders, 1 hour; intermediate riders, 2 hours.
Technical difficulty: Technically challenging due to its steeper climbs and descents and a variety of switchbacks.
Physical difficulty: Physically moderate to challenging due to the variety of terrain: sometimes flat and rolling, other times steep.
Terrain: Singletrack. The terrain rolls over hilly slickrock and sand and through open pasture.

Trail contacts: Over the Edge, 202 East Aspen, Fruita, 81521; (800) 873-3068; www.gj.net/~edge.
Schedule: April to November.
Maps: USGS maps: Ruby Lee Reservoir; *Trails Illustrated* map #208; Fruita Fat Tire Guide map.
Nearest town: Fruita.
Other trail users: Hikers and cows.
Canine compatibility: Dog friendly.

Getting There

From downtown Fruita: Drive east on Aspen Avenue, passing the Civic Center on your left. Turn north (left) onto Maple Street by two stone churches. Drive 4 miles north on Maple Street, which eventually turns into County Road 17.5. Before arriving at a sharp left curve, turn right onto CR N&3/10. County Road N&3/10 comes to a T intersection. At the T, turn left onto CR 18. (The rides in this area are more commonly referred to as located in the "18 Road Area" and the "Book Cliffs.") Drive 7 miles on CR 18, then notice a parking lot pull-out to your left. Park here and begin your ride on the singletrack located across the road. *DeLorme: Colorado Atlas & Gazetteer:* Page 42, C-3.

The Ride

For years, mountain bikers en route to Moab, Utah, would blaze right past Fruita (one of the last towns before entering Utah) without so much as a tip of the hat. What these slickrock- and arch-crazed mountain bikers failed to realize is that Fruita has the second largest concentration of natural arches in the world, not to mention miles of boundless slickrock and access to one of the most incredibly beautiful high-desert mountain biking trails. It's a wonder Fruita hasn't received the recognition

Moab has. But the tides are turning for Fruita as mountain bikers discover the juicy rides that abound in the area.

Named after the fruit trees that William Pabor envisioned planting when he founded the town in 1884, Fruita, with its 5,000 residents, is a growing agricultural center and a gateway to a number of recreational adventures. From its noteworthy fossil discoveries to its designation as the main entrance to the Colorado National Monument, Fruita has earned its place in Colorado's rich recreational and historical heritage.

The Colorado National Monument, Fruita's leading attraction, superbly illustrates the effects of a billion years of erosion: spindrift of blasting tidal seas, spiraling sands, windswept freshwater lakes, sinking swamps, and quaking ground. The 4,000-vertical-foot drive from the valley floor through the sandstone strata via the Rim Rock Drive literally shows you the history of the earth. The Colorado National Monument offers the widest variety of color found in any desert: towering red sandstone, 12-million-year-old coke ovens, stands of green juniper and piñon, and blooming yellow cacti and red Indian paintbrush. It stands to reason that John Otto, fearing the arrival of settlers in the area, petitioned Congress in 1900 to preserve this venerable place. Congress would eventually concede, and in 1911 President Taft officially designated the 32-mile plot as a national monument.

In case you didn't realize it, this is dinosaur country, and the town of Fruita boasts one of the most interactive learning centers for the study of dinosaurs, the 26,000-square-foot Devil's Canyon Science and Learning Center. The annual Fat Tire Festival in late April also brings attention to Fruita. Riders from all over the country come to compete in the four-day event. The festival welcomes riders of all abilities. Commemorative T-shirts, guidebooks, pasta dinners, parties, live music, and prizes await festival goers. The event has become quite a hit among Fruitans, providing not only amusement but also a boon to the local economy. The festival is also another way of introducing cyclists to the mountain bike trails that abound in this "Grand Valley."

One such trail, Chutes and Ladders, is a favorite among Fruita locals, and for good reason. The trail runs along the Grand Valley's northern edge, bordered entirely by the Book Cliffs. This continuous band of stark adobe cliffs and ridges runs west into Utah and bears a striking resemblance to books on a shelf. The first European settlers in the Grand Valley recognized the region's grazing potential. In the early days, cattlemen had an almost exclusive hold on the land, but as word got out, sheepmen started to arrive. Having lost much of their lands to the newly arrived sheep, the cattlemen decided to take action. The finer details of their action are still a matter of debate. Some say the cattlemen simply drove the sheep over the Book Cliffs, others say they clubbed and threw them over. Regardless, the sheep ended up dead at the bottom of the cliffs. A battle broke out between the cattlemen and the sheepmen. What resulted was legislation, the Rees-Odland Act, which permanently outlined the government's grazing rights. Today, cattle and sheep happily graze together—no hard feelings. As for the ranchers, today's herds are often managed by the same rancher.

Aside from this bit of historical controversy, what makes this area a great place to ride is its first-rate singletrack. Chutes and Ladders offers mountain bikers continuous,

Hanging it tight around some rocky singletrack.

fast, smooth-running singletrack, as well as rocky and sandy singletrack. The first 2 miles of the ride (Prime Cut) offer riders a chance to warm up. The smooth-running singletrack winds its way north, gradually ascending a small valley. With many ups and downs, the trail winds through a thick juniper forest. Visions of trolls and leprechauns come to mind as you wind your way through this Enchanted Forest. After ducking and dodging a number of low-lying branches, you come to your first real technical spot at mile 1.9. The singletrack swings right and immediately drops you into a small washout before a big rock. You have to climb out of the washout and over the rock to continue to the Book Cliffs. Here it's best that you keep your speed (as is usually the case) and pick the line directly in the center of the rock. Avoid the line to the left, as a tricky juniper branch waits to close-line.

By the end of the 2 miles, your heart rate has melded with the rhythm of the trail, vacillating from highs to lows—just in time to climb a series of three pitches. Atop these pitches you'll gain a better insight as to how Chutes and Ladders derived its name. Look to the west and you'd swear you were in the Sahara. From here, a singletrack descent awaits, as you plunge into rocky valleys via even rockier and tighter singletrack. The slope of the trail is very precipitous. Pedal against the adverse camber of the trail as you try to negotiate some tight switchbacks. Once out of the Book Cliffs section, you're treated to some sweet singletrack, described in some riding circles as "like butta." Don't knock it till you mock it. From here it's more of the same.

Miles and Directions

0.0 START at the parking lot and the trailhead for Prime Cut, which eventually leads you to Chutes and Ladders.

0.1 Arrive at a cow pond. The loop ends here. Bear left and continue on the smooth and tight singletrack, as it winds its way along the west slope of a small drainage.

1.3 Arrive at another cow pond. Ride right, around it, continuing on the singletrack.

2.2 The trail forks. This marks the beginning of Chutes and Ladders, at the base of the Book Cliffs. (Bearing left here will lead you to the dirt road and back to your vehicles, the short loop of Chutes and Ladders or Prime Cut.) Bearing right brings you to the main Chutes and Ladders Trail. Before you lie three deceptively steep climbs. Now on Chutes and Ladders, the trail crosses four drainages. Stay left at any junctions.

3.5 Sweet singletrack begins, running smooth and fast across a grassy knoll. Views of the Grand Mesa are to your left. Here's the place to hammer down.

5.0 Arrive at the Edge Loop Junction. Don't ride beyond the fence. Bear right onto singletrack running parallel with the fence. This singletrack returns you to the first cow pond you passed and ultimately to your vehicle.

8.1 Return to the parking lot.

Ride Information

Local Information

Bureau of Land Management, Grand Junction Field Office, 2815 H Road, Grand Junction, 81506; (970) 244–3000.
Colorado Welcome Center, I–70 at exit 19, Fruita, 81521; (970) 858–9335.

Local Events and Attractions

The Annual Fruita Fat Tire Festival, late April, Fruita; (800) 873–3068.

Colorado National Monument, Fruita; (970) 858–3617.
Devil's Canyon Science/Learning Center, Fruita; (970) 858–7282.

Organizations

Colorado Plateau Mountain Bike Trail Association (COPMOBA), P.O. Box 4602, Grand Junction, 81502; (970) 241–9561.

3 Troy Built Loop

The Troy Built Loop, named in honor of its builder, is an addition to the famed Kokopelli Trail, which links Grand Junction, Colorado, to Moab, Utah, via a mountain bike trail. This loop delivers some tough climbing on narrow and rocky singletrack. Views of the Grand Valley are spectacular. Some of the riding involves speedy descents along the edge of Rabbit Valley—one hell-of-a-long-way down. Once at the top of Mack Ridge, however, it's a speedy wide doubletrack back to your vehicle. The views atop Mack Ridge offer distant sights of Utah, the Grand Mesa, and the entire Grand Valley.

Start: From parking lot, just 1 mile west of exit 11, off of I–70 on dirt road.

Length: 6.3-mile loop.

Approximate riding time: Advanced riders, 1 hour; intermediate riders, 2 hours.

Technical difficulty: Technically moderate to challenging due to its rocky and narrow climbs and fast and open descents.

Physical difficulty: Physically challenging due to its steeper, rocky climbs.

Terrain: Singletrack, doubletrack, jeep road, and some slickrock. The trail travels over arid and rocky terrain, skirting, at times, precipitous canyon edges.

Trail contacts: Over the Edge, 202 East Aspen, Fruita, 81521; (800) 873-3068; www.gj.net/~edge.

Schedule: April to November.

Maps: USGS maps: Ruby Canyon; *Trails Illustrated* map 208; Fruita Fat Tire Guide; Kokopelli's Trail: Grand Junction/Fruita Area Loops Map.

Nearest town: Fruita.

Other trail users: Motorcyclist, hikers, four-wheelers, campers, and equestrians.

Canine compatibility: Dog friendly. Although short in terms of mileage, this trail can get very hot, so bring plenty of water for the pooch.

Getting There

From Fruita: Drive 8.3 miles west on I–70 to the town of Mack, exit 11. From the exit ramp in Mack, make a left under I–70 and head for the steep dirt road straight ahead. Cross the cattle guard and bear right, now heading west. You will immediately notice a parking lot. Here is where most descriptions of this ride will suggest that you start. I suggest otherwise. Continue driving west along the dirt road, passing this parking lot, for approximately 1 mile. After driving about 1 mile on this dirt road, you will notice a parking lot pull off. Park here. *DeLorme: Colorado Atlas & Gazetteer:* Page 42, C-1 to C-2

The Ride

The Troy Built Loop is part of a series of loops along Kokopelli Trail. Its completion marks the final leg of the 26.9-mile Grand Loop, which along with the Troy Built Loop includes Lion's Loop (7.8 miles) and Mary's Loop (12.8 miles). The

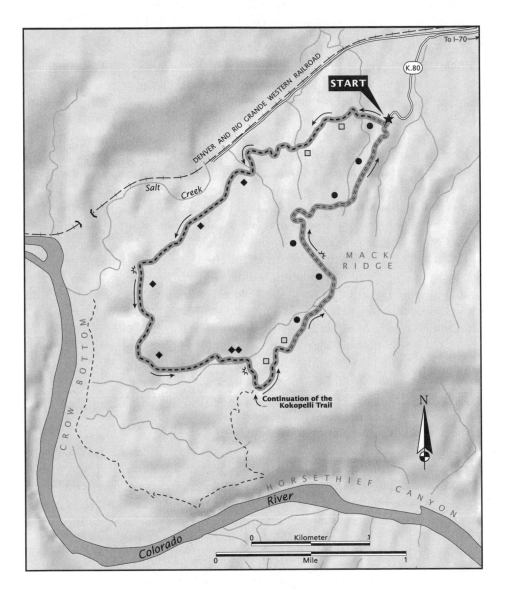

Grand Loop is a chain of three trails whose highest points intersect with the Kokopelli Trail. The route is a tribute to the hard-working mountain biking community of the Grand Valley. Of the three loops, the Troy Built Loop, due to its quality singletrack and incredible Colorado River views, is quite possibly the best. Located in the Grand Loop's northernmost section, the Troy Built Loop offers dazzling views and technical singletrack.

Although most descriptions of this trail will advise you to ride in a clockwise direction—beginning by climbing 560-foot Mack Ridge and riding down the incredible singletrack—this description advises you to begin counterclockwise. The singletrack is such that you can be challenged by its climb without being frustrated by its futility. In other words, although very challenging, the singletrack climb is ridable. All too often, trail descriptions overlook the challenges of a technical singletrack climb, opting rather to describe a trail's technical singletrack descent. The singletrack to the Troy Built Loop offers lovers of the climb a chance to strut their stuff, while allowing those who'd rather go down to see the world as others see it.

Beginning with a short singletrack descent, the trail soon transforms itself into a rigorously rocky climb. Scrambling over loose rock and dirt for 3 miles, you'll eventually arrive at the trail's trickiest section. Here the singletrack enters a short, technical descent into a sandstone creek bottom. Be patient here. Keep your speed, as this section of trail requires a couple of swift moves before hitting the last big drop off. If at first you don't succeed, give it another shot—that is, as long as you're not shot. Cairns mark the way of the trail along this creek bottom.

After this section, the toughest part of the climb begins before reaching a doubletrack at 4.0 miles. After having reached the rim, which overlooks Crow Bottom and the junction of Salt Creek and the Colorado River, relish the thought of your technical climb accomplished.

From the top of Mack Ridge, notice the rise of the 11,234-foot Grand Mesa to the east and its smaller neighbor of the Colorado Plateau, Mount Garfield. Although the Grand Mesa looms toweringly over this "Grand Valley," its 11,234-foot shadow isn't what enshrouds Mount Garfield in mysterious darkness. Rather, it's the tales told by weary locals of the deaths that have occurred in its toxic gas-filled mines of old. Like lemmings, curious adventurers and miners have succumbed to the noxious fumes emanating from this one-time coal mine.

Before spooking yourself for too long, rip down the remaining 1.3 miles to your vehicle, rounding off the Troy Built Loop and part of the Kokopelli Trail. All told, the Kokopelli Trail includes 140 miles of isolated, backcountry four-wheel-drive roads, slickrock, and singletrack. Running from Loma, Colorado, to Moab, Utah, the Kokopelli Trail was originally used by the Anasazi Indians ("Ancient Ones") as a migration route through the Colorado Plateau. It wasn't until 1989 that the Kokopelli Trail officially opened for recreational use.

Negotiating some of the tightest slickrock on the Troy Built Loop.

The Kokopelli Trail takes its name from a mythical figure recognized by many Native American tribes of the Colorado Plateau. Usually associated with the flute-playing Hopi Indians, this humped back flute player could drive back winter with his gentle music. According to legend, Kokopelli would wander from village to village with a bag of songs tucked under his arm. A symbol of fertility, Kokopelli was always welcome among villages, particularly during the spring planting season.

Although the Kokopelli Trail was originally named out of respect for Native American heritage, today's mountain bikers have adopted this legend as their own, viewing the Kokopelli as a symbol for the network of trails throughout the Colorado Plateau. Who knows which other paths of the Kokopelli's wanderings cross other area bike trails? All that is certain is that where the two meet, there is song, dance, and good rides.

Miles and Directions

0.0 START from the parking lot. Head west along the doubletrack.

0.1 The doubletrack will T. **Option:** Most descriptions of this ride will suggest you take the left route of the T, climbing the steep jeep road to the summit of Mack Ridge (560 feet), whereupon you get to descend the tricky 4 miles of singletrack. For our purposes, bear right behind the interpretive sign and continue heading west to ascend the tricky singletrack, whereupon you get to race down the steep and rocky jeep road.

0.2 You'll arrive at a map outlining the Kokopelli Trail, of which the Troy Built Loop is a part. A tight and rocky singletrack begins to the right and just beyond this map, descending for a while before beginning its gradual, southern ascent.

1.5 The singletrack once again forks. Bear left to climb, continuing on the Troy Built Loop. The right will lead you to the main Kokopelli Trail, which heads across Salt Creek and toward Rabbit Valley, offering incredible views of the Colorado River.

3.6 Begin the steepest and most technical part of the climb.

4.0 The singletrack reaches a doubletrack, which also marks the junction with Lion's Loop. From here, bear left. Both Lion's and Troy Built Loops share this section of trail. Be sure not to take any right-handed offshoots.

5.0 Reach the summit of Mack Ridge. Take in the sights and begin your fast and furious race to the bottom.

6.3 Arrive at the parking lot.

Ride Information

Local Information

Bureau of Land Management, Grand Junction Field Office, 2815 H Road, Grand Junction, 81506; (970) 244-3050.

Colorado Welcome Center, I-70 exit 19, Fruita, 81521; (970) 858-9335.

Local Events and Attractions

The Annual Fruita Fat Tire Festival in late April, Fruita; (800) 873-3068, (970) 858-3068.

Colorado National Monument, Fruita; (970) 858-3617.

Devil's Canyon Science/Learning Center, Fruita; (970) 858-7282.

Tours

Adventure Quest Expeditions, Grand Junction; (970) 245-9058 or (888) AD-Quest.

Organizations

Colorado Plateau Mountain Bike Trail Association (COPMOBA), P.O. Box 4602, Grand Junction, 81502; (970) 241-9561.

4 Crag Crest Trail

The Crag Crest Trail is located on Colorado's Grand Mesa. With 300 lakes to its credit, the Grand Mesa is truly "Land o' Lakes" country. The entire 10-mile loop of the Crag Crest Trail passes a number of these lakes and was designated a National Recreation Trail on March 14, 1978, by Forest Service Chief John McGuire. Very rarely used by mountain bikers, the trail features smooth and tacky, hard-packed terrain over exposed roots and rocks. This trail combines lake views with wild-flowering hillside meadows set between mixed aspen and conifer forests. Crag Crest Trail can be divided into two sections: the crest portion and the lower loop. This ride concerns itself strictly with the lower loop, as mountain bikes are not allowed on the crest portion. You should, however, make it a point to hike the upper crest portion of the trail, as it offers insight into the geological history of the Grand Mesa. During the height of the summer months, the mosquitoes in this area are some of the most bothersome in the state. September is usually a great time to visit.

Start: From the Grand Mesa Visitors Center.
Length: 8.6-mile loop.
Approximate riding time: Advanced riders, 45 to 60 minutes; intermediate riders, 1.5 to 2 hours.
Technical difficulty: Technically moderate due to some rockier sections.
Physical difficulty: Physically moderate due to some elevation gain at higher elevations.
Terrain: Paved state road, paved forest road, improved gravel road, and singletrack. This route passes a number of lakes as it makes its way through the forests of the Grand Mesa. Although not particularly technical, there are some short rock and root sections, as well as a few switchbacks with which to contend.

Trail contacts: Grand Mesa Visitor Center, Intersection of Colorado Highway 65 and Forest Road 121 (Trickel Park Road); (970) 856-4153.
Grand Mesa National Forest, 2250 U.S. Highway 50, Delta, 81416; (970) 874-6600.
Schedule: June to October.
Maps: USGS maps: Grand Mesa; Grand Mesa National Forest Map; Crag Crest National Recreation Trail Map; Grand Mesa Recreation Trails Map.
Nearest town: Cedaredge.
Other trail users: Hikers, picnickers, and anglers.
Canine compatibility: Dog friendly.

Getting There

From Montrose: Drive west on U.S. Highway 50 for 20 miles to Delta. Bear right onto Colorado Highway 92, by the Conoco and Diamond Shamrock stations. Drive for 4 miles on CO 92 before turning left onto CO 65, following signs for the Grand Mesa. After approximately 14.5 miles, come to the town of Cedaredge. Continue on CO 65, passing the old Grand Mesa Road to your right, and enter Grand Mesa National Forest. At 54 miles, arrive at the Grand Mesa Visitors Center, to your right. Park your vehicle here. *DeLorme: Colorado Atlas & Gazetteer:* Page 44, D-2.

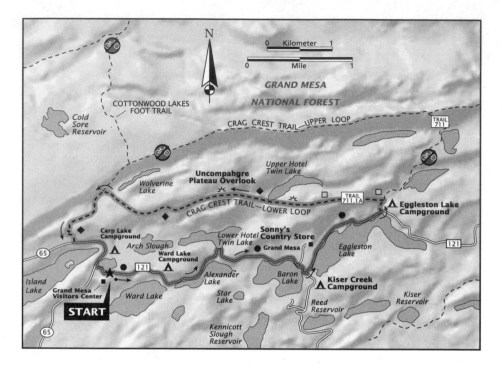

The Ride

Crag Crest Trail runs through the Grand Mesa National Forest, the second forest reserve to be set aside in Colorado. One of the world's largest flattop mountains, the Grand Mesa reaches as high as 11,234 feet atop Leon Peak. Framed in by the converging valleys of the Colorado and Gunnison Rivers, the Grand Mesa has over 300 stream-fed alpine lakes—an angler's paradise. The lakes beautifully mirror the surrounding Engelmann spruce, subalpine fir, and aspen. Dubbed "Thunder Mountain" by early Ute Indians, the Grand Mesa is a rare find in Colorado. When you visit for the first time, you'll marvel at how few people there are milling around. The Grand Mesa is definitely a sight to see, so enjoy the peace and solitude while you can.

The Grand Mesa formed 70 to 100 million years ago, the result of a series of volcanic eruptions, glaciation, and uplifts. At one time or another, a beach, a sea, and a large swamp occupied the area. The sand, silt, clay, and low-grade oil shale that were deposited some 50 million years ago when the area was a lake basin all hardened to form sedimentary rock. It is this sedimentary rock that is responsible, in part, for the crest's craggy appearance. Views from the Crag Crest tell the geological story of the Grand Mesa.

A series of lava flows starting 50 million years ago and ending 10 million years ago poured from cracks in the earth's crust onto the flat and wide sedimentary surface. Repeated lava flows poured over the surface, in turn cooling and hardening.

Eventually, the sedimentary rock became completely covered by layers of volcanic rock—layers in excess of 400 feet thick. Due to underground turmoil, this entire area reached its present elevation about 10 million years ago, exposing its lava cap (basalt rock) and the finer sedimentary rocks below the cap to wind and erosion.

The actual Crag Crest is a narrow, rocky ridge at the top of the Grand Mesa. It was formed as wind and water slowly eroded the softer sedimentary rock from its volcanic cap. Consequently, "slip surfaces" (large vertical cracks) were left in the rock. These cracks would, in effect, separate portions of smaller rock from the larger whole. These smaller portions would then slip down the sides of the opposing larger rock and tilt backward, forming large cavities that in time would fill with water. If viewed from the top of Crag Crest Trail, Upper Eggleston Lake makes a shimmering example of such slumping. Butts Lake offers an even clearer picture of how these smaller portions of rock could have slipped and tilted to form the present lake. As these separate portions of smaller rock slipped from the larger whole, what remained was a larger hole whose sides were considerably steeper than before. As this process continued, the sides grew ever steeper, as the volcanic cap grew narrower. This constant slumping has given rise both to the Crag Crest and the Grand Mesa's numerous lakes. Since this slumping is a continual process, eventually the narrow ridge of the Crag Crest will be destroyed.

▶ **Delta, Colorado, was home to the one-time brick thrower turned world champion boxer Jack Dempsey.**

Immediately after beginning the ride, you're offered views of Cobbett Lake, which lies directly to the north and through the pines. Harry Cobbett, who lends his name to the lake, moved to the Delta Valley in 1892 from England. Enamored with the valley's beauty and the Grand Mesa's silent dominion over it, he persuaded his fiancée, Lilian, to follow him in 1895. Harry and Lilian settled in a dirt-roofed cabin by the Gunnison River near the town of Delta. A short time after moving in, Harry led Lilian to view the Grand Mesa. It didn't take long before Lilian realized why her husband had been so insistent that she join him.

Harry started building dams for several of the mesa's lakes, and by the early 1900s, he was employed as a ditch rider, a person who releases water from the reservoirs into

Lands End atop the Grand Mesa.

the creeks and irrigation ditches to help irrigate the crops below the mesa. Eventually, the Cobbetts moved to Cedaredge, the town located directly below the beginning of the mesa's steepest rise, where Harry became postmaster. Due to his vigilant work clearing trails between the lakes and reservoirs and his contributions to the town of Cedaredge, Cobbett Lake is named in Harry's honor.

The ride to the singletrack of Crag Crest Trail passes no less than six of these sapphire lakes. The going is lazy but very scenic. Once you've connected with the singletrack of Crag Crest's lower loop, the trail heads west and is highlighted by wide, smooth singletrack over soft earth. After passing through meadows and mixed conifer and aspen forests, the trail starts climbing moderately, at about 3.5 miles. Rocks and roots offer a technically moderate challenge before relenting to the more commanding views of Eggleston Lake to the south. After descending through a dense lodgepole pine forest, the singletrack becomes especially tacky—nice cornering potential—as you blaze the flatter sections and across south-facing hillsides awash with bluebells, daisies, and sunflowers.

Once you've crossed the tributary of Forrest Lake, the trail again starts to ascend moderately. After reaching the hilltop meadow with views of the Uncompahgre Plateau, you begin to descend into a thick pine and aspen forest. From the western intersection of Crag Crest Trail's upper and lower loops, the trail descends rapidly on some tight, rocky singletrack—the most difficult segment of the ride. There is an immediate left-hand switchback that you'll want to keep in mind before arriving at Crag Crest's west trailhead. From the west trailhead, bear left onto Highway 65 and ride back to your vehicle.

Miles and Directions

0.0 START riding from the Grand Mesa Visitors Center on the paved Forest Road 121 (Trickel Park Road) going east, climbing gradually through the pines.

0.3 Begin descending. Expansive views of Ward Lake are to your right.

0.4 Pass Alexander Lake on your right.

1.4 Pass Sonny's Country Store on your left—burgers and drinks available.

2.0 Pass Baron Lake.

2.4 The pavement ends and FR 121 turns into an improved gravel road.

2.5 Eggleston Lake is to your right.

3.5 FR 121 intersects with Crag Crest East Trailhead (711.1A). Bear left onto the singletrack of Crag Crest Trail. The sign here reading FOOT AND HORSE TRAFFIC ONLY refers to the upper portion of Crag Crest Trail (711). You are allowed to ride on the lower looped portion of Crag Crest Trail.

3.6 After a short climb through a meadow, arrive at the Crag Crest Trail intersection and a sign reading WEST TRAILHEAD VIA CREST—6 ½, VIA LOWER LOOP—4. Bear left (west) onto the lower loop of Crag Crest Trail.

4.9 Cross a tributary of Forrest Lake. Just after crossing the creek, cross a four-wheel-drive road. You'll notice a trail sign to your right pointing in a westerly direction. Continue heading west on Crag Crest Trail.

5.3 Reach a hilltop meadow with expansive views of the Uncompahgre Plateau and the Lower Hotel Twin Lake.

7.0 Pass through a rock field and again intersect with the trailheads of Crag Crest Trail's upper and lower loops. Continue riding straight, passing the VISITOR CENTER sign.

7.1 Signs reading WEST TRAILHEAD—0.4 and VISITOR CENTER—0.8 mark another trail intersection. Bear right here, and follow the sign for the WEST TRAILHEAD—0.4.

7.5 Reach the west trailhead for Crag Crest Trail, where toilet facilities are available. Bear left onto the paved CO 65 and head east back to the Grand Mesa Visitor Center, passing Island Lake to your right.

8.6 Arrive at the VISITOR CENTER and your vehicle.

Ride Information

Local Information

Delta County Tourism Cabinet, P.O. Box 753, Delta, 81417; (800) 436-3041; www.westerncolorado.org.

Delta Area Chamber of Commerce, 301 Main Street, Delta, 81416; (970) 874-8616; www.deltacolorado.org.

Cedaredge Chamber of Commerce, P.O. Box 278, Cedaredge, 81413; (970) 856-6961; www.cedaredgecolorado.com.

Local Events and Attractions

Lands End Road: From milepost 29 on Highway 65, the Lands End Road, as part of the Grand Mesa Scenic and Historic Byway, follows the rim of the mesa for roughly 10 miles to the Lands End Overlook. Incredible views of the La Sal Mountains in Utah and the San Juan Mountains in Colorado are offered. For information, contact the Grand Mesa Visitor Center at (970) 856-4153.

Council Tree Pow-wow, in September, Delta; (970) 874-8616.

Fort Uncompahgre, Delta; (970) 874-8349.
Pioneer Town, Cedaredge; (970) 856-7554.
Applefest, in October, Cedaredge; (970) 856-6961.

Restaurants

Cozy Corner Café, Delta; (970) 874-3116.
The Apple Shed Fruit Stand, Cedaredge; (970) 856-3877 or (970) 856-7007.

Tours

Tour de Gold, in September, Montrose; (970) 249-8055 (for tour coordinator Bill Harris).
Bicycle Outfitter Touring Adventures, Grand Junction; (970) 245-2699.

Organizations

Montrose Mountain Bike Club, Montrose, CO (contact Cascade Bicycles, Montrose; 970-249-7375).
Colorado Plateau Mountain Bike Trail Association (COPMOBA), P.O. Box 4602, Grand Junction, 81502; (970) 241-9561.

Honorable Mentions

Northwest

Described here are great rides in the northwest region that didn't make the A-list this time around but deserve recognition. Check them out and let us know what you think. You may decide that one or more of these rides deserves higher status in future editions, or perhaps you may have a ride of your own that merits some attention.

A Dinosaur National Monument

Located roughly 140 miles west of Steamboat Springs and 190 miles east of Salt Lake City, Dinosaur National Monument is far from being a destination resort. In fact, it's just plain far. It is, however, close to many a traveler's heart, as it offers boundless surprises in an area all too often overlooked.

Dinosaur National Monument sits on the border of Colorado and Utah, atop a high plains desert. Its seemingly barren plateau, alive with sagebrush, greasewood, and saltbrush, turns away most quick-to-judge travelers, while the canyons of the Green and Yampa Rivers invite those who are more patient.

Named for the fossil bone deposits first unearthed here in August 1909 by Earl Douglass, a paleontologist from the Carnegie Museum in Pittsburgh, Pennsylvania, the Monument proudly boasts the Dinosaur Quarry building, an in-place museum centered around large fossil walls. The Monument's other attractions include its canyons. Access to the canyon floors is by a variety of paved, well-graded, and four-wheel-drive roads. Although Dinosaur National Monument doesn't have trails reserved strictly for mountain biking, mountain bikes are allowed on all roads.

Leading farther into the backcountry is the rugged but spectacular Echo Park Road. This road begins atop Harper's Corner Self-guiding Scenic Drive and runs a fast and rocky 12.3 miles to Echo Park, the confluence of the Green and Yampa Rivers.

After passing red-cliffed buttes and a maze of meadows, exploring mountain bikers will come upon the remains of the Jack and Rial Chew Ranch (1910–1970). Not far from the ranch, the prehistoric Fremont people carved elaborate drawings into the canyon walls, circa A.D. 1000. Here the sagebrush, greasewood, and saltbrush give way to piñon pine, juniper, cottonwoods, and boxelders, a veritable oasis in this otherwise brutal landscape. And if the sight of green doesn't immediately cool your jets, try spending a moment in the nearby "Whispering Cave," whose temperatures run approximately thirty degrees cooler than the ambient temperatures outside.

At journey's end, Echo Park, mountain bikers will enjoy a refreshing dip in either the Green or the Yampa River, or both. The park offers the perfect idyllic surprise to a day in the sun. What you need to keep in mind, however, is that your 12.3-mile descent to Echo Park must now be returned. The last 4-mile climb to the top of Harper's Corner Self-guiding Scenic Drive is a killer. Be prepared with food and water.

To reach Dinosaur, drive west on U.S. Highway 40, 90 miles from Craig, Colorado.

For more information on Dinosaur National Monument, contact the Moffatt County Tourism Association, 360 East Victory Way, Craig, 81625; www.colorado-go-west.com. *DeLorme: Colorado Atlas & Gazetteer:* Page 22, B-1.

B Tall Pines Trail

Tall Pines Trail is an incredibly beautiful ride through one of Colorado's most pristine places. Beginning roughly 6 miles west of Carbondale, which is about 10 miles south of Glenwood Springs, Tall Pines Trail leads you through some gorgeous wooded terrain to its end in Redstone. The trail weaves its sinewy course over open meadows, along a number of creeks, and through sections of forest that can only be described as enchanting. The trail combines smooth-running, well-marked single-track with tougher climbs and rockier sections, made all the more tough by being at the trail's end. If you're doing the ride as a 17-mile point-to-point, plan on leaving a shuttle in Redstone.

Lying roughly 22 miles west of Aspen, beyond the ski resort town of Snowmass Village, Redstone should be as popular as its neighbors. But with a population of only ninety-two, it's far from an Aspen. While offering all the amenities of a "civilized" mountain town—champagne Sunday brunches and gourmet dinners at the Redstone Inn and Redstone Castle—Redstone has retained a certain authenticity. The original coal-mining cottages that line the banks of the Crystal River recall a time of lost craftsmanship. The Crystal River has the distinction of being the last undammed river in Colorado. Registered as a National Historic District, Redstone enjoys its beautiful setting, backed by the Maroon Bells Snowmass Wilderness, and invites others to do the same.

To reach the trail's terminus at Redstone for your shuttle vehicle, drive south on Colorado Highway 133 from Carbondale for 18 miles. Park your vehicle near the intersection of Highway 133 and Forest Road 307. To reach Tall Pines Trailhead, drive west on Main Street through Carbondale, as it turns into County Road 108 and crosses the Crystal River. Notice the jeep road off to the left (east) at roughly 7 miles from Carbondale. Park your vehicle off of CR 108 and take the road marked County Road 1C.

For more information, contact Life Cycles, 0902 Colorado Highway 133, Carbondale, 81623; (970) 963–1149. *DeLorme: Colorado Atlas & Gazetteer:* Page 45, B-7.

Southwest

Southwest Colorado offers by far some of the most dramatic scenery and varied landscapes in the state. From Grand Junction, south to the towns of Telluride and Cortez, and then east to Durango, and all points in between, southwest Colorado is the shining jewel of all of Colorado's regions.

Included within the southwest are the high mesas and deserts of the Uncompahgre Plateau, a provincial block of land stretching from Colorado into Utah, New Mexico, and Arizona. Here the desert canyons below the plateau meld with the lush forests atop the plateau. One of Colorado's best kept secrets is the superb mountain biking opportunities atop the Uncompahgre Plateau. A ride not to be missed is the Aspen to Buck Trail. When visiting the area, take time to explore the Black Canyon of the Gunnison National Park. Gouged by the Gunnison River, the somber countenance of this gorge combines charcoal-pink cliffs half a mile high with widths shrinking to forty feet.

Considered to be the Switzerland of America, the town of Ouray lies just to the southeast of the plateau. The area surrounding Ouray is dotted with natural hot springs, the perfect complement to a day in the saddle. In the winter, Ouray features the country's only ice-climbing park. Centrally located, Portland Creek Trail offers a beautiful look at this would-be Switzerland.

To the south of Ouray rise the granite peaks of Telluride's San Juan Mountains. Known to early Ute Indians as the "land of the shining mountains," the San Juans are Colorado's most striking range. The one-time mining town of Telluride sits snugly within a box canyon, surrounded on all but one of its sides by these towering monoliths. Today, Telluride boasts some of the most challenging mountain bike terrain in all of Colorado. With its annual bluegrass and jazz festival, Telluride is considered to be the state's summer music festival capital.

Traveling farther south still, one enters the Four Corners area, the only place in the nation where four states converge to share a border. You can literally stand in Colorado, Utah, Arizona, and New Mexico at the same time. Although this area of the country is marked by its arid deserts and blazing heat, it was once home to North America's oldest known inhabitants, the Anasazi Indians (Ancient Puebloans). The Sand Canyon Trail, just outside the town of Cortez, travels past a number of small Ancient Puebloan kivas (ceremonial shelters of brick and mortar). More of these pueblos may be found at Hovenweep National Monument, 43 miles west of Cortez, or at Mesa Verde National Park.

To the east of Cortez lies Durango, the region's recreational and economic epicenter. As the undisputed mountain biking Mecca of Colorado, Durango is the southern terminus for the 470-mile Colorado Trail, was venue to the first-ever World Mountain Bike Championships, and features one of the nation's oldest bicycle races, the Iron Horse Bicycle Classic.

5 Aspen to Buck Trail

This loop enlists the help of three individual trails: Aspen Trail, Dry Creek Cutoff Trail, and Buck Trail. Each of the three delivers its own unique contribution to the whole ride. The Aspen Trail is easy and rolls beautifully over smooth singletrack and through dense aspen. Dry Creek Cutoff Trail offers some great technical riding on loose, rocky terrain before dropping to Dry Creek. Buck Trail includes a moderate ride over a variety of exposed roots, as it passes through meadows and forests of ponderosa pine—offering this route's best view at mile 12.6 miles. Situated high atop the Uncompahgre Plateau, this ride is almost never crowded. It's a solo rider's dream.

Start: From the intersection of the north Buck Trail 115 trailhead and Colorado Highway 90, ride in a southwesterly direction on Highway 90.
Length: 16.3-mile loop.
Approximate riding time: Advanced riders, 2 to 3 hours; intermediate riders, 3 to 4 hours.
Technical difficulty: Technically moderate with some challenging sections. Although most of the trail is relatively smooth, there are a few sections that offer a good degree of exposed rocks and roots.
Physical difficulty: Physically moderate due to a couple of shorter climbs at elevations exceeding 9,000 feet.
Terrain: Improved dirt roads, doubletrack, and singletrack. Most of the terrain is rolling, as it snakes atop the Uncompahgre Plateau. The trail is considerably forested, with only a couple of

eye-catching vistas. In general, this ride runs over hard-packed singletrack featuring the occasional exposed root or rock. Portions of the Buck Trail are extremely dusty.
Trail contacts: Uncompahgre National Forest, 2250 U.S. Highway 50, Delta, 81416; (970) 874-6600.
Colorado Plateau Mountain Bike Trail Association, P.O. Box 4602, Grand Junction, 81502; (970) 241-9561.
Schedule: Late May to October.
Maps: USGS maps: Antone Spring, Pryor Creek; Montrose Area Bicycling Trails; Uncompahgre National Forest Map.
Nearest town: Montrose.
Other trail users: Hunters, hikers, anglers, and picnickers.
Canine compatibility: Dog friendly.

Getting There

From Montrose: Drive southwest on Main Street, which eventually turns into Colorado Highway 90. Drive west on CO 90 toward the Uncompahgre Plateau. The pavement ends at 8.9 miles. At 20.7 miles, enter the Uncompahgre National Forest and pass the south Buck Trail 115 trailhead to your right. After 22.8 miles, you'll reach the north Buck Trail 115 trailhead to your right. Park your vehicle here. *DeLorme: Colorado Atlas & Gazetteer:* Page 65, B-7.

The Ride

On Colorado's Western Slope, along the eastern flank of the Colorado Plateau Province, lies the Uncompahgre Plateau, perhaps the most overlooked and underrated

Views of Mount Sneffles, Wetterhorn Peak,
Uncompahgre Peak, and Grand and Garfield Mesas

UNCOMPAHGRE

NATIONAL

FOREST

West

Fork

Dry

Creek

Spruce

Creek

Raspberry

Creek

To
Montrose

TRAIL
115

90

TRAIL
115

East Fork Dry Creek

To
Naturita

START

DIVIDE CREEK
CUTOFF TRAIL

90

Iron
Spring
Camp

549

UNCOMPAHGRE

NATIONAL

FOREST

SOUTH

Trailhead for
Divide Creek
Cutoff Trail

DIVIDE

565

402

ROAD

Red Canyon
Overlook

N

TRAIL
125

0   Kilometer   1

0   Mile   1

of any of Colorado's high–mountain attractions. Its 100-mile length makes the
Plateau look low, and its flat top makes it look smooth. "Low" and "smooth" are not
about to draw attention in Colorado—I guaranty you that. But the Uncompahgre
is neither low nor smooth. Topping out at 10,347 feet (Horsefly Peak), the Uncompahgre Plateau draws together a collection of steep canyons and drainages, particularly along its western rim, so it could hardly be considered low or smooth. The fact
that the Uncompahgre Plateau remains one of Colorado's greatest anomalies does

not prevent it from hosting a variety of incredible singletrack—notably the Aspen and Buck Trails.

The Aspen to Buck Trail loop features some of the area's finest singletrack, as it weaves its serpentine course through a territory the Utes called "uncompahgre"—translated by some as "hot water spring" and by others as "rocks made red by water." The Utes, Colorado's oldest permanent residents, came into Colorado along the eastern slope of the Rocky Mountains, reaching the Uncompahgre Plateau between A.D. 1200 and 1400. The Utes' powerfully built frames and bronze-colored skin identified them to other Native Americans as the "Black Indians." Until the Spanish introduced the horse to North America in the 1600s, these early Utes traveled solely on foot, relying on bow and arrow to replenish their stores.

The Utes' territorial home was the nearby San Juan Mountains, or as they called it, the "land of shining mountains." They would often winter in the low-lying areas and then move to the higher mountainous regions in the summer to hunt. The Utes so respected the land and life that should necessity dictate the killing of an animal, they'd pray for it before releasing the arrow. The Utes believed they possessed an intuitive understanding of the inner workings of nature. This ability helped them to rouse the bear from hibernation with the "Bear Dance" in early spring—the awakening of bears marked the beginning of spring, which would allow for an early growing season.

Perhaps it seems fitting that the Uncompahgre Plateau should remain relatively hidden, untainted by the development that has since disrespected so much of Colorado's mountains. Undoubtedly the Utes would agree that that which is left pure is blessed with strength. Today, the Uncompahgre Plateau remains a natural, if not formidable, monument to the earliest Americans.

As you weave your course along Aspen Trail, through thick stands of aspen and over impeccably smooth singletrack, you can imagine what it must be like to be in a Bev Doolittle painting. Herds of wapiti (American elk) stand motionless, almost invisible, in the whites, greens, and golds of the aspen trees. Although not very technical, the trail offers a beautiful ride, one that can be ridden fast without fear of high-speed impact. This fast ride lasts until you pass a vista on the right that looks out over the small town of Nucla. Soon thereafter, you reach the route's first technical climb, featuring many exposed rocks on tight singletrack.

This climb doesn't last long. The trail levels out again into another aspen glen. After 5 miles, the trail descends rapidly through a ponderosa and lodgepole pine forest. Once it connects with Dry Creek Cutoff Trail, you'll intersect and cross the Divide Road, rejoining Dry Creek Cutoff Trail on the other side. From here the riding gets considerably more technical—a definite wakeup compared to the casual Aspen Trail. The trail descends quickly over loose rocky terrain to Dry Creek and the southern tip of Buck Trail.

Buck Trail begins as a rough looking dirt road. Traveling in a northerly direction through the aspens, the road eventually disintegrates to singletrack as it makes its speedy descent, paralleling the pole-worm fence of the national forest boundary. From atop the high plateau at 12.6 miles, you're offered southeasterly views of Mount Sneffels (14,686), Wetterhorn Peak (14,017), and Uncompahgre Peak (14,309), and northerly views of the Grand Mesa and Garfield Mesa. Like white caps on a sea of green, the San Juan range rolls quietly in the distance.

From here descend through the meadows and aspens to a stock tank at 13.3 miles. Just after passing the stock tank, you'll have to grind up a tough, steep climb on loose dirt. Alan Ardizone, resident bike guru and owner of Cascade Bicycles, calls this section of trail the "50 percenter hill"—meaning that riders, if lucky, make this climb only 50 percent of the time. From the top of this hill, it's a mellow cruise back to your vehicle.

Miles and Directions

0.0 START from the intersection of north Trail 115 (Buck Trail) trailhead and Colorado Highway 90. Begin riding in a southwesterly direction on CO 90.

0.7 Reach the intersection of CO 90 and South Divide Road. Continue riding on Highway 90.

0.8 Reach the intersection of CO 90 and Forest Road 549 (States Draw Road). Bear left onto FR 549 and pass through the fence.

2.6 After passing a pond, FR 549 intersects with Trail 125 (Aspen Trail). Bear left onto Trail 125.

3.1 Trail 125 opens up onto a beautiful vista above Red Canyon. Looking to the south, one can see Lone Cone and the town of Naturita.

3.6 Intersect an old logging road. Cross the logging road and continue on the singletrack on the other side through intermittent pine and aspen.

5.3 Trail 125 intersects with Little Red Springs Trail. Bear left (west) here, continuing on the Trail 125 loop.

5.6 Reach the intersection of Trail 125 and Dry Creek Cutoff Trail. Bear right onto Dry Creek Cutoff Trail.

5.8 Dry Creek Cutoff Trail intersects with the Divide Road. Bear left onto the Divide Road and ride for roughly 25 feet before bearing right to rejoin the singletrack of the Dry Creek Cutoff Trail.

6.8 A steep and rocky doubletrack spurs off to the right of Dry Creek Cutoff Trail. Do not bear right onto this spur. It will only climb savagely back to the Divide Road. Instead, continue straight ahead on Dry Creek Cutoff Trail, descending over rocks and roots, to Dry Creek.

Atop a high plateau with the Gunnison Range in the background.

7.2 At Dry Creek, the trail forks again. Bear left here, crossing Dry Creek and continuing up the doubletrack of Dry Creek Cutoff Trail to the power lines. The right fork begins Dry Creek Trail (Pack), which eventually climbs steeply from the Dry Creek drainage to the Divide Road.

7.7 Reach the power lines. Bear right, climbing underneath the power lines.

7.9 Once you near the crest of the climb underneath the power lines, you'll be able to distinguish a singletrack trail veering off to the right into a stand of aspen and pine trees. Bear right (southeast) onto this singletrack. Descend through the aspens. The trail parallels a split-rail fence (the national forest boundary) to your right.

8.8 Pass underneath the power lines again and continue straight ahead.

9.0 Reach the intersection of south Trail 115 (Buck Trail) trailhead and Highway 90. Cross Highway 90 and continue your ride on the south Trail 115. **Option:** If you bear left onto CO 90, it will deliver you to your vehicle after 2.1 miles, cutting your ride by roughly 5 miles. In doing so, however, you miss roughly 7 miles of awesome Trail 115 singletrack.

11.8 Enter into a wide-open aspen glen where a number of singletrack spurs break from the main trail. Be careful to stay on the main trail, following the trail marker signs nailed to the trees.

12.4 Exit the aspen glen, climb moderately through a meadow, and pass through fields of scrub oak.

12.6 Arrive at a high plateau with panoramic views. From here, descend into the meadow below and then into another grouping of aspen trees.

13.3 Pass a stock tank on your right and grind up a tough and steep section of trail.

14.0 Pass another stock tank to your left. Cross a four-wheel-drive road and continue on Trail 115 on the other side, passing a multiple-use trail marker sign.

14.6 The singletrack turns into a rough dirt road. Continue riding on the road.

16.2 Cross under the power lines.

16.3 Arrive at your vehicle.

Ride Information

Local Information

Montrose Visitors and Convention Bureau, 433 South First, Montrose, 81402; (970) 240-1429, (800) 879-0244.

Montrose Chamber of Commerce, 1519 East Main Street, Montrose, 81401; (970) 249-5000 or (800) 923-5515; www.montrosechamber.com.

Visitor Information Center, Montrose; (970) 249-1726.

Bureau of Land Management, Uncompahgre Field Office, 2505 South Townsend Avenue, Montrose, 81401; (970) 249-6047.

Local Events and Attractions

Black Canyon of the Gunnison, Montrose; (970) 249-1915; for information call (970) 249-7036.

American Handgunner World Shoot-off Championship, in July, Montrose, contact the Montrose Visitors and Convention Bureau at (970) 240-1429.

Montrose County Historical Museum, mid-May to October, Montrose; (970) 249-2085.

Ute Indian Museum, Montrose; (970) 249-3098.

Tours

Tour de Gold, in September, Montrose; (970) 249-8055.

Restaurants

Sicily's Italian Restaurant, Montrose; (970) 249-9199.

Daily Bread & Bakery, Montrose; (970) 249-8444.

Sakura, Montrose; (970) 249-8230.

Organizations

Montrose Mountain Bike Club, Montrose (contact Cascade Bicycles at [970] 249-7375).

The Colorado Plateau Mountain Bike Trail Association (COPMOBA), P.O. Box 4602, Grand Junction, 81502; (970) 241-9561.

6 Deep Creek Trail

Deep Creek Trail might be one of Telluride's best. Although there's a tough climb to the Deep Creek Trail intersection, the trail itself offers a fast romp through thick aspens and pine. Deep Creek Trail runs a technically challenging descent over exposed rocks and roots before dumping you in a meadow. Views of the Wilson Peaks are outstanding. Riders will find the switchbacks down to Deep Creek Trailhead a delight. For those of you who like speed any way you can get it, you'll enjoy the mad race down Last Dollar Road to its intersection with Colorado Highway 145. Take care, though. The stop sign at the end of Last Dollar Road, right before the road meets with the highway, comes up quickly.

Start: From the clock tower in downtown Telluride.

Length: 15-mile loop.

Approximate riding time: Advanced riders, 2 to 2.5 hours; intermediate riders, 3 to 4 hours.

Technical difficulty: Technically challenging due to the rocky terrain.

Physical difficulty: Physically challenging to demanding due to the trail's steep grades and high elevations.

Terrain: Paved road, paved bike path, dirt road, and singletrack. The terrain encountered is mountainous: slide areas, talus fields, thick-wooded forests, soft and tacky earth, steep climbs and descents, and creek crossings.

Trail contacts: Paragon Ski & Sport, Telluride; (970) 728-4525.

Schedule: Mid-June to October.

Maps: USGS maps: Grayhead, Telluride; *Trails Illustrated map* 504, Durango, Silverton, Telluride, Pagosa Springs, and Cortez; Map of the Mountains of Silverton, Telluride, and Ouray; Drake Mountain Maps; Uncompahgre National Forest Map.

Nearest town: Telluride.

Other trail users: Hikers and campers.

Canine compatibility: Dog friendly.

Getting There

From downtown Telluride: Pedal east on Colorado Avenue to the courthouse and clock tower in the middle of town by the Oak Street park. Begin your ride here. *DeLorme: Colorado Atlas & Gazetteer:* Page 76, A-2 to A-3.

The Ride

Imagine a force so strong that it could wipe out a small town in seconds, leaving nothing but silent devastation in its wake. A force preceded by a thunderous boom, or sometimes no sound at all. A force that can reach speeds of over 100 miles per hour and bear the weight of thousands of tons. Now imagine riding through the path of such a force. How about twice? Yes, Deep Creek Trail passes through two avalanche paths, one below Campbell Peak and the other below Iron Mountain.

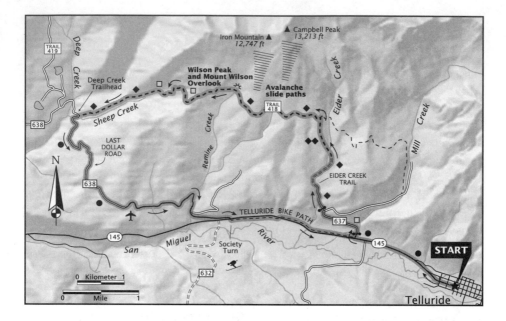

Colorado is notorious for avalanches. In fact, Colorado has the highest reported avalanche rate in the country. And no one knows, with any real degree of accuracy, exactly how many avalanches actually occur in Colorado's vast backcountry. Many of Colorado's avalanches, therefore, go unreported.

Avalanches have, quite curiously, attained somewhat of a celebrity status in Colorado. A 50-mile stretch of U.S. Highway 550 (between the Purgatory Ski Area north of Durango to Ouray) boasts over one hundred regular avalanche paths. Most of these paths can be identified by name. The East Riverside Path, just 5 miles south of Ouray, is arguably one of Colorado's most dangerous. This section of US 550 has taken a number of lives over the years. Because of the tremendous threat, a cement roof was constructed over the section of road to deflect debris into Canyon Creek.

Of all the mountain ranges in Colorado, the San Juan Range of southwest Colorado is perhaps the most noted for its high number of avalanches. The town of Telluride, home to Deep Creek Trail, is tucked in the far eastern end of a box canyon and surrounded on three sides by the sheer cliffs and soaring peaks of the San Juan Mountains. On average, Telluride receives somewhere in the vicinity of 300 inches of snow per year. The large temperature difference between the warmer, lower layers of snow and the colder surface layers creates snow layer instability. Coupled with a heavy annual snowfall, this makes Telluride a prime avalanche location. And Telluride has endured its share of avalanche hardships.

In 1902 an avalanche razed part of the Liberty Mine, located just outside of town, killing seven and injuring several more. Concussions created by the slide's thunderous roar shattered windows in Telluride. A second slide hit the Liberty

Mine's rescue team. Luckily, it hurt no one. However, while transporting some of the dead and injured back to Telluride, a third slide struck the team, killing an additional three and injuring five more. Another story tells of a home caught in the path of an avalanche. Two women on the first floor were crushed, while a baby in an upstairs room sustained only a minor scratch on the cheek. In Rico, a small town south of Telluride, a man woke to find himself sleeping under the stars. A slow-moving avalanche had slipped its way into the man's bedroom and pushed both him and his bed out under the cold night sky. These and other stories could fill volumes.

Prior to arriving at Deep Creek Trail's two avalanche paths, you must climb some rocky doubletrack as you make your way through thick aspen stands with Eider Creek to your left. Although the riding here is tough, this section is simply entrancing. Once on Deep Creek Trail, climb a brief spurt before descending on soft forest earth carpeted with pine needles. After crossing an old logging road at 4.8 miles, descend through a young aspen forest. You're dropped into the avalanche path of Campbell Peak (13,213 feet). A little farther up is Iron Mountain's (12,747 feet) avalanche path. Notice the deadfall. These torn paths are a good sign of avalanche activity.

Most slide paths lie on east and north-facing slopes, since they typically receive more snow and harsher weather. The path itself has three individual parts. The "starting zone," as the name implies, denotes where a slide begins. The "track" lies in the middle of the path. Here the avalanche is no longer accelerating but is keeping a constant speed. Generally, an avalanche doesn't "pick up" any additional snow once in the "track." Finally, the path ends, as does the avalanche, when it reaches the "runout zone." Most slope angles range from 30 to 45 degrees in the "starting zone." The "track" typically runs along a 20- to 30-degree pitch, while the "runout zone" has less than a 20-degree slope.

After passing the beautiful vistas of the Wilson Peaks, you arrive at a private property gate at 6.6. miles. From here Deep Creek Trail descends steeply over rocky singletrack through tall stands of aspen before coming to a smooth and fast, hassle-free descent into a large meadow. Cross Sheep Creek and bear left onto the road. Descend the fun switchbacks to Deep Creek Trailhead. Bear left again onto Last Dollar Road. Intersect with CO 145, and slip, slide, and away back to Telluride.

Miles and Directions

0.0 START from the courthouse and clock tower in downtown Telluride on Colorado Avenue. Ride west on Colorado Avenue out of town and intersect the paved bicycle path.

1.5 Just after passing the Texaco station, cross a cattle guard and bear right onto dirt Forest Road 637. Begin riding up FR 637.

2.2 FR 637 intersects with Eider Creek Trail, a gated doubletrack off to the left, near some camping sites. Bear left, passing through the gate, onto this doubletrack and continue climbing in a northerly direction. Soon thereafter, bear left again at another intersection and begin a steep and rocky climb on the doubletrack.

3.0 Cross Eider Creek.

3.5 Arrive at a short but technically demanding rocky climb—probably a hike-a-bike for all but the most adept.

3.7 Eider Creek Trail meets Trail 418 (Deep Creek Trail) at a T intersection. Trail 418 travels both left and right. Bear left here, continuing in a westerly direction. Note: There is no trail marker at this intersection.

4.0 Pass the Deep Creek Trail sign to your right.

4.8 Cross an old logging road and continue on the singletrack. Descend quickly through a young aspen forest.

5.0 Pass through an avalanche path of Campbell Peak.

5.8 Pass through Iron Mountain's avalanche path, with breathtaking views of Wilson Peak.

6.4 Arrive at a beautiful vista, offering expansive views of the Telluride ski resort and the San Juan Range. Intersect an old logging road that climbs sharply

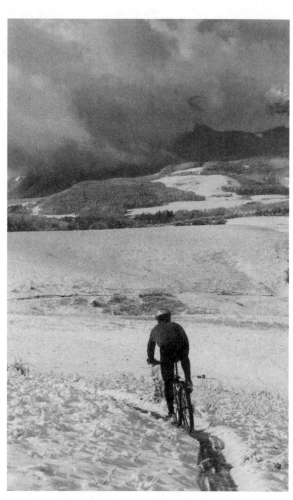

Heading toward Deep Creek Trailhead, with the Wilson Peaks in the foreground.

to the right into a stand of aspens. A sign facing the opposite direction from which you came reads DEEP CREEK TRAIL AND MILL CREEK—4. Continue straight, however, descending on this old logging road in a southwesterly direction.

6.6 This old logging road leads to a green private property gate to the left. Bear right here, continuing on Trail 418 singletrack, passing a trail marker to the right.

7.7 Reach the intersection of Trail 418 and Whipple Mountain Trail. Cross Sheep Creek and intersect a road marked with two trail signs. The sign on the left reads LAST DOLLAR ROAD (FR 638) AND DEEP CREEK TRAILHEAD—0.5 MI. The sign on the right reads DEEP CREEK TRAIL 418, WHIPPLE MTN TRAIL—3, MILL CREEK—6. Bear left here onto this dirt road, following signs for LAST DOLLAR ROAD (FR 638) and DEEP CREEK TRAILHEAD—0.5 MI.

8.2 The road forks. Bear right and pass through the barbed wire fence and descend switchbacks through the meadow to the Deep Creek Trailhead.

8.7 Reach Deep Creek Trailhead. Bear left onto FR 638 (Last Dollar Road).

9.8 Forest Road 638 turns to pavement by the stop sign. Bear left onto the paved FR 638 and descend to Society Turn and Colorado Highway 145.

11.7 Forest Road 638 intersects CO 145 at Society Turn. Cross CO 145 and bear left onto the paved bike bath back to town.

15.0 Arrive at the courthouse and clock tower in downtown Telluride.

Ride Information

Local Information
Telluride Visitor Center, 700 West Colorado Avenue, Telluride, 81435; (888) 605-2578.

Local Events and Attractions
Telluride Bluegrass Festival, in June, Telluride.
Melee in the Mines Mountain Bike Races, in July, Telluride.
Wild Mushrooms Conference, in August, Telluride.
Film Festival, in September, Telluride.
Blues & Brews Festival, in September, Telluride.

Accommodations
Town Park and Campground, Telluride; (970) 728-2173. Cost is $11.00 per night; camping, showers, and toilet facilities; available May 15 through October 15.

Restaurants
La Cocina De Luz, Telluride; (970) 728-9355 (Mexican take-out and catering company).
Rustico Ristorante, Telluride; (970) 728-4046.
Smuggler's, Telluride; (970) 728-0919. Telluride's only brew pub.

Tours
Telluride Outside, Telluride; (970) 728-3895, (800) 831-6230; www.tellurideoutside.com.
Back Country Biking, Telluride; (970) 728-0861, cell (970) 519-0874.
Telluride Sports/Adventure Desk, Telluride; (970) 728-4477, (800) 828-7547.
Telski/Mountain Adventures, Telluride; (970) 728-6900.

7 Wasatch Trail

Wasatch Trail offers a truly high-alpine adventure. Its rugged terrain is not for the faint-hearted. No Van Trapps singing here. This trail is mountain biking's equivalent to skiing in Valdez, Alaska. If it doesn't kill you, it won't just make you stronger, it'll make you fearless. Steep climbs, rocky terrain, narrow switchbacks, huge drop-offs, and hanging canyon walls all attest to this trail's dominance over any other. It's mountain biking at its most extreme. This is by far the hardest trail in the book and considered by many to be the hardest trail in Colorado—if not the country. Only expert riders in great physical shape should consider this trail. For a shorter ride that includes part of this route description, you can ride to the top of Bridal Veil Falls (Colorado's tallest waterfall at 365 feet) and return the same way.

Start: From Telluride's Town Park and Campground.
Length: 15.4-mile loop.
Approximate riding time: Advanced riders, 3 to 4 hours; intermediate riders, 5 to 6 hours.
Technical difficulty: Technically demanding due to the preponderance of rocks and large drop-offs, coupled with narrow singletrack and tight, steeply descending switchbacks.
Physical difficulty: Physically demanding due to the steep climbs at elevations exceeding 13,000 feet.
Terrain: Paved street, dirt road, four-wheel-drive road, and singletrack. The terrain of this trail includes loose rocks, tundra-like environments above timberline, steep grades, snowfields, hillside meadows, and deep-carved canyons.

Trail contacts: Paragon Ski & Sport, Telluride; (970) 728-4525.
Schedule: Mid-July to mid-September.
Maps: USGS maps: Telluride, Ophir; *Trails Illustrated* map 504, Durango, Silverton, Telluride, Pagosa Springs, and Cortez; Map of the Mountains of Silverton, Telluride, and Ouray; Drake Mountain Maps; Uncompahgre National Forest Map.
Nearest town: Telluride.
Other trail users: Hikers, backpackers, and sightseers.
Canine compatibility: Not dog friendly, due to vehicular traffic on the Bridal Veil Falls Road.

Getting There

From downtown Telluride: Pedal east on Colorado Avenue (heading toward Bridal Veil Falls) to Maple Street and the Town Park and Campground. Begin your ride from the Town Park and Campground, continuing in an easterly direction toward Bridal Veil Falls. *DeLorme: Colorado Atlas & Gazetteer:* Page 76, A-3.

The Ride

They say that the box canyon in which Telluride sits offers but one way out, west on Colorado Highway 145. To the north, south, and east of town lie the impenetrable

TRAIL SIGNS FOR:
① Bear Creek Trail
② Bridal Veil Basin and Wasatch Trail
③ East Fork Bear Creek and Trail 513

mountains of the San Juan Range. Where east CO 145 ends, the Bridal Veil Falls Road begins. At first glance, the monoliths of Mendota Peak, Telluride Peak, Ajax Peak, Ingram Peak, Ballard Mountain, and La Junta Peak form a seemingly impassable barrier at the eastern end of this box canyon. Further inspection will reveal, however, the unremitting Bridal Veil Falls Road snaking its way to the top and beyond this canyon, eventually connecting with Wasatch Trail. But like rushing the Denver Bronco's offensive line, expect to take your share of hits before breaking on through to the other side.

The route begins casually enough—riding east on Colorado Avenue to the historic Pandora Mill, located at the headwaters of the San Miguel River. Like Pandora's mythical box of evils, the Pandora Mill marks the entrance to what you might call the quintessential "To-Hell-U-Ride" ride. The cable lines you see overhead once toted ore, at the rate of 300 to 400 tons a day, from the Smuggler-Union Mine, located 3 miles above in Marshall Basin. Over 4 million ounces of gold, 21 million ounces of silver, and 12 million tons of lead, zinc, and copper were transported along this 6,700-foot aerial tramway to Pandora Mill.

In 1875 Marshall Basin was discovered to be rich in gold, silver, lead, zinc, copper, and iron. John Fallon, a prospector, opened the Sheridan Mine. Rather than develop the mine himself, Fallon leased it to other mining developers and then eventually sold it for $40,000. The Sheridan Mine became another addition to the portfolio of a group of English and Scottish bankers who were living in Shanghai at the time. Their other interests lay in the nearby Mendota, Union, and Smuggler Mines.

Roughly one year after Marshall Basin unearthed its pay dirt to Fallon, a prospector by the name of J. B. Ingram found out that the Sheridan and Union claims exceeded the legal limits of their claim by roughly 500 feet. He staked a claim on the area between these two mines, and his fortunate discovery led to the opening of the Smuggler Mine. From a single ton, the Smuggler Mine would yield eighteen ounces of gold and 800 ounces of silver. The Smuggler Mine would eventually join with the Union Mine. Their combined claim would unearth a gold vein 1 mile long. By 1900 the Smuggler-Union Mine laid claim to over 35 miles of excavated tunnels.

From the Pandora Mill, riders continue up Bridal Veil Falls Road (Lucky #13) as it switches back a number of times to the power plant. This road is simply a warm up for what lies ahead. As you climb through this rugged terrain, you can't help but marvel at the tenacity of Telluride's earliest miners. Once you pass the power plant, the trail becomes very rocky, offering even tougher climbs. Your only relief comes in the form of the cool trickle of Bridal Veil Creek to your right. The moisture from the creek and spray from the waterfall allows for wildflowers to grow very late into the season, as late as mid-September. Columbine (aquilegia caerules), roundleaf bluebell (campanula rotundifolia), Western monkshood (aconitum columbianum), and Explorer's Gentian (Gentiana calycosa) offer soft contrast to this otherwise brutal terrain.

Scrap your way to the Blue Lake turnoff, after which you'll find a grueling loose rocky climb above timberline. This climb may last upward of one to two hours, so be prepared for unexpected weather patterns. Bear right again roughly 1 mile after passing the abandoned miner's cabin and climb up this loose, shell-rock road. This is the most grueling climb of the day. Once you intersect with the road that bears the Bridal Veil Trail sign, the going gets considerably easier.

Once at the Bear Creek sign, give yourself a pat on the back. You've broken on through. From here you're offered stunning views of Bridal Veil Basin (the basin

The Lewis Mine. If you get here, you've come too far.

through which you just rode), Lookout Peak, Ophir Pass, and the town of Ophir. To enjoy a panoramic view of the surrounding San Juan Mountains, you can opt to take a 0.3-mile spur to the top of Oscar's Pass, dividing Telluride and Ophir.

Once on Wasatch Trail, the descent begins with a bone-jarring tour through a scree field before dumping you into Lena Basin and the headwaters of Bear Creek. The hillside meadows of Lena Basin are laden with tight switchbacks over loose sand and rock. These first switchbacks eventually relent to offer you a straighter ride through a drainage, as the trail continues in a westerly direction. After about 10 miles, the trail falls precipitously to Bear Creek, which lies about 60 feet below. This section demands technical skill. Aside from the steep and large drop off, the trail is tight and rock-laden.

After the junction of Wasatch Trail and the East Fork Bear Creek and Trail 513, Wasatch Trail switches back a number of times down a steep hillside meadow to meet with Bear Creek again. These switchbacks are very tight and steep. As you near the second intersection with Bear Creek at 11.3 miles, notice a snowfield over the creek. This field is usually frozen through the whole summer. Riders are ill-advised to walk on this snowfield, since it could break, dropping you some 15 feet into the creek below. Cross the creek just below the snowfield.

After crossing the creek, the trail levels out for a bit, offering views of Telluride, before delivering you to the steep canyon walls of Bear Creek Canyon, which was once a sacred ceremonial ground for early Ute Indians. Here, prayers and vision quests were conducted. Riders also may also find comfort in prayer, since this section of trail skirts the steep hanging walls of the canyon some 80 to 100 feet above the creek. With big drops and large rocks, this is no place to make a mistake. After several dizzying drop-offs, ledges, and tight switchbacks, you eventually arrive at Bear Creek Trail. Take Bear Creek Trail to Pine Street and belly up to the bar at Smuggler's Brew Pub & Grill.

Miles and Directions

0.0 START from the Telluride Town Park and Campground. Begin riding east on Colorado Avenue toward Bridal Veil Falls and the end of the canyon.

0.3 Pass the Lone Tree Cemetery to your left—the final resting place of miners killed in a fire in the 1880s.

1.4 The pavement ends and Bridal Veil Falls Road 13 begins.

4.3 Bear right as Bridal Veil Falls Road 13 meets an intersection. (The left fork travels against one-way traffic.) Duck under a gate and continue climbing above and behind the power plant on the old and rugged four-wheel-drive road.

6.2 Reach the intersection with Blue Lake Road. The left fork leads to Blue Lake, while the right fork continues in a southerly direction, making its way around La Junta Peak (13,472 feet). Bear right here, heading toward La Junta Peak.

6.8 Pass an old miner's cabin to your left. The rough four-wheel-drive road splits. Bear right here, following alongside the old rusted drainpipe to the right. Cairns begin to mark your route.

7.8 The trail meets another intersection. Bear right (south) at this intersection on the more primitive looking road. Grind up this very steep shell-rock road, heading toward the rim of Bridal Veil Basin. Continuing straight (east) will lead you to Bridal Veil Basin, passing the old Lewis Mine to your left as you make your way to Lewis Lake. If you've come to this mine, you've gone too far.

8.3 Reach the intersection of the road that cuts across the rim of Bridal Veil Basin. To your left is a trail sign for Bridal Veil Trail, pointing back in the direction from which you came. Bear left onto this road, continuing a more moderate ascent on an easier road to the saddle between Wasatch Mountain (13,555 feet) and Oscar's Pass.

8.8 A Bear Creek Trail sign is to your right. Bear right here, following the Bear Creek Trail sign to the saddle and the beginning of Wasatch Trail 508.

9.0 Arrive at the saddle (Blick's Pass) and the beginning of Wasatch Trail 508. A trail marker atop this saddle reads BRIDAL VEIL BASIN and WASATCH TRAIL. Descend in a westerly direction on the singletrack of Wasatch Trail 508 through a talus field.

10.4 Reach Bear Creek and the junction of Wasatch Trail 508, the East Fork Bear Creek, and Trail 513. Do not cross the creek at this point. Instead, bear right (north), following signs for East Fork Bear Creek and Trail 513, with Bear Creek to your left.

10.8 Cross another talus field as you descend on remarkably tight and steep switchbacks.

11.4 Cross Bear Creek and continue riding north along Wasatch Trail 508.

11.9 Cross a footbridge pressed firmly against the canyon walls of Bear Creek Canyon.

13.0 Intersect with Bear Creek Trail. Bear left onto Bear Creek Trail and head back to town.

15.0 Reach Bear Creek Trailhead and South Pine Street. Intersect with the paved South Pine Street and ride north to Colorado Avenue.

15.1 Pass Smuggler's Brew Pub & Grill to your left.

15.2 Reach the junction of South Pine Street and Colorado Avenue. Bear right onto Colorado Avenue and ride east toward the Telluride Town Park and Campground.

15.4 Arrive at the Town Park and Campground and your vehicle.

Ride Information

Local Information

Telluride Visitor Center, 700 West Colorado Avenue, Telluride 81435; (888) 605-2578.

Local Events and Attractions

Telluride Bluegrass Festival, in June, Telluride.

Melee in the Mines Mountain Bike Races, in July, Telluride.

Wild Mushrooms Conference, in August, Telluride.

Film Festival, in September, Telluride.

Blues & Brews Festival, in September, Telluride.

Accommodations

Town Park and Campground, Telluride; (970) 728-2173. Cost is $11.00 per night; camping, showers, and toilet facilities; available May 15 through October 15.

Restaurants

La Cocina De Luz, Telluride; (970) 728-9355 (Mexican take-out and catering company).

Rustico Ristorante, Telluride; (970) 728-4046.

Smuggler's Brew Pub & Grill, Telluride; (970) 728-0919 (Telluride's only brew pub).

Tours

Telluride Outside, Telluride; (970) 728-3895, (800) 831-6230; www.tellurideoutside.com.

Back Country Biking, Telluride; (970) 728-0861, cell (970) 519-0874.

Telluride Sports/Adventure Desk, Telluride; (970) 728-4477, (800) 828-7547.

Telski/Mountain Adventures, Telluride; (970) 728-6900.

8 Hermosa Creek Trail

Hermosa Creek Trail has long been considered one of the country's top rides—and for good reason. It is nearly 20 miles of descending smooth-running singletrack beside beautiful Hermosa Creek. While not overly technical, there are some off-camber sections of trail that slope precipitously toward the creek. Complicated with roots and rocks, these sections lend an element of technicality not otherwise encountered. Those packing a collapsible fishing rod will find that the north half of this ride offers great access to the creek.

Start: From Hermosa Creek Trail's northern trailhead, off Forest Road 578.
Length: 19.1-mile point-to-point.
Approximate riding time: Advanced riders, 2 hours; intermediate riders, 3 hours.
Technical difficulty: Technically moderate due to some rocky and steep sections.
Physical difficulty: Physically easy to moderate due to the fact that most of this ride descends, with only a few climbs mixed in.
Terrain: Singletrack. The trail follows the Hermosa Creek to the town of Hermosa. There are a number of creek crossings, as well as rocky sections to test your skills. Some of the terrain slopes precipitously to the creek at times, while at other times the trail delivers smooth and fast-running singletrack.
Trail contacts: San Juan Mountains Association (SJMA), P.O. Box 2261, Durango, 81302; (970) 385-1210; www.sjma.org.

Durango Cyclery, Durango; (970) 247-0747. San Juan–Rio Grande National Forests, Columbine Ranger District, P.O. Box 439, Bayfield, 81122; (970) 884-2512.
San Juan National Forest Visitor Information, (970) 247-4874.
Schedule: June to October.
Maps: USGS maps: Hermosa Peak; Elk Creek; Monument Hill; Hermosa; *Trails Illustrated* map 504, Durango, Silverton, Telluride, Pagosa Springs, and Cortez; Bicycle on Public Lands of Southwest Colorado Routes Map.
Nearest town: Hermosa.
Other trail users: Hikers, ATVs, hunters, picnickers, anglers, motorcyclists, and equestrians.
Canine compatibility: Dog friendly.

Getting There

From Durango to Hermosa Creek Trail's northern trailhead: Drive north on U.S. Highway 550 for roughly 27 miles to Purgatory Ski Area at Durango Mountain Resort. Bear left into the resort by the Purgatory sign. After passing the Purgatory sign, bear right and drive through the lower part of the ski area into the upper parking lots. FR 578 (County Road 38) starts to the right (northeast) side of the upper lots and is farthest from the ski lifts. Continue driving on FR 578, following signs for Sig Creek Campground and Hermosa Creek Trail. Pass Sig Creek Campground and drive straight for roughly 2 miles on FR 578 before bearing left into Hermosa Creek's northern trailhead. *DeLorme: Colorado Atlas & Gazetteer:* Page 76, C-2.

Shuttle Point (Hermosa Creek Trail's southern trailhead): From Durango drive north on U.S. Highway 550 for roughly 8.5 miles to Hermosa, just past the market and across Hermosa Creek. Bear left onto La Plata County Road 203 and immediately bear right onto CR 201 (Hermosa Creek Road), marked by a sign that reads HERMOSA CREEK TRAIL—4 MILES. At 9.7 miles, cross a cattle guard and enter the San Juan National Forest. Once in the national forest, the road becomes Forest Road 576. The pavement ends at 10.5 miles. At 12.8 miles, reach Hermosa Creek's southern trailhead. *DeLorme: Colorado Atlas & Gazetteer:* Page 86, A 2-3

The Ride

Durango's Hermosa Creek Trail is one of Colorado's classic rides. Located just 12.8 miles north of Durango, the trail spears directly through the heart of the San Juan National Forest. And that's no small feat considering the San Juan National Forest is 1,869,931 acres of volcanic domes, jagged aretes, and verdant forests. What this ride offers is a beautiful—that's "hermosa" in Spanish—tour through dense forests and alongside a resounding creek, all under the cover of densely grown plant life. It's absolute paradise.

Starting from behind the Purgatory Ski Area at Durango Mountain Resort, site of the 1990 World Mountain Bike Championships and the 2001 Mountain Bike World Cup, Hermosa Creek Trail runs for just under 20 miles along smooth-running singletrack to its southernmost terminus at Hermosa. Local riders like Ned Overend and Sara Ballantyne consider Hermosa Creek Trail one of their all-time favorite rides and take pride in the area's World Mountain Bike Championships association. It seems that from its earliest beginnings, the entire Animas Valley has been imbued with an incredible sense of pride.

When the Denver & Rio Grande railroad first started making its way from the silver and gold resources in Silverton through the Animas Valley, circa 1879, it was met with a certain degree of resistance. Animas City, located approximately 2 miles north of present-day Durango, had already established itself in the Animas Valley as a thriving farming and ranching community. For the Denver & Rio Grande to profit from the Silverton mines, it hoped to transport the ore to Animas City for smelting. Although the D&RG railroad offered to develop Animas City as a railroad center, the small community of farmers and ranchers who took such pride in their city's status as the region's trading center refused to be bought.

Undeterred by the town's pride, the Denver & Rio Grande threatened to establish a rival community to the south, bypassing Animas City altogether. That community turned out to be Durango. Proving to be no match against the railroad's major investors, Animas City eventually folded and became the north part of present-day Durango. The Denver & Rio Grande's William Bell and Alexander Hunt chose the site of the rival community. Hunt had been the railroad's liaison for some time, traveling as far as Mexico to rally for the rail. In fact, many speculate that Hunt chose the name Durango because of its territorial similarity to Durango, Mexico, from where he had just returned. By 1879 the Durango Trust was formed by wealthy developers from Denver & Rio Grande, whose interests included making Main Avenue, the wholesale street; Second Avenue, the retail section; and Third Avenue, the residential boulevard. Dubbed the "Denver of Southern Colorado," Durango boomed, as little Animas City became nothing more than a railroad stop on the way to Durango.

During Durango's rise to metropolitan proportions, the Denver & Rio Grande tried developing and promoting other satellite communities, which they hoped would mature as well as Durango had. Towns like Hermosa and Elbert City, which enjoyed short-lived successes, just didn't have the staying power of Durango. In spite of slipping in prosperity over the years compared to Durango, these towns still reflect a certain pride and strength that once proved critical during the early years of the

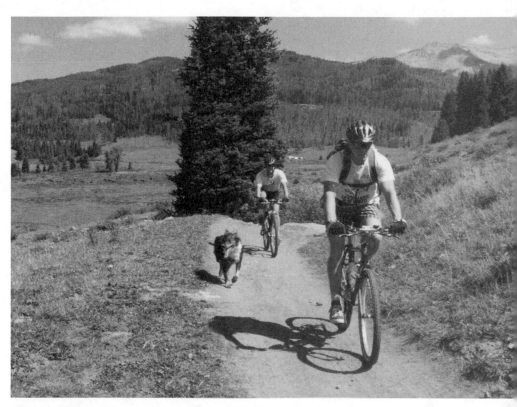

Hermosa Park and the San Juans in the background.

Animas Valley. As years pass and people move in, this pride continues and transcends all aspects of Colorado's Southwest, including its mountain biking.

The Hermosa Creek Trail begins by entering a large pine forest on smooth, wide singletrack. It heads south along the left side of the valley. Once the trail meets Hermosa Creek, it becomes a little rockier. At 3.5 miles, the trail passes underneath large cliffs, their sides covered in streaming moss and fern. Here the primeval forest offers one of the most beautiful sections of the trail. The terrain becomes increasingly muddy and rocky. Passing through an alpine meadow surrounded by large stands of Engelmann spruce, you cross Hermosa Creek and descend into Big Bend. At the intersection of Hermosa Creek Trail and Salt Creek Trail there lies a fire pit and picnic area. Here Hermosa Creek provides a small natural shower and bath. Fallen trees have blocked much of the creek's flow, allowing the water to pool atop the branches and letting soft curtains of water fall between the cracks in the limbs—thus, the perfect natural shower.

After passing Salt Creek Trail, Hermosa Creek Trail rises above the creek's eastern slopes, falling precipitously to it. This, added to some rocky sections and narrow singletrack, makes for a moderately technical ride. Here, along the sweetest section of trail, the terrain gets really playful with tight switches, roots, rocks, and a whole lot of jazz.

From Little Elk Creek you're offered a technically advanced climb. Although short, the trail is narrow and steep and combines roots and rocks to make for a tough climb. Trees hug the sides of the trail tightly. After this section the trail mellows and begins a fast and smooth descent through a lodgepole pine forest. Once you cross Dutch Creek, the trail offers the most physically challenging section of the entire ride. A series of three short climbs test a rider's staying power all the way to the finish line. Although this trail is mostly downhill, these short climbs challenge anyone who has already ridden 14 miles. After busting out 2 final miles of climbing, the trail descends speedily for another mile before delivering you to Hermosa Creek Trail's southern trailhead and your vehicle.

Miles and Directions

0.0 START at Hermosa Creek Trail's (Trail 514) northern trailhead and begin riding in a southerly direction.

0.7 Cross a cattle guard and continue riding in a southerly direction.

1.7 Cross another cattle guard, as the trail meets Hermosa Creek. Cross East Cross Creek and continue descending on the trail.

3.1 Pass Corral Draw Trail (Trail 519) to your right. Continue on the Hermosa Creek Trail.

4.8 Cross Hermosa Creek via a footbridge and blaze through a large, open meadow surrounded by pine trees. Soon thereafter, the trail climbs up a short, east-facing hillside to the right.

5.8 Cross Hermosa Creek again via another footbridge.

6.5 Hermosa Creek Trail intersects Salt Creek Trail (Trail 547). Pass Salt Creek Trail and continue riding on Hermosa Creek Trail.

10.4 Descend a rocky and tight section and cross Little Elk Creek.

14.0 Proceed down a rough, rocky descent.

14.5 Cross Dutch Creek via a footbridge and begin the first of two tough, but short, climbs to the finish.

15.4 Pass the intersection with Dutch Creek Trail and climb steadily into a beautiful stand of aspen.

16.0 Here begins the second short and steep climb before the trail's end.

18.0 Begin your final descent to Hermosa Creek Trail's southern trailhead. Near the end of the trail, the route forks. Bear left and climb the 100 feet to the trailhead.

19.1 Reach the end of Hermosa Creek Trail and your vehicle.

Ride Information

Local Information

Durango Area Chamber Resort Association, Durango; (970) 247-0312, (800) 525-8855.
San Juan National Forest, Supervisor's Office, 15 Burnett, Durango, 81301; (970) 247-4874; www.fs.fed.us/r2/sanjuan.
Durango Mountain Resort, 1 Skier Place, Durango, 81301; (970) 247-9000, (800) 982-6103.
Durango, www.durango.com.

Local Events and Attractions

Durango & Silverton Narrow Gauge Railroad, Durango; (970) 247-2733, (800) 872-4607.
Iron Horse Bicycle Classic, in May, Durango.
Trimble Hot Springs, 6 miles north of Durango on U.S. Highway 550, Trimble; (970) 247-0111.

Accommodations

Strater Hotel, 699 Main Avenue, Durango; (970) 247-4431, (800) 247-4431; www.strater.com

Organizations

San Juan Mountains Association (SJMA), Durango; (970) 385-1210.
Trails 2000, Durango; (970) 259-4682.

Restaurants

Lady Falconburgh's Barley Exchange, Durango; (970) 382-9664; www.falconburgh.com.
Stonehouse Subs, Durango; (970) 247-4882.
Nature's Oasis, Durango; (970) 247-1988.

Tours

Fat Tire Downhill, Durango; (970) 385-1778.
Southwest Adventures, Durango; (970) 259-0370.
Durango Singletrack Tours, Durango; (970) 385-7489, (888) 336-8687.

Camps

Durango Mountain Bike Camp, Durango; (970) 259-0238, (970) 259-0481.

$\mathfrak{9}$ Log Chutes Trail

Located just outside of Durango, Log Chutes Trail provides an easily accessible ride for riders staying in town or camping at Junction Creek. The section of trail along the historic Neglected Mine Road has been used in the past for the Iron Horse Bicycle Classic downhill course. This section provides a fast and fun descent. The ride can be ridden as either a short or long loop. The short loop is designated an easy ride, while the long loop is more difficult. Featured here is the long loop. The Log Chutes Road is open to motorized vehicles, so be aware.

Start: From the Log Chutes Trail parking lot.
Length: 6.5-mile loop.
Approximate riding time: Advanced riders, 45 to 60 minutes; intermediate riders, 1 to 2 hours.
Technical difficulty: Technically moderate due to some rocky and sandy sections.
Physical difficulty: Physically moderate due to some shorter climbs.
Terrain: Dirt forest road, old logging road, and singletrack. The terrain is very woodsy. There are patches of rock and sand with which to contend; however, most of the trail travels on soft forest earth among conifer trees and aspen.

Trail contacts: Durango Cyclery, Durango; (970) 247-0747.
San Juan–Rio Grande National Forests, Columbine Ranger District, P.O. Box 439, Bayfield, 81122; (970) 884-2512.
Schedule: May to October.
Maps: USGS maps: Durango West; *Trails Illustrated* map 504, Durango, Silverton, Telluride, Pagosa Springs, and Cortez; Bicycle on Public Lands of Southwest Colorado Routes Map.
Nearest town: Durango.
Other trail users: Hikers.
Canine compatibility: Dog friendly.

Getting There

From Durango: Drive north on Main Avenue for 1.5 miles to 25th Street. Turn left onto 25th Street by the Texaco and Big O Tires. This street becomes Junction Creek Road (La Plata County Road 204). Junction Creek Road intersects with La Plata County Road 205 at 4.5 miles. Bear left here, continuing on Junction Creek Road, following the sign for the JUNCTION CREEK CAMP-GROUND—2 MILES. Cross the cattle guard and enter the San Juan National Forest at 5.1 miles. Junction Creek Road turns into Forest Road 171. Continue on the dirt FR 171, passing the Junction Creek Campground at 6.6 miles to your left. Bear right into the Log Chutes parking area at 7.4 miles. *DeLorme: Colorado Atlas & Gazetteer:* Page 86, B-2.

The Ride

With regard to mountain biking, not much can be said of Durango that hasn't already been said. Durango, more than any other town in Colorado, has had, and continues to have, the greatest influence on the sport of mountain biking. Pictures dating back to 1895 show the Durango Wheel Club (the area's first bicycling club) poised across Baker's Bridge, one of the area's favorite road loops. In 1990 Durango was home to the first-ever World Mountain Bike Championships. Such renowned World Mountain Bike Champions as Ned Overend, Juli Furtado, Lisa Muhich, John Tomac, Missy Giove, and Greg Herbold have called Durango home. Durango is also home to one of the country's ten largest bicycle races, the Iron Horse Bicycle Classic (IHBC). It seems that with all the mountain biking mania going on in Durango, one would have a hard time finding a trail hidden from the hype. Well, Log Chutes Trail comes as close as it gets.

Situated just outside of Durango, Log Chutes Trail keeps a low profile among such trails as Hermosa Creek, Colorado Trail, and Kennebec Pass. But even Log Chutes Trail has had its brush with fame. Several years ago Log Chutes Trail's historic Neglected Mine Road was included as part of the downhill course for the Iron

Horse Bicycle Classic. Since the IHBC discontinued the downhill race, Log Chutes Trail has slipped into virtual anonymity, unknown to all but the most connected members of Durango's mountain biking circle.

And so, how did Durango become Colorado's premier mountain bike playground? Curiously, both the town of Durango and its status as a mountain bike mecca owe their existence to the railroad. In 1879 a workman for the Denver & Rio Grande railroad laid the first in a long line of railroad stakes that would eventually pierce the heart of the San Juan Mountains and connect Silverton with Durango. Intent on tapping the rich mining district of Silverton, the Denver & Rio Grande railroad established the town of Durango in 1881 as its depot. By 1882 the Denver & Rio Grande was hauling gold and silver unearthed in Silverton to Durango for smelting. In no time, Durango grew into the "City of the Silver San Juan."

The Denver & Rio Grande railroad conducted business as usual until mining started to wane, shortly after World War II. As other lines pulled out of the area to save what money they could, the Durango to Silverton line was full steam ahead, only now it was hauling tourists and train aficionados. The Durango & Silverton Narrow Gauge Railroad (as it's now called) has become such a part of Durango that residents are unwilling to give it up. That same steam-powered locomotive line ushered in Durango's mountain bike craze.

Jim Mayer and his younger brother Tom grew up along the tracks leading to Silverton. Jim was an engineer on the Durango to Silverton line. Tom was an avid cyclist. One day in the early 1970s, Tom challenged his brother Jim to a race—Tom on his steel 10-speed; Jim and his iron horse. The first one to reach Silverton, 47 miles and 5,500 feet later, was the winner. As the train neared their house, Jim blew the steam-engine whistle, sounding the start of the race. And the first unofficial run of the Iron Horse Bicycle Classic was initiated. When word reached Durango that Tom had actually started winning these races, all of Durango was abuzz for bicycling.

In 1972 thirty-six riders came out for the first official Iron Horse Bicycle Classic. More than twenty-five years later, still racing the iron horse, the race continues to draw a crowd. The Classic, held annually on Memorial Day weekend, has grown

Start of the IHBC downhill course.

to include a number of other bicycle events as well. Circuit races, road races, tours, BMX races, trials, and mountain bike races all have their place in Durango's Iron Horse Bicycle Classic. Although occupying its own rightful place within the Iron Horse Classic, Log Chutes Trail is one of Durango's lesser celebrated trails—a trail, nevertheless, made more intriguing by its relative anonymity among the giants of Durango's trail system.

Log Chutes Trail begins as a moderate climb up a dirt road over relatively rocky terrain. The singletrack begins once you connect with the more difficult, long-loop Log Chutes Trail. The trail begins as an easy climb through tall stands of ponderosa and lodgepole pine. The singletrack here features hard-packed forest earth with a variety of exposed rocks. At 2.4 miles the trail begins to level out, offering westerly views of Durango, the San Juans, and the hidden valley of Falls Creek. Here, the sand of the trail is intermingled with rocky, hard terrain, as it passes through intermittent fields of scrub oak and aspen glens.

At 4.1 miles you intersect with the old Neglected Mine Road, the highlight of Log Chutes Trail. As part of the Iron Horse Bicycle Classic downhill course, this trail is rocky and fast and offers many dips over which to hop. The speedy descent winds through overgrown sagebrush and tight, exposed root sections. Upon reaching the old corrals, the route continues to descend through a mixed conifer forest and crosses Junction Creek Road at 6.4 miles. From the road it's a short stretch of singletrack back to your vehicle.

Miles and Directions

0.0 START from the Log Chutes parking area and begin riding up Log Chutes Road in an easterly direction.

1.1 Log Chutes Road forks. Bear left at this fork, passing beyond the gate that bears a road closed sign. Continue climbing for 0.5 mile before leveling out. There's a bicycle-emblem signpost to the right.

1.8 The road intersects with the "Short Loop" segment of Log Chutes Trail to the left. Pass the "Short Loop" trailhead and continue riding up the road in a northerly direction. Just after passing the turnoff for the "Short Loop," bear left onto the more difficult, long loop.

2.5 The singletrack trail leads into an old logging road, offering an overgrown, wide platform through which the trail travels. Follow this trail in a westerly direction, taking note of the occasional bicycle-emblem signpost pointing the way.

4.1 Cross the dirt Junction Creek Road and immediately pick up the continuation of the singletrack on the other side. Follow this singletrack up for about 200 yards, heading in a southerly direction, before bearing left onto the old Neglected Mine Road, part of the IHBC downhill course.

4.2 Bear left onto the old Neglected Mine Road and descend to the corrals.

5.7 Pass the abandoned corrals to your right and ride approximately 200 yards past the corrals to a fork in the trail. Bear right at this fork, following trail marker signs.

6.4 The singletrack descends to Junction Creek Road again. Cross this gravel road and connect with the singletrack on the other side, completing the loop back to your vehicle.

6.5 Arrive at your vehicle.

Ride Information

Local Information

Durango Area Chamber Resort Association, Durango; (970) 247-0312, (800) 525-8855.
San Juan National Forest, Supervisor's Office, 15 Burnett Court, Durango, 81301; (970) 247-4874; www.fs.fed.us/r2/sanjuan.
Durango Mountain Resort, 1 Skier Place, Durango, 81301; (970) 247-9000, (800) 982-6103.
Durango, www.durango.com.

Local Events and Attractions

Durango & Silverton Narrow Gauge Railroad, Durango; (970) 247-2733, (800) 872-4607.
Iron Horse Bicycle Classic, in May, Durango
Trimble Hot Springs, 6 miles north of Durango on U.S. Highway 550, Trimble; (970) 247-0111.

Accommodations

Strater Hotel, 699 Main Avenue, Durango; (970) 247-4431, (800) 247-4431; www.strater.com.

Organizations

San Juan Mountains Association (SJMA), Durango; (970) 385-1210.
Trails 2000, Durango; (970) 259-4682.

Restaurants

Lady Falconburgh's Barley Exchange, Durango; (970) 382-9664; www.falconburgh.com.
Stonehouse Subs, Durango; (970) 247-4882.
Nature's Oasis, Durango; (970) 247-1988.

Tours

Fat Tire Downhill, Durango; (970) 385-1778.
Southwest Adventures, Durango; (970) 259-0370.
Durango Singletrack Tours, Durango; (970) 385-7489, (800) 336-8687.

Camps

Durango Mountain Bike Camp, Durango; (970) 259-0238, (970) 259-0481.

10 Sand Canyon Trail

Constructed in 1993 by volunteers for Outdoor Colorado, Sand Canyon Trail links the lower canyon trail to Sand Canyon Pueblo at the northern end of the canyon. Sand Canyon Pueblo is one of the largest Anasazi pueblos ever discovered. Weaving through the plastered ruins of a once thriving ancient Anasazi culture, Sand Canyon Trail strikes a fun course through desert sands and over patches of slickrock. There is no water available anywhere along the trail, so bring ample amounts. Also, riding in exposed desert terrain requires sunscreen, sunglasses, and a wide-brimmed hat.

Start: From Sand Canyon Trailhead.
Length: 7.2-mile out-and-back.
Approximate riding time: Advanced riders, 45 to 60 minutes; intermediate riders, 1.5 to 2 hours.
Technical difficulty: Technically easy to moderate due to the well-maintained trail, which rolls over relatively smooth hard-packed dirt and slickrock. Some of the trail, however, does include switchbacks and rockier sections.
Physical difficulty: Physically easy to moderate. Although there is very little elevation gain, the hot climate of this semi-arid region takes its toll on the body.
Terrain: Singletrack. This trail weaves its course through a semi-arid, desert environment. Types of terrain encountered include sand, slickrock, hard-packed earth, cacti, and cryptobiotic crust.
Trail contacts: San Juan Public Lands Center, San Juan National Forest and San Juan BLM Office, 15 Burnett Court, Durango, 81301; (970) 247-4874.
Schedule: April to October.
Maps: USGS maps: Battle Rock, Woods Canyon; *Trails Illustrated* map 504, Durango, Silverton, Telluride, Pagosa Springs, and Cortez.
Nearest town: Cortez.
Other trail users: Hikers, equestrians, geologists, and anthropologists.
Canine compatibility: Not dog friendly, due to the dry, hot climate and the lack of water in this area.

Getting There

From Cortez: Drive west on U.S. Highway 160 (Main Street) from the Cortez Visitors Center and Chamber of Commerce. After 1.2 miles, bear left by the Burger King, following signs for US 160 South and US 666 South. Now on US 160 South, pass a Phillips 66 truck stop and gas station on your left and bear right onto Montezuma County Road G (McElmo Canyon Road) at 3.8 miles, passing the airport sign. At 5.0 miles, pass the Cortez Municipal Airport on your left. After crossing McElmo Creek at 16.2 miles, via a steel bridge, drive for another 0.6 mile to Sand Canyon Trailhead. Park your vehicle at Sand Canyon Trailhead on the right side of McElmo Road at 16.8 miles. *DeLorme: Colorado Atlas & Gazetteer:* Page 84, B-2.

The Ride

Sand Canyon Trail lies in the Four Corners Region, where the borders of Colorado, Utah, New Mexico, and Arizona all converge at right angles. Here, in this plateau country of Colorado, the landscape begins to take on the ruddy-colored, bone-dry features more commonly associated with Utah and New Mexico. Water is limited, and towns are separated by large stretches of flat, windswept desert and canyon. It is here, among this dry and seemingly barren landscape, that the Four Corners region's first known inhabitants, the ancient Anasazi Indians, thrived.

The early Anasazi Indians ("Anasazi" being Navajo for "The Ancient Ones") first settled the area around A.D. 450. This period is commonly referred to as the "Modified Basketmaker Period" (from A.D. 450 to 750). These so-called basketmakers hunted with spears and gathered desert plants to survive. Their dexterous craftsmanship is evidenced in what we find of their woven baskets. The Anasazi began to evolve, trading their spears for bows and arrows, creating pottery, growing yellow flint corn, and building underground pit houses. These pit houses were shallow, saucer-like dwellings topped with logs bound by fibrous yucca plant strips and chinked with mud mortar. They served as ceremonial meeting places—forebears to today's conference halls. Between A.D. 750 and 1100, their achievements would finally culminate in the building and establishing of large communal dwellings, virtual cities of stone and adobe built into the sand-blasted cliff sides. This period marked the emergence of the "Pueblo" culture. The Cliff Palace in Mesa Verde National Park is a perfect example of the Ancestral Puebloans' architectural mastery.

Sand Canyon Trail passes a number of these cliff dwellings as it leads to one of the largest pueblos ever built, the Sand Canyon Pueblo. The trail begins on slickrock, with cairns marking the route to the wide singletrack. Rolling over hard-packed desert sand, it passes through piñon-juniper forests and sagebrush. There are a number of playful dips and natural velodromes highlighting the beginning portion of the trail. The trail also passes one of the desert's most unique and important, but very fragile, life forms: cryptobiotic crust.

Appearing as a miniature city of dark sand castles, cryptobiotic crust is actually a living organism. The crust has anti-erosional and nitrogen-enriching qualities that prepare the ground for future plant life. Growing on barren ground and requiring little nutrition from the soil, cryptobiotic crust is a self-sustaining biological unit, a critical part of the desert's soil-building processes. Since it can take as long as one hundred years to mature—and less than one revolution of a bicycle tire to be destroyed—it is imperative that you avoid disturbing this organism and only admire it from the trail.

Within 3 miles, you pass four Ancestral Puebloan cliff dwellings. Sand Canyon is unique in that it offers the mountain biker a chance to examine these ruins more intimately than you could otherwise at places like Mesa Verde National Park (where bicycles are restricted to paved and designated roads). These ruins have a certain presence about them, one that envelops the entire canyon with an air of arcane inventiveness. Donald G. Pike writes in his book *Anasazi:* "The old cities have weathered well, retreating only slightly, and then only into a more harmonious union with the face of the land. They, like the earth, abide in a quiet strength, a presence that betokens an assurance of permanence." This lasting power is testimony to the Ancestral Puebloans' craftsmanship, as well as their understanding of the land. The droves of

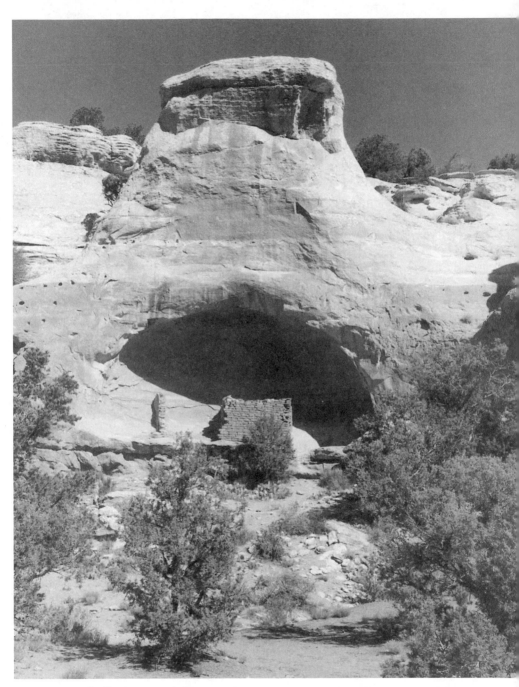

First Anasazi dwelling.

cacti growing before most of these ruins act as a warning to unwary travelers who might think to disrespect these ancient dwellings.

Just over a half mile from the fourth cliff dwelling is the turnaround point. From this point, riding your bike to Sand Canyon's northern end may prove more foolhardy than adventurous, as the trail becomes considerably sandier, rockier, and steeper, combining no less than thirty switchbacks on its way to the top of the canyon. A better option would be to hike these last remaining 3 miles to the canyon's northern end and the Sand Canyon Pueblo.

In cooperation with the Bureau of Land Management, research and excavation at the Sand Canyon Pueblo was first conducted in 1983 by the Crow Canyon Archeological Center staff. The Sand Canyon Pueblo is believed to have been inhabited in the latter part of the thirteenth century and may well have been a social and ceremonial center. A community of an estimated 735 residents once occupied this area. No less than 420 rooms, 90 kivas (underground rooms used for ceremonial and social gatherings), and 14 towers make up the village. Most of the excavations are being backfilled for preservation, so aside from pueblo mounds and room outlines, there are few structures to view from afar. Thus, a tour of the Sand Canyon Pueblo is best suited for people with a serious archeological interest, as opposed to those having only a casual interest in archeology.

No one knows with any real certainty why these Ancestral Puebloans mysteriously disappeared around A.D. 1300. A long drought in the area (from A.D. 1276 to 1299) may have been the cause of their sudden departure. Others hold that raiding Shoshonean hunters, who had begun to roam the plateau at that time, forced the Ancestral Puebloans to leave. Researchers at the Sand Canyon Pueblo hope to uncover the answers to this and other questions that have gone unanswered for nearly 700 years, regarding the life and culture and customs of these "Ancient Ones."

Miles and Directions

0.0 START from Sand Canyon Trailhead and begin your ride by heading north over the slickrock. Cairns atop the slickrock mark the route.

0.2 Reach Sand Canyon Trail sign to your left. Continue riding in a northeasterly direction, passing the sign.

1.1 Arrive at your first Anasazi ruin off to your left (west).

1.9 Reach the top of a juniper and piñon field, across from which lie two Anasazi ruins imbedded in a natural amphitheater. Descend four technically moderate switchbacks to this juniper and piñon field and arrive below these two ruins.

2.9 Arrive at the fourth and largest of all the cliff dwellings in this area. This site has been roped off due to erosion. Access to this ruin is pending stabilization.

3.6 Arrive at a sign that reads THE NEXT MILE IS ROCKY AND STEEP. RECOMMENDED FOR FOOT TRAFFIC ONLY. Turn around here and return the way you came to your vehicle. (Note: You may wish to stash your bike and hike the 3 miles to Sand Canyon's northern trailhead and the Sand

Canyon Pueblo. You may opt to bike the 3 miles. Be advised that half of these next 3 miles include a very sandy, dried-up creek bed and some thirty switchbacks that rise steeply from the creek bed to the northern end of Sand Canyon, making riding virtually impossible.)

7.2 Reach your vehicle.

Ride Information

Local Information

Crow Canyon Archeological Center, 23390 Road U, Cortez, 81321; (970) 565–8975, (800) 422–8975.

Cortez Area Chamber of Commerce and Colorado Welcome Center, P.O. Box 968, 928 East Main, Cortez, 81321; (970) 565–3414; www.cortezchamber.org.

Mesa Verde Country Visitor Information Bureau, P.O. Box HH, Cortez, 81321; (970) 565–8227, (800) 253–1616; www.mesaverdecountry.com or www.swcolo.org.

Local Events and Attractions

Mesa Verde National Park; (970) 529–4461; www.mesaverde.org.

Ute Mountain Tribal Park, Towaoc; (970) 565–3751 (ext. 282), (800) 847–5485.

Hovenweep National Monument, c/o Mesa Verde National Park; (970) 749–0510; www2.educ.ksu.edu/projects/hovenweep/hovenhome.html.

Anasazi Heritage Center Museum, Dolores; (970) 882–4811.

Cortez CU Center, Cortez; (970) 565–1151; www.fone.net/~cucenter.

Tours

Crow Canyon Archeological Center, 23390 Road U, Cortez, 81321; (970) 565–8975, (800) 422–8975.

Restaurants

Main Street Brewery, Cortez; (970) 564–9112.

Francisca's, Cortez; (970) 565–4093.

Honorable Mentions

Southwest

Described here are great rides in the southwest region that didn't make the A-list this time around but deserve recognition. Check them out and let us know what you think. You may decide that one or more of these rides deserves higher status in future editions, or perhaps you may have a ride of your own that merits some attention.

C Portland Creek Trail

It's been called the "Switzerland of America" and for good reason. Ouray, Colorado, is quite possibly one of the most beautiful places in Colorado. Nestled safely in an alpine cathedral at the bottom of the treacherous Red Mountain Pass, in the heart of one of America's most scenic drives, the San Juan Skyway, Ouray offers jaw-dropping views of towering San Juan peaks. Coupled with Ouray's head-tilting scenery are the many waterfalls that veil its walls. The dramatic waterfalls of Box Canyon, Cascade, Bear Creek, and Twin Falls in Yankee Boy Basin are all testimony to the town's relation to Switzerland. In winter, these falls turn into an ice climber's paradise. Ouray recognizes this, boasting the world's only man-made ice park in existence. Among these highest of heights lies Portland Creek Trail, a short but sweet ride.

As one of the Amphitheater trails, Portland Creek Trail is a great acclimatization ride for travelers. With views of the Amphitheater cliffs and peaks to the west and south of Ouray, this trail travels directly above America's Switzerland.

If you were to travel south through the town on U.S. Highway 550, you'd bear left just after passing the turnoff for Box Canyon and follow the signs for Cascade Falls. After turning left, make your first right where you'll see the sign for Portland Creek Trail to your left.

For more information contact Ouray Mountain Sports at (970) 325–4284 or the Ouray County Chamber of Commerce at (800) 228–1876. *DeLorme: Colorado Atlas & Gazetteer:* Page 66, D-4

D Ute Mountain Ute Tribal Park

The Ute Mountain Ute Tribal Park offers riders a unique look into early Native American culture. Personal tour guides will inform riders about regional archeology, history, rock art, geological land formations, artifacts, and dwellings. The Utes of Ute Mountain (the Weenuche band) are one of the seven original Ute bands who once thrived throughout all of Colorado.

Following an old jeep road along the Mancos River, riders descend 800 feet to a group campground 13 miles later. The route passes by several Anasazi archeology ruin sites, which can be accessed by short side hikes. The riding is remote, with spectacular Mancos River valley views, but the area offers no water or food, so riders should carry their own.

To reach the Ute Mountain Ute Tribal Park, drive south on Main Street from the Mancos Visitors Center at the intersection of U.S. Highway 160 and Colorado Highway 184 in downtown Mancos. Main Street will shortly merge with County Road 41. Drive on CR 41 for 10 miles to a sign identifying the Ute Mountain Tribal Park. Park your vehicle here. Due to the extensive Ute artifacts and dwellings, the Ute Mountain Ute Tribe strictly controls trips into the Tribal Park. Riders must first call and reserve their space. Bike tours may be arranged by calling the Tribal Park at (800) 847–5485. For a full-day tour the cost is $30.00. For a half-day tour it's $17.00. *DeLorme: Colorado Atlas & Gazetteer:* page 85, C-6.

North Central Mountains

N orth central Colorado is likely the state's principal destination, receiving more visitors than any other region. It's where more people go to play when visiting Colorado, as it typifies the Colorado mountain experience.

Lying to the northwest is the Yampa River Valley, a vast expanse of rolling green mountains. Here the traditional ranching and cowboy communities of Hahns Peak Village, Clark, and Steamboat Springs coalesce with a burgeoning recreational destination to deliver western congeniality with first-rate recreation. One of the premier rides in the area, the Nipple Peak Loop challenges the hardiest of riders. Moving east into Steamboat Springs, the Yampa Valley comes alive with a vast network of trails guaranteed to delight. Try soaking your bum in the hot springs of Strawberry Park or marvel at the 90-meter long jump sliding precipitously down Howelsen Hill.

The area east of Rabbit Ears Pass and the Continental Divide is more appropriately known as North Park, the moose-viewing capital of Colorado. Just west of Cameron Pass lies the Bockman Campground Loop, offering great moose-viewing potential. The stark and sheer face of the Nokhu Crags is breathtaking. Here the landscape is marked by towering ponderosa and lodgepole pine. During the autumn months, golden aspen appear as a patchwork in North Park's mountains.

Centrally located in this region lies the town of Winter Park, in the Fraser Valley. With over 600 miles of maintained trails for every ability level and the most extensive trail system in the Colorado high country, it's no surprise that Winter Park and the Fraser Valley bill themselves as "Mountain Bike Capital USA™." Typifying the riding in this area, the Tipperary Creek Loop offers soft singletrack, fast descents, and moderate climbs.

Just south of Winter Park and the Fraser Valley are bustling Summit and Eagle Counties, the modern heart of Colorado. With I–70 running straight through Colorado's heart, Summit and Eagle Counties are among the most accessible mountain regions in the state. Since these counties have the highest concentration of ski resorts of any other area in the state (Vail was even host to the 1999 World Alpine Ski Championship), they provide a treasure trove of lift-accessible mountain bike terrain after the winter snowmelt. That's not to say, however, that the trails described herein offer easy and immediate access to the top. Far from it. We earn our turns here. Vail's famed Grand Traverse Trail passes by views of the Holy Cross Wilderness and the Gore, Sawatch, and New York Mountain ranges, while Breckenridge's Wise Mountain Trail is one of the most impressive stretches of the 470-mile-long Colorado Trail. Some of the area's other highlights include the historic gold-mining town of Breckenridge, which is surrounded by the Tenmile mountain range, the Vail Valley, the Colorado Ski Museum and Hall of Fame, and the Dillon Reservoir.

11 Nipple Peak Loop

By all accounts, the Nipple Peak Loop is a stellar trail, but not for the faint-hearted. It requires advanced skills in climbing and descending. Covering 20.5 miles, this loop offers an elevation gain of roughly 3,000 feet, with the highest elevation topping off at 9,600 feet. Bring lots of sandwiches for this ride and expect to be out most of the day. The challenging climbs and incredibly fast and technical singletrack place this trail on equal par with any of Colorado's finest. Although area locals seem to prefer riding it clockwise, the loop can be done just as enjoyably counterclockwise. If ridden counterclockwise, the climbing comes early, but makes for more hike-a-bike sections up the steeper and rockier sections of trail. Also, riding it counterclockwise allows the rider to return to his or her vehicle via easier gravel roads. If ridden clockwise, the rider descends more technically challenging sections but will also have to contend with much of the climbing toward the end of the loop. This ride follows the loop clockwise.

Start: At the Nipple Peak Loop Trailhead.
Length: 20.5-mile loop.
Approximate riding time: Advanced riders, 3 to 3.5 hours; Intermediate riders, 4 to 4.5 hours.
Technical difficulty: Technically moderate to challenging due to the variety of roots, rock, and ruts.
Physical difficulty: Physically challenging to demanding due to the taxing climbs at high elevations.
Terrain: Paved road, dirt road, doubletrack, and singletrack—includes thick roots, loose rock, and steep inclines and offers soft, pine-needled surfaces, muddy sections, and sandy patches.
Trail contacts: Routt National Forest, Hahns Peak/Bears Ears Ranger District, 925 Weiss Drive, Steamboat Springs, 80487; (970) 879-1870.
Schedule: July to October.
Maps: USGS maps: Elkhorn Mountain, Hahns Peak, Meaden Peak, Shield Mountain; Routt National Forest map.
Nearest town: Hahns Peak Village.
Other trail users: Hikers, equestrians, backpackers, and motorcyclists.
Canine compatibility: Dog friendly.

Getting There

From Steamboat Springs: Drive west on U.S. Highway 40. Turn right onto Elk River Road (County Road 129), just after the 7-Eleven. Drive on Elk River Road for 32.5 miles, passing through the towns of Clark, Hahns Peak Village, and Columbine. At 30.5 miles, Elk River Road turns to dirt and changes its name to Forest Road 129. After 32 miles, look to your right for the brown Nipple Peak East/Trail 1147 sign. Just beyond the sign, turn left onto the fire road. Cross the cattle guard and pass through the gate before parking your vehicle. *DeLorme: Colorado Atlas & Gazetteer:* Page 16, A and B 1–2

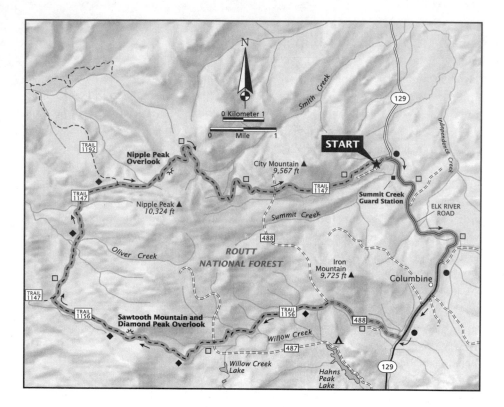

The Ride

The Nipple Peak Loop takes its name from the protruding promontory located in the northernmost reaches of Routt National Forest, near the Wyoming border. Nestled roughly 15 miles to the northwest of Hahns Peak, the wind-scoured mountain visible from downtown Steamboat Springs, Nipple Peak is far less distinguished than its neighbor. That's not to say, however, that area locals don't appreciate Nipple Peak. On the contrary, Nipple Peak is, perhaps, even more appreciated, if only for its association with that particular body part. Although some may argue that referring to a mountain peak as a nipple is brash at best, I wonder what those same people would think if it were known that the nipple in question actually belonged to someone at one time.

"Maggie's Nipple" (the one-time name of Nipple Peak) was named after Maggie Baggs, the common-law wife of George Baggs (who lent his name to Baggs, Wyoming). According to the cowhands on the Baggs' Double Eleven Ranch, Maggie enjoyed belittling and bossing the hired help, and on occasion would take certain less-than-honorable liberties with them. One can only imagine the sport made of Maggie behind her back.

On a routine roundup, cowhand Jack Farrell referred to the infamous peak as "Maggie's Nipple." When word reached Maggie that her honor had been attacked, she had Jack publicly horsewhipped. Otherwise unaffected by the slur, Maggie ran off to California with a red-haired, freckle-faced cowboy named Mike Sweet. After the money from her divorce settlement was exhausted, Sweet skipped town. When last anyone heard, Maggie was managing "rooming apartments" as a "social matron" in Galveston, Texas. Maggie Baggs's story notwithstanding, the Nipple Peak Loop remains one of the most sought after mountain bike trails in all of Northwest Colorado.

Nipple Peak stands within close proximity to Hahns Peak, its slightly more dignified neighbor. The Ute Indians (the so-called Top-of-the-Mountain People) were the first to appreciate Hahns Peak, which they called "Old Baldy." They would use the peak's massive 10,839-foot crown as a lookout. From atop the peak, scouts could see well into what today are Wyoming, Utah, and Colorado.

Hahns Peak owes its present name to the German immigrant Joseph Hahn, who came to Colorado in 1860 prospecting for gold and found it in the Hahns Peak Basin. Delayed by the Civil War, Hahn returned to the area in 1865 with William Doyle and Captain George Way. Together they established the Hahns Peak Mining District. Having left Hahn in camp one summer day, Doyle and Way climbed to the yet-unnamed peak's summit with a waterproof Preston and Merrill baking powder tin. Inside the tin Doyle had placed a scrap of paper upon which he had written: "This is named Hahns Peak by his friend and comrade, William A. Doyle, August 27, 1865." The tin was left atop the peak, anchored in stones.

Although the Hahns Peak Mining District failed to strike the mother lode, the town was the county seat for thirty-five years and remains Routt County's oldest permanent town. As for Hahns Peak, perhaps its greatest distinction came in 1912, when the federal government authorized the Routt National Forest to build one of the first fire lookout stations in the Rocky Mountain region. It seems fitting that after all the digging and scrambling for gold over its rocky slope, Hahns Peak had become once again a lookout. In a way, Chief Colorow, the stubborn Ute Indian who fought to keep his tribe's mountain from being exploited, finally succeeded in securing "Old Baldy" for his Top-of-the-Mountain People.

With a nod to Chief Colorow, modern-day guardians of the mountain pedal their way to surrounding heights scouting for prospective singletrack. And considering the singletrack of Nipple Peak Loop, they have hit pure pay dirt.

Nearing the top of the first ridge climb to views of Sawtooth Mountain and California Park.

The route begins by heading south on County Road 129. From CR 129 you connect with Forest Road 488 and begin to climb moderately. Hahns Peak lies to the east. Once you pick up the singletrack Trail 1156 (Prospector Trail), the terrain offers fast, root- and rock-filled descents through tall aspen and lodgepole pine. After two short climbs, you cross Willow Creek, before arriving at a large area of deadfall. The climb from out of the deadfall area is beset with steep and rutted terrain.

Once you cross FR 488, be prepared for a long grunt of a climb through aspens and hillside meadows. This is a good place to fuel up for the long climb ahead. At the top of the ridge, gorgeous views of Sawtooth Mountain await the diligent climber. Your climb to this overlook is rewarded with 3 miles of prime, rocky real estate. From here, it's a 3-mile assault on some very steep and technical terrain through old-growth forests. The singletrack eventually drops you onto a service road at 10.3 miles. Cross the road and continue descending down the singletrack.

After crossing the forks of Oliver Creek, a tough sandy section awaits, as well as a grueling climb through the aspens ahead. After climbing sharply for roughly 1 mile, the forest turns to pine and the pitch begins to level off as the trail snakes over rocks and roots. From the top of this ridge at 15.3 miles, the trail descends rapidly over technical root sections, through a couple of creeks, and past the south side of an old logging area. Sections of trail hug the hillside rather precariously, sometimes causing you to slip a little. Careful. Once you cross Forest Road 487, pick up the singletrack on the other side. This final descent is sandy, so take care when ripping around corners and over berms. Continue descending, bearing right at all junctions, to your vehicle.

Miles and Directions

0.0 START at the Nipple Peak Loop Trailhead. Return to Elk River Road and ride back (south) toward Columbine.

2.5 Elk River Road turns to pavement.

3.0 Pass through the town of Columbine.

4.0 Bear right onto FR 488.

5.5 A singletrack trail veers off to the left of FR 488. This is the trailhead for Trail 1156 (Prospector Trail) and the beginning of the singletrack for the Nipple Peak Loop. Bear left here onto Trail 1156 and descend through a stand of aspen.

8.2 Cross FR 487 and continue on the singletrack on the other side, following the sign for Trail 1156.

9.4 Reach the top of the ridge and take in the stunning views of Sawtooth Mountain and California Park directly in front of you.

11.3 Trail 1156 intersects with Trail 1147 (Nipple Peak Trail). Bear right onto Trail 1147.

12.3 Cross the two forks of Oliver Creek and begin your long grunt of a climb through the aspens.

14.1 Reach the junction of Trail 1147 and Trail 1192 (Burton Creek Trail). Continue climbing on Trail 1147, passing Trail 1192 on your left.

15.3 Reach the top of the ridge, elevation 9,410 feet.

17.7 Reach the scree section, offering views of Nipple Peak.

17.9 Cross FR 488 and pick up the final stretch of trail on the other side.

18.6 The trail intersects with a doubletrack trail. Veer right, continuing your descent to your vehicle.

20.5 Reach your vehicle.

Ride Information

Local Information

City of Steamboat Springs, P.O. Box 775088, Steamboat Springs, 80477; (970) 879-2060; www.ci.steamboat.co.us.

Steamboat Springs Chamber Resort Association, 1255 Lincoln Avenue, Steamboat Springs, 80477; (970) 879-0880; www.steamboat-chamber.com.

Local Events and Attractions

Strawberry Park Hot Springs, Steamboat Springs; (970) 879-0342.

Tread of Pioneers Museum, Steamboat Springs; (970) 879-2214.

Steamboat Lake State Park, North of Steamboat Springs along FR 129; (970) 879-7019.

A Walking Tour of the Springs of Steamboat, Steamboat Springs; (970) 879-2214 (pick up area map at Tread of Pioneers Museum).

Organizations

Routt County Riders Bicycle Club, Steamboat Springs; (970) 879-1735.

Restaurants

Backcountry Provisions, Steamboat Springs; (970) 879-3617.

Steamboat Brewery & Tavern, Steamboat Springs; (970) 879-2233.

12 Lower Bear Trail

One of the appeals of this ride, indeed, one of the appeals of many rides in the Steamboat area, is that you can start riding from downtown Steamboat Springs. Lower Bear Trail was recently built to replace the old "Two-track" Trail that had previously run through private property. By rerouting the old "Two-track" Trail, Lower Bear Trail circumvents any private property. Although it may seem that this ride offers more climbing than descending, there is plenty of screaming descent awaiting you once you reach the trail's high point. Aside from the short but sweet singletrack descent from the top, the descent on Elk Park Road, straight and steep, more than makes up for any burn you may have felt while climbing. Indeed, the descent on Elk Park Road ranks among one of the best mountain bike descents along any road.

Start: At the corner of 3rd Street and Fish Creek Falls Road, by the Steamboat Springs Post Office.
Length: 16.6-mile loop.
Approximate riding time: Advanced riders, 1.5 hours; intermediate riders, 2–2.5 hours.
Technical difficulty: Technically moderate, with some more challenging sections along the descent of Elk Park Road.
Physical difficulty: Physically moderate to challenging, due to the extended and steep climbs at higher elevations.
Terrain: Paved road, four-wheel-drive dirt road, and singletrack. Riders encounter rocky singletrack, sand, ruts, and soft forest singletrack.
Trail contacts: Medicine Bow–Routt National Forest, Hahns Peak/Bears Ears Ranger District, 925 Weiss Drive, Steamboat Springs, 80487; (970) 879-1870.
Sore Saddle Cyclery, Steamboat Springs, 80487; (970) 879-1675.
Schedule: Mid-June to early October.
Maps: USGS maps: Steamboat Springs, Rocky Peak; *Trails Illustrated* maps 117, Clark, Buffalo Pass and 118, Steamboat Springs, Rabbit Ears Pass; Routt National Forest Map.
Nearest town: Steamboat Springs.
Other trail users: Hikers, campers, four-wheelers.
Canine-compatibility: Dog unfriendly, due to the vehicular traffic along this route.

Getting There

From downtown Steamboat Springs: Drive east on U.S. Highway 40 (Lincoln Avenue) to 3rd Street. At the light, turn left by the Steamboat Springs Post Office and Wells Fargo Bank. Drive for one block and intersect Fish Creek Falls Road. Park your vehicle along 3rd Street or in the Wells Fargo Bank parking lot across 3rd Street and begin riding up Fish Creek Falls Road. *DeLorme: Colorado Atlas & Gazetteer:* Page 16, D-3.

The Ride

From downtown Steamboat Springs, riders begin climbing up Fish Creek Falls Road. Fish Creek Falls Road takes its name from a popular Steamboat tourist attraction, Fish Creek Falls. The falls start from between two large granite rocks surrounded by a stately row of thick evergreens and fall more than 100 feet to the creek below. Including the several cascades below and above the falls, Fish Creek Falls is estimated to be 283 feet long. Some say that Coors Brewing Company took Fish Creek Falls as its model when it designed its beer bottle label.

Unless yours is a dehydration pack, this is the closest to beer that you'll be getting until after the ride. Upon passing the Steamboat Springs Health and Recreation Center to your right, you may notice aromas usually associated with someone in serious gastrointestinal distress. What you probably smell is the Health and Rec's three spring-fed, natural bicarbonate and lithium pools. Early Ute

Catching a bit of air on the speedy Elk Park Road.

Indians made their camp along the banks of where the Heart Springs Pool sits today. Local legend identifies the hill behind the heart-shaped, cement-lined pool as the site of the last great battle in Steamboat Springs between the Arapaho and the Ute Indians. From here continue climbing up Fish Creek Falls Road to its intersection with Amethyst Drive. Amethyst Drive will weave through a residential neighborhood before intersecting with Routt County Road 36 (Hot Springs Road).

Hot Springs Road passes through the broad expanse of Strawberry Park Valley. As you ride through this valley, you'll be able to see Rocky Peak directly to the north. Just before crossing Soda Creek, Hot Springs Road will turn to dirt before intersecting with Elk Park Road.

The intersection of Hot Springs Road and Elk Park Road marks the beginning of the road's toughest climb as well as the point you return to on Elk Park Road. After this section, though, it's a relatively short distance to a great overlook of Mount Werner and the road's high point. The tall, cool aspens at the top of Hot Springs Road provide an inviting place to catch your breath, sip on some water, and take a bite out of your Backcountry Provision's sandwich. From here, it's a speedy descent to the Lower Bear Trailhead.

In 2000 Steamboat's Routt County Riders bicycling organization received a $13,000 grant from GOCO to construct Lower Bear Trail. A RockShox Club Assistance Grant also helped fund the construction of the trail. Routt County Riders, along with the Forest Service, the Rocky Mountain Youth Corps, and the International Mountain Bicycling Association (IMBA), completed the trail in September 2001. Replacing the old "Two-Track Trail," Lower Bear Trail delivers 800 feet of elevation gain that is less steep than the old "Two-Track Trail." The project resulted in a newly constructed 1.5-mile connector to the old "Two-Track Trail" and a 1-mile reconstruction of the old "Two-Track Trail."

From the trailhead, pass the Forest Service trail sign and ride between two boulders to connect with the singletrack. The trail switches back a number of times as it climbs steeply across a western-sloping hillside covered in scrub oak. The singletrack at this point is smooth. Just after 7 miles into your ride, you're offered easterly views of Buffalo Pass and Mount Werner. Behind you lie views of Elk Valley and the Sleeping Giant. Nearing 8 miles, the trail will begin to level off a bit, as it continues to offer views of Yampa Valley through intermittent stands of aspen and scrub oak.

Arriving at the trail's high point, you begin descending through tall stands of aspen over smooth singletrack. Just after 9 miles into your ride, you'll arrive at the trail's "lunarscape section." Here, marked by cairns, the route travels over imbedded rock toward its final descent to Elk Park Road. As the trail descends in a more southerly direction, you are rewarded with a fast run through a mixed conifer and aspen forest.

Once on Elk Park Road, it's a fast, steep, and rutted descent to Hot Springs Road, all under a cover of quaking aspen and mixed conifers. Excessive speeds are easily attainable, so watch out for vehicular traffic or stray elk. At roughly 10 and 11 miles into your ride, you come to two particularly steep, sandy, and rutted sections. Some riders have been known to launch themselves during these sections, so check your speed. After the second steep section, you can let it ride and cruise down the rest of the way. The banked sections toward the end of Elk Park Road make for a fun, "velodromatic" finish to the descent. Once connected with Hot Springs Road, bear left and return the way you came.

Miles and Directions

0.0 START at the junction of 3rd Street and Fish Creek Falls Road, by the Steamboat Springs Post Office. Bear right and begin riding up Fish Creek Falls Road, passing above the Steamboat Springs Health and Recreation Club on your right.

0.3 Bear left onto Amethyst Drive, following signs for Buffalo Pass, Perry Mansfield, and the Hot Springs. Once on Amethyst, after passing through the first block of residential homes, you'll pass Spring Creek Trail to your right, another great ride. From the Spring Creek Trail intersection, continue climbing on Amethyst through a residential neighborhood before passing the Steamboat Springs high school at 1.3 miles.

2.0 Amethyst Drive intersects CR 36 (Hot Springs Road). Bear right and continue riding on CR 36 in a northerly direction, through Strawberry Park Valley.

3.7 CR 36 turns into a dirt road. Cross Soda Creek via Soda Creek Bridge and continue riding along CR 36.

4.6 Pass the Lowell Whiteman School on your left.

5.1 Pass Elk Park Road to your right. This is where you will be returning later on in the ride.

5.9 As the road cuts sharply to the left, you're offered one of the best views of Mount Werner (the Steamboat Springs ski mountain). An aspen glen marks the end of the climb on Hot Springs Road.

6.7 Hot Springs Road will intersect with the primitive Lower Bear Trail campground and trailhead. Bear right into the Lower Bear Trail campground and connect with the singletrack to the north of the campground.

8.3 Lower Bear Trail will intersect with the old "Two-Track Trail" to your right. From here, the old "Two-Track Trail" and new Lower Bear Trail follow the same route for roughly 1 mile. Continue riding along Lower Bear Trail, heading in a northerly direction.

8.7 Arrive at the trail's high point. Continue riding in a northerly direction over smooth singletrack.

9.6 Lower Bear Trail intersects with Elk Park Road. Bear right onto Elk Park Road and descend in a southerly direction to Hot Springs Road.

11.5 Elk Park Road intersects with Hot Springs Road. Bear left on Hot Springs Road and return the way you came.

16.6 Arrive at your vehicle.

Ride Information

Local Information

City of Steamboat Springs, P.O. Box 775088, Steamboat Springs, 80477; (970) 879–2060; www.ci.steamboat.co.us.

Steamboat Springs Chamber Resort Association, 1255 Lincoln Avenue, Steamboat Springs, 80477; (970) 879–0880; www.steamboat-chamber.com.

Local Events and Attractions

Strawberry Park Hot Springs, Steamboat Springs; (970) 879–0342.

A Walking Tour of the Springs of Steamboat, (pick up area map at Tread of Pioneers Museum).

Steamboat Springs Health and Recreation Center, 136 Lincoln Avenue, Steamboat Springs; (970) 879–1828.

Organizations

Routt County Riders Bicycle Club, Steamboat Springs; (970) 879–1735.

Restaurants

Backcountry Provisions, 635 Lincoln Avenue, Steamboat Springs; (970) 879–3617.

Harwigs, 911 Lincoln Avenue, Steamboat Springs; (970) 879–1980.

Steamboat Brewery & Tavern, 435 Lincoln Avenue, Steamboat Springs; (970) 879–2233.

13 Bockman Campground Loop

Linking the Cache La Poudre–North Park Scenic and Historic Byway and old logging roads, the Bockman Campground Loop offers a mostly mellow ride with 2 miles of somewhat difficult climbing over 10,000 feet. The loop introduces the rider to pristine North Park, the moose-viewing capital of Colorado. The many logging roads make for a variety of mountain bike options. Caution should be observed when riding these roads. The Bockman Campground Loop is a great loop to do during the week, when motor traffic is considerably reduced. Be sure to carry insect repellent, as the mosquitoes in North Park can be dreadful.

Start: From the turnout for Lake Agnes, approximately 2.5 miles from the summit of Cameron Pass on the south side of Colorado Highway 14.
Length: 19.9-mile loop.
Approximate riding time: Advanced riders, 1.5 hours; intermediate riders, 2.5 to 3 hours.
Technical difficulty: Technically easy, since the trail travels over a forest service road.
Physical difficulty: Physically moderate. Although most of this ride is a casual cruise through North Park, portions are quite steep and travel over 10,000 feet.
Terrain: Surface includes paved highway, improved dirt roads, and rougher jeep roads. Bockman Road was recently improved, so many of the ruts and washouts have been replaced by drainage dips.

Trail contacts: Colorado State Forest State Park, 2746 County Road 41, Walden, 80480; (970) 723-8366.
Colorado State Parks, North Region Office, 3745 East Prospect Road, Suite 2, Fort Collins, 80525; (970) 226-6641.
Schedule: Late June to October.
Maps: USGS maps: Gould; Clark Peak; *Trails Illustrated map* 112, Poudre River and Cameron Pass and 114, Walden and Gould; Never Summer Nordic Mountain Bike Trail Map, Yurts of Never Summer Nordic.
Nearest town: Walden.
Other trail users: Equestrians, campers, anglers, four-wheelers, hikers, and picnickers.
Canine compatibility: Dog friendly, but dogs must be under control and on a 6-foot or shorter leash.

Getting There

From Fort Collins: Take U.S. Highway 287 north to Colorado Highway 14 west. Drive on CO 14 for 61.9 miles, passing through the Poudre Canyon and going over 10,276-foot Cameron Pass, before turning left into the Lake Agnes turnout. The Lake Agnes turnout is approximately 2.5 miles west of Cameron Pass. Park your vehicle here and begin by riding west on CO 14. *DeLorme: Colorado Atlas & Gazetteer:* Page 18, D-2 to D-3.

The Ride

The Bockman Campground Loop is nestled in the northern reaches of Colorado's North Park. Within the Colorado State Forest State Park's 70,768 acres lie endless

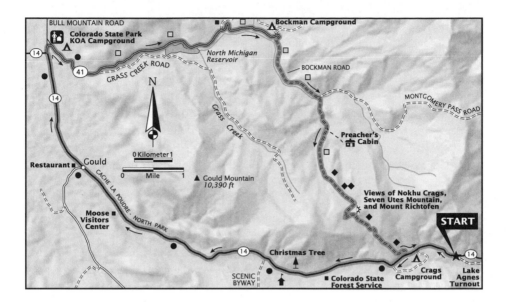

logging roads on which to observe area wildlife and explore the region's rich logging history.

North Park stretches along the west side of the Medicine Bow Mountains and into the north end of the Never Summer Range. Originally called "Bull Pen" by native Ute Indians, North Park provided a natural grazing environment for large herds of buffalo. With the buffalo long since removed from Colorado's injured reserve list, the "Bull Pen" now boasts the highest concentration of moose in Colorado.

Although native to Colorado, moose were rarely seen in North Park until the late 1970s when the Colorado Division of Wildlife (DOW) decided to establish a moose herd here. In March 1978, twelve moose were rounded up near the Bear River in Utah. Financed by private donations, the moose were tranquilized, removed by helicopter, and transported in cattle trucks to North Park. Having been tested for disease, the moose were released on the upper end of North Park's Illinois River.

Due to its ideal habitat of willow-lined streams, North Park is now home to an estimated 550 to 600 moose. In recognition of the proliferation of moose in the area, the Colorado Senate in 1995 designated North Park and the nearby town of Walden the "Moose Viewing Capital of Colorado."

The Bockman Campground Loop is an ideal introduction to this celebrated area. The first 9 miles of the 19.9-mile route pass over the 101-mile Cache La Poudre–North Park Scenic and Historic Byway. The route passes the band-saw spires of the 12,400-foot Nokhu Crags—that's NO-koo, a corruption of the original Arapaho word "Neaha-no-xhu," meaning "eagle's nest"—and leads through the Colorado State Forest. Then it's on to the site of the largest logging camp ever to have operated in Colorado.

The first 1.5 miles is a fast-cruising descent past the Nokhu Crags and the Seven Utes Mountain. At mile 0.8, Bockman Road will be to your right. Here is where the Bockman Campground Loop reconnects with the highway. Heading toward the tiny town of Gould, you pass on your right the never-out-of-season Christmas Tree—a pine tree that's decorated year-round with garland and ornaments—and to your left, the Ranger Lakes Campground and the Moose Visitors Center. Once you officially enter the state forest, the route turns onto County Road 41, a dirt road.

Passing through a densely populated lodgepole pine forest, CR 41 forks just after 10 miles. Bear left, following the signs to Bockman Campground, and ride along the north rim of North Michigan Reservoir. Traveling along the willow-lined banks of the North Michigan drainage, you'll encounter perfect moose-viewing settings. As you ride away from the reservoir, the great expanse of Bull Mountain lies directly in front of you.

Heading toward the Bockman Campground, the route pierces the heart of North Park's prosperous logging tradition. By 1949 the Bockman Lumber Camp, now the Bockman Campground, was Colorado's largest operating logging camp. Derelict log loading ramps and sawdust piles—relics of logging days gone by—are all that remain of the camp's former glory. Albeit to a lesser degree, logging continues to be an important source of revenue for the state forest.

Starting from the Bockman Campground, Bockman Road threads its way through the forest and travels over 10,000 feet. You may notice the forest beginning to thin to your left at roughly 14 miles into your ride. A plaque here commemorates a boy scout who, in order to receive the highest rank of Eagle Scout, had to organize and conduct a community project. The project here was to thin the forest. Thinning forests is a means of regeneration whereby competition among existing trees is lessened, thereby adding to the natural diversity of the forest.

After passing the Eagle Scout's community project, the route becomes increasingly tougher. At 15.3 miles, Bockman Road intersects with Montgomery Pass Road. Continue on Bockman Road and splash through the North Fork Michigan River. By mile 16.5 the steepest section of the route begins, ending only after a lung-busting 1-mile climb to the top. At 17.6 miles, Bockman Road levels. In stark

Bull Mountain.

contrast to the otherwise thick forest, a large clearcut lies to your left. Hike through the clearcut to the very top and take in the beautiful views of the Nokhu Crags and Seven Utes Mountain to the south, Bull Mountain to the north, and the Mount Zirkel Wilderness Area to the west.

From here it's a speedy and steep descent to CO 14. You'll come to an intersection at 17.8 miles. An unidentified road leads off to the right. Continue left, along Bockman Road as it drops you past gray slab piles of logging remains and through a lush green meadow replete with aspen, lupine, and thistle. Descend onto CO 14 and bear left for the 0.8-mile return to your vehicle.

Miles and Directions

- **0.0** START at the Lake Agnes turnout. Head back onto CO 14 and continue riding west down the highway.
- **3.0** The Colorado State Forest Service is to your left.

4.5 Christmas Tree is to your right.

5.6 The Moose Visitors Center for the Colorado State Forest is to your left.

6.2 Enter the tiny town of Gould.

8.9 Turn right into the KOA Campground and the Colorado State Park and immediately bear left onto CR 41. Stop at the ranger station and purchase your $2.00 daily pass. The general store at the KOA Campground is a good place to stock up on snacks for the rest of the ride.

10.2 County Road 41 forks. Take the left fork, following signs for the Bockman Campground and the moose-viewing deck.

12.6 County Road 41 forks again. Veering off CR 41, take the right fork, following signs to Bockman Campground. The left fork leads to the moose-viewing.

13.8 Again, the road forks. The left fork leads you over a cattle guard to Bockman Campground, while the right fork leads you to CO 14 along Bockman Road. Bear right onto this road.

14.5 Bockman Road intersects Montgomery Pass Road, which leads to Montgomery Pass and the Montgomery Pass yurts. Continue riding straight on Bockman Road, following signs for CO 14.

15.3 Bockman Road intersects Diamond Peaks Road. Continuing on Bockman Road, blast through the North Fork of North Michigan River and resume your Bockman Campground Loop.

16.0 Bockman Road forks again. Bear left. The right side only leads to a locked gate. From here the going gets a lot tougher, all the way to the top at 17.6 miles. Expect drainage dips.

17.6 As you near the top, there's a clearcut off to the left. Hike through it and take in the views of the Nokhu Crags to your south, Bull Mountain to the north, and the farthest stretches of the Mount Zirkel Wilderness due west.

17.8 Come to an intersection. Continue left on Bockman Road.

19.1 Bockman Road connects with CO 14. Bear left and ride the last 0.8 mile to the Lake Agnes turnout and your vehicle.

19.9 Arrive back at your vehicle.

Ride Information

Fees and Permits
$2.00 daily park pass is required for each bicycle entering the Colorado State Forest State Park; $5.00 daily park pass is required for any motorized vehicle to enter the Colorado State Forest.

Local Information
North Park Chamber of Commerce, 491 Main Street, Walden, 80480; (970) 723–4600.
U.S. Forest Service Visitor Information Center, 240 West Prospect, Fort Collins, 80526; (970) 498–2770.

Local Events and Attractions
The North Park Pioneer Museum, Walden; (970) 723–8371, (970) 723–4212, (970) 723–4711 (located behind the Jackson County courthouse).
North Park Fair, Walden; (970) 723–4600.
Yurts of Never Summer Nordic, Fort Collins; (970) 482–9411; www.neversummernordic.com.

14 Hot Springs to Mad Creek to Red Dirt Trail Loop

Mountain bike riders in Steamboat Springs are tough. When one trail isn't long enough to fill up the space of a day, local riders combine two or more trails. The Hot Springs to Mad Creek to Red Dirt Trail Loop is more than just a ride—it's three rides combined. A favorite among area locals, this loop spotlights the Strawberry Park Hot Springs, the steep-walled canyon of Mad Creek, and the quiet solitude of Red Dirt Trail. Each one of these rides can be ridden separately or fashioned into shorter loops.

Start: From the corner of 3rd Street and Fish Creek Falls Road, by the Steamboat Springs Post Office.

Length: 24.3-mile loop, with options to shorten.

Approximate riding time: Advanced riders, 2 to 2.5 hours; intermediate riders, 3 to 3.5 hours.

Technical difficulty: Technically moderate. Most of the trail rolls over smooth, hard-packed singletrack, although there are a couple of challenging rocky sections (predominantly on the hot springs segment of the route).

Physical difficulty: Physically moderate to challenging. The climb to the top of the Hot Springs is challenging, and the road is steep in sections and climbs to heights above 8,000 feet.

Terrain: Paved road, improved dirt road, and singletrack. Riders encounter rocky singletrack, sand, creek crossings, ruts, and soft forest singletrack.

Trail contacts: Hahns Peak/Bears Ears Ranger District, 925 Weiss Drive, Steamboat Springs, 80487; (970) 879-1870, Blowdown Hotline (970) 870-2192; www.fs.fed.us/r2/mor.
Sore Saddle Cyclery, Steamboat Springs; (970) 879-1675.
Medicine Bow–Routt National Forest (Blowdown Hotline), Steamboat Springs; (970) 870-2192; www.fs.fed.us/mrnf.

Schedule: Mid-June to early October.

Maps: USGS maps: Steamboat Springs, Rocky Peak, Mad Creek; *Trails Illustrated* maps 117, Clark, Buffalo Pass and 118, Steamboat Springs, Rabbit Ears Pass; Routt National Forest Map.

Nearest town: Steamboat Springs.

Other trail users: Hikers, campers, equestrians, and bathers.

Canine compatibility: Dog friendly.

Getting There

From downtown Steamboat Springs: Drive east on U.S. Highway 40 (Lincoln Avenue) to 3rd Street. At the light, make a left by the Steamboat Springs Post Office and Wells Fargo Bank. Drive for one block and intersect Fish Creek Falls Road. Park your vehicle and begin riding up Fish Creek Falls Road. *DeLorme: Colorado Atlas & Gazetteer:* Page 26, A-3.

The Ride

To reach the hot springs, riders pass through a long and verdant meadowland surrounded by expansive views of Steamboat Ski Resort and Buffalo Pass. This area is known as Strawberry Park (formerly called Sheddeger Park). From 1900 to 1916, Strawberry Park bore fields of commercially grown strawberries. The area was named after the Kansas farmer Lester J. Remington, who first noticed the marketability of the strawberries that grew in his hay meadows at the base of Buffalo Pass. The berries were harvested and then shipped to Denver. The newly built railroad afforded Remington accessibility to Denver's affluent market. Denver's lavish hotel and restaurant, the Brown Palace, became one of Strawberry Park's first accounts. Remington learned that his berries would continue to grow long after plants at lower elevations had stopped bearing fruit. Spurring the town's first economic boon, Strawberry Park became home to two flourishing general stores and provided Steamboat Springs with sixteen years of fruitful strawberry production. Area old-timers speak of Remington's strawberries as too big to fit into a drinking glass, and as sweet as they were large. Rising competition among other berry growers, coupled with a killing frost in the early summers of 1915 and 1916, ultimately caused Strawberry Park to cease its operations for good.

Long before strawberries blanketed this meadowland, summering Ute Indians used the open meadows to dry the roots of the yampa plant (a turnip-like plant that grows along the banks of the Yampa River) for winter storage. As winter approached, they would set up camp near the hot springs, basking in its warmth and bathing in its curative geothermal waters. Elk, too, would often descend from the higher elevations to drink from these waters and warm themselves, giving Ute Indians all the more reason to camp near the springs. Oftentimes after battle, Indians would visit these springs to rejuvenate their strength and vitality. For the Utes, these springs were sacred ground, under which Manitou, the supernatural force pervading the natural world, resided. Elaborating on this idea of the spiritual force beneath the ground, Dr. R. E. Jones writes, "Mineral Springs are magical in their charm for man. All people have an abiding faith in nature and the mysterious workings that are constantly taking place in her unseen laboratories deep below the earth's surface."

It wasn't long before Europeans discovered the curative powers of hot springs. During Colorado's rise as a health spa paradise in the latter part of the 1800s, bathers were known not only to soak in the hot springs' mineral-rich waters but also to drink from them. Lulita Crawford Pritchett, daughter of Steamboat Springs' founding father, describes the delicious taste of "iron water lemonade" in her book, *The Cabin at Medicine Springs.* A 1946 article in the Steamboat Springs paper, the *Pilot,* tells of a peculiar pastime among area residents. They would march down to the hot springs with picnic baskets and tea pots containing a few spoonfuls of tea. They would first boil their eggs in their tea pots full of spring water. After the eggs were boiled, a cup of tea was made from the leftover water to wash the eggs down.

From the Strawberry Park Hot Springs, riders descend along the north edge of Hot Springs Creek. In many places the trail slopes precipitously to the creek. Although this segment of trail isn't overly technical, there are a number of short technical sections that require advanced bicycle handling skills. With Hot Springs Creek to your left, the trail weaves in and out of lodgepole pine and aspen forests before letting out onto Mad House Road and the second part of the ride.

As you pedal north up the Mad Creek drainage along the wide, sometimes sandy and rocky trail, you'll notice the crashing waters of Mad Creek directly below. The nerve-jarring echoes from Mad Creek Canyon suggest why this creek is "Mad."

Strawberry Park Hot Springs.

Deriving its name, as you might assume, from its fast flowing waters, Mad Creek has taken its fair share of casualties. In 1877 a weary traveler narrowly escaped drowning in its current. His horse, not so lucky, was beaten to death on the rocks. So take pains not to get too close to the trail's edge, as it tightly hugs an east-facing slope on its way to the Mad House (a Forest Service guard station).

On the morning of October 25, 1997, easterly winds blowing over the Continental Divide and traveling in excess of 120 miles per hour razed roughly 20,000 acres of trees surrounding the Mad House. A wall of wind nearly 5 miles wide and 30 miles long destroyed over 4 million of Routt National Forest's Engelmann spruce and subalpine fir. One of the hardest hit areas of this Routt Divide Blowdown was the Mad Creek drainage. Although this route through Mad Creek Canyon lies to the south of the drainage's hardest hit areas, riders should nevertheless use caution when cornering around blind curves. The Forest Service is responding to this crisis by implementing salvage logging programs, conducting impact research projects, organizing trail rerouting procedures, and analyzing insect infestation probabilities.

Escaping the mad-running waters and the wind-torn forests, one finally finds sanctuary in the peaceful solitude of the Saddle Trail, a short connector to the Red Dirt Trail. After connecting onto the Saddle Trail, dense rows of golden aspen run alongside the singletrack and bow overhead like drawn swords at a West Point wedding. Riding through this peaceful, gold-leafed gauntlet, you pass rows of beautiful pearly everlasting (anaphalis margaritacea) before intersecting with Red Dirt Trail.

Red Dirt Trail combines exquisite hard-packed singletrack through some of the area's most undisturbed terrain. As you ride through varying aspen and fir forests, you're delivered a cool and quiet ride. You're thrown from your blissful reverie at 14.3 miles, when washboard ruts 12 inches deep and wide jostle the unsuspecting rider. Once you've connected with Elk River Road (County Road 129), bear left for the mellow highway ride back to Steamboat Springs.

Miles and Directions

0.0 START at the junction of 3rd Street and Fish Creek Falls Road, by the Steamboat Springs Post Office. Bear right and begin riding up Fish Creek Falls Road, passing above the Steamboat Springs Health and Recreation Club on your right.

0.3 Bear left onto Amethyst Drive, following signs for Buffalo Pass, Perry Mansfield, and the hot springs. Once on Amethyst, after passing through the first block of residential homes, pass Spring Creek Trail to your right (another great ride). From Spring Creek Trail, continue climbing on Amethyst through a residential neighborhood before passing the Steamboat Springs high school at 1.3 miles.

2.0 Amethyst Drive intersects County Road 36. Continue riding on CR 36 in a northerly direction, through Strawberry Park, following signs for the hot springs. Pass CR 38 to your right and the sign for Dry Lake Campground, 3 miles; Buffalo Pass, 11 miles; Fish Creek Reservoir, 16 miles; and Colorado Highway 14, 32 miles.

3.7 County Road 36 turns into a dirt road. Cross Soda Creek via Soda Creek Bridge and continue riding along CR 36.

5.9 As the road cuts sharply to the left, you're offered one of the best views of Mount Werner (the Steamboat Springs ski mountain). This point marks the end of the climb. The road weaves its way through dense aspen before descending to the Strawberry Park Hot Springs.

7.3 Arrive at the Strawberry Park Hot Springs. Ride through the red iron gate, entering the hot springs area, and ride down the hill. A private dirt road will be immediately to your right. Pass this road and pass another turnoff to your left that leads down to the hot springs. Continue riding straight ahead to the singletrack, toward the outhouse.

7.4 Reach the trailhead for the Hot Springs 1169 singletrack.

9.9 Arrive at the junction of the Hot Springs 1169 trail and Mad House Road. Here, the rider has a number of options from which to choose. **Option One:** (which we are featuring in this chapter) Bear left onto Mad House Road and descend to the paved CR 129 (Elk River Road). Once on CR 129, bear right and head for the singletrack climb up through Mad Creek Canyon. **Option Two:** Bear right onto Mad House Road and climb to high-alpine meadows. Reach the Mad House (Forest Service guard station), and ride down either Mad Creek Trail or Red Dirt Trail to CR 129. **Option Three:** Bear left onto Mad House Road and descend to the paved CR 129 (Elk River Road). Once on CR 129, bear left again and return to Steamboat Springs.

10.7 After following Option One, Mad Creek Trailhead will appear to your right. Ride into the Mad Creek parking lot and begin riding up the singletrack of Mad Creek Canyon, following signs for Mad Creek and Swamp Park.

12.2 Arrive at a gate and go through it. Continue riding straight ahead, along the wooden fence, and toward the Mad House.

12.4 Mad Creek Trail intersects with Saddle Trail 1140. Bear left onto Saddle Trail 1140. Saddle Trail heads in a southwesterly direction and eventually connects with Red Dirt Trail.

13.5 Saddle Trail 1140 intersects with Red Dirt Trail 1171. Bear left onto Red Dirt Trail, as it descends back down to CR 129 (Elk River Road). Bearing right leads to the Mount Zirkel Wilderness Area.

15.4 Red Dirt Trail 1171 intersects with CR 129 (Elk River Road). Bear left (south) onto CR 129.

21.0 The Steamboat Springs Airport is to your right. Pass the airport and ride down a speedy descent to U.S. Highway 40.

22.2 County Road 129 intersects with US 40. Bear left (east) onto US 40 and return to Steamboat Springs to complete the loop.

23.4 Enter the town of Steamboat Springs and intersect the Core Trail, a 10-foot-wide paved multi-use trail along the Yampa River. Bear left at the Yampa River Bridge, and right onto Lincoln Avenue. Then left on 3rd Street.

24.3 Arrive at the intersection of 3rd Street and Fish Creek Falls Road and your vehicle.

Ride Information

Local Information

City of Steamboat Springs, P.O. Box 755088, Steamboat Springs, 80477; (970) 879-2060; www.ci.steamboat.co.us.

Steamboat Springs Chamber Resort Association, 1255 Lincoln Avenue, Steamboat Springs, 80477; (970) 879-0880; www.steamboat-chamber.com.

Local Events and Attractions

Strawberry Park Hot Springs, Steamboat Springs; (970) 879-0342.

Tread of Pioneers Museum, Steamboat Springs; (970) 879-2214.

Steamboat Springs Health and Recreation Center, Steamboat Springs; (970) 879-1828.

Steamboat Lake State Park, north of Steamboat Springs along FR 129; (970) 879-7019.

Sweet Pea Tours, Steamboat Springs; (970) 879-5820 (hot springs tours).

Peak Experience Tours, Steamboat Springs; (970) 879-1873 (hot springs tours).

Organizations

Routt County Riders Bicycle Club, Steamboat Springs; (970) 879-1735.

Restaurants

Harwigs, Steamboat Springs; (970) 879-1980.

Backcountry Provisions, Steamboat Springs; (970) 879-3617.

15 Howelsen Hill Loop 6

As a skiing hill, Howelsen Hill has already been the proving grounds for more than thirty-seven Olympians, fourteen members of the Colorado Ski Hall of Fame, and six members of the National Ski Hall of Fame, and has sent more skiers to international competition than any other area in the nation. As a mountain biking hill, Howelsen Hill offers great singletrack riding immediately accessible from downtown Steamboat Springs. Billed as a quick ride to squeeze in before work, the Howelsen Hill Loop climbs 2.3 miles to a rock quarry before ripping down incredibly steep, rocky, and hard-packed singletrack.

Start: From the base of Howelsen Hill by the Tow House.

Length: 4.1-mile loop.

Approximate riding time: Advanced riders, 45 minutes; intermediate riders, 1 to 1.5 hours.

Technical difficulty: Technically moderate to challenging. There are a couple of tough rocky and steep sections with which to contend, but the majority of the route follows over hard-packed dirt singletrack and improved dirt road.

Physical difficulty: Physically moderate due to a short but steep section of road.

Terrain: Improved dirt road, doubletrack, and singletrack. The terrain includes sandy and rocky sections, creek crossings, and hard-packed dirt through meadows and aspen and fir forests.

Trail contacts: Howelsen Hill Ski Area, Steamboat Springs Parks and Recreation Department, P.O. Box 755088, Steamboat Springs, 80477; (970) 879-4300.

Schedule: June to early October.

Maps: USGS maps: Steamboat Springs; *Trails Illustrated* map 118, Steamboat Springs, Rabbit Ears Pass.

Nearest town: Steamboat Springs.

Other trail users: Hikers, joggers, and equestrians.

Canine compatibility: Dog friendly.

Getting There

From Steamboat Springs: Drive east on U.S. Highway 40 (Lincoln Avenue) and turn right onto 5th Street. Cross the 5th Street Bridge and the Yampa River. Turn right by the Rodeo Grounds and drive toward the softball fields. Bear left by the softball fields and park in the Howelsen Hill parking lot. Begin your ride by the Tow House at the base of Howelsen Hill. *DeLorme: Colorado Atlas & Gazetteer:* Page 26, A-2 to A-3.

The Ride

Howelsen Hill is holy ground—though you wouldn't necessarily know it, given its "other side of the tracks" heritage. Riders from downtown Steamboat Springs access the trails to Howelsen Hill by crossing the Yampa River via the 5th Street Bridge. Dividing the north from the south sides of Steamboat Springs, the Yampa River flows directly through the middle of town. Back in the early 1900s, the 5th Street

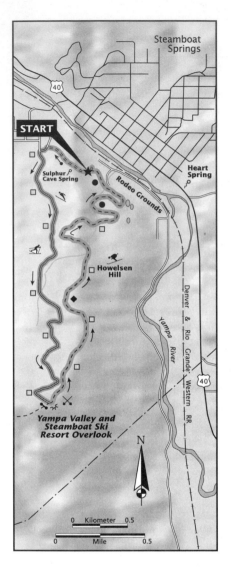

Bridge was more commonly referred to as the "Brooklyn Bridge"—more for its corrupt city-like connotations than for any physical similarity to the famous New York City bridge. As riders head toward Howelsen Hill via the 5th Street Bridge, they cross over into what was Steamboat Springs' red light district. While the north end of town had its bible thumpers, the south end of town enjoyed all the comforts whiskey, women, and cards could afford. Given this history, it seems unlikely that anything holy could arise from this side of the tracks.

Howelsen Hill gets its name from the Norwegian ski-jumping champion Carl Howelsen, who came to America in 1905. Barnum and Bailey Circus first discovered Howelsen while he was working as a stone mason in Chicago. The circus set up a makeshift ski jump inside arenas from Chicago to New York. Howelsen descended this slick ramp on his skis and soared through the air, not unlike the way he used to do as a boy growing up in Norway. His daring flights through the air, covering over 80 feet, thrilled audiences in New York City's Madison Square Garden. Having played the star attraction for the "Greatest Show on Earth," Howelsen found it not nearly as gratifying as the simple pleasures of living in Ski Town, U.S.A. He moved to Steamboat Springs in 1913. Although he would never become an Olympian, Howelsen would become a legend.

Almost immediately after arriving in Steamboat Springs, Howelsen was jumping and performing for the local crowds. In 1914 he organized the town's first Winter Carnival on Woodchuck Hill (the present site of Colorado Mountain College). This is not to say that the people of Steamboat didn't know what skiing was prior to Howelsen's arrival. As early as the 1880s, men like George Wren and Elmer Brooks skied to Morrison Creek to meet the mail carriage and ski the mail back to town. Among the Steamboat people, Howelsen found the same passion for skiing that he had. This is the connection he had been missing in the concrete jungles of Chicago and New York City.

In the summer following the first Steamboat Springs Winter Carnival, Howelsen helped organize the Steamboat Springs Winter Sports Club, the first nationally recognized ski club west of the Mississippi. By this time Howelsen had recognized the need for a first-class jumping hill, so in 1915 he had a Winter Carnival committee cutting underbrush and timber to make way for the first ski jump below Emerald Mountain. In February 1917, during the 4th Annual Winter Sports Carnival, the new ski jumping hill was officially christened Howelsen Hill.

Howelsen continued to promote ski jumping throughout Colorado. Enthusiasm for ski jumping grew by leaps and bounds. Howelsen's reward came in 1921 when he won the National Professional Ski Championships at Gennesee Mountain. Perhaps it was this final achievement that prompted him to return to the "old country" in the fall of that same year. Howelsen soon married a fellow Norwegian and lived out the remainder of his days in his homeland—no doubt on a pair of skis.

Left without their "Flying Norseman," the people of Steamboat Springs continued skiing. By the late 1930s, Howelsen Hill included not only a ski jump, but slalom and downhill courses as well. By 1934 a "boat tow," powered by a car motor, pulled skiers to the top of Howelsen Hill via cable and two sleds. The 1940s saw the construction of a log ski lodge at the base of Howelsen Hill, another rope tow, and one of the United States' longest ski lifts at that time, running from the hill's base to the top of Emerald Mountain. During the 1950s, a 90-meter ski jump was built and is still in use today.

In fact, all of Howelsen Hill is still being enjoyed, making it one of the oldest jumping complexes in the nation. Today, Howelsen Hill is an official city park and is managed by the Steamboat Springs Parks and Recreation Department. Just as the mountain brought the Steamboat Springs community together through skiing, it now brings people together through mountain biking.

It wasn't until 1998 that the first mountain bike trail signs appeared on Howelsen Hill. Prior to that, the trails were there; they just weren't marked. Today, the Parks and Recreation Department has marked six loop rides for added convenience. Loop

6 (the area's longest official ride) takes us to the top of Howelsen Hill and delivers us to the Rodeo Grounds. To access Loop 6, riders begin from the Tow House and pedal past the 90-meter jump before reaching the dirt access road. As the road climbs to the south, views of the Sleeping Giant lie to the west. Looking from the east, the mountain resembles a giant sleeping on his back, his knees drawn up. This road eventually takes you to the beginning of Loop 6 and a beautiful overlook. From the overlook, panoramic views from east to west include Mount Werner, Fish Creek Canyon, Buffalo Pass, Soda Mountain, Hahns Peak, and the Mount Zirkel Wilderness Area.

Loop 6 descends rapidly over rocky and sometimes steep terrain. After passing through intermittent forests of pine and aspen, the trail descends through a number of meadows before reaching the cow ponds. Once past the cow ponds, bear left to finish your ride with a narrow and steep descent to the Rodeo Grounds and the base of Howelsen Hill.

Miles and Directions

0.0 START riding on the doubletrack by the Tow House at the base of Howelsen Hill, following signs for Loops 1 through 6 and Howelsen Hill Hiking Trail. Bear right around the Tow House and ride up in front of the 90-meter ski jump.

0.2 After a brief descent, the doubletrack intersects with a singletrack. Bear left onto this singletrack, following signs for Loops 1 through 6. This singletrack immediately connects with another dirt road. Bear left onto the dirt road and continue climbing.

0.4 This dirt road intersects with another dirt road. Bear right here, continuing in a southerly direction, riding on the same road on which you started.

0.8 Arrive at a fork, noticeable by a squat wall of river stone encased within wire. A singletrack trail bears to the right as the road continues to the left. Bearing left here leads you to trail signs for Loops 1 through 6, while bearing right on the singletrack leads you to another dirt road. Either fork will lead you to the top and the beginning of Loop 6. At this junction, bear right onto the singletrack, passing the wall of river stone, and continue climbing.

0.9 The singletrack intersects with another dirt road. Veer left onto this dirt road. This road leads you to the top of Howelsen Hill, passing signs for Option Meadows cross-country and Loops 2 through 6.

1.3 Pass the beginning of Loop 2.

1.5 Pass the beginning of Loop 3.

1.7 Pass the beginning of Loop 4.

2.0 Pass the beginning of Loop 5.

2.3 Reach the top of Loop 6. Begin your descent by ripping down the shale-torn singletrack, past the Loop 6 sign on the right. The initial descent on Loop 6 heads straight for the road that delivered you to the top. Approximately 25 feet before you reach this road again, another singletrack trail veers off to the right (at 2.4 miles). Veer right onto this singletrack. It drops you in a northeasterly direction through a forest of scrub oak.

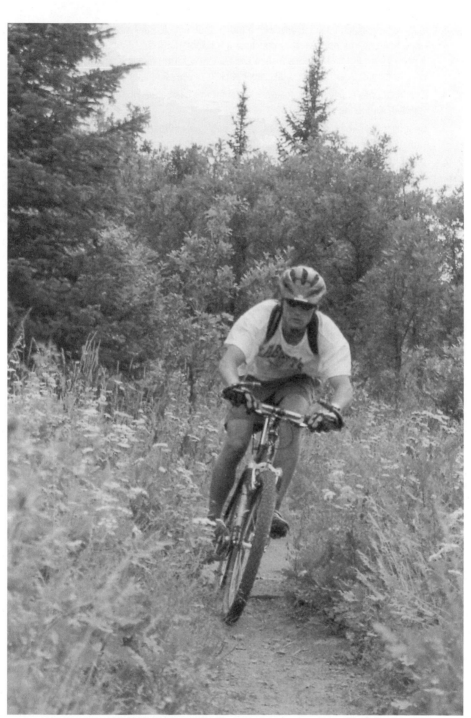

Making short work of the "Hill's" singletrack.

3.1 The Loop 6 singletrack intersects with a rough doubletrack. Bear left onto this double-track, heading in a northwesterly direction. If you look down this doubletrack, you'll notice a point where the trail reaches a short crest. Just over this crest is a singletrack that bears off to the right. Bear right onto this singletrack. It passes a couple of cow ponds.

3.5 Bear right onto a singletrack, following signs for the base area. Howelsen Hill will be to your left. Notice the chairlifts.

3.8 Bear right again onto the singletrack. It will lead to a dirt road directly behind the Rodeo Grounds. Once on this dirt road, bear left and descend to the parking lot.

4.1 Reach the base of Howelsen Hill and your vehicle.

Ride Information

Local Information

City of Steamboat Springs, P.O. Box 755088, Steamboat Springs, 80477; (970) 879–2060; www.ci.steamboat.co.us.
Steamboat Springs Chamber Resort Association, 1255 Lincoln Avenue, Steamboat Springs, 80477; (970) 879–0880; www.steamboat-chamber.com.

Local Events and Attractions

Strawberry Park Hot Springs, Steamboat Springs; (970) 879–0342.
Tread of Pioneers Museum, Steamboat Springs; (970) 879–2214 (offers a walking-tour map).

Steamboat Lake State Park, north of Steamboat Springs along Forest Road 129; (970) 879–7019.

Organizations

Routt County Riders Bicycle Club, Steamboat Springs; (970) 879–1735.

Restaurants

Harwigs, Steamboat Springs; (970) 879–1980.
Backcountry Provisions, Steamboat Springs; (970) 879–3617.

16 Arapaho Ridge Trail

This Continental Divide–brushing ride, bordering on the Routt and Arapaho National Forests, is great for anyone seeking an awe-inspiring 360-degree view, coupled with a savage descent. Although the view and descent do come at a price, the climb to the top of the Divide shouldn't deter any dreamy-eyed mountain biker. Once you reach the top, you're rewarded with a narrow, rutted, rocky, and switchbacking singletrack descent. The trail continues its vertical fall over rocky hillsides, through creeks, meadows, ponds, and evergreen forests before entering into the lower elevations and increasingly smoother singletrack. Speed was never so pretty.

Start: From the trailhead for Arapaho Ridge Trail and Hyannis Peak Trail 1135.
Length: 12.2-mile out-and-back.
Approximate riding time: Advanced riders, 2–2.5 hours; intermediate riders, 3–4 hours.
Technical difficulty: Technically demanding due to the amount of rocky, rutted, and sloping terrain upon reaching the higher elevations.
Physical difficulty: Physically challenging to demanding due to grueling climbs.
Terrain: Singletrack. Travels over soft, forest earth, coupled with exposed rocks and roots; sloping, marshy meadows; rocky and rutted tundra-like terrain; and a number of creek crossings.
Trail contacts: Medicine Bow–Routt National Forests Parks Ranger District, P.O. Box 1210,
2103 East Park Avenue, Kremmling, 80459; (970) 724-3437.
Motion Sports, Kremmling; (970) 724-9067.
Schedule: July to mid-October.
Maps: USGS maps: Hyannis Peak, Buffalo Peak; *Trails Illustrated* map 106; Routt National Forest Map; Kremmling Area Mountain Bike Map (this map incorporates Arapaho Ridge Trail as part of the larger "Continental Divide Loop"; however, locating the "jeep road" off of Arapaho Ridge Trail to connect the loop is an ascetic's lesson in patience, if not futility).
Nearest town: Kremmling.
Other trail users: Hikers, campers, and anglers.
Canine compatibility: Dog friendly.

Getting There

From Kremmling: Drive west on U.S. Highway 40 for 15.6 miles before turning right onto County Road 27 (Chimney Rock Road), following signs for Chimney Rock. After 6 miles (from when you turned onto CR 27) enter the Arapaho National Forest. County Road 27 becomes Forest Road 103. Drive on FR 103 for another 4 miles before bearing right onto FR 700. Soon thereafter, FR 700 intersects FR 104. Bear left at this intersection and continue on FR 700 for another 5 miles before FR 700 forks again. Bear right at this fork and continue on FR 700. Drive for another 4 miles to the trailhead for the Arapaho Ridge Trail. After crossing the Middle Fork Arapaho Creek, the trail will be to your right, marked by a bulletin board. *DeLorme: Colorado Atlas & Gazetteer:* Page 27, A-6 to A-7.

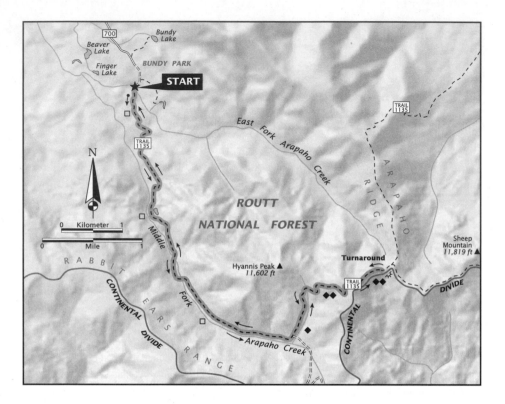

The Ride

Arapaho Ridge Trail remains one of Colorado's most anomalous trails. Located in the Routt National Forest, the trail leads to the top of the Continental Divide, the geographical dividing line of the Platte River watershed, which flows to the Atlantic Ocean, and the Colorado River watershed, which flows to the Pacific Ocean. The Divide also marks the boundary between the Arapaho and Routt National Forests. Although the Arapaho National Forest includes land on both sides of the Continental Divide, a vast majority of its land lies near the high population communities of the Front Range. As such, the Arapaho National Forest is one of Colorado's most visited national forests.

The 1,126,346-acre Routt National Forest, on the other hand, lies on Colorado's Western Slope and receives far less traffic. Of the trails within the Routt National Forest, the one that receives perhaps the least number of visits is Arapaho Ridge Trail, as it lies along the forest's easternmost boundary. While Front Range cyclists enjoy most of the Arapaho National Forest east of the Continental Divide, mountain bikers of the Routt National Forest tend to enjoy the more interior trails west of the Continental Divide. Since Arapaho Ridge Trail lies on the cusp of each of these forests, it typically gets overlooked by both camps. As a result, Arapaho Ridge

Trail remains relatively unused, hidden in a kind of no-man's-land amid the wilds of Colorado's Western Slope. With neither Front Range nor Western Slope riders claiming Arapaho Ridge Trail as their own, the trail would certainly remain an orphan were it not for its close proximity to Kremmling, a tiny town nestled in a valley at the confluence of the Colorado and Blue Rivers.

Kremmling seems a fitting surrogate for this orphaned trail since its own birth shares a similar kind of isolation. Kremmling's first settlement, and later its first business, rose from a cave located on the banks of the Muddy River, just north of the town's present location. James Crawford settled alone in the cave in 1873 with hopes of securing a place to live for his family. Before he'd move his family into what was then a wild and inhospitable country, Crawford led a relatively solitary life, mostly tending his cattle. He made his way out from the cave only to carry milk to his family, whom he'd left in Hot Sulphur Springs. On these few and infrequent occasions, Crawford loaded a wooden sled and dragged it himself the 15 miles to Hot Sulphur Springs. Deciding that a cave was no place to raise a family, Crawford moved west to Steamboat Springs, this time bringing his family with him.

With the cave vacant, and somewhat of a curiosity, Rudolph Kremmling, a retail businessman from Dillon and Kremmling's founding father, decided that the cave would make an excellent shop. In 1874 the town of Kremmling had its first business. Run by the Dillon retailer, the cave became a supply store for settlers traveling west. With the promise of the coming Denver, Northwestern & Pacific Railroad and the good ranch land available in the area, Kremmling found it necessary to move his shop to a bigger location. In 1875 his outfitter shop moved to its present site, now the Dan Hoare Village Smithy building, north of the Town Square. Out of this new location grew his business and eventually the town's first post office. By 1900 Kremmling was a town on the rise, with 270 people building for a promising future.

When the railroad arrived in 1906, Kremmling had already established itself as one of the Colorado West's premier social towns, complete with eight libation stations. And who could ask for a better setting. The town is surrounded by the peaks of the Gore Range to the south; to the west by Gore Canyon's steep crevasse, through which flows the Gore River; to the north by monolithic cliffs; and to the east by the William's Fork Range and the Continental Divide. Today, Kremmling is poised as one of Colorado's premier playgrounds.

Taking care of business along the trail's rockier sections.

We begin exploring the playground on Arapaho Ridge Trail's hard-packed singletrack through a densely mixed conifer forest. As the route climbs moderately over hilly terrain, the trail courses through the best of Colorado woodlands. During the summer, the Arapaho Indians frequently hunted these woodlands, perhaps following this same trail as it courses through prime elk, moose, and deer real estate. After crossing Arapaho Creek three times, you reach the Carter Creek sign.

Although not particularly technical to this point, the trail becomes increasingly so after you leave the sign. After 4 miles the trail begins to climb significantly over tight and gravely singletrack. As you near the timberline, at about 4.5 miles, the trail opens up onto an east-facing slope. Here the trail climbs sharply to the north. Loose rock, deep ruts, narrow singletrack, and high elevations all take their toll on your struggling body—but never your will.

As the route dips into an enormous valley, trees fall from view as surrounding Hyannis Peak (11,602 feet) rises like the sun. Here, all is mountain. If the trail were the thread and the route, the stitching, you'd find yourself nothing more than a spec of lint in the huge pocket of a mountainous coat. A south-facing gully provides easy access to the deepest recesses of this pocket before delivering you to the last remaining switchback to the top.

Although the climb to the top is very demanding, the views upon reaching the Continental Divide are unbelievably well worth the strain. The panoramic view offers up the Mount Zirkel Wilderness to the north, the Gore Range to the south and west, and the Never Summer Wilderness to the east. The view will no doubt delay your descent for a time.

Miles and Directions

0.0 START at the Arapaho Ridge and Hyannis Peak trailhead. Begin riding in a southerly direction through a dense evergreen forest, climbing moderately over hilly terrain.

1.4 Arrive at a beaver pond, lying to the southwest. Bear right, riding around the pond.

2.1 Cross Arapaho Creek for the first time and again at 2.2 miles.

2.6 Cross Arapaho Creek for the third time. After riding out of the drainage, the route leads across a hillside. This hillside is marked by slippery, exposed rock.

3.4 Enter a hillside and meadow, and ride toward the Forest Service sign CARTER CREEK—5 MILES. This is a good spot to rest and refuel, as the toughest part of the route begins here.

4.6 A rocky technical section awaits. Here the tight and rocky route descends into a small gully, before cutting sharply to the right at the bottom and rising steeply from the gully to the top.

6.1 Reach the top of Arapaho Ridge and the Continental Divide. Return the same way you came.

12.2 Arrive at your vehicle.

Ride Information

Local Information

Kremmling Chamber of Commerce and Information Center, P.O. Box 471, Kremmling, 80459; (970) 724-3472.

Local Events and Attractions

Junction Butte, Kremmling. Called "Elk Mountain" by locals, it's located south of town and features the outline of a buck on its north face.
Gore Canyon, located roughly 5 miles southwest of Kremmling, offers Class IV and V whitewater rafting on the Colorado River. For details contact AdventureQuest.com, Colorado Blue Adventures (970) 724-9419, or Monarch Guides (970) 653-4210, (888) 463-5628.
Green Mountain Reservoir, 12 miles south of Kremmling on Colorado Highway 9. For more information, contact the Kremmling Chamber of Commerce and Information Center (970) 724-3472.
Wolford Reservoir, just 6 miles north of town, off of U.S. Highway 40, offers some of the area's best gold medal fishing. For more information, contact the Kremmling Chamber of Commerce and Information Center (970) 724-3472.
Annual Roadkill Supper, in October, Kremmling; (970) 724-3472 (an all-you-can-eat dinner featuring wild game).
Middle Park Fair & Rodeo, in September, Kremmling; (970) 724-3436 (children's games, food and crafts).
Kremmling Days, in June, Kremmling; (970) 724-3472 (parade, kids' games, crafts, family activities).
Fire at the Cliffs, July 4, Kremmling (close to Junction Butte), (970) 724-3472 (fireworks display).

Accommodations

Hotel Eastin, Kremmling; (970) 724-3261, (800) 546-0815.
Stagecoach Country Inn, Hot Sulphur Springs; (800) 725-3919.

17 Base Camp to Mountain View Trail

Starting from Rabbit Ears Pass, riders travel over steep, rocky descents and ascents and through fast, smooth high-alpine meadows and bone-chilling creeks on their way to the top of the Steamboat Springs Ski Resort. Commanding views of the Yampa Valley and Routt National Forest reward the tireless rider as he or she approaches the resort. From the top of the resort there are a variety of trail options to the bottom, ranging from technical singletrack (described herein) to dirt service roads.

Start: From the Rabbit Ears Trailhead.
Length: 26.5-mile point-to-point.
Approximate riding time: 3 to 4 hours.
Technical difficulty: Technically moderate to challenging due to rocky and rutted terrain.
Physical difficulty: Physically challenging due to long miles and extended climbs at higher elevations.
Terrain: Improved dirt roads, singletrack, and doubletrack. You'll pass a number of lakes and cross a variety of creeks, traveling mostly in dense woodlands. The ride extends over very mountainous terrain.
Trail contacts: Medicine Bow–Routt National Forest, Hahns Peak/Bears Ears Ranger District, 925 Weiss Drive, Steamboat Springs; (970) 879-1870.
Steamboat Ski and Resort, 2305 Mount Werner Circle, Steamboat Springs, 80487; (970) 879-6111, (879) 237-2628; www.steamboat-ski.com.
Schedule: July to early October.
Maps: USGS maps: Rabbit Ears Peak, Mount Werner; *Trails Illustrated* map 118, Steamboat Springs and Rabbit Ears Pass; Steamboat Springs Ski Resort Bike Map.
Nearest town: Steamboat Springs.
Other trail users: Hikers, campers, anglers, back-country skiers, and snowmobilers.
Canine compatibility: Dog friendly.

Getting There

From Steamboat Springs: Drive east on U.S. Highway 40 toward Rabbit Ears Pass. Turn left (north) onto Forest Road 315, 2 miles before the east summit of Rabbit Ears Pass (or 7 miles past the west summit)—a sign for Dumont Lake marks the entrance. Follow FR 315 for nearly 2 miles as it winds its way eastward. Just beyond the Dumont Lake Campground, on the north (left) side of the road, you'll notice a large boulder monument commemorating Rabbit Ears Pass. Turn here and drive into the parking lot. Begin your ride through the wooden gate (not the trail to the right of it) and onto FR 311, Base Camp Road. *DeLorme: Colorado Atlas & Gazetteer:* Page 27, A-4.
Shuttle Required: Leave one vehicle parked in the municipal parking lot on the corner of Mount Werner Circle and Ski Time Square. Park the second vehicle at the Rabbit Ears Trailhead, at the start of Base Camp Road.

The Ride

Base Camp Trail to Mountain View Trail is located at the top of Rabbit Ears Pass in the Routt National Forest. Riders typically access this trail from the Steamboat

Views from the top of Pete's Wicked Trail.

Springs Ski Resort at the top of Mount Werner; however, starting, as this ride does, from Rabbit Ears Pass allows the rider to explore a network of trails along the Continental Divide, while testing his or her climbing strength.

Rabbit Ears Pass takes its name from an enormous rock formation located to the north of the pass. Rabbit Ears Peak, as it's called, consists of twin 100-foot pinnacles, which bear a striking resemblance to a pair of rabbit ears. The "ears" are actually a single volcanic plug split in half. This lava-filled artery is all that remains of a Precambrian plug that has since been done in by time and erosion. The cementing of broken volcanic material with reddish lava has given the formation its mahogany-colored shadings. Iron oxide remains the dominant color influence. The base of the Rabbit Ears' south face is steeped in this agglomerate rock. Since this rock's consistency closely resembles that of cooled cinders, hikers to the peaks make sport of jumping down the Rabbit Ears' south face as if it were a snow-covered hillside. One can literally "ski" down the south face in the summertime, redefining the sport of ski jumping.

Just west of Rabbit Ears Peak lies the Meadows Campground, an early Ute Indian campsite. On a larger scale, the area surrounding the Base Camp Trailhead used to be a general meeting ground for a variety of Native Americans. The mountain tribes, Arapahos and Gros Ventres; the Great Plains tribes, Sioux and Cheyenne; and the Colorado and Great Basin tribes, the Utes, would travel the great natural wilderness highways to partake of the area's excellent hunting and fishing.

Rabbit Ears Pass saw little more than foot traffic until 1914, when, funded by private investors, it saw its first highway. Dedicated later as a memorial to those who lost their lives in World War I, the Victory Highway (now U.S. Highway 40) provided the first transcontinental link between New York and San Francisco. In the early days of the Victory Highway, a well was placed in the Meadows Campground to aid the boiling radiators of vehicles ambitious enough to cross.

Beginning at 9,573 feet, Base Camp Road climbs to a modest 10,320 feet within the first 4 miles—a good warm up by anyone's standards. The well-worn jeep road meanders through thick evergreen forests and past open meadows and marshes, offering stunning views of Rabbit Ears Peak and Dumont Lake. Although the terrain is physically and technically moderate, it should take approximately 45 minutes to arrive at the Base Camp Trailhead.

There are a number of tricky dips on Base Camp Trail, with a fair amount of rocky, technical sections. The trail eventually dances its way out of the forest to meet with the siren song of Fishhook Lake, a subalpine lake whose banks caress the heart of the forest in the shape of a fishhook. From Fishhook Lake the trail climbs through thick rows of evergreens and polished aspen until arriving at the junction of Percy Lake Trail (Forest Road 1134), Wyoming Trail (FR 1101, which runs along the Continental Divide to Buffalo Pass), and the beginning of Fish Creek Falls Trail (FR 1102). Known to local riders as the 7-Eleven spot, this junction's only edible treats come in the form of huckleberries. Continue riding west on Fish Creek Falls Trail to Long Lake.

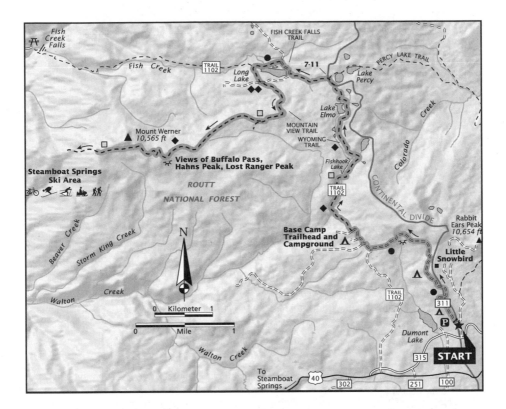

Once you arrive at Long Lake—a century-old watershed at the head of Fish Creek—the singletrack gives way to a service road. Avoid the unmarked, bushwhacked trail to the left, which crosses a Long Lake tributary near a solar-paneled post. Bear right and continue on Fish Creek Falls Trail as it flanks the north side of the lake. Eventually the road forks, and you notice a sign for Fish Creek Falls Trail, directing you to the left. Continue on this trail for a mile until arriving at Mountain View Trail.

Mountain View Trail begins with a steep but short climb until eventually leveling off in the thick of the woods. From here, the trail winds its way through dense stands of pine and aspen and past meadows and beaver ponds. Just past the beaver ponds, at roughly 14.1 miles, the sun-warmed scree off to the right of the trail provides a great spot to dry wet socks and warm cold feet. The toughest climbing of the day begins here.

You'll encounter two switchbacks at the trail's steepest gradient. Northern views of Buffalo Pass, western views of Hahns Peak and the Lost Ranger Peak, and southern views of the Never Summer Mountain Range surround you and complement the dizzying sensation one experiences while climbing at altitudes in excess of 9,000 feet. The trail eventually crests and offers outstanding views of the Flat Tops

Wilderness Area and the Yampa Valley. Follow the trail as it makes its way to the top of Storm Peak, passing through stellar wintertime backcountry skiing terrain.

At 17.5 miles you arrive at the top of Storm Peak. From here, there are a variety of options to reach the bottom; Pete's Wicked to Duster to Zig Zag or Creekside is a fine option. From the top of Mount Werner, plan on taking at least an hour to reach the bottom, covering roughly 9 miles in the process.

Miles and Directions

0.0 START on Base Camp Road.

1.4 "Little Snowbird" is to your right—a popular backcountry skiing site for Steamboat Springs locals.

4.3 On your right, leading into the forest due north, is the start of the singletrack. Notice the sign for Forest Road 1102. This is the Base Camp Trailhead. There may be vehicles parked here.

6.5 Here the trail intersects. A short hike will bring you to Lost Lake. Bear left, however, and continue on Base Camp Trail, following signs for Lake Elmo.

8.8 Base Camp Trail meets Wyoming Trail (FR 1101, Continental Divide Trail), Percy Lake Trail (FR 1134), and the Fish Creek Falls Trail (FR 1102). Bear left and continue westward on Trail 1102, now Fish Creek Falls Trail, for about 1 mile until arriving at Long Lake.

9.8 Arrive at Long Lake. Bear right following the Fish Creek Falls Trail signs.

10.7 Mountain View Trail starts to your left as it splits from Fish Creek Falls Trail and immediately begins to climb.

17.5 Reach the top of Storm Peak and intersect Storm Peak Challenge Trail. Veer right heading for Pete's Wicked Trail. Just past the top of the Storm Peak Express Lift, veer right onto the singletrack of Pete's Wicked Trail. With the exception of one short climb at the bottom of the Sunshine Lift, it's all downhill from here.

20.2 Arrive at the bottom of the Sunshine Lift. Continue climbing up the road until you reach the Rendezvous Saddle, where refreshments are available. At this point, Pete's Wicked Trail ends. Take Duster, a long and fast cruise with luscious views of the valley.

21.5 Arrive at the Rainbow Saddle. Take the middle of three roads to your left and climb for approximately 0.3 mile. Come to a SLOW sign on your right. Veer right onto this doubletrack, which is now the Zig Zag Trail. Zig Zag will immediately come to an abrupt fork. Take the fork hard to the right. It winds down to the Arrowhead Lift line, where the trail once again turns into a dirt road. In just 0.6 mile dive left onto a singletrack trail that eventually leads out onto another service road.

24.2 This road winds past the bottom of the Storm Peak Express Chairlift until reaching the Creekside Trailhead on the right. Continue on the doubletrack of Zig Zag, but be careful to check your speed as dips across the trail make for hazardous high-speed travel.

26.5 Once you reach the bottom of the ski resort, you'll find tasty margaritas at the Dos Amigos and frothy brews at Slopeside Grill.

Ride Information

Local Information

City of Steamboat Springs, P.O. Box 755088, Steamboat Springs, 80477; (970) 879–2060; www.ci.steamboat.co.us.

Steamboat Springs Chamber Resort Association, 1255 Lincoln Avenue, Steamboat Springs, 80477; (970) 879–0880; www.steamboat-chamber.com.

Local Events and Attractions

Steamboat Ski Area, Steamboat Springs; (970) 879–6111; www.steamboat-ski.com.

Strawberry Park Hot Springs, Steamboat Springs; (970) 879–0342.

Tread of Pioneers Museum, Steamboat Springs; (970) 879–2214.

Accommodations

Steamboat Bed and Breakfast, Steamboat Springs; (970) 879–5724.

Rabbit Ears Motel, Steamboat Springs; (970) 879–1150; www.toski.com/rabbitears/summer.

Restaurants

Backcountry Provisions, Steamboat Springs; (970) 879–3617.

Steamboat Brewery & Tavern, Steamboat Springs; (970) 879–2233.

Organizations

Routt County Riders Bicycle Club, Steamboat Springs; (970) 879–1735.

18 Muddy Slide and Morrison Divide Trails

Muddy Slide Trail is one of Routt County's oldest and best trails. The trail leads riders to the geological oddity after which this ride is named. Atop Green Ridge lies a mountain with half of its side missing. The trail was built expressly to deliver tourists to this particular view, and it has been doing so for some seventy-five years. Due to its age and its historical and geological significance, Muddy Slide Trail is eligible to be listed on the National Register of Historic Places. In the summer of 1999, a two-panel interpretive sign was constructed atop Green Ridge and includes geological and historical accounts of the muddy slide. The Rocky Mountain Youth Corps (an organization designed to foster leadership and teamwork in high-risk junior and high school–aged youths), in partnership with the Routt National Forest, has maintained the trail's integrity by building a number of "turnpikes" (banked sections of trail designed to prevent erosion) through its muddier sections. By all counts, Muddy Slide Trail just gets better with age.

Start: From the trailhead of Morrison Divide Trail 1174.

Length: 20.2-mile loop.

Approximate riding time: Advanced riders, 2 to 2.5 hours; intermediate riders, 3 to 3.5 hours.

Technical difficulty: Technically moderate to challenging due to off-camber terrain, roots, and rocks.

Physical difficulty: Physically moderate to challenging due to extended climbs over rougher terrain.

Terrain: Improved dirt road, doubletrack, and singletrack—portions include ruts, mud, tree roots, and rocks; however, most of the route runs over hard-packed forest earth.

Trail contacts: Medicine Bow–Routt National Forests, Yampa Ranger District, P.O. Box 7, 300 Roselawn Avenue, Yampa, 80483; (970) 638-4516.

Schedule: Mid-June to early October.

Maps: USGS maps: Green Ridge, Gore Mountain, Lynx Pass; *Trails Illustrated* map 119 Yampa, Gore Pass; Routt National Forest Map.

Nearest town: Yampa.

Other trail users: Equestrians, hikers, campers.

Canine compatibility: Dog friendly.

Getting There

From Steamboat Springs: Travel east on U.S. Highway 40. Turn right onto Colorado Highway 131, heading south. Drive for 7 miles before turning left onto County Road 14, just beyond the brown sign for Stagecoach State Park. Drive for another 7 miles on CR 14 before turning left onto CR 16, following signs for Lynx Pass. Drive around Stagecoach Reservoir and turn left by the Eagles' Nest condominiums (approximately 2 miles from where you turned onto CR 16). Still on CR 16, bear right at the yield sign and drive for approximately 10 miles. The sign for Trail 1174 and Morrison Divide will be on your right. Park on the right just beyond this sign, before the bulletin board. *DeLorme: Colorado Atlas & Gazetteer:* Page 26, C-3.

The Ride

Although officially dubbed Morrison Divide Trail 1174 by the Forest Service, area locals more affectionately refer to this trail as "Muddy Slide." The trail takes its provincial name from the geological wonder high atop the east slope of Green Ridge. There, surrounded by the shimmering greens of tight-fitting lodgepole pine trees, lie in stark contrast the remains of a mountain with half of its side missing . . . Muddy Slide.

To reach this surreal sight, riders first pedal up Routt County Road 16 to Lynx Pass. Paralleling the road, Morrison Creek flows north from Lynx Pass some 15 miles to its confluence with Stagecoach Reservoir just east of Oak Creek in Stagecoach State Park. Legend has it that Morrison Creek was named by James Harvey Crawford, Steamboat Springs' founding father and first permanent settler.

In 1878 some local Ute Indians reported having spotted a starving "crazy man" along the banks of the creek. James Crawford organized a search party to find the lost man. When the men found Joe Morrison, he was near death and cooking his last remaining stores of food: the tails of his burros. When asked how he had gotten lost, the crotchety old prospector told Crawford that he had been looking for the Phantom Gold Pillar, a finger-like rock of almost pure gold believed to be in an area just east of Lynx Pass. In those days, any hint of the existence of gold would have sparked any would-be prospector's curiosity, and Morrison was no exception. After Morrison's return to town, news of the pillar's existence spread fast throughout the Yampa Valley. As many people back then were wont to do, living in the milieu of gold fever, area would-be prospectors sought to find the Phantom Gold Pillar for themselves. Although several prospectors returned from their searches claiming to have found the pillar, no one ever produced any evidence of its existence, nor could any one find their way back to where they allegedly had found it. The Phantom Gold Pillar's location and existence remain a mystery.

Continuing along the banks of Morrison Creek, westerly views reveal Muddy Slide high atop Green Ridge. Once on Lynx Pass, the Muddy Slide singletrack begins. Within the first 0.5 mile, two short but steep climbs await you. The trail then levels out, snaking its way in and out of logging areas and through thick stands of pine and aspen on smooth, hard-packed terrain.

The trail climbs steadily on its way to Muddy Slide. As the trail passes through sandy, rocky, and rooty sections, riders are offered small, intermittent dashes of downhill delight. One such descent comes after passing under a set of power lines at 9.4 miles. After veering onto the dirt road a mile later, the route gradually disintegrates into a rough doubletrack and offers a fast and rocky descent to its intersection with the continuation of the Muddy Slide singletrack. Once reconnected with the singletrack, the trail climbs through an open hillside meadow awash with wildflowers. This section of the route, which is sometimes severely rutted, eventually delivers you onto some off-camber singletrack through an aspen grove. At this point, you're only two miles from Muddy Slide and the beginning of your savage descent. Having persevered on this grueling singletrack climb, follow the road to Muddy Slide and spend a few moments taking it in.

The Slide is unlike anything you've ever seen. It overlooks the entire Morrison Valley, with northeasterly views of Rabbit Ears Peak, northwesterly views of Hahns Peak, and southeasterly views of the Eagles Nest Wilderness and the Gore Range. Consisting of mostly glacial out-wash, the Muddy Slide debris was part of the alluvial valley formed by the uplifting of the nearby Flat Tops Mountains millions of years ago. This uplift deposited large amounts of unconsolidated rock directly in the

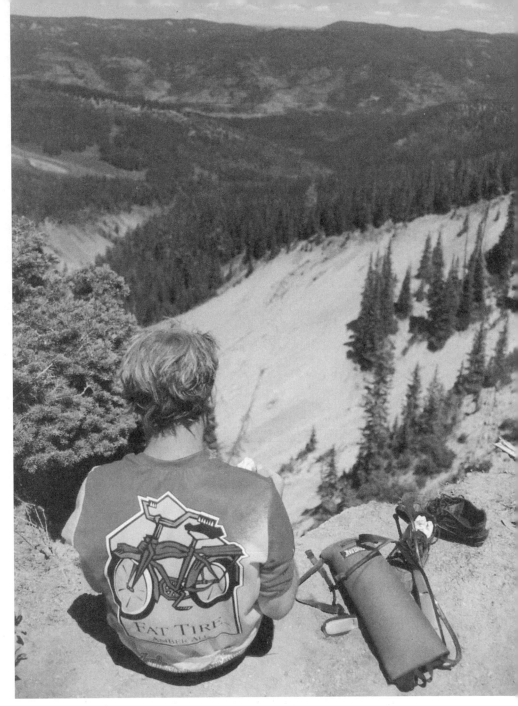

Taking a powder after grunting to the Slide. Dig the shirt?

path of slow-moving glaciers. During glaciation, which carved the Morrison Valley, loose rock was pushed to the tops of steep, high valley walls. Over time, the effects of wind, water, and erosion caused this rock to slide all at once in a large-scale rotational slump, referred to in geological circles as a "mass movement."

From the Slide's highest point, 10,240 feet above sea level, layers of different colored rock—tan, gray, yellow, and pink—mark the passing of Earth's billion-year-old history. Looking down from the top of the Slide, a gash nearly 800 feet long and a quarter-mile wide breaks almost perpendicularly from Green Ridge. At its base lies Muddy Creek. Continually receiving eroded soil from the Slide, Muddy Creek stays murky the whole year through and delivers more silt to the upper Yampa River than any other waterway in the county.

From the Slide, the trail begins as a fast descent through mixed conifer forests. The 5-mile descent from the Slide is technically challenging and offers many thrills, if not spills, for the weary rider. Crossing over sloped-singletrack, roots, rocks, and ruts, the trail weaves its way through creeks and meadows before letting out by your vehicle. Although the push to the top of Green Ridge is a considerable effort, the descent from the Slide is well worth the pains taken to reach the top.

Miles and Directions

0.0 START at the Morrison Divide Trail 1174 (Muddy Slide) Trailhead. From the trailhead, begin riding south down County Road 16 through Morrison Valley to Lynx Pass. **Option:** Riders can choose to leave one car atop Lynx Pass at Morrison Divide Trail 1174 Trailhead, and another at the trail's lower trailhead (where this trail description begins). This will cut out 6.5 miles of climbing on CR 16.

6.5 After passing the sign for Morrison Divide/1174, veer right onto the service road. Ride up this service road for roughly 0.1 mile before turning right onto the Muddy Slide singletrack, just beyond the bulletin board.

8.8 Cross a dirt road and continue along the singletrack on the other side.

10.4 The trail will let out onto a dirt road. Bear left onto the fire road and begin a steady descent. There will be a locked iron gate to your right.

12.7 Reach the junction of Morrison Divide Trail 1174. Bear right onto the singletrack.

13.5 The trail will let out onto another dirt road. Bear left onto it, following signs for Trail 1174 as you head to the Slide.

14.6 Reach the Slide. Pass beyond the red iron gate and ride southwest along the rim of the Slide on the fire road.

15.0 The fire road will intersect with the Muddy Slide singletrack. Bear right onto the singletrack.

17.5 Encounter a root and rock section.

19.8 The trail lets out into a wide meadow. Follow the trail through the meadow as it delivers you to your vehicle.

20.2 Arrive at your vehicle.

Ride Information

Local Information

City of Steamboat Springs, P.O. Box 755088, Steamboat Springs, 80477; (970) 879-2060; www.ci.steamboat.co.us.

Steamboat Springs Chamber Resort Association, 1255 Lincoln Avenue, Steamboat Springs, 80477; (970) 879-0880; www.steamboat-chamber.com.

Local Events and Attractions

Steamboat Springs Health and Recreation Center, Steamboat Springs; (970) 879-1828.
Tread of Pioneers Museum, Steamboat Springs; (970) 879-2214.
Steamboat Lake State Park, north of Steamboat Springs along Forest Road 129; (970) 879-7019.

Stagecoach State Park, Oak Creek; (970) 736-2436.
Flat Tops Trail Scenic Byway, connecting the towns of Yampa and Meeker, (970) 638-4516.

Organizations

Routt County Riders Bicycle Club, Steamboat Springs; (970) 879-1735.
Rocky Mountain Youth Corps., Steamboat Springs; (970) 879-6960.

Restaurants

Harwigs, Steamboat Springs; (970) 879-1980.
Backcountry Provisions, Steamboat Springs; (970) 879-3617.

19 Tipperary Creek Loop

The Tipperary Creek Loop is a shorter version of the famed Tipperary Creek Classic (the main attraction at the Winter Park Mountain Bike Festival). Although it doesn't include the entire Classic route, the Tipperary Creek Loop does include the legendary Tipperary Creek Trail, and it provides access to a number of other Fraser Valley and Winter Park singletrack trails. Though not overly technical or physically demanding, the Tipperary Creek Loop exemplifies how neat and clean singletrack riding can be—something "Mountain Bike Capital, USA" takes pride in. Its soft, smooth-running singletrack will delight, as well as excite a playfulness in the spirit of any mountain biker.

Start: From Elk Creek Road, heading west past the Frasier Valley Center.
Length: 20.4-mile loop.
Approximate riding time: Advanced riders, 1.5 to 2 hours; intermediate riders 2.5 to 3 hours.
Technical difficulty: Technically easy to moderate, due to smooth-running singletrack.
Physical difficulty: Physically moderate. Although there is some climbing involved, it isn't very long, and it doesn't travel over too rough terrain.
Terrain: Paved road, dirt road, and singletrack. Most of the singletrack is very smooth, not much in the way of rocks and roots.

Trail contacts: Winter Park Sports Shop, Ltd., Winter Park; (970) 726-5554; (800) 222-7547; www.winterparkbike.com. Arapaho National Forest, Sulphur Ranger District, 9 Ten Mile Drive, Granby, 80446; (970) 887-3331.
Schedule: July to October.
Maps: USGS maps: Bottle Pass, Fraser; *Trails Illustrated* map 503, Winter Park, Grand Lake; Winter Park and Fraser Valley Chamber of Commerce Mountain Bike Trail Map.
Nearest town: Fraser.
Other trail users: Equestrians, hikers, and campers.
Canine compatibility: Dog friendly.

Getting There

From Denver: Travel west on I-70, taking exit 232 onto U.S. Highway 40 west. Follow the signs to Winter Park. Drive over Berthoud Pass and into Winter Park. From Winter Park drive west to the town of Fraser and turn left at the light by the Fraser Valley Center. This will be Elk Creek Road (County Road 72). Park your vehicle in the Fraser Valley Center parking lot and begin your ride heading west on Elk Creek Road under the railroad tracks. *DeLorme: Colorado Atlas & Gazetteer:* Page 38, A-3 to A-4.

The Ride

With over 600 miles of marked, mapped, and maintained mountain biking trails, the town of Winter Park and the area surrounding the town, Fraser Valley, enjoy one of the world's largest trail systems. Add to that the legendary 30-mile point-to-point

Tipperary Creek Classic racecourse, voted one of the world's best, and you begin to see why Winter Park and the Fraser Valley's trademark "Mountain Bike Capital, USA" is far from hyperbole.

What sets the Fraser Valley and Winter Park apart from other mountain biking destinations is, in large part, the lay of the land. The Fraser Valley is very open and fairly level, while Winter Park's mountains rise gradually above the valley to the top of the Continental Divide—yin to Telluride's yang.

From their beginnings the Fraser Valley and Winter Park were destined for mountain biking greatness. Ute and Arapaho Indians considered the Fraser Valley a favorite hunting ground. They created within the valley a network of unidentified hunting and game trails, which area locals estimate to travel well over 2,400 miles. When pioneers began settling the valley in 1850, railroad and logging industries started to flourish. These industries proved to be the impetus behind Mountain Bike Capital, USA.

David H. Moffat spearheaded the building of a transcontinental railroad line that extended from Denver to Salt Lake City and the West Coast. The line over Rollins Pass, which lies roughly 7 miles to the east of Fraser atop the Continental Divide, was completed in 1905 and remained in service until 1928 when the 6.2-mile Moffat Tunnel was opened. The tunnel provided a safer and more direct alternative to crossing over the Western Slope mountains. Winter Park now sits at the west portal of the Moffat Tunnel.

As the railroad pushed farther west, it provided easier access for boomtowns to acquire timber. The forests west of the Continental Divide provided ample stores of timber for burgeoning cities. By providing Denver with valuable raw materials, Fraser Valley's logging industry helped secure Denver's state capital status. And the Fraser Valley, for its part, had begun bidding for capital claims of its own—that is, becoming America's mountain bike capital. The many logging roads and trails that were being created to supply Denver with timber would eventually evolve into one of the world's largest mountain biking trail systems.

Since Mountain Bike Capital, USA grew in response to the needs of the people, it seems fitting that its trails remain intimately connected with the people. Names of trails reflect the sacrifices made to construct them, as well as recognizing the industries upon which the Fraser Valley's strong mountain biking foundation was laid. Twisted Ankle, Northwest Passage, Flume, Chainsaw, and WTB (named for trailbuilders Wade, Todd, and Bill), all attest to the close relationship the Fraser Valley residents share with their mountain biking.

The Fraser Valley's local Forest Service branch is one of the only branches to employ a full-time mountain bike ranger in the summer, while Winter Park's Adopt-A-Trail program has fostered the adoption of more than 300 miles of trails by local bike shops, hotels, and restaurants. The fantastic condition of area trails speaks for their success in trail maintenance.

While the Tipperary Creek Loop incorporates part of the Tipperary Creek Classic racecourse, it also includes a number of other fine area singletrack. Funded with Colorado Lottery dollars, the Givelo Trail, for instance, runs alongside County Road 73 over nap-worthy earth. Here bicycles are so heralded that they adorn nearby trees. Retired bicycles literally hang like ornaments on evergreens. Passing these now ornamental war horses, you connect with the Northwest Passage Trail.

Northwest Passage Trail delivers 2 miles of tacky, soft-forest earth through thick stands of lodgepole pine. Rest assured, Henry Hudson and the Half Moon never had it this good. An easy, woodsy trail with two major creek crossings, Northwest Passage Trail eventually connects with an access road at 3.8 miles. Follow this road

On the slick Tipperary Creek Trail.

straight past the old softball fields to connect with County Road 50. Once you pass the old, red log cabin on your right, the softball fields should follow immediately.

Once on CR 50, you can either ride for 3.5 miles to the Tipperary Creek Trailhead or pedal up the short "Whoop–Di–Doos" singletrack paralleling CR 50 on the right. The "Whoop–Di–Doos" trail eventually leads back onto CR 50 after 0.5 mile.

At the Tipperary Creek Trail fork, bear right, crossing Tipperary Creek. Begin a slow and steady climb to Morse Pass. With Tipperary Creek to your left, ride through alternating forests of aspen and pine on relatively smooth singletrack. The ridge across Morse Pass travels up to 10,351 feet before descending 1,000 feet over fast and rocky terrain to St. Louis Creek Road.

Flume Trail, named after the water flume that loggers once used to transport timber to Fraser in the early 1900s, passes through lodgepole pine forests and meadows. Although it has some rooty and rocky sections, Flume Trail is mostly smooth and delivers you to a serene meadow at 15.7 miles, offering views of Byers Peak. From there, Chainsaw Trail delivers some tough climbing but features the quietness of a dark forest. By 17.7 miles you'll arrive at the junction of Chainsaw Trail and Zoom Trail. Continue riding on Chainsaw Trail to Elk Creek Road. Bear left onto Elk Creek Road and ride the 2 miles back to your vehicle.

Historian Margaret Cole describes this home of the ancient Arapaho Indians as a "boundless land," where there were "always opportunities to test their independence by racing their ponies wildly across the plains, whooping and hollering, far away from the security of the village?" Who can't appreciate the connection between we modern-day Arapaho and our horse-backed predecessors?

Miles and Directions

0.0 START at the Fraser Valley Center parking lot. Ride west on Elk Creek Road (CR 72) and head under the railroad tracks. Once having gone underneath the railroad tracks, immediately bear right onto Fraser Parkway. There will be a tubing hill off to your left.

1.0 Fraser Parkway intersects CR 73. Cross CR 73 and bear left onto Givelo Trail as it parallels CR 73.

2.6 Givelo Trail will let out onto CR 73. Travel on CR 73 for roughly 0.1 mile before turning right onto Northwest Passage Trail, just before the Fraser Experimental Forest sign.

4.6 Northwest Passage Trail connects with CR 50. Bear left and ride on CR 50 for approximately 3.5 miles before arriving at the Tipperary Creek Trailhead.

8.3 After passing over a cattle guard, pick up Tipperary Creek Trail off to the left side of CR 50, as it cuts sharply to the right.

10.5 Reach the junction of Tipperary Creek Trail and Back Scratch Trail. Continue heading straight, passing Back Scratch Trail to your right. Now Tipperary Creek Trail becomes Spruce Creek Trail.

12.1 Reach the junction of Spruce Creek Trail and Deadhorse Loop. Pass the Deadhorse Loop and continue descending Spruce Creek Trail.

13.4 Spruce Creek Trail drops to St. Louis Creek Road. Turn right onto St. Louis Creek Road and immediately turn left onto CR 59.

13.6 Veer left onto the Flume Trail.

15.8 Reach the junction of Flume Trail and Chainsaw Trail. Connect with Chainsaw Trail and begin a steady climb to Elk Creek Road.

18.0 Reach the junction of Chainsaw Trail and Elk Creek Road. Turn left onto Elk Creek Road and follow the road back to your vehicle.

20.4 Arrive back at your vehicle in the Fraser Valley Center parking lot.

Ride Information

Local Information

Winter Park–Fraser Valley Chamber of Commerce, P.O. Box 3236, Winter Park, 80482; (970) 726-4118, (800) 903-7275; www.winterpark-info.com.

Winter Park Resort, P.O. Box 36, Winter Park, 80482; (970) 726-5514, (800) 979-0332; www.skiwinterpark.com.

Local Events and Attractions

King of the Rockies Off-Road Stage Race and Mountain Bike Festival, August, Winter Park; (970) 887-2519.

American Red Cross Fat Tire Classic, June, Winter Park; (970) 722-7474.

Tours

Purple Sage Multi-Sport Adventures, Winter Park; (888) 342-6789.

Winter Park–Fraser Valley Chamber of Commerce, Winter Park; (970) 726-4118, (800) 903-7275 (offers free guided town rides, acquainting riders with the trails of Winter Park and the Fraser Valley).

In Addition

Extreme Snow Bikes—Alpine Snow Bicycle Association

Berthoud Pass, which straddles the Continental Divide at 11,307 feet, traditionally has tempted only the best backcountry skiers and snowboarders to swoosh through its 400 to 500 inches of annual snowfall. Until now.

There's a new breed of adventurer on Colorado's winter mountains. He or she doesn't fall within the skier/snowboarder camp or the mountain biker camp, but rather somewhere in between. Expanding the boundaries of what can be done on snow, snow bikers are taking to the hills in their modified BMX and vintage Laguna bicycles and ripping it up, smiling all the way.

"We were up here one day taking photos for ESPN," says Richard Fischer. "The wind blew so hard that it lifted my Ford 250's rear suspension four to five inches." Fischer owns and manages the Extreme Snow Bikes and Alpine Snow Bicycle Association.

According to Fischer, snow biking has been around since the mid-1970s. Out of necessity, Coloradoans started studding their bicycle tires with screws as a way to get to and from work without having to contend with the hazards of driving in snowy conditions.

Today, thanks to the efforts of Fischer and Butch Bendele (creator of the Wake Board), snow biking has made its way to the X-Games, found a home among NORBA-sanctioned events, and been officially recognized by the Union Cyclist International (UCI), the world governing body for cycling.

For the past several years Colorado has held a variety of snow biking races. Extreme Snow Bikes has competed in Leadville, at Breckenridge, and Arapahoe Basin—to name just a few. Their proving grounds are the windswept mountains of Berthoud Pass, where speeds in excess of 70 miles per hour are reached on bulletproof snow.

Racing is only part of the new snow bikers' paradigm. Unlike snowboarding, which began life at Colorado ski areas as a recreational vehicle, snow biking has emerged as a competitive vehicle. The goal of Fischer and the Alpine Snow Bicycle Association is to bring snow biking more into the mainstream—as snowboarding has since become.

Fischer admits: "Everything I've done since day-one—working with NORBA, creating a dialogue with ski areas, racing with Extreme Snow Bikes—has been for the ultimate goal of recreational snow biking at ski areas." In response to this single goal, the Alpine Snow Bicycle Association—a union of promoters and snow bikers

Richard Fischer demonstrates his snow biking skills through the thick white stuff on Berthoud Pass.

from Alaska to Maine—was created in 1996 as a way to bring snow bikers together and exchange ideas. With no membership fee, the Alpine Snow Bicycle Association is intended for anybody.

Although the future of snow biking remains uncertain, no one can dispute the fact that it's an intriguing concept, not to mention a lot of fun. To Fischer's credit, people will never be able to look at a mountain bike quite the same way. With an air of boastful triumph, Fischer laughs, "always that preconception of a bicycle as a summer vehicle, not any more."

Extreme Snow Bikes
Alpine Snow Bicycle Association
Richard Fischer, Owner/Operator
620 South Knox Court
Denver, CO 80218
(303) 935–8494

20 Grand Traverse and Cougar Ridge Trail

This ride incorporates the widely popular Grand Traverse Trail on Vail Mountain to access the more obscure Cougar Ridge Trail to Minturn. Via Village Trail, riders get an overview of the Vail Ski Resort, as it winds its mellow way from the base of the Vista Bahn Express Lift to the top of Eagle's Nest. From there, 2 miles along the Grand Traverse Trail deliver stellar views of the Sawatch Range and the Mount of the Holy Cross. After picking up the unpatrolled Cougar Ridge Trail, the rider is afforded a blasting descent to Minturn before connecting with U.S. Highway 24 and the Vail Bike Path back to your vehicle.

Start: From the base of the Vista Bahn Express Lift.
Length: 21-mile loop.
Approximate riding time: Advanced riders, 2 to 2.5 hours; intermediate riders, 3 to 3.5 hours.
Technical difficulty: Technically easy to moderate, with a few short, challenging sections along Cougar Ridge Trail.
Physical difficulty: Physically moderate to challenging due to the elevation gained from the base of Vail Ski Resort to its summit.
Terrain: Dirt access road, paved road, paved bicycle path, and singletrack. Most of the terrain is smooth and nontechnical; however, the Cougar Ridge portion offers a variety of roots, rocks, and washboards.

Trail contacts: Wheel Base (two locations), Vail; (970) 479-0913; (970) 476-5799. Mountain Pedaler of Vail, Minturn; (970) 827-5522.
White River National Forest, Holy Cross Ranger District, 24747 U.S. Highway 24, P.O. Box 190, Minturn, 81645; (970) 827-5715.
Schedule: July to October.
Maps: USGS maps: Vail East, Vail West, Minturn, Red Cliff; Vail and Eagle Valley Mountain Biking and Recreation map by Latitude 40; Vail and Beaver Creek Summer Biking and Hiking maps.
Nearest town: Vail.
Other trail users: Equestrians, hikers, anglers, rafters, and kayakers.
Canine compatibility: Dog friendly.

Getting There

From Denver: Travel west on I-70 to Vail. At 29.5 miles past Silverthorne, take exit 176 and turn left onto Vail Road, crossing under I-70. At the circle, bear right onto the South Frontage Road for roughly 0.5 mile. Park at the Lionshead parking lot, just before the Vail Valley Tourism and Convention Bureau. From the Lionshead parking lot, ride your bicycles east on West Meadow Drive, which will turn into East Meadow Drive. Make a right onto Bridge Street through Vail Village to the Vista Bahn Express Lift. Begin your ride from the base of the Vista Bahn Express Lift. *DeLorme: Colorado Atlas & Gazetteer:* Page 37, C-6, C-7, D-6, and D-7.
Public Transportation: From Beaver Creek and Edwards, take the Eco-Transit shuttle bus to the Lionshead gondola.

The Ride

Described as a jewel, Grand Traverse is Vail's hallmark mountain bike trail. What most people know of Grand Traverse is that it offers mountain bikers rolling single-track past Vail's hyped back bowls. What many do not know is that Grand Traverse—by way of unmarked singletrack—links with Cougar Ridge Trail, a 5-mile stretch of unmaintained and unpatrolled, descending singletrack that ends in the quirky old railroad town of Minturn. Aside from dirt, dust, and endless delight, these two seemingly unrelated trails share in the unmistakable presence of higher power.

"Sawatch," a derivative of a Native American word meaning "water of the blue earth," is the name given to the range that overlooks Grand Traverse and Cougar Ridge Trail. The first recorded use of the name dates back to 1853, when it originally identified a large lake in the San Luis Valley. How this range came to acquire the name is a mystery, as is much of the history surrounding its mountains. Steeped in legend and lore, the Sawatch Mountains demand reverence. The Mount of the Holy Cross is perhaps the Sawatch Range's most prominent mountain and sits within view of Grand Traverse and the beginning of Cougar Ridge Trail. Although the stories of the Mount of the Holy Cross tend to stem from legend rather than life, they provide meaning for the holy land upon which your wheels tread.

A sign to commemorate the soldiers of the Tenth Mountain Division.

One such legendary story recalls the tale of a friar who had been part of the expedition led by the Spanish explorer Hernando de Soto. After having explored much of America's interior and claimed much of the explored land for Spain, de Soto finally concluded his expedition along the banks of the Mississippi River. Upset that the expedition had come to an end, the Franciscan friar questioned de Soto's decision. As penalty for his insolence, the Franciscan friar was stripped of his holy habit and crucifix by an angry soldier of de Soto. Ashamed for his actions, the friar set out alone, continuing his travels through America's interior. A Chickasaw brave who had witnessed the event at the Mississippi River decided that he would follow the friar. Having thought himself alone for several days since his falling out with de Soto, the friar no doubt was surprised to see that he had been followed by the brave. The friar drew a cross in the sand to show the brave that his intentions were peaceful. Seeing this, the Chickasaw Indian led the friar to join his tribe in the Mississippi Delta.

While living with the Chickasaw, the friar came upon a smattering of de Soto's army. Included among the rambling few was the soldier who had stripped the friar of his vestments. Trying to disguise himself from the friar, the soldier had now been dressed in the friar's own garb. Enraged, the friar stabbed the soldier, killing him instantly. Ashamed at what he had done, the friar left the Chickasaw in search of divine forgiveness. His search led him west, toward the Rocky Mountains. With his strength failing, the friar knelt in prayer upon a fog-covered mountainside. As he asked for forgiveness one last time, the fog lifted, revealing a snow-white cross imbedded in a dark mountainside—a sign of spiritual redemption.

This story and others like it spawned a massive pilgrimage campaign to seek out this most blessed place. Mountain men and early fur traders sought furiously after this snowy symbol of Christianity. It wasn't until the Hayden Survey Team of 1873 that the site's exact location was documented in photographs taken by the famed western photographer William H. Jackson. Legend had turned to life, and life would shortly thereafter turn to art.

Impressed with Jackson's photographs, the famed English artist Thomas Moran visited the mountain in 1874. On his return, Moran painted a variety of pictures of the Mount of the Holy Cross, the most famous of which now hangs in England and measures 6 feet 10 inches by 6 feet. The American poet Henry Wadsworth Longfellow also immortalized the mountain in his poem "The Cross of Snow":

There is a mountain in the distant West
That, sun-defying, in its deep ravines
Displays a cross of snow upon its side.

With this kind of exposure, it's no wonder that in 1912 three Episcopal priests held Eucharist on the summit of nearby Notch Mountain, setting a precedent for the famous Mount Holy Cross pilgrimages. What began with three priests in 1912 grew to 2,000 by 1932. Colorado became the American version of Canterbury, as tales of miraculous healings were reported by returning pilgrims.

By today's standards, the cross in the mountainside can best be understood, perhaps, as a vertical couloir, running 1,500 feet long and 25 to 50 feet wide. An outward-sloping shelf runs across and near the top of this couloir, collecting more snow on its flatter surface than what would normally collect on the mountain's steeper sides. When snow fills the couloir and collects atop the shelf, the two combine to offer the appearance of a downy white cross on the northeast peak of the Mount of the Holy Cross. This geological explanation, however, hasn't detracted from the spiritual air surrounding the Mount of the Holy Cross. Riders reaching the top of Vail Mountain, near the Eagle's Nest restaurant and concession stand, are offered a dazzling view of this sacred mountain. An overlook nearby is site to nondenominational sunrise services.

Returning from this natural altar, Grand Traverse invites the rider to reflect on the grandness that is the Sawatch Range. For 2 miles Grand Traverse rolls over moderate rolling terrain before connecting with Cougar Ridge Trail. The unmanaged singletrack of Cougar Ridge Trail recalls the hardships earlier explorers and traders had to endure in their search for truth. Today, however, truth is yours and found among pools of blue columbine and organ-jarring descents. Like life in the high country, this trail is definitely not for everybody. Those expecting a smooth ride should look elsewhere. Those who enjoy a bit of pounding will relish this trail's unmaintained terrain.

Since this is an unmaintained trail, expect a lot of low-lying tree branches and rutted singletrack. The first mile descent travels west from Vail Mountain and offers expansive views of the Sawatch Range and the Mount of the Holy Cross. One short burst of a hill climb comes at roughly 10 miles. From there the singletrack runs its course through intermittent stands of pine and aspen, offering a beautiful view atop the Lionshead rock formation above Minturn and a fast switchback descent to the Game Creek Trail. The Game Creek Trail provides some tricky rocks before picking up U.S. Highway 24 in Minturn. Turn right onto US 24 and connect with the Vail Bike Path back to the Lionshead parking lot and your vehicles.

Miles and Directions

0.0 START at the base of the Vista Bahn Express Lift. Begin riding on the Village Bike Path toward Eagle's Nest.

1.0 The Village Bike Path intersects with Gitalong Road. Although both lead to the top, Gitalong Road follows much of Vail's ski routes whereas the Village Bike Path follows the eastern route to the top of Eagle's Nest. Cross under the Vista Bahn Express Lift and continue riding up the Village Bike Path.

3.2 Encounter the first little descent of the Village Bike Path. Ride past the gate and around Chairlift 10, the Highline Lift. From the Highline Lift, the Village Bike Path begins to climb more steadily.

5.6 Reach Mid-Vail and the top of the Vista Bahn Express Lift. As the trail levels out, continue riding across the mountain to Eagle's Nest.

6.8 Arrive at Eagle's Nest, where you're offered food, drink, and recreation amid a beautiful alpine setting. Bear left around Eagle's Nest, following the sign for Grand Traverse.

8.4 Cross under the Vail Ski Area boundary ropes.

8.7 Grand Traverse cuts sharply to the left, as it climbs to Wildwood, Vail's westernmost summit (10,950 feet). Here is where you break from Grand Traverse and pick up Cougar Ridge Trail. As Grand Traverse cuts sharply left, continue straight along the singletrack heading into the pine forest. This junction is marked by two blue signs: one pointing in the direction from which you came and designating the way back to Eagle's Nest via Grand Traverse, the other pointing to Wildwood and the continuation of Grand Traverse. Note: There is no designation for Cougar Ridge Trail at this junction.

8.9 Reach the trailhead for Cougar Ridge Trail. Marked by a red sign, Cougar Ridge Trail breaks right from the trail you are on.

11.3 Reach the Lionshead overlook of Minturn.

13.4 Connect with Game Creek Trail. Cross Game Creek and head left down Game Creek Trail.

13.9 Come to the end of Game Creek Trail and to its trailhead. Veer left onto the gravel/dirt road, and ride alongside the railroad tracks, keeping them to your right. Cross the tracks and ride around the old depot, now the International Trade Center.

14.6 Intersect with U.S. Highway 24. Bear right onto US 24, and ride north to the intersection with I–70 and the Vail Bike Path.

16.5 Having crossed underneath I–70, reach the Vail Bike Path. Bear right onto the bike path, crossing the Eagle River, heading east back to Vail.

18.0 Pass Stephens Park, a local watering hole, to your right.

21.0 Reach the Eagle Bahn Gondola and Clock Tower of Lionshead. Walk through the square to your vehicle at the Lionshead parking lot.

Ride Information

Local Information

Vail Resort, P.O. Box 7, Vail, 81658; (970) 476–5601, (877) 204–7881; vail.snow.com. **Vail Valley Chamber and Tourism Bureau,** 100 East Meadow Drive, Suite 34, Vail, 81657; (877) 750–8245; www.vailalways.com. **Vail Information Booth,** Vail; (970) 479–1394.

Local Events and Attractions

Colorado Ski Heritage Museum, in the Vail Village Transportation Center); (970) 476–1876. **Taste of Vail,** early April, Vail; (970) 476–1000.

Restaurants

Cougar Ridge Café, under the Lionshead Rock in Minturn; (970) 827–5609 (the best pizza in Minturn, highlighted by New Belgium Brewing Company's Fat Tire Amber Ale).

In Addition

The Tenth Mountain Division

Colorado's vast hut systems provide backcountry bikers with solitude and peace of mind in the deepest reaches of Colorado's wilderness. It's interesting that these huts were born of a threat to our national security.

To combat the growing threat of Nazi infiltration in Europe during World War II, the United States established in 1942 a winter training facility for an elite corps of champion skiers, mountain climbers, and European mountaineers—a group known as the Tenth Mountain Division, America's only mountain winter warfare unit. Just one year after the bombing of Pearl Harbor, Camp Hale (elevation 10,000 feet) was established along Leadville's northern boundaries in Pando, Colorado, just south of Vail Pass in Alpine Valley. Camp Hale (nicknamed Camp Hell) was home for over 14,000 mountain soldiers trained to battle the Nazis in the snow-covered mountainous regions of Europe.

Donning coveralls of all white, carrying over ninety pounds of gear in their army-issued rucksacks, and skiing on 7.5-foot-long hickory boards, these soldiers trained at altitudes in excess of 13,000 feet on nearby Copper Hill and atop Tennessee and Vail Passes. Temperatures would sometimes fall forty degrees below zero. These "phantoms of the snow" honed their fighting skills by engaging in alpine military tactics under the most severe and strenuous conditions imaginable—and yet, great pains were taken to make these conditions as bearable as possible. The first snowmobile, the first motorized toboggan, and the first snow cat were all created for the ski troops.

Their skills would eventually be brought to bear on the night of February 18, 1945, near Florence, Italy. The Tenth Mountain Division climbed the 2,000-vertical-foot escarpment of Riva Ridge in a single file line in the dead of night. By 5 A.M. the next morning, the Tenth reached the top of the ridge. In the dense fog that had enshrouded the entire ridge, the Tenth Mountain Division ambushed the Germans, taking Riva Ridge. The next day, the Tenth Mountain Division stormed Mount Belvedere. Their assault on Riva Ridge and Mount Belvedere proved to be turning points in the war.

After their tour was over, many of the men of the Tenth Mountain Division returned to Colorado to take up permanent residence. Two such corps members, Pete Seibert and Earl Eaton, took what they learned from training and living in the farthest reaches of Colorado's backcountry and established Colorado's first ski resort, at Loveland Pass. Pete Seibert also played a pivotal role in developing the Vail Valley's ski industry. Larry Jump, a Tenth Mountain veteran, established Arapahoe Basin in 1946. In all, 2,000 Tenth Mountain men became ski instructors, and sixty-two American ski resorts were either founded, managed, or had their schools directed by members of the Tenth Mountain Division.

Of course, not all of the former members of the Tenth Mountain Division pursued a life in the ski industry. David Brower became the first executive director of the Sierra Club. Fritz Benedict created the Tenth Mountain Hut and Trail System. Paul Pelzoldt founded the Wilderness Education Association. Bob Lewis created the "Braille Trail"—the first hiking trail for the blind. Bill Bowerman, the track coach for the University of Oregon, was introduced to a new fitness exercise while his team was competing in New Zealand. The Kiwis called it "jogging." Bringing the idea back to the States, Bowerman began making jogging shoes. His waffle iron became the inspiration for a sole that wouldn't pick up mud. He called these shoes "The Waffle" and would later call his new shoe company Nike.

In 1988 the Tenth Mountain Division helped create the International Federation of Mountain Soldiers, a worldwide alliance of mountain troops dedicated to world peace. Germans included. On February 18, 1995, fifty years after their assault on Riva Ridge, a group of these septuagenarian mountain men climbed the ridge again. At the top, the Germans joined them in peace. Of the 14,300 Tenth Mountain men, 992 were killed and more than 4,000 were wounded. A memorial to these 992 men stands at the top of Tennessee Pass.

Today, the Tenth Mountain Trail Association Hut System, established in 1980, offers backcountry thrill seekers thirty-four square miles of adventure within the White River and San Isabel National Forests. Aside from the thirteen huts in the Tenth Mountain Hut System, Colorado boasts over forty other established huts and yurts throughout the state, most of which are accessible by mountain bikes.

21 Searle Pass and Kokomo Pass Trail

This portion of the Colorado Trail delivers you above timberline via the beautiful Guller Gulch. On the other side of Copper Mountain Ski Resort, the singletrack passes high above Janet's Cabin to Searle Pass and on to Kokomo Pass. This entire area proved to be an invaluable resource to America during World War II. You'll pass by an area where soldiers of the Tenth Mountain Division once trained for wintertime warfare. Visible from Searle Pass, the Climax Molybdenum Mine supplied the Allied Forces with most of their molybdenum, an element used to reinforce steel alloys, which was critical to the war effort. With incredible singletrack over smooth and rocky terrain leading well above timberline, Searle/Kokomo Passes Trail is a true Rocky Mountain gem.

Start: At the Union Creek parking lot in the Copper Mountain Ski Resort.
Length: 13.6-mile out-and-back from Searle Pass; 19.6-mile out-and-back from Kokomo Pass.
Approximate riding time: Advanced riders, 2.5 to 3 hours; intermediate riders, 3 to 3.5 hours.
Technical difficulty: Technically moderate to challenging due in large part to the rockiness of much of the trail, particularly above treeline, and the commonness of tree roots.
Physical difficulty: Physically moderate to challenging since the trail starts at 9,877 feet and reaches 12,320 feet.
Terrain: The route begins with a short stint on a paved bicycle path before connecting to singletrack. The singletrack includes rocky terrain and many roots.
Trail contacts: White River National Forest, Dillon Ranger District, 680 River Pathway, P.O. Box 620, Silverthorne, 80498; (970) 468-5400.
Schedule: July to September.
Maps: USGS maps: Vail Pass, Copper Mountain; *Trails Illustrated* maps 108, Vail Pass and Map 109, Breckenridge South.
Nearest town: Frisco.
Other trail users: Equestrians, hikers, backpackers, and backcountry skiers.
Canine compatibility: Dog friendly.

Getting There

From Denver: Drive west on I-70 through the Eisenhower Tunnel and into Silverthorne. From Silverthorne continue traveling west on I-70 for 10 miles before taking exit 195 for Copper Mountain Resort. Turn right at Copper Road and drive through the resort. After 1.8 miles from where you turned onto Copper Road, turn right at Beeler Place. The Telemark Lodge will be to your right and Club Med to your left. Drive up Beeler to the Union Creek parking lot. *DeLorme: Colorado Atlas & Gazetteer:* Page 48, A-1.

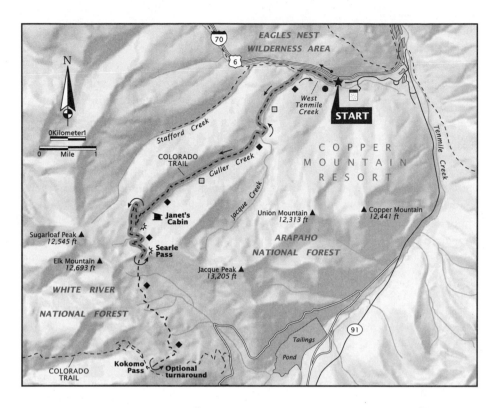

The Ride

Located at the base of Copper Mountain Ski Resort, Searle Pass and Kokomo Pass Trail is one of the most easily accessible routes of the entire 470-mile Colorado Trail. The trail's somewhat boring beginning along the paved bike path of Vail Pass quickly redeems itself once it connects with the singletrack to Searle Pass. The singletrack winds its way under I-70, crossing Guller Creek a number of times. Split-log foot-bridges span these creek crossings, a challenge to ride no matter how fat your tires. Winding its way through Guller Gulch, a beautiful willow-filled valley, the trail snakes over varied terrain of root and rock. After 2.5 miles, the drainage opens widely, offering expansive views of Elk Ridge. Dilapidated cabins, left over from an old sawmill, dot the first 4 miles of Guller Gulch. After negotiating a series of sharp climbing switchbacks, you reach the head of the gulch, marked by a wooden bench and fire ring. Just barely in sight at the end of this long gulch is Janet's Cabin, tro-phy of the Summit Huts Association.

Although quite far away, a sharp eye can make out the black tin roof of Janet's Cabin as it sits hidden in a stand of trees. Named after Janet Boyd Tyler, an icon of the Colorado ski scene, Janet's Cabin was built in 1990 and sits at 11,610 feet. In response to the growing popularity of hut-to-hut skiing, the Breckenridge-based

Summit Huts Association began work on its own hut system. With Janet's Cabin as its inaugural hut, the Summit Huts Association began its plan to connect eastern and western Summit County via a network of backcountry huts. Janet's Cabin stands as a skillfully crafted and luxurious retreat for backcountry skiers and winter enthusiasts. In addition to a wood-burning stove, cookware, and other requisite backcountry hut amenities, Janet's Cabin includes a $10,000 toilet, solar-heated showers, and the Nancy Dayton Memorial Sauna, which had to be airlifted in.

Continue riding through thick stands of lodgepole pine and blue spruce. Here begins the final push to Searle Pass. After crossing a wide mountain runoff at 5.5 miles, cairns mark the rest of your way above and beyond timberline. Both oxygen-depleted air and rocky terrain make the going rough. Take care to stay on the trail, though. The tundra-like environment above the timberline is a very fragile ecosystem and may suffer irreparable damage if heavily treaded. The trail winds its way left above Janet's Cabin. With a sneering, contemptible heart for the luxuries that lie below, continue on to Searle Pass.

Once atop Searle Pass, bask in the luxury that only eyes can afford. To the southeast lie the spirey peaks of the Tenmile Range and 13,205-foot Jaque Peak. On all other sides are the Gore and Holy Cross ranges. Via mountain bike, you've just accessed the one-time winter-training grounds for the U.S. Army's Tenth Mountain Division.

Notice the dirt roads and pools of water to the south and below Searle Pass. These are the remains of the Climax Molybdenum Mine, once the world's largest underground mine, producing 1.9 billion tons of molybdenum. Nearby Bartlett Mountain provided the world's single largest deposit of molybdenum. As mountain bikers, we owe a debt of gratitude to this hard gray metallic element that is used to reinforce steel alloys. It was molybdenum that added the "moly" to chro-moly bicycle frames.

During World War II, the Climax Mine worked feverishly, supplying roughly 72 percent of the world's molybdenum stock needed for the war effort. Sadly, the ponds you see below Searle Pass are remnants of the billions of tons of mill tailings that the Climax Mine has dumped into Tenmile Valley over the years. In fact, the Climax Mine dumped enough mill tailings in the valley to literally bury the sites

Searle Pass.

where the 1880s silver-mining camps of Recene and Kokomo once stood—a fitting end to these silver-mining camps. There is presently a program underway to cover these tailings.

From Searle Pass, veer right and traverse upward along Elk Ridge to reach Kokomo Pass. The ride ends once you arrive at Elk Ridge's high point; Kokomo Pass is actually below this point. The trail does continue, however, to Kokomo Pass, taking you on to Camp Hale, the site of the original winter camp for the Tenth Mountain Division.

From either Searle or Kokomo Pass, it's a wild ride back down. Starting from above timberline, the trail descends with surprising speed over rough terrain. The first section after returning to the trees is full of tight switchbacks and smooth-running singletrack. Snaking through intermittent spans of forest and meadow, the trail crosses over some tricky rock and root sections. The last 3 miles of singletrack offer more than enough occasion for speed, but they also include an assortment of technical, rocky terrain.

Passing over Guller Creek and under I–70, the singletrack once again meets with pavement. This time, however, the bike path offers more in the way of remission than resistance. Like a fine sipping whiskey, the bike path back to your vehicles makes for a mellow and smooth finish to your feast of a ride.

Miles and Directions

0.0 START from the Union Creek parking lot. Begin riding on the paved bike path beyond the bulletin board, passing the horse stables to your right and following West Tenmile Creek upstream.

0.7 Veer left over the bridge at the Colorado Trail sign. Once over the bridge, look for the Searle and Kokomo Pass sign. Here begins the singletrack portion of the route.

2.2 Pass a collapsed cabin and horse trail to your left. Once you pass these, bear right and continue along the Colorado Trail.

3.8 A series of lodgepole pine trees have fallen and now lie across the trail. Carefully maneuver around them and continue your ride on the other side.

4.3 Encounter switchbacks and a tougher section of the climb.

5.2 The trail becomes very smooth and soft through forest.

6.4 Reach Janet's Cabin.

6.8 Reach the top of Elk Ridge; Searle Pass is actually below this point. You have the option of turning around here. **Option:** To continue to Kokomo Pass, veer right and traverse in a southwesterly direction along Elk Ridge for roughly 3 miles. A number of switchbacks bring you to the route's high point. Turn around here; Kokomo Pass is actually below this point.

13.6 Arrive at your vehicle.

Ride Information

Local Information

Summit County Chamber of Commerce, P.O. Box 2010, Frisco, 80443; (970) 668-2054, (800) 530-3099; www.summitchamber.org.

Local Events and Attractions

Janet's Cabin, Tenth Mountain Hut Association, Breckenridge; (970) 925-5775 (not available in the summer.)

22 Wise Mountain and the Colorado Trail

On top of offering the whole enchilada, this section of the Colorado Trail smothers it in green chili. Sink your knobby teeth into this: mellow cruising along Breckenridge's Tiger Road, roaring descents on smooth-like-butter singletrack, and climbs that would impress even Sir Hilary. This trail is particularly well suited for mountain biking novitiates and anyone you're hoping to recruit to the sport. One word of caution: The switchbacks at the end of the ride descend quite steeply, so watch your speed. If you haven't ridden this trail yet, you don't know what you're missing.

Start: From the Gold Hill Trailhead.
Length: 24.8-mile loop.
Approximate riding time: Advanced riders, 2.5 hours; intermediate riders, 3 to 3.5 hours.
Technical difficulty: Technically moderate; although, a number of severe switchbacks do challenge even the most technical of riders.
Physical difficulty: Physically moderate to challenging due to the length, altitude, and amount of climbing involved.
Terrain: Improved dirt roads and singletrack. Singletrack is very smooth, most of which is made up of soft, forest earth; some roots and rocks with which to contend, but nothing that would pose too technical a challenge to the intermediate mountain biker.
Trail contacts: White River National Forest, Dillon Ranger District, 680 River Parkway, P.O. Box 620, Silverthorne, 80498; (970) 468–5400.
Schedule: July to October.
Maps: USGS maps: Boreas Pass, Keystone, Frisco; *Trails Illustrated* map 104.
Nearest town: Frisco.
Other trail users: Hikers, equestrians, backpackers, campers, and anglers.
Canine compatibility: Dog friendly.

Getting There

From Denver: Travel west on I-70 through the Eisenhower Tunnel. Take exit 203 to Colorado Highway 9 south. Once on Highway 9 drive south for 6.4 miles, passing through the town of Frisco, then turn right onto County Road 950 and park at the Gold Hill Trailhead, just off the paved bike path. *DeLorme: Colorado Atlas & Gazetteer:* Page 38, D-2.
Public Transportation: From Frisco, take the Summit Stage Breckenridge bus to the intersection of CO 9 and CR 950. Ride west on CR 950 to the Gold Hill Trailhead.

The Ride

This 25-mile section of the Colorado Trail may be the finest example of singletrack ecstasy ever to be experienced within the limits of law (divine or otherwise)—a kind of hedonism, basking within the gray shades that separate the spiritually holy from the sinisterly evil. Even the most stoic mountain bikers have succumbed to fits of frenzy before the base of Wise Mountain—and understandably so, owing to the trail's close proximity to that brain-beleaguered town of Breckenridge.

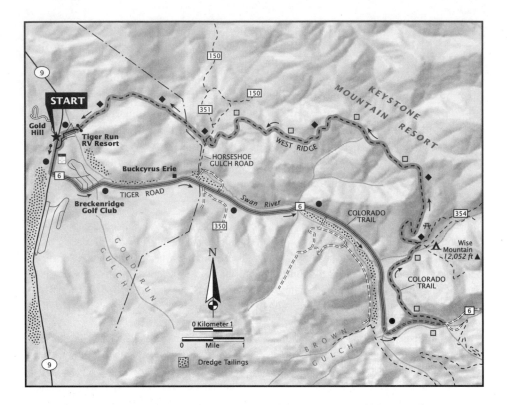

You might say Breckenridge hangs in the balance of a hybrid identity. Owing to its earliest scrambles for gold, Breckenridge is home to the largest gold nugget ever unearthed in Colorado—the thirteen-pound, seven-ounce "Tom's Baby." Of more recent fortune, Breckenridge boasts a relatively new, multibillion-dollar ski industry and offers the dreamy-eyed tourist Colorado's largest historic district: over 250 authentically maintained structures. Its quaint 1890s Victorian downtown offers a charming first impression, thanks to its ski industry economy. But ride down any one of a number of its back streets and you'll see the dilapidated remains of its notorious nineteenth-century gold-mining history.

The Colorado Trail leads the historically minded mountain biker down one such back street. Adhering to the maxim "a spoon full of sugar helps the medicine go down," the trail passes alongside the world's only publicly owned Jack Nicklaus–designed golf course before offering the rider views of the area's more sinister past.

Littered alongside Tiger Road and the banks of the Swan River, and indeed throughout Summit County, are miles of river stone churned up by dredging boats that operated in the area from 1898 to 1942. The first of nine dredging boats to operate in Colorado was brought here by Ben Stanley Revett. Revett's boats, weighing as much as 500 tons and measuring 100 feet long by 30 feet wide, ripped through surrounding river valleys in an effort to mine gold. These massive wooden boats dredged the river beds to depths of 50 feet, in a swell 200 feet wide. The tons of dredged glacial rock were separated from the river bed's finer sands and tossed to the banks. With the river stones laid aside, these mechanical miners could easily wash the gold deposits from the separated sands.

Today, the glacial rocks that were left behind and piled high atop one another now lie like exposed sores along the otherwise verdant slopes of the Swan River Valley. Painstaking efforts are being made, however, to rid the valley of these sores. Stones are being collected, loaded onto trucks, and driven to mills where they're pulverized and added to cement mixtures. As you near 3 miles into your trip, an abandoned Buckcyrus Erie model dredger, the kind once used for dredging the Swan River, sits in a still pond surrounded by some exhumed river stone.

Ripping down some of the fastest singletrack along the Colorado Trail.

Your cathartic 8.9-mile ride along the dirt roads eventually leads you to the salvation of the Colorado Trail singletrack. This trail takes you over rolling terrain along the base of Wise Mountain. As smooth as a buttered baby's bottom, and on occasion every bit as tacky, the singletrack descends to the North Fork of the Swan River, snaking its way through switchback-laden hillside meadows and past crowded stands of pine.

After crossing the Swan River, the trail will veer sharply to the left, before a camping site, at mile 11.5. A cairn marks the way to the left, while a Colorado Trail marker validates the move soon thereafter. Here begins your long grunt of a climb to West Ridge. This climb is not for the faint of heart, but it can be ridden without having to walk your bicycle. Stay on the main trail at all junctions; you'll pass two singletrack trails to your right that drop you to Keystone Resort. With Keystone now lying across the valley on the East Ridge, the trail levels out, offering smooth-running singletrack through a pine forest.

At 16 miles, the trail starts descending fast. Although this section invites speed, there are a number of tight switchbacks with which to contend. After descending for approximately 4 fast miles, you cross Horseshoe Gulch Road and begin the final climb of the ride. The trail eventually forks right into a meadow, offering expansive views of the Tenmile Range. After roughly 2 miles of moderate climbing, the trail's final descent through several tight switchbacks leads you to the Tiger Run RV Resort. The switchbacks above the resort are not easily managed and should not be taken lightly. Ride quickly and quietly to the front of the resort. Cross Colorado Highway 9 and turn right on the paved bike path back to your vehicle.

Miles and Directions

0.0 START at the Gold Hill Trailhead. Travel south on the bike path, heading toward Brecken-ridge.

0.7 Cross CO 9 and turn left onto Tiger Road by the Breckenridge Golf Club.

3.3 The abandoned *Buckcyrus Erie* dredging boat is on your left.

5.4 There's a dilapidated mine off to your right.

6.5 Reach the junction of North and Middle Fork Roads. Turn right onto Middle/South Forks Road.

7.0 Reach the junction of Middle and South Fork Roads. South Fork Road bears to your right and heads over Georgia Pass. Continue riding straight on Middle Fork Road.

8.9 Two entrances to the Colorado Trail will be on both sides of the road. Turn left onto the Colorado Trail singletrack. (The right fork climbs steeply to Georgia Pass, and the main road climbs above timberline, eventually dropping into Montezuma.)

11.1 Cross the North Fork of the Swan River. There are a number of picnic and camping sites here. Noticeable are the man-made log foot bridges.

11.5 Cross North Fork Road, which climbs to a high-alpine valley. The trail continues across the road. After crossing North Fork Road, the trail will cross over a stream and come to another road and a log fence. Cross through the log fence area and continue on the trail.

13.7 Arrive at a fire line. Keystone Ski Resort will be to your right. Notice the chair lift.

14.5 The trail will fork. The right fork will lead into Keystone Ski Resort. Bear left, continuing on the Colorado Trail.

17.9 Pass through a gate.

20.7 Cross Horseshoe Gulch Road, underneath the power lines, and continue on the trail directly in front of you, climbing over the hill.

22.0 Enjoy the final fast descent, ending with a number of very tight switchbacks as the trail descends to Tiger Run RV Resort.

24.8 Reach your vehicle.

Ride Information

Local Information

Breckenridge Resort Chamber, 311 South Ridge Street, P.O. Box 1909, Breckenridge, 80424; (970) 453-2913, (888) 251-2417; www.gobreck.com.

Organizations

Summit Fat Tire Society, Breckenridge; (970) 949-8057.

Breckenridge Fat Tire Society, Breckenridge; (970) 453-5548 or (970) 453-INFO, push #FATT.

Honorable Mention

North Central Mountains

Noted below is one of the great rides in the north central region that didn't make the A-list this time around but deserves recognition nonetheless. Check it out and let us know what you think. You may decide that it deserves higher status in future editions or, perhaps, you may have a ride of your own that merits some attention.

E Baker's Tank Loop

Located in the heart of Summit County, Baker's Tank Loop is accessed by climbing up Boreas Pass Road. Named after the god of wind, Boreas Pass Road connects with many shorter singletrack trails, one of which is the Baker's Tank Loop. This moderately challenging 5.5-mile loop gains little elevation, only traveling between 10,360 and 10,850 feet. The attraction riders have to this trail is its relatively "hidden" location within one of Colorado's more recognized mountain areas. From the road the singletrack descends through dense pine forests on an old four-wheel-drive road to Baker's Tank, site of one of the earlier mining operations in Summit County. From Baker's Tank, riders intersect the singletrack on the left that begins near a fence. This section of trail clings to a steep slope, so riders beware. Due to its predominantly shaded route, this trail may remain too wet to ride until late June.

With views of Bald Mountain (13,684 feet), this trail is a gem of a ride in the heart of outdoor Colorado. To access the Baker's Tank Loop, drive south through Breckenridge on Colorado Highway 9. After the stoplight on the south end of town, bear left onto Boreas Pass Road. Drive for 3.5 miles on Boreas Pass Road until the pavement ends. Park your vehicle here in a pullout on the left and begin riding up the road.

For more information on this ride and other Summit County rides, contact the Knorr House at 303 S. Main St., Breckenridge, (970) 453–2631; or the Breckenridge Resort Chamber in Breckenridge, (970) 453–2913 or (970) 453–6018. *DeLorme: Colorado Atlas & Gazetteer:* Page 48, A-3.

South Central Mountains

Colorado owes much to its south central region. Many of the state's "firsts" happened here. Founded in 1849, Garcia is Colorado's first and oldest town. Our Lady of Guadalupe (built in the town of Conejos during the Spanish settlement of the 1800s) is the state's oldest church. Fort Garland, established in 1858 by Kit Carson, is Colorado's oldest military post. Colorado mountain biking was first discovered in Crested Butte in 1976. Aside from these "firsts," however, south central Colorado also enjoys a rich geography.

This region is truly a land of contrasts. The San Luis Valley, one of the largest alpine valleys in the world, is surrounded by the 14,000-foot peaks of the Sangre de Cristo Mountains to the east, the San Juan Mountains to the west, and the Sawatch Mountains to the north. Colorado's tallest mountain, Mount Elbert (14,433 feet), is located at the northern tip of this region. Northeast of the town of Alamosa, near the region's eastern flank, lie the Great Sand Dunes, a veritable 700-foot-high mountain range of sand, the tallest in North America.

Owing to its sun-drenched terrain, the San Luis Valley provides a longer riding season than most other areas in Colorado. Ironically, however, the valley remains relatively unknown as a mountain biking destination. Zapata Falls Trail is a fun, stacked singletrack loop that offers incredible views of the Great Sand Dunes and the Sangre de Cristo Mountains. Traveling west, near the little-known town of South Fork, Cat Creek Trail provides an intermediate ride through tall stands of spruce and fir. In the winter of 1999, lynx were reintroduced into this area. As one heads north toward Salida and the Fourteeners region of Chaffee County, the landscape does an acrobatic turnaround, providing fifteen of Colorado's fifty-four Fourteeners (mountains that are 14,000 feet or higher). Typifying the riding of this area is the Colorado classic, Monarch Crest Trail. To the northwest of Salida lies the birthplace of Colorado mountain biking, Crested Butte, Colorado. Crested Butte is considered by many to have the best riding in all of Colorado.

From exploration, to agriculture, to mining, south central Colorado's cultural influences are as varied as its landscape. To the credit of Colorado's first explorers, this region is steeped in Spanish influences. In 1596 Juan de Zaldivar, on behalf of the Don Juan de Onate expedition into New Mexico, came into Colorado through the San Luis Valley to track troublesome Indians. This early exploration into the valley laid the groundwork for a region founded on ancient Spanish culture and tradition.

The fertile San Luis Valley turns into a veritable sea of green in the spring. With a growing agricultural economy, the San Luis Valley owes much of its success to the Rio Grande del Norte. Flowing through the middle of the valley, this river is the agricultural lifeblood of the economy of the San Luis Valley.

Farther north, in towns like Crested Butte, Buena Vista, and Salida, mining was the area's mainstay, that is, before giving way to mountain thrill seekers. Remnants of the bygone mining days can still be seen throughout the mountainsides. Today, however, these mountainsides serve better to wow the crowds with steep singletrack descents and jaw-dropping views.

23 Deer Creek Trail

With the Gunnison National Forest blanketing nearly 85 percent of the entire county, Crested Butte is a mountain biker's town. Deer Creek Trail is one of the town's most celebrated trails. This trail has one of the longest stretches of singletrack of any single trail in Crested Butte and offers incredible views after a grueling but short climb through the aspens. Since Deer Creek Trail is open for cattle grazing toward the latter end of the mountain biking season, the trail does tend to become "ripped up," particularly near the end as you ride through the meadows into Gothic. Because of this, it's a good idea to do this trail around mid-season. The trail features hard-packed singletrack, tight aspens, and rutted and rocky ascents and descents. It's a Crested Butte favorite.

Start: From the Alpineer bicycle shop in downtown Crested Butte.
Length: 28.9-mile loop.
Approximate riding time: Advanced riders, 3 to 4 hours; intermediate riders, 4 to 5 hours.
Technical difficulty: Technically moderate to challenging with some demanding sections. Some route segments combine steep single-track grades (both ascending and descending) with exposed roots and rocks.
Physical difficulty: Physically moderate to challenging due to the significant climbing at high altitude.
Terrain: Paved state road, dirt forest road, and singletrack. The terrain includes tough-climbing dirt road and singletrack. Most of the route travels over mountainous terrain at higher elevations and rolls over a number of rocks and roots.
Trail contacts: Bureau of Land Management, Gunnison Field Office, 216 North Colorado, Gunnison, 81230; (970) 641-1928. Gunnison National Forest, Gunnison Ranger District, 216 North Colorado, Gunnison, 81230; (970) 641-0471.
Schedule: Mid-June to October.
Maps: USGS maps: Crested Butte, Gothic; *Trails Illustrated* map 133; Crested Butte Bike Trails Map; Aspen, Crested Butte, Gunnison Recreation Topo Map, Latitude 40° Inc.
Nearest town: Crested Butte.
Other trail users: Hikers and equestrians.
Canine compatibility: Dog friendly.

Getting There

From Gunnison: Drive north on Colorado Highway 135 into Crested Butte. Once in Crested Butte, drive through the all-way stop intersection at 0.2 mile to the next four-way stop at 0.4 mile. Turn left into the shopping complex before the Bullion King sign. Park your vehicle in the lot just outside the Alpineer, Crested Butte's ski and bike shop. *DeLorme: Colorado Atlas & Gazetteer:* Page 58, A-2.

The Ride

Although mountain biking has saturated many of Colorado's mountain towns, one town remains relatively untracked by the mountain biking masses, and curiously, it

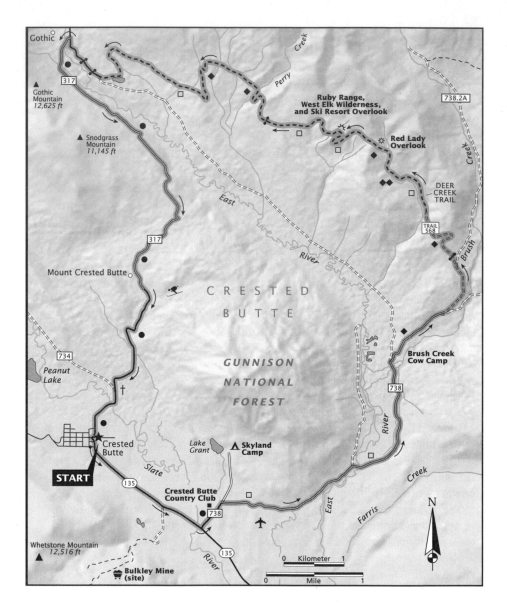

offers some of the state's best singletrack trails. Crested Butte enjoys clandestine cranking like Durango and Moab could only dream of. Virtually endless trails weave their sinuous courses through the region's terrain, from its highest (above timberline) to its lowest (the high-desert sands). Among Crested Butte's best and most beloved rides is Deer Creek Trail.

As you begin riding south out of town on Colorado Highway 135, you pass through the shadow of 12,516-foot Whetstone Mountain—just as the miners did who worked the Bulkley Mine over one hundred years ago. During the winter months, miners, clothes darkened from the bituminous coal, formed long processionals on their way to the mine. The scene looked like a trail of chucked coffee on virgin snow as the miners slogged single-file from Crested Butte to the Bulkley Mine through waist-deep drifts. When the lead miner would get tired from breaking trail, he'd hand off the duty to the second-in-line and fall to the rear for his rest. This would continue until it was his turn again.

Situated along the steep sides of Whetstone Mountain, the Bulkley Mine was quite susceptible to avalanches. In 1912 an avalanche ripped over the head house of the mine, carrying six men 500 feet before burying them alive. Workers quickly began their search for the buried men. All of the men were eventually found, but not before the avalanche claimed one of them.

After reaching the ominous shadow of Whetstone Mountain, riders intersect Brush Creek Road. Here the mood lightens considerably, as high-alpine valleys and expansive views of the 1,700,000-acre Gunnison National Forest greet you. The first big climb of the day comes after roughly 8 miles. This climb features steep grades and rocky terrain, before topping out at 9.5 miles. Having connected to the singletrack, the second big climb arrives after crossing Deer Creek. Luckily, this climb lasts only half a mile, as it passes through a beautiful aspen glen. Steep grades, ruts, and exposed root sections make this climb physically demanding and technically challenging. Upon reaching the top, you're offered expansive westerly views of the Ruby Range, the West Elk Wilderness, and Mount Crested Butte's ski resort. In full prominence stands the 12,392-foot Mount Emmons. This mountain is home to the Red Lady Bowl, and one of Crested Butte's most heated disputes.

Frank Orazem, a Crested Butte elder, recalled first seeing the bowl: "I saw the red ore glowing in what we call Mount Emmons Basin. Then I saw her, shaped by the ore or shadows or a trick of light . . . an Oriental empress . . . her kimono was bright red. . . . I called her the *Red Lady* because that's what the basin looked like to me." Needless to say, the locals take their mountains quite seriously.

In 1977 the Cyprus-Amax Mining Company discovered the world's largest known molybdenum deposit approximately 1,200 feet below Red Lady Bowl and threatened to mine it. The molybdenum deposit, with a diameter of 2,500 feet and an average thickness of 300 feet, is estimated to have a market value of $7 billion.

The Black Hole section of the Deer Creek Trail with Crested Butte Ski Resort in the background.

Amax's proposal included not only the building of the molybdenum mine, but also the building of a mill and a sludge pond, all to be located on surrounding national forest and ranch land. The town of Crested Butte rallied against the proposal and formed the High Country Citizens' Alliance. The dispute was described by the *High Country News* on December 8, 1997, as "a classic David vs. Goliath battle." The article went on to say that the "residents of the ski-resort town of Crested Butte, Colorado, chased the world's largest mining conglomerate out of their valley."

Now, over twenty years later, the battle rages on. In an attempt to supply the would-be mine with water, Cyprus-Amax has filed in Colorado Water Court for rights to tap the Slate River. If approved, Cyprus-Amax's access to water would mark the first step to molybdenum mining atop Red Lady, a project whose current estimates propose mining 6,000 tons (with the ability to extend) of molybdenum a day. In their continued fight against Cyprus-Amax, the members of the High Country Citizen's Alliance worry that a mine of this proportion might deliver negative environmental, social, and economic blows to Crested Butte. Presently, the High Country Citizen's Alliance, in cooperation with local volunteers, is gathering more information about mining and molybdenum. They're conducting educational lectures on what a mine would mean to Crested Butte, showing slide shows of previous mining activity, and hiking to the proposed site below Red Lady Bowl. Lawyers for the High Country Citizen's Alliance are fighting Cyprus-Amax's appeal for water rights.

From the site of this bone of contention, you descend through hillside meadows and aspens where large herds of elk are frequently bugling. Skirting the rim of the "black hole" (a large slide out area), you continue into a sun-drenched, tightly packed aspen grove. From here the trail descends through a variety of meadows to Perry Creek. Climb from Perry Creek and top out approximately at 15 miles. Starting at the top of this climb lies the most technical riding of the entire route. As you pass through intermittent meadows and aspen glens, steep ruts and large rocks mark your way into the town of Gothic at the base of Gothic Mountain (12,625 feet). From Gothic it's a fast descent through Mt. Crested Butte to the town of Crested Butte and your vehicle.

Miles and Directions

0.0 START from the Alpineer bike shop in downtown Crested Butte and begin riding south on Highway 135, heading out of town.

2.0 Bear left onto Forest Road 738 (Brush Creek Road), by the Crested Butte Country Club sign, heading toward the airport.

2.6 FR 738 turns into an improved dirt road. Continue riding on the road. The Crested Butte Country Club is to your left.

3.9 After crossing a second cattle guard, Upper Upper Loop Trail is to your left. Pass this trail and descend on FR 738.

4.5 The Brush Creek Trailhead is on your left. Continue riding on FR 738.

6.6 Cross Brush Creek.

7.7 FR 738 reaches a trail intersection marked by a sign that reads DEER CREEK TRAIL 568–3 MILES and TEOCALLI RIDGE TRAIL 557–5 MILES. Bear left here and climb up the rough double-track, heading in a northeasterly direction en route to Deer Creek Trail.

8.6 Arrive at another trail intersection marked by a sign that reads DEER CREEK TRAIL 568–2 MILES and TEOCALLI RIDGE TRAIL 557–4 MILES. Bear left at this trail intersection and head in a north-westerly direction, following signs for Deer Creek Trail 568.

9.5 Pass through a gate (closing it behind you) and descend quickly into an aspen and lodge-pole pine forest.

9.7 The trail forks. Bear left at this fork, following signs reading DEER CREEK.

10.1 Intersect the Deer Creek singletrack and continue riding in a northwesterly direction.

11.0 Cross Deer Creek and begin a slow grunt of a climb through the aspens.

11.6 Arrive at the crest and a beautiful vista. From here, descend through slope-side meadows, past a slide area, and into a dense aspen forest.

13.4 Arrive at a stock tank. Pass around the tank and continue riding due west.

13.7 Cross over the barbed wire fence via a step ladder and descend through Dry Basin.

14.1 Cross Perry Creek and climb up another hillside meadow through another stand of aspen.

15.1 Top out and descend through meadows and aspen glens toward the town of Gothic.

17.1 The trail meets with a barbed wire fence and a cattle tank. Continue riding due west on the trail with the fence running alongside the trail to your left.

19.6 After crossing underneath the telephone lines, arrive at the west Deer Creek Trailhead and a dirt road. Bear right onto the dirt road, heading toward the town of Gothic.

19.8 Pass through an orange gate and continue up the dirt road.

20.0 Pass through another orange gate and continue up the dirt road.

20.3 After passing through a couple of gates, the dirt road intersects with an improved dirt road in Gothic. Bear left onto this improved dirt road and cross the East River to FR 317.

20.4 Bear left onto FR 317 and ride south, back to Crested Butte.

24.0 Reach Mount Crested Butte. FR 317 becomes paved and turns into Gothic Street. Ride on Gothic Street through Mt. Crested Butte to the paved bicycle path.

24.4 Intercept the bike path and ride back to Crested Butte and your vehicle.

28.0 Pass the Crested Butte Cemetery to your left.

28.8 Pass the Crested Butte Chamber of Commerce to your left.

28.9 Arrive at your vehicle.

Ride Information

Local Information

Crested Butte/Mt. Crested Butte Chamber of Commerce, P.O. Box 1288, Crested Butte, 81224; (970) 349-6438, (800) 545-4505; www.crestedbuttechamber.com.
High Country Citizens' Alliance, 724 Elk Avenue, P.O. Box 1066, Crested Butte, 81224; (970) 349-7104; www.hccaonline.org.

Local Events and Attractions

Mountain Bike Hall of Fame and Museum, Crested Butte; (970) 349-6817, (800) 454-4505.
Crested Butte Mountain Heritage Museum, Inc., Crested Butte; (970) 349-1880.
Fat Tire Bike Festival, in June, Crested Butte; (970) 349-6438, (800) 545-4505.
Annual Wildflower Festival, in July, Crested Butte; (970) 349-6438, (800) 545-4505.
One World Music Festival, in September, Crested Butte; (970) 349-6438, (800) 545-4505.
Rendezvous Gallery, Crested Butte; (970) 349-6804.

Organizations

Crested Butte Mountain Bike Association (C.B.M.B.A), Crested Butte; (970) 349-5517, (970) 349-6817.

Accommodations

Irwin Lodge, Crested Butte; (970) 349-9800, (888) GO-IRWIN.
Crested Butte International Hostel LLC, Crested Butte; (970) 349-0588, (888) 389-0588; www.gunnison.com/~hostel.

Restaurants

Idle Spur, Crested Butte; (970) 349-5026.
Donita's Cantina, Crested Butte; (970) 349-6674.
Wooden Nickel, Crested Butte; (970) 349-6350.

Tours

No Limits Center, Crested Butte, Mt. Crested Butte; (970) 349-4247, (888) 954-4247.
Pioneer Guide Service, Crested Butte; (970) 349-5517; www.pioneer@crestedbutte.net.
Paddle Trax & Syngltrax, Crested Butte; (970) 349-1100.
Alpine Outside, Crested Butte; (970) 349-5011, (800) 833-8052; Almont; (970) 641-1303, (888) 761-FISH; www.3rivers resort.com.

24 Deadman Gulch

Deadman Gulch Trail is one of Crested Butte's finest, running the gamut of Rocky Mountain riding. Burning climbs, savage descents, technical singletrack (both up and down), and the famed Deadman's switchbacks all contribute to this trail's legendary status. The views of the Elk Mountains, where innumerable clashes between Ute Indians and the early prospecting parties of the 1860s and 1870s occurred, are fantastic. Since most of Crested Butte's trails are multi-use, some sections may be rutted from motorcycles—particularly the climb from Deadman Gulch. Due to the preponderance of creeks that flow throughout the area, this trail is best ridden during the latter half of the season.

Start: From the Deadman Gulch Trailhead.
Length: 20.1-mile loop.
Approximate riding time: Advanced riders, 3 to 3.5 hours; intermediate riders, 4 to 5 hours.
Technical difficulty: Technically challenging to demanding due to a variety of exposed roots and rocks. The numerous switchbacks down Deadman Gulch to your vehicle are particularly technical.
Physical difficulty: Physically challenging to demanding due to sustained climbs at high elevations over rough terrain.
Terrain: Dirt forest road, logging road, and singletrack. Types of terrain over which you'll be riding include steep ascending and descending singletrack, large amounts of exposed roots and rocks, slippery creek-side moss-covered roots and rocks, tough switchbacks, hard-packed dirt, sand, and ruts.

Trail contacts: Bureau of Land Management, Gunnison Field Office, 216 North Colorado, Gunnison, 81230; (970) 641–1928. Gunnison National Forest, Gunnison Ranger District, 216 North Colorado, Gunnison, 81230; (970) 641–0471.
Schedule: Mid-July to October.
Maps: USGS maps: Cement Mountain, Pearl Pass, Italian Creek; *Trails Illustrated* map 133; Crested Butte Bike Trails Map, available at the Alpineer; Aspen, Crested Butte, Gunnison Recreation Topo Map, Latitude 40° Inc., available at select area bike shops.
Nearest town: Crested Butte.
Other trail users: Hikers, equestrians, motorcyclists, campers, and anglers.
Canine compatibility: Dog friendly.

Getting There

From Crested Butte: Drive south on Colorado Highway 135 for 6.9 miles (from the Alpineer bike shop) before turning left onto County Road 740 (Cement Creek Road). At 7.8 miles the pavement ends. Cross a cattle guard at 8.9 miles. Cement Creek Road forks at 10.3 miles. Continue straight (left) here, passing a sign for Cement Creek. Enter into the Gunnison National Forest at 10.6 miles. Pass the Mad Creek Ranch to your right at 11.6 miles. At 14 miles bear right into the Deadman Gulch Trailhead. *DeLorme: Colorado Atlas & Gazetteer:* Page 58, B-3 to A-3.

The Ride

After the Big Mine closed in 1952, effectively putting an end to coal mining in Crested Butte, a new breed of settlers started to move into town. There were the summer vacationers—among them Dick Eflin and Fred Rice, co-founders of the Crested Butte Ski Resort. And there were the hippies. By the late 1960s and early 1970s, Crested Butte had become a skiing commune for nature lovers. Surrounded by three wilderness areas and over a million acres of national forest, Crested Butte offered a good deal of elbow room. Skiing would prove to be too limited an endeavor upon which to build a recreation paradise, so the sport of mountain biking soon arrived to fill the void.

Mountain biking came to Crested Butte, and indeed the rest of Colorado, in the summer of 1976. Before then, town bikes were nothing more than a means of transport, from the market to the post office to home. Local firefighters, after the threat of summer fires had passed, would return from their mountain posts on their town bikes. After ripping down rough mountain roads at hair-raising speeds (helmetless, of course), they'd drop into Crested Butte and skid to a stop at the local watering hole. Well, in 1976, a group of motorcyclists from Aspen rode their bikes over Pearl Pass (12,705 feet) and descended upon Crested Butte. Before the dust from their bikes had settled, the bikers were already bragging about their high-alpine accomplishments. Not to be outdone, the firefighters decided to cross Pearl Pass and descend into Aspen with their town bicycles. The passage took two days and featured a Deadheaded campout in Cumberland Basin. The riders descended upon Aspen and set themselves up at the Hotel Jerome, their bikes piled in a clunking heap outside. This has since become an annual event. What began on a cold September morning with only fifteen fat-tire faithfuls has today evolved into a multimillion-dollar industry. We owe a certain debt of gratitude to Crested Butte for its accomplishments and its continued support of the sport.

Seven years after the "birth of mountain biking" in Colorado, Crested Butte formed the Crested Butte Mountain Bike Association, a volunteer, nonprofit organization designed to preserve and protect trails and the surrounding ecosystem, while informing and educating users on proper trail etiquette. In 1988 Crested Butte founded the country's first Mountain Biking Hall of Fame and Museum (MBHOF). The MBHOF preserves and displays vintage bicycles, classic photos, and numerous press clippings. Since its inception as a nonprofit organization, the MBHOF has inducted sixty-six of the sport's major players.

A major player in its own right, Deadman Gulch Trail is one of Crested Butte's rowdier rides. The ride begins by paralleling rushing Cement Creek. It continues its way through the steep rock walls of Cement Canyon. After crossing Cement Creek, you climb moderately and are offered views of Crystal Peak and Mount Tilton. The space between the two mountains is where a rush of Leadville prospectors descended in 1879 and 1880. Their silver discovery prompted the building of the Red Cloud, Tilden, Moonlight, and Climax Mines near the headwaters of Cement Creek. The inaccessibility of the mines eventually led to their downfall. But a prospector's misfortune is a mountain biker's gain. You'll appreciate this as you continue riding to the top of Reno Divide.

Reno Divide Road climbs steeply via switchbacks through a dense conifer forest and passes an old miner's cabin to the left. In 1892 Reno Divide served as a halfway station for freighters serving local area mines. Italian Mountain (13,378 feet) and Lambertson Peak lie to the north. From Reno Divide, connect with Flag Creek Trail, which offers the first of several great descents. After crossing Flag Creek, you may notice a singletrack spur that breaks left. This is not the trail. Continue straight on the main trail for a mile before reaching a very sandy, rooty, and rocky section, which climbs steeply through dense forest.

Once you connect with Bear Creek Trail, the ride descends rapidly through a meadow and crosses a wooden footbridge. After crossing Bear Creek, you have to descend through sections of tricky, technical sand and rock. After this tricky descent, the trail becomes a fast and smooth tour through the pines. With Bear Creek flowing to your left, you ride along a precipitous west-facing slope, with slippery rocks and roots. From here, the trail opens up onto a beautiful high-alpine valley. The singletrack through this valley is fast and smooth and leads to Deadman Gulch. The gulch received its foreboding name in 1859, when Ute Indians massacred six miners here who had trespassed on their land in search of gold. Today, however, the gulch's killer climb may better serve to identify the spot.

Although most of this climb is manageable, save the last 200–300 yards where the climbing gets considerably steeper, it does arrive late in the ride—around 15.4 miles. Its late arrival makes this final push that much more challenging. Once you reach the top, the dark pine forest offers cool relief after a burning climb. From the top of Deadman Gulch, descend down the famed switchbacks through tight aspens and over large exposed rocks. After ripping the switchbacks, you pass a private home before descending steeply to Cement Creek. The trail travels upstream for 100 yards. A large, fallen tree with notched stairs carved into its ends lies across the creek. Cross the creek via the tree and climb to your vehicle.

Miles and Directions

0.0 START from the Deadman Gulch Trailhead and begin riding up County Road 740 (Cement Creek Road).

1.0 Pass a small hillside waterfall to your left and continue riding up the rocky road through narrow Cement Creek Canyon.

1.3 County Road 740 crosses Cement Creek. Continue riding up the road. Pass a singletrack trail to your left before crossing the creek and a campground to your right after crossing the creek.

2.2 County Road 740 intersects with Forest Road 759 (Reno Divide Road). Bear right onto the FR 759, following signs for Reno Pass.

3.5 Pass a dilapidated cabin to your left.

This footbridge is a good landmark for knowing you're on the Bear Creek Trail.

4.2 The climb begins to level somewhat.

5.9 Reach the summit of Reno Divide. As you bear right (east) atop the ridge, pass through the gate and ride to the junction of Italian Creek Road and Flag Creek Trail 422.

6.0 Reach the Flag Creek 422 trailhead. A sign here marks SPRING CREEK—4 MILES and BEAR CREEK—6 MILES. Continue riding on the singletrack of Flag Creek Trail, heading east.

8.9 Cross an eroding wooden footbridge and continue descending Flag Creek Trail.

9.1 Arrive at the intersection of Trail 426 and Spring Creek Trail. Bear right at this intersection, following the sign for Trail 426 and BEAR CREEK—9.1 MILES. Immediately after bearing right here, notice a sign posted on a lodgepole pine tree for DEADMAN GULCH—7 MILES pointing you in the right direction. Cross Flag Creek and continue riding due west.

11.4 After climbing through a meadow, the trail intersects with an old logging road. Bear left onto this old logging road and continue riding south. Be sure not to cross this logging road to connect with the continuation of the singletrack on the other side.

12.0 The logging road forks. Bear right to the intersection of Bear Creek Trail 415, passing signs for DEADMAN GULCH—4 MILES and SPRING CREEK—7 MILES. Continue riding on Bear Creek Trail 415 as it heads south through a meadow.

12.3 Cross a wooden footbridge.

13.4 Cross Bear Creek.

15.4 Reach the intersection of Bear Creek Trail and Deadman Gulch Trail. Bear right (west) onto Deadman Gulch Trail 420.

17.8 Reach the top of the Deadman Gulch, climbing and descending the switchbacks.

18.9 Reach a beautiful aspen forest.

19.8 Pass a private home to your left, as the trail parallels a barbed wire fence.

20.1 Arrive at your vehicle.

Ride Information

Local Information

Crested Butte/Mount Crested Butte Chamber of Commerce, P.O. Box 1288, Crested Butte, 81224; (970) 349-6438, (800) 545-4505; www.crestedbuttechamber.com.

High Country Citizens' Alliance, 724 Elk Avenue, P.O. Box 1066, Crested Butte, 81224; (970) 349-7104; www.hccaonline.org.

Local Events and Attractions

Mountain Bike Hall of Fame and Museum, Crested Butte; (970) 349-6817, (800) 454-4505.

Crested Butte Mountain Heritage Museum, Inc., Crested Butte; (970) 349-1880.

Fat Tire Bike Festival, in June, Crested Butte; (970) 349-6438, (800) 545-4505.

Annual Wildflower Festival, in July, Crested Butte; (970) 349-6438, (800) 545-4505.

One World Music Festival, in September, Crested Butte; (970) 349-6438, (800) 545-4505.

Rendezvous Gallery, Crested Butte; (970) 349-6804.

Organizations

Crested Butte Mountain Bike Association, Crested Butte; (970) 349-5517, (970) 349-6817.

Accommodations

Irwin Lodge, Crested Butte; (970) 349-9800, (888) GO-IRWIN.

Crested Butte International Hostel LLC, Crested Butte; (970) 349-0588, (888) 389-0588; www.gunnison.com/~hostel.

Restaurants

Idle Spur, Crested Butte; (970) 349-5026.

Donita's Cantina, Crested Butte; (970) 349-6674.

Wooden Nickel, Crested Butte; (970) 349-6350.

Tours

No Limits Center, Crested Butte, Mt. Crested Butte; (970) 349-4247, (888) 954-4247.

Pioneer Guide Service, Crested Butte; (970) 349-5517; www.pioneer@crestedbutte.net.

Paddle Trax & Syngltrax, Crested Butte; (970) 349-1100.

Alpine Outside, Crested Butte; (970) 349-5011, (800) 833-8052; Almont; (970) 641-1303, (888) 761-FISH; www.3rivers resort.com.

25 Dyke Trail

The Dyke Trail Loop is another trail in Crested Butte's long list of incredible rides. Combining long climbs, lakeside views, towering mountains, fast singletrack, and aspen forests, Dyke Trail is sure to please. With the exception of the road climb to Kebler Pass and the short distance from Irwin Lake to Dyke Trailhead, this ride is composed mostly of unbeatable singletrack. Even though your ride takes you to the top of Kebler Pass, don't be fooled that the way from Irwin Lake is all downhill. There are a couple of steep, rocky, and sandy climbs en route to Horse Ranch Park, one of which arrives just as you near the dyke.

Start: From Horse Ranch Park.
Length: 14-mile loop.
Approximate riding time: Advanced riders, 2 hours; intermediate riders, 3 hours.
Technical difficulty: Technically moderate to challenging due to a number of steep-walled creek crossings.
Physical difficulty: Physically moderate to challenging due to the climbing involved at higher elevations. As you reach the middle of the ride there is one long sustained climb that travels steeply through the aspens.
Terrain: Improved dirt road and singletrack. This trail runs its mountainous course along hard-packed forest earth. There are a number of exposed roots and rocks with which to contend. Several creek crossings, coupled with one major rock field, round out this ride's terrain.

Trail contacts: Bureau of Land Management, Gunnison Field Office, 216 North Colorado, Gunnison, 81230; (970) 641–1928. Gunnison National Forest, Gunnison Ranger District, 216 North Colorado, Gunnison, 81230; (970) 641–0471.
Schedule: Mid-June to October.
Maps: USGS maps: Oh-Be-Joyful, Mount Axtell, Marcellina Mountain, Anthracite Range; *Trails Illustrated* map 133; Crested Butte Bike Trails Map, available at the Alpineer; Aspen, Crested Butte, Gunnison Recreation Topo Map, Latitude 40° Inc., available at select bike shops.
Nearest town: Crested Butte.
Other trail users: Hikers, equestrians, and picnickers.
Canine compatibility: Dog friendly.

Getting There

From Crested Butte: Drive west on Colorado Highway 135 from the Alpineer store to the four-way stop intersection at Elk Avenue. Bear left on Elk Avenue, passing the sign for the Crested Butte business district and Kebler Pass. At 0.5 mile, bear left onto 1st Avenue, passing the sign for Kebler Pass Road. Make your next immediate right onto Whiterock Avenue. Whiterock Avenue turns into County Road 12 (Kebler Pass Road). At 1.8 miles the pavement ends. Bear left at 2.4 miles, passing the sign for Kebler Pass. Continue on CR 12. Bear left (still on CR 12) at the Irwin Lake intersection (7.2 miles), passing the sign for Kebler Pass. Reach Kebler Pass at 7.9 miles. Begin your descent to Horse Ranch Park. At 12.5 miles bear right into Horse Ranch Park. Park your vehicle here. *DeLorme: Colorado Atlas & Gazetteer:* Page 58, A-1 and A-2 to B-1 and B-2.

The Ride

As you begin riding up Kebler Pass Road to Kebler Pass, views of the Anthracite Range are to the south (right), with Ohio Peak (12,271 feet) standing out most prominently. The ruddy-looking Anthracite Range takes its name and its color from the hard natural coal found in abundance in its mountains. In Crested Butte's early mining days, fired coal from the surrounding mountains filled the crisp alpine air with a glow reminiscent of a city under siege. Lewis Lathrop, a Rio Grande engineer, recalled: "Both anthracite and soft coal poured in never-ending streams from the surrounding mountains. . . . Long banks of coke ovens made the night sky lurid with leaping red flames and the sickening-sweet odor of coal being baked into coke hung heavily over the snow-covered town." Although these now dilapidated coke ovens can be dismissed as nothing more than a minor pox on an otherwise unblemished Colorado landscape, they nevertheless whisper of the fortunes, foibles, strengths, and triumphs of the human spirit. This spirit now lies quietly captured in the Irwin Cemetery atop Kebler Pass.

Dejected, penniless, and disgusted after not having reaped the benefits of a twelve-year prospecting venture, A. T. Gilkerson decided to pack what little belongings he had and move his impoverished family back across the Great Plains. After his mule gave out, Gilkerson left his family with some provisions and went out in search of work. Gilkerson paused one day for lunch. There, on that warm July afternoon in 1879, in a ledge laid bare by horses' hooves, Gilkerson discovered Ruby Gulch, a deposit rich in ruby and wire silver.

Word of Gilkerson's discovery soon spread—perhaps by none louder than Richard P. Irwin, a well-respected prospector who had prospected the entire length of the Rocky Mountains from Canada to Mexico. Miners and prospectors descended on Ruby Gulch in record numbers in the spring following Gilkerson's discovery, causing a mushroom of competing mining towns. Perhaps no other mining town grew as aggressively in the area as did the town of Irwin.

With the town speedily coming of age, an ambitious printer from the town of Rosita saw his chance to set up Irwin's first newspaper. After arriving in Gunnison on March 3, 1880, John E. Phillips awaited the arrival of a Washington hand press he had sent for from Chicago. In the interim, Phillips walked the 30 miles to Irwin in 10 feet of snow and bought himself a lot—which also happened to be under 10 feet of snow. When the press equipment arrived, Phillips organized a team of freighters equipped with homemade snowshoes to transport the goods to Irwin. George Crofutt, author of *Crofutt's Grip-Sack Guide of Colorado,* best described their journey over Ohio Pass and the descent into Irwin as being "in a style peculiarly western, . . . American in the extreme." Irwin's first newspaper press was set up in a cabin without doors, windows, or a floor—the town had no milled lumber yet. The first edition of the *Elk Mountain Pilot,* dated June 17, 1880, was displayed atop a whiskey barrel in the middle of the street and auctioned off at $56, along with the whiskey in the barrel. "American in the extreme," indeed.

The town flourished during the summer of 1880 and grew from a population of fifty to one hundred times that number in just two months. Early miners built their cabins from trees felled just above the snowline, since digging through the snowline to the bottom of the trees proved to be too labor–intensive for miners eager to strike it rich. As a result, Irwin's first cabins sat 10 feet above the ground, on top of the snow-pack. As the snows melted and the cabins sank some 10 feet to the ground, the cabins began to look as though they could have been built by the procurer of the town's first newspaper edition. Large quantities of snow like this and the failure to obtain a railroad eventually led to the demise of Irwin. Its boom only lasted from 1879 to 1881. By the late 1880s, most of the area mines had been shut down. All that remains of this once bustling boomtown is the Irwin Cemetery.

Take a moment to tour through the cemetery upon reaching Kebler Pass. There's a footpath that weaves past a number of old headstones. Then, passing the old Irwin Cemetery to your left, descend toward Lake Irwin and the intersection with Dyke Trail.

Surrounded by Ruby Peak (12,644 feet), Mount Owen (13,058 feet), and Purple Peak (12,810 feet), Lake Irwin bears peaceful testimony to the strength of will and depth of courage exhibited by the now-vanished community of Irwin. From the lake, you ride to Dyke Trail. A fast initial descent through a hillside meadow delivers you to the first of many steep–walled creek beds. After descending through thick aspen and lodgepole pine forests and scurrying across a sloping rock field, you arrive at the bottom of the dyke. The large igneous rocks you see before you are the cooled remains of liquid magma forced through narrow vertical slits in a mountainside. Resembling a backbone, this natural dyke runs down the southern shoulder of Ruby Peak and terminates in the forests just before crossing the trail.

The descent from the dyke leads you to the junction of the Raggeds Wilderness Area and Dyke Trail. The descent from this junction is savage, as the trail runs over a variety of mountainous terrain on its way through a pristine aspen forest. This section of the trail is very sinewy, so hip-steering is a must. Upon reaching the Dark Canyon Trailhead, bear left and descend to your vehicle.

Miles and Directions

0.0 START from Horse Ranch Park. Bear left back onto Kebler Pass Road and begin riding east back to Kebler Pass.

3.0 Cross over Ruby Anthracite Creek.

4.7 Reach Kebler Pass (10,007 feet). To your left is the Irwin Cemetery.

5.3 Bear left onto FR 826, following signs for the Lake Irwin Campground.

7.7 Enter the Gunnison National Forest. Continue riding on FR 826, passing alongside Lake Irwin's western banks.

7.8 Pass the FISHERMAN PARKING to your right.

7.9 Pass the Lake Irwin Campground to your right.

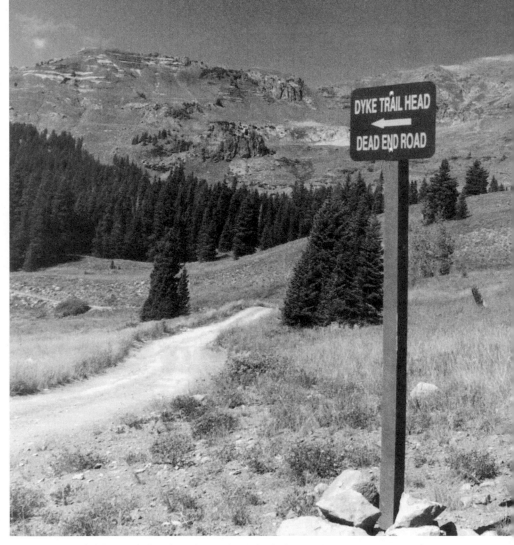

The beginning of Dyke Trail with Ruby Peak in the background.

8.3 FR 826 breaks hard to the right. Bear left onto the dirt road that heads due west, by the brown signs to Dyke Trailhead and Dead End Road. The road to the right continues on to Irwin Lodge.

8.5 Dead End Road forks. Bear left at the fork and follow the sign for Dyke Trail (Trail 837).

8.6 The Dyke Trail singletrack begins. Descend swiftly in a southerly direction on Dyke Trail through a meadow.

8.8 Descend into a thick lodgepole pine forest. Notice the black-and-white Dyke Trail marker pointing you to the right. Bear right here and descend steeply to a creek.

11.3 Descend along a sloping and rocky section of trail to a rock field (the dyke). From the rock field area, a long and arduous climb through the aspens awaits.

12.5 Dyke Trail intersects the Raggeds Wilderness Area. Bear left (south), continuing on Dyke Trail and following signs for Horse Ranch Park. Descend savagely to Horse Ranch Park.

13.8 Arrive at Horse Ranch Park and the trailheads for Dark Canyon Trail 830, Oh-Be-Joyful Pass 9, and Erickson Springs 13. Bear left onto the dirt Horse Ranch Park road and ride back to your vehicle.

14.0 Reach your vehicle.

Ride Information

Local Information

Crested Butte/Mount Crested Butte Chamber of Commerce, P.O. Box 1288, Crested Butte, 81224; (970) 349-6438, (800) 545-4505; www.crestedbuttechamber.com.

Gunnison National Forest and Bureau of Land Management, Gunnison Resource Area, Gunnison; (970) 641-0471.

High Country Citizens' Alliance, 724 Elk Avenue, P.O. Box 1066, Crested Butte, 81224; (970) 349-7104; www.hccaonline.org.

Local Events and Attractions

Mountain Bike Hall of Fame and Museum, Crested Butte; (970) 349-6817, (800) 454-4505.

Crested Butte Mountain Heritage Museum, Inc., Crested Butte; (970) 349-1880.

Fat Tire Bike Festival, in June, Crested Butte; (970) 349-6438, (800) 545-4505.

Annual Wildflower Festival, in July, Crested Butte; (970) 349-6438, (800) 545-4505.

One World Music Festival, in September, Crested Butte; (970) 349-6438, (800) 545-4505.

Rendezvous Gallery, Crested Butte; (970) 349-6804.

Organizations

Crested Butte Mountain Bike Association (C.B.M.B.A), Crested Butte; (970) 349-5517, (970) 349-6817.

Accommodations

Irwin Lodge, Crested Butte; (970) 349-9800, (888) GO-IRWIN.

Crested Butte International Hostel LLC, Crested Butte; (970) 349-0588 or (888) 389-0588, www.gunnison.com/~hostel.

Restaurants

Idle Spur, Crested Butte; (970) 349-5026.

Donita's Cantina, Crested Butte; (970) 349-6674.

Wooden Nickel, Crested Butte; (970) 349-6350.

Tours

No Limits Center, Crested Butte, Mount Crested Butte; (970) 349-4247, (888) 954-4247.

Pioneer Guide Service, Crested Butte; (970) 349-5517; www.pioneer@crestedbutte.net.

Paddle Trax & Syngltrax, Crested Butte; (970) 349-1100.

Alpine Outside, Crested Butte; (970) 349-5011, (800) 833-8052; Almont, (970) 641-1303, (888) 761-FISH; www.3rivers resort.com.

26 Mount Princeton to Raspberry Gulch

The Mount Princeton to Raspberry Gulch ride offers a great introduction to Colorado's Fourteener region. Incorporating sections of the Colorado Trail, this ride provides fat-tire enthusiasts with great views of the Arkansas Valley and the Sawatch Range's Collegiate Peaks. Although the ride is both technically and physically challenging, a soak in the Mount Princeton Hot Springs at the trail's end is inspiration enough to grunt up Raspberry Gulch Road. The singletrack portion of the ride provides challenging access to two of the Sawatch Range's most dominant peaks: Mount Princeton and Mount Antero. You'll enjoy passing through gorgeous stands of aspen and mixed conifer forests.

Start: From the parking lot of the Mount Princeton Hot Springs, begin your ride on County Road 162.

Length: 19.6-mile loop.

Approximate riding time: Advanced riders, 2 to 2.5 hours; intermediate riders, 3 to 3.5 hours.

Technical difficulty: Technically moderate: Although 7 miles of the route pass over paved county road, there are some rough sections of singletrack, offering near impossible switchbacks and rocky descents.

Physical difficulty: Physically moderate to challenging due to lung-busting steep climbs over rutted and off-camber terrain.

Terrain: Paved highway, county roads, forest roads, and singletrack. Forest Road 273 becomes very rutted and rocky as it nears its end. The singletrack includes it all: nearly impassable rock sections, softened forest earth, and sand.

Trail contacts: Greater Buena Vista Area Chamber of Commerce, 343 U.S. Highway 24 South, P.O. Box 2021, Buena Vista, 81211; (719) 395-6612; www.fourteenernet.com.

Schedule: Late April to early October.

Maps: USGS maps: Mount Antero, Nathrop; *Trails Illustrated* map 130, Salida, St. Elmo, Shavano Peak; 14ers Region Mountain Bike Guide.

Nearest town: Buena Vista.

Other trail users: Hikers, campers, backpackers, and equestrians.

Canine compatibility: Dog friendly.

Getting There

From Buena Vista: Drive south on Colorado Highway 24 until you intersect U.S. Highway 285 at around 2.3 miles. Continue traveling south on US 285 for roughly 6 miles. In the town of Nathrop, turn right onto CR 162 at 8.1 miles, by the Mount Princeton Hot Springs Resort sign. Drive 4.5 miles before turning left into the resort parking lot at 12.6 miles. Park here and begin riding east on CR 162. *DeLorme: Colorado Atlas & Gazetteer:* Page 60, C 1-2

The Ride

The Mount Princeton to Raspberry Gulch trail is located in the heart of Colorado's Fourteeners region (the highest concentration of 14,000-foot peaks in the continental United States). Fifteen Colorado peaks, all reaching over 14,000 feet, lie within a region no larger than 30 by 20 miles. Here the impressive Sawatch Mountains stretch across the west side of the Arkansas Valley from southwest of Salida north to Leadville. Of these fifteen peaks, four (including Mount Princeton) are typically referred to as the Collegiate Peaks.

At 14,197 feet, Mount Princeton is the second highest of the Collegiate Peaks, second only to Mount Harvard. The Collegiate Peaks include Mount Princeton, Mount Harvard (14,420 feet), Mount Columbia (14,073 feet), and Mount Yale (14,196 feet). Each peak gets its name from the institution that sponsored its study and survey in the mid- to late 1800s. Of the four Collegiate Peaks, and perhaps of all the mountains in the Sawatch Range, Mount Princeton remains one of the most striking. Looking west from the Arkansas Valley, Mount Princeton displays an almost perfect symmetry, with two smaller peaks flanking the central summit. But Mount Princeton's symmetry is not all that attracts the eye. No doubt your curiosity will be sparked by the mountain's south-sloping escarpment.

As if someone took a giant cleaver to the mountain, Mount Princeton's south slope falls abruptly from the mountainside to form the Chalk Cliffs. Though chalk-like in appearance, the white, crumbly composition of these cliffs is actually an admixture of quartz, K-feldspar, and plagioclase called white quartz monzonite. Strikingly unique, these cliffs have developed over the years an identity and a history that are almost independent of the mountain to which they cling.

One story tells of a band of Spaniards who raided a nearby Ute village more than 200 years ago. With the stolen booty in hand, the Spaniards headed for the sanctuary of the Chalk Cliffs. Undeterred by the Spaniards' dangerous route, the Ute Indians followed. Sensing the Utes hot on their trail, the Spaniards buried the booty somewhere in the Cliffs. The Utes finally caught up with the thieves, but the Spaniards wouldn't say where they had hidden the stolen possessions. The Utes summarily killed the raiders. According to legend, the treasure still remains buried somewhere in the dusty recesses of the Chalk Cliffs.

With the Chalk Cliffs to the north (left), pedal your way from the Mount Princeton Hot Springs to Mount Antero. The hot springs once served as a mining camp for the Hortense Mine, located on the southern peak of Mount Princeton. The Hortense Mine, one of the most productive silver mines in the Sawatch Range, drew much attention from itinerant traffic, and, consequently, so too did the Mount Princeton Hot Springs.

By 1915 the hot springs had a hundred-room hotel, complete with stained glass windows and a gigantic ballroom. The market crash of 1929 dealt a serious blow to the hot springs' popularity, and in 1930 the hotel was reopened as the Antero Hotel (named after the nearby mountain). It too would struggle, until 1950 when the wrecking ball destroyed the opulent hotel and laid waste what little semblance of luxury and refinement these Colorado wilds could afford. Today, the Mount Princeton Hot Springs is back in business. With the Princeton Club dining room, three separate lodging units, convention facilities, and packaged recreational activities, the Mount Princeton Hot Springs has recaptured much of its Roaring Twenties grandeur.

From the hot springs, the trail skirts the westernmost border of the Arkansas Valley on its way to Mount Antero. Mount Antero takes its name from Chief Antero, the one-time leader of the Uintah band of Ute Indians. Chief Antero was among those who signed the 1878 treaty that allotted portions of Ute land in the San Juans to the silver-mining camps of the day. An advocate for peace, Chief Antero quelled many Indian uprisings and kept his own tribe at peace during the White River Utes' uprising in 1879.

Mount Antero is one of Colorado's most mineral-rich Fourteeners. Aquamarine, topaz, and clear and smoky quartz crystals color all of Antero's 14,269 feet. To preserve and display the mountain's mineral wealth, the Colorado Mineralogical Society created the Mount Antero Mineral Park on August 1, 1949. A bronze plaque imbedded in a granite boulder marks Mount Antero as North America's highest mineral site.

As you approach Mount Antero along Forest Road 273, you pass through flat, open stands of lodgepole pine before climbing steeply to the point where the forest road closes to motor vehicles. The singletrack that connects this point to the Colorado Trail delivers short, rocky sections; smooth-tracking terrain; and tight turns. Once on the Colorado Trail, the route descends over very technically challenging rocky terrain before opening up to fast runs through mixed conifer forests and sandy meadows.

Once you cross FR 273, the trail passes through a small aspen glen and winds its way up a hillside laden with pine saplings and scrub oak. This section of the route offers incredible views of the Chalk Cliffs. Meadows of roundleaf bluebell (campanula rotundifolia), Indian paintbrush (castilleja miniata), scarlet bugler (penstemon centranthifolius), and Richardson's geranium (geranium richardsonii) dot the landscape around Mount Antero. After crossing a four-wheel-drive road at 14.3 miles, technically steep singletrack over rocks, sand, and silt await the tireless rider.

After another mile, the trail begins its descent into Chalk Creek and runs over incredibly demanding technical sections, requiring most riders to dismount. Once across Chalk Creek, it's a smooth coast through Chalk Creek Canyon back to your vehicle and a 105-degree geothermal soak in the Mount Princeton Hot Springs.

Miles and Directions

0.0 START from the Mount Princeton Hot Springs and bear right onto County Road 162, riding east.

0.7 County Road 162 intersects with CR 270. Bear right onto CR 270.

4.5 Cross a cattle guard.

4.7 County Road 270 intersects with CR 272. At the T intersection, bear right onto dirt CR 272 following the signs for Browns Creek.

5.6 Cross a cattle guard and enter the San Isabel National Forest. Camping is available once you pass into the national forest.

6.9 Arrive at the junction of CR 272 and Forest Road 274. CR 272 turns left (south). Bear right onto FR 274.

Mount Princeton.

7.2 Forest Road 274 intersects with FR 273 (Raspberry Gulch Road). Bear left onto FR 273 and climb steadily over rocky and rutted terrain. You'll climb over 1,000 feet in 2 miles. As FR 273 nears its end, the trail becomes increasingly narrow, to the point of becoming a wide doubletrack.

9.4 From this point on, FR 273 is closed to motor vehicle travel. A few yards beyond the rusted ROAD CLOSED TO MOTOR VEHICLES sign lies the singletrack. Signs here indicate Browns Creek to be 2 miles to the south and Chalk Creek 3 miles to the north. Bear left here onto the Colorado Trail and head south, following signs for Browns Creek.

10.5 Arrive at the intersection of the Colorado Trail (Trail 1776) and Trail 1430 (Little Browns Creek Trail). The Colorado Trail spurs left and also continues straight ahead, while Trail 1430 bears right. The spur directly in front of you will eventually start leading south, crossing Browns Creek, while the spur to your left follows a northerly route back to the Mount Princeton Hot Springs. Bear left, following the Colorado Trail in a northerly direction.

11.8 The Colorado Trail drops to a flat pine-forested meadow. The trail is fast here.

12.2 Cross an old four-wheel-drive road and continue straight ahead on the Colorado Trail. From the meadow, beautiful views of the Sawatch Range and Chalk Cliffs are offered.

12.8 Cross Raspberry Gulch Road, just before the beautiful stands of aspen, and continue climbing up the other side of the hill.

14.3 Cross another four-wheel-drive road and begin a steep singletrack climb.

15.1 Here are the best views of the Chalk Cliffs.

15.4 Catch some great views of Mount Princeton. From here, follow the trail west over some loose rocky terrain.

16.5 Cross the dirt road and continue on the Colorado Trail, heading toward Chalk Creek.

16.9 Cross over Chalk Creek and turn right onto CR 291, heading east through Chalk Creek Canyon.

18.2 Arrive at the junction of CR 291 and CR 162. CR 291 ends where CR 162 begins. Continue on CR 162 east to the Mount Princeton Hot Springs.

19.6 Arrive at the Mount Princeton Hot Springs and your vehicle.

Ride Information

Local Information
Greater Buena Vista Area Chamber of Commerce, 343 U.S. Highway 24 South, P.O. Box 2021, Buena Vista, 81211; (719) 395-6612; www.fourteenernet.com.

Local Events and Attractions
Buena Vista Heritage Museum, Buena Vista; (719) 395-8458 (open daily June, July, August, and part of September).
Mount Princeton Hot Springs Resort, Nathrop; (888) 395-7799; www.mtprinceton.com.

Gold Rush Days and Music Festival, August, Buena Vista; (719) 395-6612.

Restaurants
Casa del Sol, Buena Vista; (719) 395-8810 (reservations advised).
Bongo Billy's, Buena Vista; (719) 395-2634, (719) 395-4991.

Mountain Bike Tours
Buffalo Joe River Trips, Buena Vista; (800) 356-7984, (719) 395-8757.

27 Bear Creek to Methodist Mountain

Bear Creek to Methodist Mountain Trail is part of the annual Banana Belt Mountain Bike Loop Race, one of the most time-honored mountain biking traditions in Salida, if not in Colorado. The nonsanctioned race pays tribute to the grassroots beginnings of mountain biking by including riders of all ability levels in the festivities. A favorite of Salida locals, Bear Creek to Methodist Mountain Trail travels up the beautiful Bear Creek drainage into the San Isabel National Forest to its intersection with the famed Rainbow Trail. This route incorporates a section of the 100-mile Rainbow Trail. Rainbow Trail itself extends from the Continental Divide, southwest of Salida, to Music Pass and travels along the east side of the Sangre de Cristo Mountains.

Start: From the USDA Forest Service Office, Salida Ranger District, in downtown Salida.
Length: 20-mile loop.
Approximate riding time: Advanced riders, 2 to 2.5 hours; intermediate riders, 3 to 3.5 hours.
Technical difficulty: Technically moderate due to a number of rocky and sandy sections.
Physical difficulty: Physically moderate to challenging due to its extended climbing over 8,000 feet.
Terrain: Paved highway, county road, four-wheel-drive road, and singletrack. The route passes through semi-arid terrain along the Arkansas River to narrow, high-mountain valleys lined with wildflowers. Expect smooth-running singletrack, pavement, and exposed rocks and roots. After crossing Rock Creek, the terrain becomes somewhat gravely and sandy.
Trail contacts: San Isabel National Forest, Salida Ranger District, 325 West Rainbow Boulevard, Salida, 81201; (719) 539-3591.
Schedule: Late May to late September.
Maps: USGS maps: Salida West, Salida East, Wellsville, Poncha Pass; 14ers Region Mountain Bike Guide.
Nearest town: Salida.
Other trail users: Hikers, campers, and equestrians.
Canine compatibility: Dog friendly.

Getting There

From Poncha Springs: Drive east on U.S. Highway 50 for 3.1 miles to the Pike, San Isabel National Forest office in Salida, which is to the right. Park your vehicle and begin riding east on US 50 through Salida. *DeLorme: Colorado Atlas & Gazetteer:* Page 60, D-3.

The Ride

"Welcome to Colorado . . . the way it Used to Be," touts the welcoming sign to Fourteener country's southernmost town. Surrounded by the Collegiate Peaks to the west, the Mosquito Range to the east, and the Sangre de Cristo Mountains to the south, Salida typifies the Colorado experience, yesterday and today. Owing to its prime location and the genuine warmth of its people, Salida inspires awe and provides thrills galore for

those seeking to play in and around its majestic mountains. Grounded in every John Denver colloquialism, Salida sets the standard by which all other outdoor-oriented Colorado towns are judged.

Members of the Colorado Historic Preservation Review Board determined that downtown Salida has not only one of the largest but also one of the finest collections of historically significant buildings in all of Colorado. Receiving its listing in the National Register of Historic Places in July 1984, Salida recalls much of the state's old-world charm. The relatively private location of its historic district—located behind the motels, chain restaurants, and gas stations lining U.S. Highways 50 and 285—attests to the unassuming nature of Colorado's past. Downtown buildings stand in quiet memorial to the dreams and determination of the city's earliest inhabitants.

In 1880 the town of Salida (originally named South Arkansas) was established along the track beds of the Denver & Rio Grande Railroad. As the railroad grew, expanding its services to the nearby mining districts of Monarch and Turrent, so too did Salida grow. Salida's farmers and ranchers profited by supplying produce and meat to railroad and mining crews. The town mushroomed in the early half of the 1880s. But as it grew, Salida was dealt its share of blows when major fires ripped through its downtown in both 1886 and 1888. Not to be slowed by this unfortunate turn of events, residents created Salida Fire Blocks, an ordinance requiring all new downtown buildings to be built of brick. From Front Street (now Sackett) to Fourth Street and between C and H Streets, Salida Fire Blocks now make up Salida's historic district.

The Corner Stone Pub (formerly known as Club Rio) is believed to be Salida's oldest commercial building. Once a flourishing general store, the building's original wooden frame got its brick face-lift in 1883 from proprietors Edward W. Corbin and Elias H. Webb. It later became a tavern and currently holds the distinction of having Colorado's second oldest liquor license. A huge mural inside the tavern depicts the history of Salida. Joe "Kidd" Orr, champion boxer and one-time owner of the club,

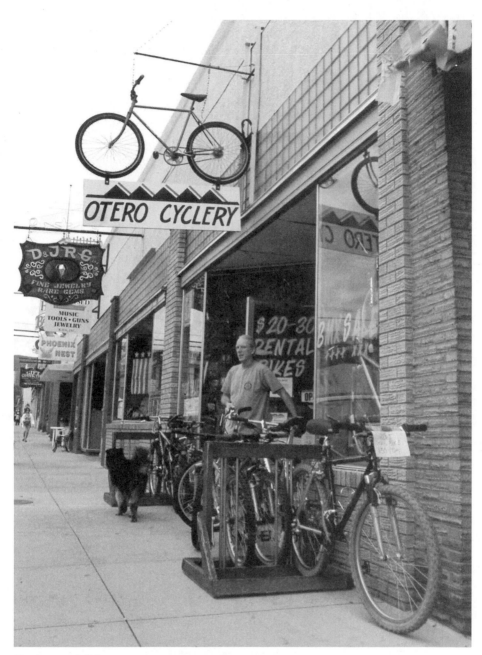

Downtown Salida.

named the bar "Club Rio" in honor of his father, Ralph Edward Orr. Dad's initials, phonetically at least, provided Kidd with "Rio."

After the passing of the Denver & Rio Grande Railroad and the mining booms and busts of the early 1970s and 1980s, Salida turned itself into a thriving recreational community, rallying mostly around mountain biking and river boating. The people of Salida now commemorate themselves through shared outdoor activities.

Located within the "Banana Belt," Salida and the towns of Buena Vista and Poncha Springs enjoy a unique environment that's highly conducive to outdoor recreation. Guarded by a veritable wall of Fourteeners and nestled in the relatively low-lying Arkansas Valley (6,800–8,500 feet), these three towns receive a mere 10 to 12 inches per annum of rainfall. What little precipitation does find its way over the Sawatch Range is usually evaporated in the drier, warmer atmosphere of the Arkansas Valley. Just 35 miles north of these towns, in the mountains surrounding the town of Leadville (10,430 feet), snowfall arrives in excess of 10 feet per year, while in Salida, Buena Vista, and Poncha Springs conditions remain remarkably dry.

In an effort to bring the community together in a sharing and healthy environment, the now defunct Banana Belt Fat Tracks Club organized the first Banana Belt Mountain Bike Loop Race in 1989. That year seventy-six local riders turned out to enjoy the festivities. Since then, the number of participants has grown to well over 150. In response to the many high-profile mountain biking events throughout Colorado, the Banana Belt Mountain Bike Loop Race remains a nonsanctioned, grassroots memorial to the community and welcomes every rider, regardless of ability level.

The Bear Creek to Methodist Mountain Trail covers a large portion of the race's course and invites you to become part of the community. From downtown Salida, ride east on US 50 to its intersection with CR 101. County Road 101 is bordered east and west by private property, so stay on the road. Once in the San Isabel National Forest, the road becomes the single-lane FR 101.3. This road will fork at 7.1 miles. Bear right and continue climbing. The road becomes steep, rocky, and rutted, with views of the peaks Simmons and Hunts through the trees at 8 miles.

Once on the singletrack of Rainbow Trail, the riding becomes generally smooth with only a few exposed rocky sections, making the trail moderately technical as it cuts across pine-filled hillsides in a westerly direction. Views of the surrounding San

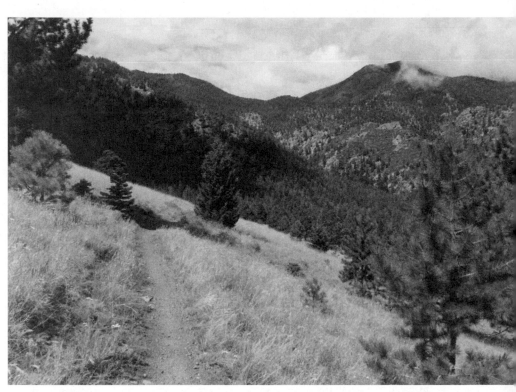
Rainbow singletrack with views of Methodist Mountain.

Isabel National Forest and Salida are to the northwest. Rather than providing sustained lengths of high speed, Rainbow Trail mixes short, rocky sections with blind curves and small hill climbs, making for a colorful ride.

From FR 108, the descent is steep and rocky. Almost immediately you're thrown a sharp hairpin turn to the right, after which the road becomes steep and rocky. This rough section lasts for about 2 miles until FR 108 becomes a graded two-lane road, the route gets speedy. You'll be able to fly down this section to your vehicle, making up for any lost time on the climb.

Miles and Directions

0.0 START from Salida Ranger Station in downtown Salida and head east on U.S. Highway 50 through Salida.

0.5 Pass the sign for Methodist Mountain, elevation 11,655 feet.

3.7 U.S. Highway 50 intersects with CR 101. Bear right (south) onto CR 101 and ride over the cattle guard.

4.6 Cross the Chaffee/Fremont County line. (Here Chaffee County Road 101 becomes Fremont County Road 49.)

6.9 Cross over the cattle guard and enter the San Isabel National Forest. (Here Fremont County Road 49 becomes FR 101.3.)

9.1 Forest Road 101.3 intersects with Trail 101A on the left. Pass by Trail 101A and continue climbing straight ahead.

9.4 Ford Bear Creek. After crossing Bear Creek, head up a short but rocky climb before arriving at the Rainbow Trail singletrack.

9.5 Arrive at the trailhead for Rainbow Trail (Trail 1336) on your right. There'll also be signs for HOWARD CREEK—3 MILES and METHODIST MOUNTAIN—6 MILES. Bear right onto Rainbow Trail, following signs for Methodist Mountain.

9.9 Cross a four-wheel-drive road where a sign on the left reads BEAR CREEK—0.25 MILE and METHODIST MOUNTAIN—6 MILES. Pass the sign and continue heading west along Rainbow Trail.

10.2 Cross Bear Creek again.

11.4 Cross Rock Creek and begin a short climb through a gravely and sandy section. As the trail continues heading north through fields of scrub oak, see the meadow across the gully through which you've just ridden.

12.4 Cross another four-wheel-drive road and continue riding on Rainbow Trail.

14.3 Arrive at another beautiful hillside meadow, offering the best views of Salida and the San Isabel National Forest. Notice the S on the hillside. A collection of white painted rocks, S marks the spot for the town of Salida and offers yet another area ride, known simply as the S Trail. Here's a great spot to have a snack and take in the view. Continue riding through the meadow and descend on plush singletrack through the pine forest.

15.4 Arrive at FR 108, the road that leads to the top of Methodist Mountain. Bear right onto FR 108 and descend to US 50.

17.0 Forest Road 108 becomes a graded, two-lane road, as you leave the San Isabel National Forest. Here FR 108 becomes CR 107. Bear right, heading down CR 107.

18.7 Woodlawn Cemetery is off to your left. Pass the old cemetery and continue heading for US 50.

19.4 County Road 107 intersects US 50. Bear left (west), heading back to your vehicle.

20.0 Reach your vehicle at the Salida Ranger Station.

Ride Information

Local Information

Heart of the Rockies Chamber of Commerce, 406 West Highway 50, Salida, 81201; (877) 772-5432; www.salidachamber.org.

Fourteener Net at www.fourteenernet.com or www.nowthisiscolorado.com.

Local Events and Attractions

Salida Hot Springs Aquatic Center, Salida; (719) 539-6738.

Banana Belt Mountain Bike Loop Race, in September, Salida; (719) 539-2068.

Restaurants

The County Bounty, Salida; (719) 539-3546.

Cornucopia Bakery & Cafe, Salida; (719) 539-2531.

First Street Café, Salida; (719) 539-4759.

Amica's Pizzeria & Brewery, Salida; (719) 539-5219.

Mountain Bike Tours

Buffalo Joe River Trips, Buena Vista; (800) 356-7984, (719) 395-8757.

Bill Dvorak's, Salida; (800) 824-3795.

28 Hartman Rocks

The Hartman Rocks area offers high-desert riding in a 6,000-acre basin. Funky granite formations, slickrock, sand, and sage add to this geological curiosity's appeal. The "Rocks," as Gunnison locals call it, is a mountain biking area replete with interconnecting trails. This route skirts the perimeter of the Hartman Rocks area and follows, in part, the Rage in the Sage course, Gunnison's annual mountain bike race. Although the trails throughout Hartman Rocks can get confusing, this shouldn't deter you from riding the Rocks, as efforts are continually being made to distinguish the right from the wrong way. Take notice of smaller rocks or sticks imbedded in the ground across a trail, signifying a wrong way. Observe branches lying parallel to a trail, seemingly pointing the right way. In general, look for "natural" reference points, which might otherwise seem out of place: a stacked pile of rocks (cairns), orange tape, painted arrows, or even arrows drawn in the sand.

Start: From the Hartman Rocks parking lot.
Length: 18.5-mile loop, with many options to either shorten or lengthen.
Approximate riding time: Advanced riders, 2.5 to 3 hours; intermediate riders, 3 to 4 hours.
Technical difficulty: Technically moderate with a few tight rocky sections. Most of the singletrack is smooth.
Physical difficulty: Physically moderate. There are some steeper climbs, coupled with sandy sections that make for a tough ride in spots.
Terrain: Jeep road and singletrack. The trail rolls over hilly terrain and through sagebrush meadowland. Much of the terrain is hardpacked, but there are a number of rocky and sandy sections. Some sections go through riparian areas. The area offers seemingly endless miles of singletrack and dirt road that break off in every direction.

Trail contacts: Bureau of Land Management, Gunnison Field Office, 216 North Colorado, Gunnison, 81230; (970) 641-1928. Gunnison National Forest, Gunnison Ranger District, 216 North Colorado, Gunnison, 81230; (970) 641-0471.
Schedule: May to September.
Maps: USGS maps: Gunnison, Iris NW; *Trails Illustrated* map 132; Gunnison Area Mountain Bike Map; Aspen, Crested Butte, Gunnison Recreation Topo Map, Latitude 40° Inc.
Nearest town: Gunnison.
Other trail users: Campers, hikers, motorcyclists, rock climbers, and picnickers.
Canine compatibility: Not dog friendly, due to exposed terrain and vehicular traffic in the area.

Getting There

From Gunnison: Drive west on U.S. Highway 50 for 1.5 miles before bearing left on Gunnison County Road 38 (south). County Road 38 is also called Gold Basin Road. After crossing Tomichi Creek, drive for another mile before turning right onto CR 56 and into the Hartman Rocks parking lot at 4.0 miles. *DeLorme: Colorado Atlas & Gazetteer:* Page 58, D-2.

The Ride

Gunnison, Colorado, offers you a sandy twist to your everyday trip through the timbers. Located in the southwestern region of the state, the town of Gunnison sits at nearly 8,000 feet. But don't let its elevation fool you into believing that Gunnison is your typical mountain town. On the contrary, its nearest mountain is located roughly 25 miles north in Crested Butte. Gunnison, rather, sits on a plateau and features high-plains desert riding, as opposed to high-mountainous alpine riding. The dwarfed colonies of chaparral, the sandy mesas, and the red, 100-foot undulating granite formations that make up the lunar landscape all contribute to Gunnison's overall feeling of eerie otherworldliness.

Gunnison began its life as a mining town, resting at the northern edge of the San Juan mining district. The town took its name from Captain John Gunnison of the Army Topographical Engineers. In 1853 Congress enlisted Gunnison to survey the central railroad route between the 38th and 39th parallels to settle the debate over which would be the best route between the East and West via a transcontinental railroad. Departing from Fort Leavenworth, Kansas, on June 15, Gunnison, an experienced explorer with eleven years of wilderness surveying to his credit, was put in charge of thirty-two mounted riflemen, sixteen six-mule wagons, a four-mule drawn carriage full of instruments, and a four-mule medical supply carriage. By September the team had crossed Cochetopa Pass (10,032 feet) and the Continental Divide in south central Colorado. They camped near what is today the town of Gunnison. Gunnison and his team continued west until, on October 25, 1853, while seeking winter quarters near Sevier Lake in Utah, they were attacked and killed by Paiute Indians. Few escaped to tell of the horrid events that transpired that day.

As if naming a town after a man slaughtered by Indians isn't enough to put the voodoo on you, the town of Gunnison would again be haunted twenty years later, this time by one of Colorado's most notorious acts of barbarism. During the winter of 1873–1874, Alferd Packer set out from Provo, Utah, to prospect a new gold strike in Breckenridge. (Yes, it's "Alferd." A tattoist misspelled his name and Packer happened to like it.) Upon reaching the Uncompahgre Valley, Ute Indian Chief Ouray advised Packer and his party not to continue, for the snowfall had been especially heavy that winter. Not bothered by Ouray's concerns, Packer pressed on, leaving the morning of February 9 and taking only seven days' worth of provisions. Packer expected to reach the Los Pinos Indian Agency in the Cochetopa Mountains, just southeast of present-day Gunnison.

Sixty-six days passed without word from Packer or anyone in his party. Then, on the morning of April 6, agency officials spotted the bedraggled Packer walking alone through Los Pinos. Lost and with frostbitten feet, Packer spoke of being abandoned by his party and forced to fend for himself. Curiously unaffected by his traumatic ordeal, Packer continued on to Saguache, still intent on reaching Breckenridge. While in Saguache, Packer began to arouse suspicion. He had been carrying a Winchester rifle that belonged to a member of his prospecting party, as well as a skinning knife that belonged to another. And some noted that he was looking a little too rosy-cheeked for a man who had endured such privation. Placed in the Saguache jail pending investigation, Packer managed to escape on August 8, 1874. For nine years he roamed free, with no one having a clue as to his whereabouts.

On March 11, 1883, Packer was spotted in Cheyenne, Wyoming, living under the alias John Schwartze. After returning to Saguache for trial, Packer was found guilty

Riding beside the million-years-old lunarscape formations of Hartman Rocks.

of murder and cannibalism. While awaiting sentence in the Gunnison jail, Packer's attorneys seized on a technicality in the trial, explaining that these horrific crimes occurred on Ute land when Colorado was still a territory, so Packer should not have been tried under state law, but instead, territorial law. Appealing his conviction to the Colorado Supreme Court on October 10, 1885, under this grandfather clause, Packer's attorneys successfully spared their client the noose. As a result, the court threw out the case—striking the record clean. Interestingly, Colorado had become a state in between the murders and his first trial, so Packer could now be tried again, under newly appointed state laws, since he in effect had never been tried for these crimes under state law. So on August 5, 1886, Packer was tried in Gunnison and once again found guilty, his sentence now upheld by the Colorado Supreme Court. Sentenced to forty years in prison, Packer was paroled in 1901. He died six years later—his death certificate reading: "of senility - trouble & worry."

In 1989 a forensic team led by James Starrs located the bodies of Packer's party on a bluff above the Lake Fork River near Lake City. Among their findings were crushed skulls (thought to be struck while the men were sleeping), signs indicating a struggle, and chipped bones—all indicating that these men hadn't been murdered without a struggle. There is a historical marker and sign at the site of the massacre.

Careful not to chip any bones, cross over imbedded slickrock at 2.0 miles, where beautiful views of Gunnison lie to the north. Views of the Hartman Rocks give you a perspective of how far you've come. From here you skirt alongside the rocks themselves. The Hartman Rocks area is one of only five igneous ring dykes in the world. Millions of years ago lava-injected magma cooled several miles below the earth's surface. Over time, this magma formed into granite. A subsequent series of uplifts forced the granite through the earth's surface, forming the Hartman Rocks. The porous nature of granite allows Douglas fir, ponderosa pine, and juniper to grow in an area that otherwise would be too dry. This gives the area a surreal feel.

From these rocks, you intersect with Luge Trail, one of the Rage in the Sage's highlights. Its fast and smooth course offers many banked turns on which to rip before dropping you into one of the area's most unique features: a beautiful riparian segment of the ride. Thick cottonwoods and tall plants abound, as the rushing of the Gunnison River can be heard just to the right, behind the trees.

Once you've connected with Outback Trail, you're offered sweet slickrock with variable sandy sections through hard-packed, sagebrush meadows. From the meadows, return back to the Rocks and descend the harrowing V-drop back to your vehicle.

Miles and Directions

0.0 START by riding west on County Road 58 from the Hartman Rocks parking lot.

0.2 As CR 58 veers sharply to the right, bear left through the yellow gate and continue riding up a rough dirt road. Bear right onto Hartman Rocks Road (Kill Hill) and begin your steep, granny gear ascent to Hartman Rocks, heading in a northerly direction.

0.6 Upon reaching the crest of this initial climb, Hartman Rocks Road comes to a T intersection. Bear left at this intersection, crossing a yellow cattle guard.

0.7 Just after crossing the cattle guard, notice the large pullout area to your right. Bear right into this pullout and onto a smooth doubletrack, following the brown trail marker sign, as the trail descends northerly through a sage-filled meadow. The doubletrack eventually disintegrates to sandy singletrack, leading out onto a rough, four-wheel-drive road.

0.9 Bear right onto the road and begin climbing, following the brown trail marker sign.

1.6 The road cuts sharply to the left (west) alongside a barbed wire fence. Bear right, passing through this fence, following the brown trail marker sign.

2.0 The road starts to level out, as it crosses a field of embedded slickrock. Riding in an easterly direction across the slickrock, intersect with the singletrack on the other side.

2.5 The singletrack intersects with another jeep road. Here, bear right onto this road, following the trail marker sign. Ride in a northerly direction.

3.1 The road intersects with Luge Trail. Bear right onto the smooth singletrack of the Luge and descend in a northerly direction.

4.8 Luge Trail breaks sharply to the left. Continue due west alongside a barbed wire fence. Bear left at this point, riding to the right of the fence. Soon thereafter, notice another brown trail marker sign that directs you to ride away from this fence. As you make your way from the fence, descend into a beautiful riparian segment of the route.

5.6 After descending speedily through this riparian ecosystem, Luge Trail forks. Bear left here and begin climbing in a southerly direction. The right fork reaches down to the Gunnison River and private property.

6.1 Descend to a treatment plant and the very northwest corner of the loop. Bear left here, climbing moderately and heading due south, as the trail continues alongside another barbed wire fence to your right.

6.8 Veer right, passing through an opening in the fence. Now the fence is on your left, as the trail continues in a southerly direction, passing a trail marker. Continue climbing to the crest of the hill.

7.1 Reach the crest. From here, a jeep road passes through the fence to your left and descends steeply to McCabe Lane to your right. Bear right here and rip steeply down this rough jeep road to the junction with McCabe Lane and CR 32B.

7.6 Reach CR 32B and bear left onto it, continuing south.

9.2 From CR 32B, bear right (west) onto the singletrack identified by the brown trail marker. Climb up a short ridge. Follow past the trail marker sign and descend over some moderately technical rocky terrain and through a flat, sage-filled meadow.

10.4 Having descended past some large rocks on either side of the trail, arrive at another dirt road. Bear left onto this dirt road, following the brown trail marker sign.

10.8 The road intersects with a rough jeep trail that descends to the right. An old motorcycle trail marker signals the jeep trail. Bear right onto this trail and descend sharply. **Option:** You can forgo the jeep trail and continue straight on the current road. If you do this, you'll rejoin the main course in about a mile and avoid approximately 1 mile of moderate climbing.

11.1 After passing the long and deep rut cutting through the center of this jeep trail, bear left (east) onto another singletrack, following a brown trail marker sign. If you encounter a gate and a dilapidated cabin, you've gone too far. Turn around and ride back to intersect with the singletrack, now on your right.

11.5 The trail arrives at a gate and a barbed wire fence. Pass through the gate and veer right (south), following the singletrack to the left of the fence.

11.7 Cross under the power lines and continue on the singletrack of Outback Trail. Ride on Outback Trail to this route's southernmost location.

13.5 The Outback Trail's singletrack intersects with a road. Bear right onto this road, riding in an easterly direction through a vast, open plateau of sagebrush.

13.6 Bear left onto Wiensy'z Trail and continue riding north.

14.5 Cross under the power lines again and bear right onto the four-wheel-drive road. Riding directly under the power lines, you're now back on the Rage in the Sage course. Continue riding in an easterly direction, following the brown trail marker signs.

14.7 Once you pass through the barbed wire fence gate, veer left, following the brown trail marker sign. From here you're offered a view of the Hartman Rocks.

16.4 The four-wheel-drive road forks in a variety of directions. Bear left and continue toward Hartman Rocks, passing the entrance to the "Upper Luge."

17.2 Bear right onto the singletrack of "V-drop" for an exciting technical descent to the Hartman Rocks parking lot.

18.5 Arrive at your vehicle.

The Ride

Local Information

Gunnison Country Chamber of Commerce, 500 East Tomichi Avenue, Gunnison, 81230; (970) 641-1501, (800) 274-7580; www.gunnison-co.com.

Local Events and Attractions

Black Canyon of the Gunnison, Montrose; (970) 249-1915.

Rage in the Sage, in May, Gunnison; (970) 641-0285.

Blue Mesa Reservoir and the Dillon Pinnacles, (970) 641-1501 or (800) 274-7580.

Gunnison Pioneer Museum, Gunnison; (970) 641-4530.

Hinsdale County Museum, Lake City; (970) 944-9515 (boasts most extensive collection of Alferd Packer memorabilia).

Accommodations

Hylander Inn, Gunnison; (970) 641-0700.

Mary Lawrence Inn, Gunnison; (970) 641-3343.

Restaurants

Café Silvestre, Gunnison; (970) 641-4001 (closed Tuesdays).

Firebrand Deli, Gunnison; (970) 641-6266.

W. Café, Gunnison; (970) 641-1744.

Tours

Gunnison Valley Adventure Guides, Gunnison; (970) 641-5541.

29 Monarch Crest Trail

Epic is the only word for it. Monarch Crest Trail is considered the premier mountain bike ride in the entire Fourteeners region. Touted by *Bicycle Magazine* as one of the top five rides in the United States, the trail covers roughly 40 miles of descending singletrack over tundra-like terrain, across talus fields, through old-growth forests and high-plains desert. This ride is one not to be missed, an impressive addition to anyone's mountain biking resume.

Start: From atop Monarch Pass on the Continental Divide Trail.
Length: 35.1-mile point-to-point (shuttle required); many break-off points allow for shorter rides.
Approximate riding time: Advanced riders, 3 to 4 hours; intermediate riders, 4 to 5 hours.
Technical difficulty: Technically challenging due to the route's rocky terrain, sloping trail, and steep grades.
Physical difficulty: Physically challenging to demanding due to the trail's length, altitude, and extended climbs.
Terrain: Singletrack, four-wheel-drive road, improved dirt road, and highway. The terrain includes mountaintop granite and quartz, tundra, talus fields, dark forest, and high-plains desert.
Trail contacts: San Isabel National Forest, Salida Ranger District, 325 West Rainbow Boulevard, Salida, 81201; (719) 539-3591 Monarch Crest Shuttle Service, High Valley Center, Poncha Springs; (800) 871-5145, (719) 539-6089.
Schedule: July to September.
Fees and permits: Shuttle costs $11.50; the fee is apt to change from year to year.
Maps: USGS maps: Bonanza, Poncha Pass, Pahlone Peak, Mount Ouray, Salida West; 14ers Region Mountain Bike Guide, available free at area locations and chambers of commerce.
Nearest town: Poncha Springs.
Other trail users: Hikers, equestrians, backpackers, and sightseers.
Canine compatibility: Not dog friendly. Due to the length of this ride and the harsh terrain over which it travels, bringing a dog is ill-advised.

Getting There

To Reach Monarch Pass: From Poncha Springs and the intersection of U.S. Highway 285 and US 50: Drive west on US 50 for 18.4 miles, passing the Monarch Pass Ski Resort at 16.7 miles, to Monarch Pass (11,312 feet). *DeLorme: Colorado Atlas & Gazetteer:* Page 69, A-7
Shuttle Point. From Buena Vista: Drive south on US 24 until it intersects with US 285. Continue driving south on US 285 for approximately 22 miles before entering the town of Poncha Springs. In Poncha Springs, bear left and continue on US 285 south for another 0.7 mile before turning left into the High Valley Center. *DeLorme: Colorado Atlas & Gazetteer:* Page 60, D-2.

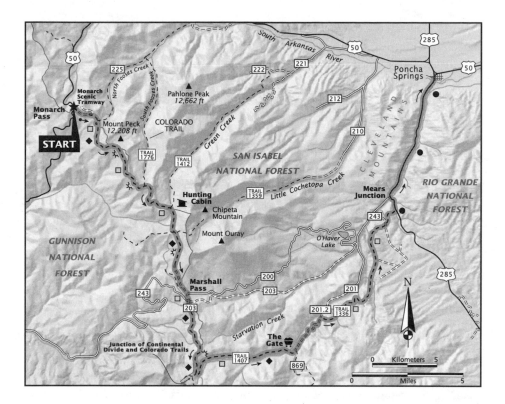

The Ride

Monarch Crest Trail descends an Odyssean 3,500 feet, from high atop Monarch Pass (11,312 feet) to the ride's lowest point at U.S. Highway 285. The trail leads around Mount Peck and reaches its highest point at 12,145 feet. As you near Mount Peck, three distinct peaks come into view: Mount Ouray (13,971 feet), named after Chief Ouray; Chipeta Mountain (12,050 feet), named after Ouray's wife; and Pahlone Peak (12,667 feet), named after their son.

Born in 1833, Chief Ouray was the first chief of the Ute Nation appointed by the United States. As such, Chief Ouray acted as liaison between the government of the United States and the Ute Nation. Many hold Chief Ouray out to be a hero, but there are just as many who consider him a sell-out. Chief Ouray's "political" career began with the Tabeguache Treaty of 1863, which first recognized Ouray as head of all the Utes. The treaty forced the Utes back from the Eastern Slope of the Rockies and the San Luis Valley, resulting in the loss of significant amounts of Ute land. Since not all of the Utes abided by the Tabeguache Treaty, Chief Ouray was asked to visit Washington again for another treaty.

After some tough bargaining at the Treaty of 1868 (or the Hunt Treaty), the first definitive boundaries were set for the Utes' territorial relocation. Essentially, the Utes were limited to 15,120,000 acres (approximately the western third of Colorado). This move called for them to abandon the San Luis Valley, the Yampa River Valley, and the Middle and North Parks. In exchange, the United States briefly halted white settlement in the Ute's ancestral lands of the San Juan Mountains, or "The Shining Mountains." At the treaty's signing, Chief Ouray expressed his people's helplessness: "The agreement an Indian makes to a United States treaty is like the agreement a buffalo makes with his hunter when pierced with arrows. All he can do is lie down and give in."

Today, regardless of any negative opinions, Chief Ouray is considered one of Colorado's founding fathers. High in the rotunda of Colorado's Capitol Building hang stained glass portraits of the sixteen most highly regarded pioneers of the state. Of these, Chief Ouray is the only Native American. Moreover, Ouray was the only one to receive a unanimous vote.

As you ride atop this seemingly barren alpine tundra, take time to smell the wildflowers. Their squat, fibrous stems are well adapted to the harsh and unpredictable weather experienced above timberline. Tiny, hair-like fibers create an air space around the stems that help the plants retain the requisite moisture in this windy environment. Alpine primrose (primula angustifolia), western yellow paintbrush (castilleja occidentalis), white marsh marigold (caltha leptosepala), snow buttercup (ranunculus adoneus), and rock primrose (androsace septentrionalis) are all endemic to the Rockies and may be found along Monarch Crest Trail.

From this alpine tundra, descend 400 feet into a mixed conifer forest until you reach a hunting cabin. The cabin marks the beginning of the ride's last major climb. The climb, which may get bogged down in wet weather, eventually rejoins the crest, but not before testing your technical skills with some short, rocky sections. Cross Agate Creek and descend through the trees before arriving at a bone-jarring talus field at 8.5 miles. Ride over this field and descend to a four-wheel-drive road (County Road 234.2G).

The 600-foot descent to Marshall Pass offers a number of dips over which to either bunny or bonk. Pass an old mine to your right and cross a cattle guard before connecting with the old Denver & Rio Grande Railroad grade. Marshall Pass (10,846 feet), located on Mount Ouray's southern flank, is the lowest crossing of the

Sawatch Range. In a race to rail link Colorado's east and west slopes via the mighty Sawatch Range, the Denver South Park & Pacific Railroad bored a third-of-a-mile tunnel through the range, while the Denver & Rio Grande Railroad opted for the Marshall Pass route. Although longer, the Marshall Pass route did not require a tunnel bore, and so proved the better. On August 8, 1881, the Denver & Rio Grande Railroad made it into Gunnison via Marshall Pass, beating the Denver South Park & Pacific Railroad by nearly a year. For seventy years afterward, the Marshall Pass line was a featured addition to "The Scenic Line of the World," a collection of the world's most scenic railroad lines. The Marshall Pass route remained in use until 1954 when coal mines in Crested Butte ceased operations.

From Marshall Pass connect with Silver Creek 1407/Rainbow Trail. The descent is wicked. Beginning with steep and rocky switchbacks through a sloping meadow awash with wildflowers, the trail runs its scree-filled course through intermittent stands of pine and aspen on its way to the Kismuth Mine.

From the trail's intersection with the four-wheel-drive road (Silver Creek Road 201.2), riders connect with Rainbow Trail. Resembling a rainbow in shape, the trail was blazed by settlers of the Upper Arkansas River and Wet Mountain Valley. As the need for timber grew, foot-beaten trails provided access into surrounding mountains. Similarly, miners and prospectors carved their own trails to mines like the Kismuth. Other trails owe their existence to foraging animals. In 1912 a program to connect these trails was implemented, resulting in the present-day 100-mile-long Rainbow Trail.

As Rainbow Trail rolls in and out of hillside gullies, the scene is something out of Kauai's Na Pali Coast. In contrast to the stark landscape near Mount Peck, Rainbow

Celebrating a ride atop the Continental Divide.

Trail winds its way through gardens ripe with evergreens, aspens, creeks, wildflowers, and ferns. The lush old-growth forests of Rainbow Trail occasionally give way to hillside meadows, where surrounding rocky peaks offer dimension to the distances already traveled. The last 3 miles before intersecting with US 285 offer a fast and rocky technical descent as Douglas fir and lodgepole pine eventually give way to oak and piñon-juniper woodlands. Once on US 285, it's a smooth 5-mile coast back to your vehicle in Poncha Springs.

Miles and Directions

0.0 START at the top of Monarch Pass (11,312 feet). Begin riding up the single-lane Forest Road 906 under the Monarch Scenic Tramway.

0.3 At the sign reading SOUTH FOOSES CREEK—5 MILES, GREEN CREEK—6 MILES, LITTLE COCHETOPA CREEK—8 MILES and MARSHALL PASS—10 MILES, bear right onto the singletrack of the Continental Divide Trail, heading toward Marshall Pass.

1.0 The Continental Divide Trail intersects with a four-wheel-drive road. Bear right onto this four-wheel-drive road and head under the power lines, following signs for the CONTINENTAL DIVIDE TRAIL, SOUTH FOOSES CREEK—4, and MARSHALL PASS—9.

1.5 After two switchbacks, continue climbing on the four-wheel-drive road heading into the trees. Bear right onto the singletrack Continental Divide Trail.

5.0 Arrive at the junction where the Continental Divide Trail and Colorado Trail 1776 merge and continue to share the same route to Marshall Pass and Rainbow Trail. Continue on the Continental Divide Trail, heading in a southeasterly direction.

6.5 Arrive at the hunting cabin. Pass the sign for Green Creek Trail and continue on the Continental Divide Trail.

7.9 Pass a sign for Little Cochetopa Creek Trail to your left and continue on the Continental Divide Trail.

10.7 Arrive at the Marshall Pass Trailhead. Toilet facilities are located here. Bear right onto the old Denver & Rio Grande Railroad grade, now CR 200. **Option.** Bear left onto the old Denver & Rio Grande Railroad grade (CR 200) and follow this graded road to Gray's Creek, just over a mile after crossing the Chaffee-Saguache county line sign. Continue down the embankment on the right to O'Haver Lake. Ride along the lake's southern rim and leave the campground on CR 202. After 0.5 mile, you'll ride through an intersection. Continue riding for another mile before arriving at another T with a stop sign. Bear left, heading in an easterly direction onto CR 200 to US 285. This is a very easy cruise back to US 285 and will shorten the entire length of the ride by 8 miles.

11.0 County Road 200 forks. Bear left (now CR 203), following Colorado Trail signs. Continue on CR 203. After a short climb, pass two trails on your left, as you continue heading straight.

11.1 County Road 203 intersects CR 486 by the gate. Bear left onto the singletrack trail marked by a sign reading SILVER CREEK—3 MILES, CONTINENTAL DIVIDE TRAIL, COLORADO TRAIL AND SAGUACHE—28 MILES. Begin climbing up this singletrack on your way to Silver Creek and Rainbow Trails.

13.5 The singletrack intersects with an old logging road. Bear left onto this logging road, following signs for Silver Creek.

13.9 The singletrack of Silver Creek/Rainbow Trails veers off to the right from this road. The words SILVER CREEK and RAINBOW TRAIL are spray-painted yellow on a placard to the left of the trail. The logging road descends to the left. Bear right onto this singletrack, following signs for Silver Creek and Rainbow Trails.

14.7 Reach the trailhead for Silver Creek Trail 1407. Bear left (east) onto Silver Creek Trail 1407.

19.0 Pass the Kismuth Mine to your right and cross Silver Creek. Ride past a Silver Creek Trail 1407 sign before connecting with four-wheel-drive CR 201.2 (Silver Creek Road).

19.2 Come to the intersection of Silver Creek Road and Toll Road Gulch (FR 869). Bear left, continuing on the Silver Creek Road, passing Toll Road Gulch (FR 869) on the right.

19.3 Come to the intersection of Silver Creek Road and the continuation of the singletrack Rainbow Trail 1336. Bear right onto the famed Rainbow Trail. **Option:** You can choose to continue descending on Silver Creek Road (now CR 201) to US 285. Although CR 201 to US 285 is a faster and easier alternative, both options cover roughly 9 miles each. For tired riders, choosing CR 201 to US 285 is the best option. Its smooth and fast downhill run is accentuated by many dips across the road. Riders should, however, be aware of the vehicular traffic on this road. After 4.5 miles from the intersection of Silver Creek Road and Rainbow Trail, you'll arrive at a spot known as Shirley, the junction of CR 200, CR 201, CR 203, and CR 243. At this junction, continue on CR 243 to US 285.

25.9 Cross a dirt road and pass a sign for HIGHWAY 285–3 MILES, continuing on the singletrack of Rainbow Trail. This marks the beginning of a short grunt of a climb, as the trail passes through a number of hillside meadows.

28.6 The Rainbow Trail singletrack intersects with an old four-wheel-drive road. Passing a Rainbow Trail sign reading SILVER CREEK 7.5 and HIGHWAY 285 1.5 on your left, continue down the steep singletrack descent to US 285.

30.0 Arrive at US 285. Bear left (north) onto US 285 and return to your vehicle at the High Valley Center in Poncha Springs.

35.1 Arrive at your vehicle.

Ride Information

Local Information
Heart of the Rockies Chamber of Commerce, 406 West U.S. Highway 50, Salida, 81201; (877) 772-5932; www.salidachamber.org. **FourteenerNet** www.fourteenernet.com or www.nowthisiscolorado.com.

Local Events and Attractions
Salida Hot Springs Aquatic Center, Salida; (719) 539-6738.
Monarch Crest Scenic Tram, Salida; (719) 539-4789 or (719) 539-4091.

Restaurants
Monarch Crest Scenic Tram Sandwich & Gift Shop, on U.S. Highway 50, Monarch Pass.

The County Bounty, Salida; (719) 539-3546.
Cornucopia Bakery & Cafe, Salida; (719) 539-2531.
First Street Café, Salida; (719) 539-4759.
Amica's Pizzeria & Brewery, Salida; (719) 539-5219.

Mountain Bike Tours
Buffalo Joe River Trips, Buena Vista; (800) 356-7984 or (719) 395-8757.
Bill Dvorak's, Salida; (800) 824-3795.

30 Wheeler Monument

Located in Mineral County (95 percent of which is national forest public access land), the Wheeler Geologic Area is truly one of Colorado's most unique and fascinating attractions. The result of numerous volcanic ash flow eruptions, this geological phenomenon has shaped itself into a city of spiny pinnacles and dark-seated caverns. Its towering spires and sheer cliff walls, rising directly from the middle of the forest like petrified trees, give the impression of a ghost's castle. But as with anything worthwhile, the way to the Wheeler Monument is not an easy one. The route begins at 10,840 feet and climbs to 12,000 feet and includes tough climbs, fast descents, deep ruts, and large rocks. Mountain bikers must leave their bicycles outside of the Wheeler Geologic Area, but a short half-mile hike delivers you to this bizarre geological wonder.

Start: From Hanson's Mill on Forest Road 600.
Length: 28.9-mile out-and-back.
Approximate riding time: Advanced riders, 3.5 to 4 hours; intermediate riders, 4.5 to 5 hours.
Technical difficulty: Technically moderate due to the four-wheel-drive road—rocky and rutted in sections.
Physical difficulty: Physically challenging, as you're riding just below timberline, between 10,840 and 12,000 feet.
Terrain: Four-wheel-drive road—most of which is quite manageable, although there are a number of steep rock and rooty sections.
Trail contacts: South Fork Visitors Center, P.O. Box 1030, South Fork, 81154; (719) 873-5512, (800) 571-0881; www.south fork.org.

Rio Grande National Forest, Divide Ranger District, Third and Creede Avenue, Creede, 81130; (719) 658-2556.
Schedule: Forest Road 600 to the Wheeler Monument usually opens the last week in May (or the first week in June) and closes the first week in October, all depending on the snow pack.
Maps: USGS maps: Wagon Wheel Gap, Pool Table Mountain, Half Moon; *Trails Illustrated* map 142, South San Juan/Del Norte; Chamber of Commerce Wheeler Geological Area map.
Nearest town: Creede.
Other trail users: Hikers, campers, and backpackers.
Canine compatibility: Not dog friendly. FR 600 receives a good deal of vehicular traffic.

Getting There

From Creede: Drive south on Colorado Highway 149 for 7.6 miles. After crossing the Rio Grande, turn left onto Forest Road 600 (Pool Table Road/Spring Gulch), following signs for Hanson's Mill. Drive on FR 600 for roughly 10 miles before reaching the site of the old Hanson's Mill at 17.5 miles. Pass the big sawdust pile on your left and pull up to the bulletin board for the WHEELER AREA and WHEELER TRAIL 790. The route begins here. *DeLorme: Colorado Atlas & Gazetteer:* Pages 78 to 79, B-3 to B-4.

The Ride

San Juan's "Badlands." That's how one leaflet describes the Wheeler Geological Area. Nestled in a remote region of the San Juan Mountains, occupying sixty acres of the Rio Grande National Forest, the Wheeler Geological Area is, if not badlands, certainly bad-ass. From the 40-million-year-old remains of violent volcanic eruptions rise fiendish spires and ghoulish mounds, which Dante himself could never have envisioned. As if the Great Creator forgot to put away the plans for the netherworld, the Wheeler Geological Area leaves us with a hint of what Hades must look like.

Forming the largest volcanic region in Colorado, the San Juan Mountains proved the perfect setting for this geological ghost town. Lava from erupting volcanoes coalesced to form a rise 4,000 feet thick and 9,000 square miles wide. After lying dormant for 1 million years, these volcanoes erupted again, with ash flows accumulating to depths of 3,000 feet.

The volcanic debris thrown from these eruptions, consisting of dust particles and pebbles, settled on the ground in layers called volcanic tuff. Occasional rock fragments (breccia), sometimes as large as 3 feet in diameter, were also spat from erupting volcanoes and found perches on these relatively soft tuff beds. Since tuff particles have weak bonds, they became more susceptible to wind and rain erosion. Over time, the wind and rain cut away at the volcanic tuff, leaving behind spindly minarets topped precariously with breccia. The pinnacles regularly developed vertical cracks, which soon widened as erosion took its toll to form towering legions of stony specters, silently standing abreast.

In December 1908 President Theodore Roosevelt proclaimed the site a National Monument in honor of George M. Wheeler, a member of the U.S. Army Corps of Topographical Engineers. Although Wheeler conducted extensive geological research in the area from 1873 to 1884, it's unclear whether he ever actually visited the site. Due to its remoteness and a lack of funds, the Wheeler National Monument lost its designation on August 3, 1950.

For a time the Wheeler Geologic Area remained in the custody of the Forest Service and the Rio Grande National Forest. Fortunately, in 1993, with the passing of the Colorado Wilderness bill, the area was protected by its inclusion in the La Garita Wilderness Area. Today the Wheeler Geologic Area enjoys complete wilderness protection, preventing any and all logging, mineral exploration, road building, new water diversion structures, or mechanized travel—yes, mountain bikes included.

Twenty miles west of the Wheeler Geologic Area, on the north side of the San Luis Peaks, lies Mineral County's only town: the quirky, onetime mining camp of Creede. During its silver-mining heyday, Creede was notorious for its wild goings-on. As one visitor once wrote: "I couldn't sleep with all the noise . . . hollering, yelling, horses galloping, wagons chuckling, hammering, pounding, sawing, shooting."

Three of Colorado's most notorious characters were Creede residents: McGinty, Jefferson Randolph "Soapy" Smith, and Bob Ford. McGinty, whom the rest of Colorado knew as the "Solid Muldoon," was a 7-foot figure cast out of Portland cement and passed off as a petrified man. By 1842 this missing link became one of Creede's most profitable attractions. Jefferson Randolph "Soapy" Smith, a con man of the highest order, duped the Creede townspeople but chose to put his earnings into building churches and helping the poor. His altruism also extended to the canine population, as he would frequently befriend lost dogs.

Bob Ford, perhaps Creede's most infamous citizen, was the proprietor of the Ford Exchange saloon. Ford, the James gang's newest member, rocketed into infamy when on April 3, 1882, he sneaked in and shot the famous outlaw Jesse James in the back while James was standing on a chair, straightening a picture. Ten years later, a wandering cowboy named Ed O'Kelley moseyed into Creede and returned the favor, killing Ford in his saloon. Although little is known of O'Kelley's background or his motive, his comment to the arresting officer after he had turned himself in for murder was: "I don't rob and I don't insult women, but I kill rats like Bob Ford." During O'Kelley's trial, the court received thousands of letters asking for a pardon of James's avenger. These letters were all postmarked from James's home state of Missouri, where James had retired just prior to his death, vowing to lead an honest life.

The road to discovery is beset by toil and pain, and so too is the road to the Wheeler Geological Area. The ride begins on Forest Road 600, not on the single-track of the FR 790 (Wheeler Trail), which begins immediately from the bulletin board. (FR 790 descends for 2.5 miles to East Bellows Creek, across from which lies the La Garita Wilderness Area. After East Bellows Creek, the trail is open to horses and hikers only, as it makes its way to the Wheeler Monument. No bikes!) Riders need to take FR 600 to reach the Wheeler Monument. The route's first half runs its rutted and rocky course for 14.4 miles at elevations exceeding 11,000 feet. Passing through montane and subalpine bio-geographic zones, the route offers long stretches of intermittent climbs and descents through high-alpine meadows and evergreen forests.

At these higher bio-geographic zones, the terrain is very fragile and damaged if trodden upon needlessly. Though fragile and, at times, inhospitable, the terrain at these higher elevations does offer an abundance of life. The hardy yet beautiful northern fairy candelabra (androsace septentrionalis), whose bunches of flowers resemble tiny star bursts; the spring beauty (claytonia lanceolata), whose hurried attempts to flower will usually give rise to its location along the receding snowline; and the subalpine buttercup (ranunculus eschscholtzii), whose cups are the largest of any North American species—all reside at these higher elevations. After you climb through the first meadow and cross East Bellows Creek at 4.3 miles, you arrive at the intersection of FR 600 and FR 600/3A.

Descend through another high-alpine meadow to Trujillo Creek and climb moderately for 1 mile. Here, surrounding mountain walls pulsate with the echoes of howling coyotes. By 7.2 miles, a 2-mile descent delivers you through another high-alpine meadow and Cañon Fernandez. The only good thing about climbing out from Cañon Fernandez is the thought of savagely ripping down its rock-torn road on your return.

After passing the brown Wheeler arrow sign at 12.5 miles, ride for another 0.5 mile to a beautiful overlook with views to the west of the San Juan Mountains. A cursory glimpse reveals the seemingly out-of-place formations of the Wheeler Geologic Area. From here descend to the southern boundary of the Wheeler Geologic Area, where you'll have to park your bicycle and hike 0.5 mile to the Wheeler site.

San Juan's "Badlands."

The return trip has you climbing almost immediately. By 17.7 miles, however, all that changes. A fast and rocky descent just below timberline delivers you to Cañon Fernandez at 18.9 miles. From Cañon Fernandez, climb steadily. A few short descents keep you from going mental. Cross Trujillo Creek and head for the intersection of FR 600 and FR 600/3A at 24.4 miles. Once atop the last meadow, enjoy the fast descent to your vehicle.

Miles and Directions

0.0 START riding on Forest Road 600 across from the WHEELER AREA and WHEELER TRAIL 790 bulletin board.

0.4 A sign for the Wheeler Geologic Area is to your right, with views of the San Juans to the west.

3.4 Arrive at a large meadow. Climb eastward through the meadow.

4.5 Come to the junction of FR 600 and FR 600/3A. Forest Road 600/3A goes right to Agua Ramon Tie. Bear left, continuing on FR 600 in a northwesterly direction.

6.0 Cross Trujillo Creek.

9.9 Pass through Cañon Fernandez.

11.2 Pass through Cañon Nieve.

12.5 A brown WHEELER arrow sign is to your left.

13.3 Come to the junction of FR 600 and FR 790 (Wheeler Trail).

14.4 Reach the Wheeler Geologic Area and Trailhead. No bicycles are allowed. When you've finished looking around, turn around and retrace your tracks back to the start.

28.9 Arrive back at your vehicle.

Ride Information

Local Information

South Fork Visitors Center, P.O. Box 1030, South Fork, 81154; (719) 873-5512, (800) 571-0881; www.southfork.org.

Creede-Mineral County Chamber of Commerce, P.O. Box 580, Creede, 81130; (719) 658-2377, (800) 327-2102; www. creede.com.

Local Events and Attractions

Silver Thread Colorado Scenic and Historic Byway (beginning in South Fork on CO 149, the byway weaves 75 miles through the historic communities of South Fork, Creede, and Lake City; and through the Gunnison and Rio Grande National Forests.

Creede Underground Mining Museum, Creede; (719) 658-0811.

Creede Repertory Theater, Creede; (719) 658-2540.

Tours

Mountain Man Tours Highway, Creede; (719) 658-2663.

Organizations

Creede Mountain Bike Club, Creede; (719) 658-2351.

31 Trout Creek Trail

The Trout Creek Trail is a great date ride. A short 4.5 miles up and over two hills delivers you to an idyllic picnic setting in the meadows surrounding Trout Creek. Composed entirely of smooth singletrack, the trail is lined on either side by wild raspberry bushes, and the meadows of Trout Creek offer droves of wild mint. The enormous rock outcroppings near Trout Creek have great bouldering potential. Although not particularly technical, there are brief sections of rocky, off-camber trail, and moderate switchbacks that add an element of surprise to this predominantly user-friendly trail. Trout Creek Trail is great for those interested in a short and sweet ride.

Start: From the Trout Creek Trail 831 Trailhead.
Length: 9-mile out-and-back.
Approximate riding time: Advanced riders, 1 to 1.5 hours; intermediate riders, 2 to 2.5 hours.
Technical difficulty: Technically moderate due to the smooth-running singletrack that passes over only a few rocky sections.
Physical difficulty: Physically moderate due to shorter hill climbs at relatively low elevations.
Terrain: Singletrack and doubletrack—mostly smooth-running over two hills and through thick pine/aspen forests. There are a few tough rocky sections.

Trail contacts: San Luis Valley Cycling Club, Kristi Mountain Sports, Villa Mall, Alamosa; (719) 589-9759.
Rio Grande National Forest, Supervisor's Office, 1803 West Highway 160, Monte Vista, 81144; (719) 852-5941.
Schedule: Late spring to early autumn.
Maps: USGS maps: South Fork West; Colorado's San Luis Valley Mountain Bike Guide; National Forest's Best Trails of Colorado's San Luis Valley; Rio Grande National Forest Map.
Nearest town: South Fork.
Other trail uses: Hikers, picnickers, and equestrians.
Canine compatibility: Dog friendly.

Getting There

From Monte Vista: Drive west on U.S. Highway 160 to South Fork. Once in South Fork, continue driving on US 160 to its intersection with Colorado Highway 149. From this intersection (location of the South Fork Visitor Center), continue southwest on US 160 for 3 more miles. After 3 miles, a gravel parking lot will be on the right side of the road. Pull into this parking lot. There you'll notice a sign for Trout Creek Trail 831. *DeLorme: Colorado Atlas & Gazetteer:* Page 78, C-3 and D-3, Page 79, C-4 and D-4.

The Ride

Put on your finest silver because we're going for a ride on Colorado's Silver Thread Scenic and Historic Byway. And the first stop is South Fork, Colorado. Just 5 miles from the Trout Creek Trailhead lies the small timbering town of South Fork.

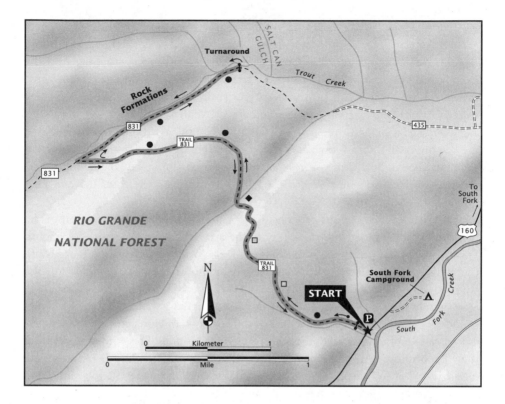

Located at the junction of the Rio Grande and its south fork, where U.S. Highway 160 abuts Colorado Highway 149, South Fork is the gateway to one of Colorado's most scenic and historic roads.

The Silver Thread Scenic and Historic Byway extends over 75 miles, following the winding Rio Grande to its headwaters in the San Juan Mountains of southwestern Colorado. It crosses the Gunnison and Rio Grande National Forests on its way through the quaint historic towns of South Fork, Creede, and Lake City. The present-day route follows the old toll roads Del Norte & Antelope Park and Antelope Park & Lake City, roads instrumental in developing the forbidding San Juan Mountains in the 1870s.

Interested in securing the "gateway city" title for the rich mining discoveries being made near Bakers Park in the upper Animas Valley, the town of Del Norte, neighbor to South Fork, started building the Del Norte & San Juan Toll Road in 1873. The road stretched 55 miles from Del Norte up the Rio Grande to Antelope Park. From Antelope Park, it continued up Crooked Creek, over Stoney Pass, and through Cunnigham Gulch into Bakers Park. To further increase its stranglehold on mining discoveries, Del Norte constructed a second road called the Antelope Park & Lake City Toll Road.

The Antelope Park & Lake City Toll Road split from the Del Norte & San Juan route at Antelope Springs (then a stage stop). From the Springs, this new road skirted past Mirror Lake and over the Continental Divide, eventually dropping into the Lake Mining District, where in 1874 the town of Lake City was established. These early roads to the rich San Juan mines were hardly paved with gold—in fact, they weren't paved at all. One early traveler remarked: "With a pitch and a jolt and a jerk, and a jerk and a jolt and a pitch, down, down you go till you think you have reached the bottom of all things. Down, down till the bottom of all things seems an elevated peak, and down, down till you lose all sense of every thing, but the awful downwardness of life—and here you are at Lake City, the very heart of the San Juan mines."

The rich mining exploits of Creede and Lake City caught the attention of the Denver & Rio Grande Railroad. Up until the arrival of the railroad in 1882, South Fork existed simply as a stage stop along the Del Norte & San Juan Toll Road. With the arrival of the railroad, cheap and reliable transportation was brought into the Animas Valley. South Fork could now exploit its vast stores of timber.

Sawmills started popping up like bubbles in boiling water. Timber from surrounding mountains (which today make up nearly two million acres of national forest) were brought down and processed through these mills. The refined timber was then shipped to the more populated areas of Denver and Durango. In addition, the wood processed by these sawmills provided the building materials for mines and miners' homes and supplied ties to the railroad boom of the late 1880s through the early 1900s.

The brothers Orville and Charlie Galbreath owned and operated the O. S. Galbreath Tie & Timber Company, the area's most productive timber company. Providing South Fork with a hotel, post office, and company store, the O. S. Galbreath Tie & Timber Company provided the lifeblood for the "company town" of South Fork. Its influence stretched so far as to control the lumber interests of South Fork, Del Norte, Pagosa Springs, and Juanita. Workers for the company were paid with script, forbear to our modern-day coupons. Scripts were written documents, essentially IOUs, which entitled workers to receive goods for their exchange. The script, however, was only redeemable at the company store. How's that for owning your soul?

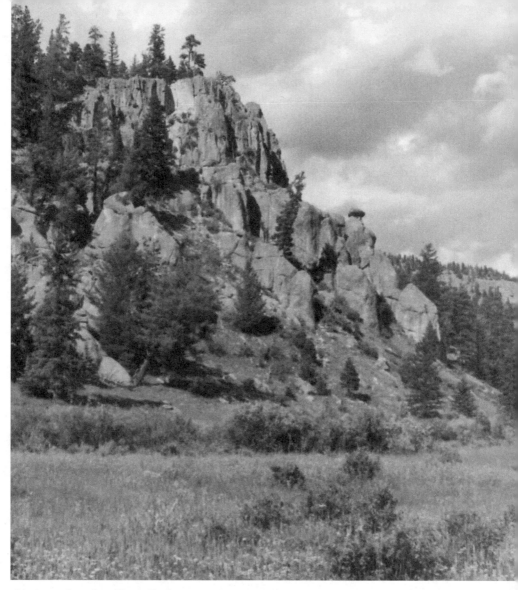

Picnic meadow along Trout Creek.

Today South Fork, still a vibrant timber town, remains a hub for tourism, offering up for show its colorful past. One of the town's most notable tourist attractions is a 24-foot-tall lumberjack called "Biggin." Carved out of a 450-year-old Douglas fir by Ron McDowel in the summer of 1987, Biggin stands at the junction of US 160 and CO 149. Positioned at the extreme southern end of the Silver Thread Scenic and Historic Byway, Biggin marks the beginning of a 75-mile journey past such attractions as the spiraling rock towers of the Palisades on the east side of the Rio Grande, the stagecoach travelers' inscriptions on Post Office Rock, the important stage stop of Antelope Springs, and the incredible views of the mountain peaks surrounding Lake City at Windy Point Scenic Overlook. Toll roads and byways aside, the real area attraction for mountain bikers is Trout Creek Trail.

Located at the base of Wolf Creek Pass, Trout Creek Trail offers a fun out-and-back ride comprising eight parts. The first mile switchbacks up a hillside and delivers views of the next hill to climb. From there you descend for roughly 1 mile through intermittent stands of lodgepole pine and aspen, catching as much air as you can off of the dips strewn about the trail. The switchbacks at 2.5 miles include loose sand and rocks, offering a little challenge to this otherwise smooth ride.

By 3.2 miles, the trail starts to bear south, as it begins its second descent to Trout Creek. Before reaching Trout Creek, however, the trail forks, with a left spur climbing up the west-facing slope. Pass this spur to the left and continue descending in a southerly direction. Once on Forest Road 831, the trail continues in a northeasterly direction along the banks of Trout Creek. Upon reaching the fence, turn around and return to your vehicle.

STEPHEN'S TRAIL BARS

Nothing quite satisfies a hunger on the trail like a wholesomely delicious snack. My trail bars have wowed crowds from backcountry hut trips to backyard Bar-B-Qs. They will wow you too.

½ cup whole wheat flour

½ cup white flour

¼ cup wheat germ

½ cup dry milk powder

3½ cups uncooked oatmeal

½ cup honey

1 cup margarine

1 egg

½ cup nuts

1 cup raisins or dates

2 cups strawberry jam

Mix both kinds of flour, wheat germ, dry milk powder, and oatmeal in a large bowl. In a smaller bowl, melt margarine. Add honey and beat in the egg. Combine the two mixtures thoroughly. Stir in nuts and raisins (or dates). Pour into a greased 13-by-9-inch pan. Press slightly as you spread it around. Form a smooth layer—this will keep it from becoming too crumbly. Bake at 300° for forty to fifty minutes. After cooling, cut the 13-by-9-inch mixture in half. Spread the strawberry jam on one half and place the other half on top. Cut into squares. Eat!

Miles and Directions

0.0 START from the Trout Creek Trail 831 Trailhead. Pass through the wooden gate and ride due west.

1.2 Reach the top of the first climb, which offers a nice campsite and a fire ring off to the left. Cross over the white, nylon cord gate and begin your first descent.

2.3 Cross a tributary of Trout Creek after your first descent.

2.7 Pass through the barbed wire gate, closing it behind you.

3.2 The second hill climb tops out.

4.0 Arrive at FR 831 (more like a rough doubletrack) and bear right.

4.5 Reach the private property fence. Turn around.

9.0 Arrive at your vehicle.

Ride Information

Local Information

South Fork Visitor Center, P.O. Box 1030, South Fork, 81154; (719) 873-5512, (800) 571-0881; www.southfork.org.

Local Events and Attractions

Logger Days, third weekend in July, South Fork. **Silver Thread Colorado Scenic and Historic Byway** (beginning in South Fork on Highway 149, the byway weaves 75 miles through the historic communities of South Fork, Creede, and Lake City; and through the Gunnison and Rio Grande National Forests).

Organizations

San Luis Valley Cycling Club, Kristi Mountain Sports, Villa Mall, Alamosa; (719) 589-9759.

32 Zapata Falls

Zapata Falls Trail offers a short but scenic tour of the San Luis Valley, the Great Sand Dunes, and the Sangre de Cristo Mountains. An easy, stacked-loop ride, Zapata Falls Trail is a great family ride, offering 4 to 10 miles of well-maintained singletrack—an excellent trail for the beginner mountain biker. Although the Zapata area is composed of four distinct numbered loops, the loop described here actually includes sections of each loop, introducing the rider to all four. It's best to consult interpretive area map signs when deciding which loops to add or subtract from this description. A short 0.25-mile hike beginning at 9,000 feet delivers you to Zapata Falls. The falls are 50 feet high and enter into an open-air cavern. To reach the falls, you must hike through the Zapata Creek bed upstream—be prepared to get your feet wet. But once there, the falls and cavern offer chilling relief from even the most sweltering of summer days.

Start: From the trailhead for Loop 1 at Zapata Falls.

Length: 2.5-mile loop, with at least 4 miles of trail that you can ride without duplication.

Approximate riding time: Advanced riders, 20 minutes; intermediate riders, 30 minutes.

Technical difficulty: Technically easy due to its mellow singletrack terrain.

Physical difficulty: Physically easy due to its lack of elevation gain.

Terrain: Singletrack—mostly hard-packed earth that weaves through piñon pine and juniper forests and scrub oak trees; a few rocky sections.

Trail contacts: Rio Grande National Forest, Conejos Ranger District and Bureau of Land Management, LaVara Field Office, 15571 County Road T5, LaVara, 81140; (719) 274-8971.

Schedule: May to October.

Maps: USGS maps: Zapata Ranch, Twin Peaks; Colorado's San Luis Valley Mountain Bike Guide, available at local bike shops.

Nearest town: Alamosa.

Other trail users: Hikers, picnickers, and gold panners.

Canine compatibility: Dog friendly.

Getting There

From Alamosa: Drive east on U.S. Highway 160 for 15 miles. Turn left onto Colorado Highway 150 (Great Sand Dunes Road) and drive for another 11 miles. After driving roughly 26 miles, look for the brown, wooden Zapata Falls Recreation Area sign to your right. Bear right onto the gravel road by the sign and drive up it for roughly 3.5 miles. Pass the first pullout parking area at 28.4 miles and continue up the road for another mile. Park your vehicle at the second pullout parking area to your left at 29.4 miles. This is the trailhead for Loop 1. *DeLorme: Colorado Atlas & Gazetteer:* Page 81, D-6.

The Ride

If contradiction and contrast are the realities of life, then the San Luis Valley—home to the Great Sand Dunes National Park, the Sangre de Cristo Mountains, and Zapata Falls—is truly alive.

Just 5 miles north of the Zapata Falls Trailhead is the entrance to the Great Sand Dunes National Park. President Herbert Hoover designated the Great Sand Dunes a National Monument in 1932. It was designated a National Park and Preserve in 2000. The snowcapped Sangre de Cristos provide a unique backdrop to the teeming sands below. Lieutenant Zebulon Pike (of Pike's Peak fame) came upon the Great Sand Dunes while leading an expedition to the southwestern borders of the Louisiana Purchase. His journal entry of January 28, 1807, describes the encounter: "We discovered sandy hills. . . . Their appearance was exactly that of a sea in a storm except as to color."

The San Luis Valley's prevailing southwest winds wash these desert sands to heights rising above 14,000 feet. During spring and fall, winds blowing in excess of 40 miles-per-hour funnel sand from the valley's floor through three low-lying Sangre de Cristo passes—Mosca, Music, and Medano. As these winds sweep up and over the mountains, they deposit sand along the western foothills of the Sangre de Cristos.

The sand is composed of mostly rounded grains of quartz and metamorphic rocks from the San Juan Mountains, giving the dunes a darker color than one might expect. Since darker surfaces absorb solar radiation more readily than lighter surfaces, these dunes can reach temperatures in excess of 140 degrees. In the early 1970s, Jim Ryan, the famous Kansas miler, ran to the top of the high dune and back in 30 minutes—no doubt encouraged by the burning sands.

These winds, functioning in a cycle that has been repeating itself for over 12,000 years, have deposited sand accumulating to depths of 750 feet and covering 39 square miles. Sheltering this continent's tallest sand dunes from erosion is the patriarch of the Sangre de Cristos, the 14,345-foot massif Blanca Peak. The fourth highest mountain in Colorado, Blanca Peak towers over Zapata Falls as well. The series of lesser summits surrounding Blanca Peak help create the geological hierarchy that has since become synonymous with the Sangre de Cristo Mountains. "Such a beautiful subordination of parts we had not seen before anywhere among the mountains of Colorado," wrote Franklin Rhoda in 1875 when mapping the region for the Hayden Survey.

The Sangre de Cristos' history stands apart from most other Centennial mountain histories. While other ranges have their stories of harrowing exploits during the Anglo mining rushes of the 1800s, the story of the Sangre de Cristos had to be translated from its original language: Spanish.

After the founding of Santa Fe in 1609, Spanish missionaries traveled north, naming prominent geographic features. The name Sangre de Cristo (or "Blood of Christ") is attributed to an unknown missionary who apparently witnessed the reflection of a crimson sunset upon its peaks. Moved by this divine sight, the missionary gave the range its religious name.

As the southernmost range in the Rocky Mountain chain, running for roughly 200 miles from south of Salida well into New Mexico, the Sangre de Cristos became sought after as a sanctuary for many Mexicans. When Mexico declared its independence from Spain in 1820, the new government distributed large parcels of land

One of many views of the Great Sand Dunes with the peaks of the Sangre de Cristos in the background.

along its northern frontier. The Sangre de Cristo Grant included much of the south-eastern San Luis Valley. With Mexicans moving into the valley in hopes of creating new lives for themselves, the new Mexican government stood a better chance of maintaining its presence in the recently annexed area.

Settlement began in the valley in 1849. In 1851 the community of San Luis (Colorado's oldest) was founded. Today, thanks to the Colorado Wilderness Bill of 1993, 226,455 acres of the Sangre de Cristos—the length of the range from south of Salida to the Great Sand Dunes National Park—is a protected Wilderness Area.

Respectfully skirting the protected domain of the Great Sand Dunes National Park, Blanca Peak, and the Sangre de Cristos is Zapata Falls Trail. Named after the spectacular 50-foot waterfall located on the west slope of the Sangre de Cristos, Zapata Falls Trail offers scenic views of the San Luis Valley, the Great Sand Dunes, and the Blanca Wetlands.

Beginning as a nicely manicured and hard-packed singletrack trail, Zapata Falls Trail loops its way through piñon pine and juniper forests and over a few short rocky sections. This stacked-loop trail system exhibits the docile side of mountain biking. Four clearly marked loops lead you through the entire Zapata Falls area. The water from Zapata Falls flows through a rock dike left by a retreating glacier. As the glacier melted, a large amount of runoff collected behind the dike. Eventually, the water began to work its way through a weak spot in the dike and carved its natural course through the rock gorge. This area provides 4 miles of trail that can be ridden without duplication.

The 2.5-mile route described here includes portions of each loop. Longer or shorter loops can be made if desired. Since the area is somewhat limited in terms of rideable miles, it's best to combine hiking, picnicking, and riding in your day.

Miles and Directions

0.0 START at the trailhead for Loop 1. Go through the wooden fence and immediately bear right at the fork marked by an island of rocks. This is the beginning of Loop 1.

0.2 Arrive at a second fork. Bear left here.

0.5 The trail starts descending moderately, heading in a southwesterly direction.

0.8 Connect with the north rim of Loop 2. At this point, veer right. A pine sapling in the middle of a rock island marks the intersection.

1.1 Connect with Loop 3 as it travels north. Bear right, directly behind the Zapata Falls area trail map sign.

1.2 Arrive at the junction of Loop 3 and Loop 4. Bear right onto Loop 4, heading west.

1.4 Loop 4 forks. Bear left, heading for the connection with Loop 3.

1.8 Connect with Loop 3 and cut sharply to the left.

2.0 Reach the intersection of Loop 3 and Loop 2. At this junction, veer right, heading south on Loop 2.

2.2 Loop 2 forks. Bear right.

2.3 Loop 2 intersects with Loop 1. Bear right, heading south on Loop 1.

2.5 At the intersection, veer right and ride south back to your vehicle.

Ride Information

Local Information

Alamosa Visitor Information Center, Cole Park, Alamosa, 81101; (719) 589-4840; www.alamosa.org.
Alamosa County Chamber of Commerce, Cole Park, Alamosa, 81101; (719) 589-3681, (800) 589-3681; www.alamosachamber.com.

Local Events and Attractions

Great Sand Dunes National Monument, Mosca; (719) 378-2312; www.nps.gov/grsa.
Alamosa/Monte Vista National Wildlife Refuge Complex, Alamosa; (719) 589-4021.

Organizations

San Luis Valley Cycling Club, Kristi Mountain Sports, Villa Mall, Alamosa; (719) 589-9759.

33 Cat Creek Trail

Since a vast majority of the route passes through dense stands of aspen, Cat Creek Trail makes for a great autumn ride. With a total elevation gain of 1,400 feet, this ride is moderately difficult. If done at a conservative pace, nearly anyone in good physical condition can enjoy this ride. Forest Road 271 can get quite muddy after a rainstorm, making its steeper sections a grueling challenge, if not a chore. Nevertheless, the easterly views of the San Luis Valley more than make up for a little mud in the face. The singletrack is smooth and fast and virtually unused, but it does see a fair share of deadfall, so be aware when ripping around blind turns. Views of Blowout Pass display a wind-eroded, cup-shaped hollow in the side of a mountain.

Start: From the junction of FR 271 and Cat Creek Trail 704.

Length: 14.4-mile loop.

Approximate riding time: Advanced riders, 1.5 hours; intermediate riders, 2 to 2.5 hours.

Technical difficulty: Technically moderate with a few minor rocky and root sections.

Physical difficulty: Physically moderate to challenging, due to the climbing on the rutted FR 271.

Terrain: Forest road and singletrack through high-alpine meadows and aspen forests. Though predominantly smooth, parts of the route include steeper climbs and descents over rocks and roots.

Trail contacts: Rio Grande National Forest, Supervisor's Office, 1803 West Highway 160, Monte Vista, 81144; (719) 852-5941.

Schedule: June to October.

Maps: USGS maps: Greenie Mountain, Jasper; Colorado's San Luis Valley Mountain Bike Guide; National Forest's Best Trails of Colorado's San Luis Valley

Nearest town: Monte Vista.

Other trail users: Hikers, equestrians, and anglers.

Canine compatibility: Dog friendly.

Getting There

From Monte Vista: Drive south on Colorado Highway 15 for roughly 12.7 miles. Bear right onto Forest Road 250, by the bulletin board. Heading west, cross a cattle guard at 19.4 miles, and enter the Rio Grande National Forest. To your right will be a brown sign for Cat Creek, Cat Creek Park, and Deer Creek. At 19.9 miles, turn right onto FR 271 and drive approximately 4.5 miles to the intersection of FR 271 and Cat Creek Horse Trail. Cat Creek Horse Trail is off to your left. Park your vehicle here. You have traveled 24.3 miles from Monte Vista. *DeLorme: Colorado Atlas & Gazetteer:* Page 89, A-7.

The Ride

Cat Creek Trail lies south of Monte Vista in the 1.86-million-acre Rio Grande National Forest. Located on the eastern slope of the Continental Divide in southern

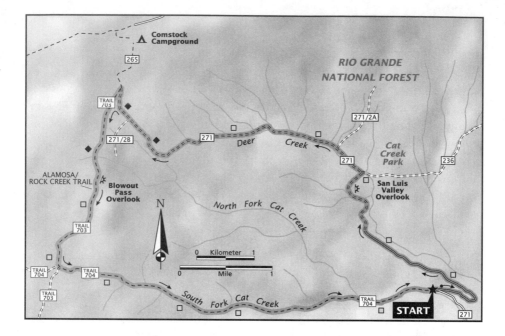

Colorado, the Rio Grande National Forest is composed of four major interrelated land forms: the San Juan Mountains, the Sangre de Cristo Mountains, the San Luis Valley, and the Rio Grande del Norte. The elevation within the forest ranges from 7,500 feet to over 14,000 feet, and the average yearly precipitation can vary from under 8 inches to over 50 inches. As the natural depository of all this potential precipitation, the San Luis Valley is a fertile basin for agriculture.

Located in the heart of the San Luis Valley, Monte Vista enjoys all the spoils that the world's largest alpine valley can offer. An area the size of Connecticut, the San Luis Valley is bordered on the east by the Sangre de Cristo Mountains and along the west by the San Juans. At the valley's southern tip lies the town of Monte Vista. Since the valley's southern section lies above its northern section, precipitation in the south drains to the north. Were it not for the desertlike climate of the northern stretches of the San Luis Valley, the naturally closed basin of the north would have certainly become a lake by now—and indeed, it almost did.

In 1880 ambitious valley farmers constructed large canals in an effort to divert water from Rio Grande tributaries into the northern half of the valley. Ultimately, these canals proved to be ill conceived. When the water table rose to the surface of the ground, fields flooded. Farmers were forced to move south to Monte Vista to cultivate their crops.

Hardship would again strike the farmers, this time in the form of a long drought beginning in the early 1930s. Runoff continued to fall below normal levels until as late as 1955. Desperate, farmers turned to subsurface water, drilling wells into the valley floor. The trough-shaped San Luis Valley floor, in concert with porous gravel and impenetrable layers of clay, ash, and lava, provided farmers with artesian wells. Today, more than 7,000 artesian wells exist throughout the valley.

Monte Vista enjoys a fertile agricultural economy, relying on these wells to irrigate its fields. Potatoes, head lettuce, peas, and cauliflower are all cultivated in and around Monte Vista. And according to W. H. Odin, a state agricultural official, Monte Vista's future looks secure. "We have the soil, the altitude, the climate, and the irrigation that insures quality in our mountain truck crops and vegetables."

With its green fields surrounded by snow-covered mountains, Monte Vista sits like an emerald in snow, a rare Colorado gem inspiring many to appreciate its people, its places, and its potatoes. The Cat Creek Trail facilitates this appreciation. From its intersection with FR 271, begin the route with a moderate climb up the road, passing large open meadows that lie to the northwest.

Besides intersecting with FR 236 at 3.2 miles, FR 271 crosses only two other roads: one at 3.7 miles, where FR 271/2A veers off to the right; and the second at 5.1 miles, where FR 271/2B veers off to the left. At either location, continue straight ahead in a northwesterly direction.

After 5 miles, the road steepens, climbing through pine forests and meadows. Once you reach the road's highest point at 6.6 miles, you'll need to look for the connecting singletrack of the Alamosa/Rock Creek Trail 703. It lies out of plain view and is hidden among a stand of thick aspens. After 6.6 miles, FR 271 levels off through a small meadow, continuing through it before descending to the town of Comstock. If you start descending after reaching this meadow, you've gone too far. Before reaching the end of the meadow, start looking for the Alamosa/Rock Creek Trail 703 after the road levels. It will be marked by a sign reading NO VEHICLES – MORE THAN 40 INCHES WIDE. The trail begins 50 feet to the left of FR 271 and disappears into aspen timber, following in a southerly direction.

Once on Alamosa/Rock Creek Trail 703, climb over wide and soft singletrack through aspen and pine forests. After crossing the north fork of Cat Creek, the climbing becomes more severe. By 7.5 miles, the trail starts descending rapidly along narrow, rock- and root-filled terrain to the Blowout Pass overlook. Ride west over the cracked shale and descend to a fork at 8.5 miles.

The left fork crosses a barbed wire fence and leads into a meadow, while the right fork climbs through a stand of aspens. Bear right. After crossing Cat Creek, pass

Passing a lonely barn on the way to the trail.

through a barbed wire fence and begin a fast and smooth cruise down to the junction of Cat Creek Trail 704.

Cat Creek Trail 704 offers smooth, soaring descents past aspen and mixed conifer forests, through creeks and across marvelous meadows. At 10.4 miles, the trail hugs a sloping south face as it switchbacks into the aspen-lined drainage of Cat Creek's south fork. Here the singletrack becomes rockier.

At 12.8 miles, pass through another lush meadow—although this time the meadow is surrounded by sky-piercing granite walls. From here, it's a final rocky descent past a wooden gate and beaver ponds to your vehicle.

Miles and Directions

- **0.0** START at the junction of FR 271 and Trail 704 (Cat Creek Trail). Notice the squat stone wall behind the trail sign and begin riding east on FR 271.
- **3.2** Intersect with FR 236 and Cat Creek Park to your right. Continue heading west on FR 271.
- **6.6** FR 271 connects with the singletrack of Trail 703 (Alamosa/Rock Creek Trail). Follow Trail 703 into aspen timber.
- **8.2** Reach the Blowout Pass Overlook.
- **9.4** Come to the junction where a sign says ALAMOSA RIVER, 2 MI.; SOUTH ROCK CREEK, 3 MI.; BLOW OUT PASS, 5 MI.; and SOUTH CAT CREEK, 5 MI. From Trail 703, bear left onto Trail 704, heading east. Caution: Do not miss this turnoff, as Trail 704 will deliver you right to your vehicle.
- **14.4** Arrive at your vehicle.

Always wear your helmet.

Ride Information

Local Information
Monte Vista Chamber of Commerce, 1035 Park Avenue, Monte Vista, 81144; (719) 852-2731, (800) 562-7085; www.monte vista.org.
San Luis Valley Information Center, 947 First Avenue, Monte Vista, 81144; (719) 852-0660, (800) 214-1240; shell.amigo.net/~slvic.

Local Events and Attractions
Monte Vista National Wildlife Refuge, on Highway 15, 6 miles south of Monte Vista (for information, contact the U.S. Fish and Wildlife Service, Alamosa; 719-589-4021).

Monte Vista Crane Festival, during February and March, Monte Vista; (719) 852-3552 (more than 20,000 sandhill cranes migrate through the Monte Vista National Wildlife Refuge).
Sky High Stampede, in July, Monte Vista; (719) 852-2731 (Colorado's oldest pro rodeo).

Organizations
San Luis Valley Cycling Club, Kristi Mountain Sports, Villa Mall, Alamosa; (719) 589-9759.

In Addition

Colorado's Off-Road Wheelchair Racing

Jackie Robinson did it for African-Americans and baseball in 1947 when he first took the field as a Brooklyn Dodger. Roberta "Bobbi" Gibb did it for women and marathon racing when she broke the "men-only" Boston Marathon rule in 1966. John Davis did it for off-road riders and mountain biking in 1991 when he wheeled himself to the starting gate of a NORBA-sponsored mountain bike race, becoming the sport's first wheelchair athlete.

No one can contest the significance of Jackie Robinson's actions, nor can anyone question the contribution of Bobbi Gibb—such is the luxury of hindsight. It may be too soon to tell, but Michael Whiting, manager of Team Phoenix and owner of Denver-based Wildernet—a designing and manufacturing company of off-road wheelchairs—realizes the significance of Davis's actions. For Whiting, Davis's bold move in 1991 was the necessary first step in the evolution of off-road wheelchair competition in the National Off-Road Biking Association (NORBA).

Davis rode on a "Cobra" hardtail, the original off-road wheelchair designed by John Castellano specifically for Davis. Since the "Cobra" was custom fit to Davis, an elite athlete, its design hampered the development of off-road wheelchairs for the average rider.

"The first time I met David Noonan," remembers Whiting, speaking of the man who inspired him to create his first off-road wheelchair, "he had just wheeled himself into my mountain bike shop. We started talking about mountain biking, and he told me of his frustrations with his inability to do the things he used to do prior to his injury, so we started kicking around the idea of building an off-road wheelchair."

Whiting began by making a list of performance parameters for a person in a wheelchair. The chair would need a suspension system that would enable a 150- to 200-pound individual to mock down a rough stretch of trail in excess of 50 miles per hour without being bounced out. It would also need a braking system that offered four times the braking power of traditional bicycles, as well as a frame that would be light enough and strong enough to handle the rigors of mountain racing. What he came up with was the Phoenix, named after the mythical bird that rose from its own ashes and took to flight.

Today, Wildernet offers two different off-road wheelchairs: the Phoenix, a full-suspension downhill racing bike with hydraulic brakes and independent dual-wishbone suspension; and the Razor, a suspended cross-country chair and Wildernet's first production model. The Razor offers an unprecedented amount of adjustments that enable the rider to get a dialed-in fit without paying top dollar.

These two off-road wheelchairs provide the fire power for Team Phoenix, Colorado's only off-road wheelchair racing team.

Team Phoenix's mission statement focuses on enhancing and highlighting ability rather than compensating for disability. In 1994 Team Phoenix built and raced the first full-suspension wheelchair in the world. In 1995 Team Phoenix member Gretchen Schaper became the first disabled woman to compete in a NORBA event and was the recipient of the first NORBA medal for a disabled person. The first quadriplegic mountain biker ever to race in a NORBA downhill raced with Team Phoenix. In the summer of 1997, Team Phoenix hosted the first off-road wheelchair race with a cash purse at Winter Park, Colorado. The team gained international exposure at the 1997 All Japan Mountain Bike Cup, Japan's largest mountain bike event.

Ultimately, Whiting sees mountain biking as a form of self-expression, and his adaptive off-road wheelchair technology offers the disabled person an opportunity to express himself or herself. "People with disabilities," says Whiting, "need their own way of self-expression, and every time someone sees our product, it changes the size of the planet for them."

Off-road wheelchair mountain biking is well on its way to becoming the next niche in the mountain bike racing scene. In fact, off-road wheelchair racing has already furnished the mountain biking community with its own list of major players: Matt Feeny of Winter Park, Colorado; Gerard Morano of Los Angeles, California; and H. D. Baily—off-road wheelchair racing's own Iggy Pop.

The concerns of latter-day mountain bikers arguing over the gram weights of little nuts and bolts fade from view when confronted by questions like "How is an off-road wheelchair going to enhance my life?" and "What will I be able to do now that I couldn't do before?" These questions demand a shift in perspective from the mountain biking community, a perspective heretofore missing in the endless gram debates.

Honorable Mentions

South Central Mountains

Described here are great rides in the south central region that didn't make the A-list this time around but deserve recognition. Check them out and let us know what you think. You may decide that one or more of these rides deserves higher status in future editions or, perhaps, you may have a ride of your own that merits some attention.

F Old Midland Railroad Grade

The Fourteeners region of Chaffee County is a veritable home to the giants—including four of Colorado's five highest peaks—but you don't have to be a colossus to enjoy the Old Midland Railroad Grade. This intermediate, 8-mile ride is one of Buena Vista's most popular trails and has had a long-standing reputation as a favorite among visitors. In fact, the Midland is the Fourteeners region's, and the San Isabel National Forest's, first designated mountain bike trail. In cooperation with the Bureau of Land Management and the town of Buena Vista, the USDA Forest Service began construction on the trail in 1990. It connects riders to a number of other area rides as well, most notably the Lenhardy Cutoff and Buena Vista River Road.

The Old Midland Railroad Grade follows the historic and long-abandoned Midland rail line. Old ties, hillside cuts, and telegraph poles remind us of a bygone era whose pioneers conquered many hardships to establish flourishing communities. One look around and these hardships are colorfully evident in the views of the surrounding Sawatch Range's Collegiate Peaks: Mount Princeton, Mount Harvard, Mount Columbia, and Mount Yale. The grade is very rideable, with only a few difficult stretches where the cut walls have collapsed. These tougher sections serve as a good introduction to technical singletrack.

Although short, this trail will require a shuttle. Park your shuttle vehicle at the Shield's Gulch Trailhead. To reach Shields Gulch, drive south on U.S. Highway 24 from Buena Vista to Johnson Village. Bear left onto US 285 in Johnson Village and drive east for 5 miles to Forest Road 315. Turn left (north) onto FR 315 and drive for another 0.5 mile. The trailhead will be to your left. Leave your second vehicle at the trail's end, at the Arkansas River footbridge at the end of Buena Vista's East Main Street.

For details on this and other rides in the area, contact the Greater Buena Vista Area Chamber of Commerce, 343 U.S. Highway 24 South, Buena Vista, 81211; (719) 395–6612; www.fourteenernet.com. *DeLorme: Colorado Atlas & Gazetteer:* Page 60, B-2.

G Reservoir Hill

Reservoir Hill is Pagosa Springs' centrally located trail system. On land owned by the town, this system combines singletrack and dirt road routes of varying difficulty. The annual "Gone to the Hill" mountain bike race is held here every September. The area boasts two main bike routes up the hill: a moderate-grade singletrack and an even mellower road. The singletrack delivers you to the water tower on top, while the road leads you to a cabin where it forks. Riders can go in either direction from the fork. From the top a network of mellower terrain abounds. Upon returning from the top of the hill, riders can descend the west side of the hill on either one of two options, the road or the singletrack. There are also descents off the hill's north and east sides, but these routes won't bring you directly to your vehicle and are considerably steeper.

The hill, however, includes more than just bicycling, as this trail system is located near the town park, visitor center, and hot springs. These springs serve up warm relief after a day's ride and are as a much a part of the town as its residents. Indeed, "Pagosa" hails from the Ute Indian name meaning "Healing Waters." Hot springs aren't the only attraction, however. Pagosa Springs' country also boasts a number of waterfalls such as Treasure Falls, Piedra Falls, and Four Mile Falls.

To reach Reservoir Hill, drive south through Pagosa Springs to the stoplight at the center of town. Turn southeast on Hot Springs Boulevard toward the visitor center. After crossing the San Juan River, bear left onto San Juan Street. Drive for another block before turning right onto a gravel road, climbing a short hill, to the parking area and the trailhead.

For more information on this ride and the surrounding area, contact the Pagosa Springs Area Chamber, 402 San Juan Street, Pagosa Springs; (800) 252–2204, (970) 264–2360. *DeLorme: Colorado Atlas & Gazetteer:* Page 88, B-1.

Front Range

The length of Rocky Mountain foothills running south from Fort Collins to Colorado Springs, where amber waves of grain meet the purple mountains' majesty, is generally referred to as the Front Range. It is Colorado's most populated region (home to nearly 80 percent of the state's population). The Front Range's terrain is predominantly semi-arid and rocky. Offering cacti, steep grades and loose rocks, the Front Range delivers some of the most technical riding in the state. Although the views are not as dramatic as the ones found in Colorado's inner Rocky Mountains, the trails here are just as good, albeit somewhat more crowded.

Unlike most major metropolitan areas, those found along the Front Range—Fort Collins, Boulder, Golden, Denver, and Colorado Springs—are all within an easy thirty minutes' drive of incredible riding. Since trails along the Front Range typically receive a higher volume of use, their routes tend to be considerably easier to follow. That's not to say, however, that Front Range riding is all user-friendly. Front Range trails often travel through rattlesnake and mountain lion habitats, something to consider if ever riding alone. Moreover, the Front Range's semi-arid terrain is an ideal growing environment for the weed commonly referred to as "Goathead" or "Puncturevine" (Tribulus terrestris). The fruits these weeds produce are also known as goatheads. After these goatheads fall from their host weeds, they harden and dry (with the seed of the weed inside). Becoming a three-pointed, thorn-like enemy on the trail, goatheads have an uncanny ability of finding their way into your tires. Their pervasiveness throughout the Front Range demands riders to ride with thicker and/or spare tubes, a pump, and a stocked patch kit.

To the north, Fort Collins lies in the Cache la Poudre River Valley. Here, riders enjoy over 20 miles of multi-use recreational trails, over 3,000 acres of open space, and over 80 miles of designated bikeways, including paved trails, bike lanes, and bike routes. The Poudre Canyon, Horsetooth Reservoir, and Lory State Park offer the best in area mountain biking. Just south of Fort Collins lies Rocky Mountain National Park. With 410 square miles of forests, meadows, tundra, and opaline ponds, in addition to Trail Ridge Road, the country's highest continuous highway reaching above timberline into the tundra, Rocky Mountain National Park is a must see.

Roughly 60 miles south of Fort Collins, Boulder is perhaps the region's reigning recreational town. With the sheer granite walls of the Flatirons as a backdrop, Boulder provides a healthy lifestyle. To accommodate the number of bicycle commuters in Boulder (which, incidentally, is seven times greater than the national average), the town boasts 60,000 acres of open space and 150 miles of trails. Moreover, the International Mountain Bicycling Association (IMBA) has its headquarters in Boulder. The Walker Ranch Loop, as well as Sourdough Trail, are two of Boulder's classic rides. To the south of Boulder, near Golden, White Ranch offers a venous network of trails, accommodating riders of every ability.

Although Denver, Colorado's capital, provides as much art, shopping, and dining as any other city, it also contributes to Colorado's health-conscious attitude. *Bicycling Magazine* rated Denver City sixth in its "Best Bicycling Cities" feature for cities whose populations were greater than 100,000. The Hogback, boasting technical descents and offering incredible views of the geological phenomenon of Red Rocks Amphitheater, is a great ride and just twenty minutes from downtown Denver. Waterton Canyon is another Denver riding destination and marks the beginning of the 470-mile Colorado Trail.

Just an hour's drive south of Denver is Colorado Springs, home to Pikes Peak. Colorado Springs also does its part in keeping up with Colorado's active lifestyle. A major city in its own right, Colorado Springs is home to USA Cycling (888-405-7223), the national governing body of bicycling, which includes the National Off-Road Mountain Biking Association (NORBA), the national governing body for mountain bike racing. Colorado Springs is also home to the U.S. Olympic Training Center. Some of the better rides in the area include Rampart Reservoir Shoreline Loop and Waldo Canyon. Each trail features singletrack lined with Pikes Peak granite, which helps in the absorption of water, keeping trails drier and extending the riding season.

34 Hewlett Gulch

Hewlett Gulch is a favorite among mountain bikers in and around Fort Collins. Its fast singletrack, big drop-offs, creek crossings, killer climbs, and one very rocky descent will satisfy any mountain biker's idea of a good ride. Although technically and physically moderate to challenging, the ride serves first-time mountain bikers well, as it can be ridden at any pace. For those who like to grab air, there's a great spot at the 2.3-mile mark where the trail dips into a small gully. With enough speed, you'd swear you were flying.

Start: From Poudre Canyon, just past Poudre Park.

Length: 8.5-mile loop (with an additional 4 miles added if you opt for the out-and-back).

Approximate riding time: Advanced riders, 1.5 hours; intermediate riders, 2.5 hours.

Technical difficulty: Technically challenging, due to a very rocky, steep descent on the return.

Physical difficulty: Physically moderate to challenging due to an extended climb midway through the ride.

Terrain: Rough doubletrack and singletrack. This trail crosses many creeks and enters in and out of mixed conifer forests before climbing up through a meadow. Though generally manageable, there are big drop-off sections,

as well as one of the rockiest singletrack descents in all of the Front Range.

Trail contacts: Diamond Peaks Mountain Bike Patrol, Timnath; (970) 482–6006, ext. 22; DPMBP@aol.com.
Arapaho and Roosevelt National Forests, Supervisor's Office, 240 West Prospect, Fort Collins, 80526; (970) 498–1375.

Schedule: April to November.

Maps: USGS maps: Poudre Park; *Trails Illustrated* map 101, Cache La Poudre and Big Thompson; Arapaho and Roosevelt National Forests map.

Nearest town: Poudre Park.

Other trail users: Hikers, campers, equestrians, and hunters.

Canine compatibility: Dog friendly.

Getting There

From Fort Collins: Head north on U.S. Highway 287. Turn left onto Colorado Highway 14 following signs for the Poudre Canyon. Drive 10 miles. After passing the tiny town of Poudre Park, you'll spot a bridge to the north spanning the Cache la Poudre River. The bridge is blocked by an iron bar, but biking is allowed. Park on either side of CO 14—additional parking is located 100 yards down the road on the right. Respect residents of the Poudre Canyon by not parking in front of their driveways or mailboxes. *DeLorme: Colorado Atlas & Gazetteer:* Page 19, C-7.

The Ride

As the crashing waves of the Cache la Poudre River blaze through the Poudre Canyon in Roosevelt National Forest, the echoes of a distant pioneering past resound from its granite walls. The very name of the canyon (and more specifically the river) recalls the struggles that the early pioneers had to endure to come to terms with this western wilderness.

The story goes that a party of French-Canadian trappers and traders, led by Antione Janis of John Jacob Astor's American Fur Company, was en route to a prescribed rendezvous on the Green River when bad weather hit. It was November 1836. The snowstorm made it impossible for the company to safely ford the Poudre Canyon's river, so Janis gave the order to lighten the wagon loads. The men dug a large pit, lined it with pine boughs and animal skins, and filled it with what could be spared from each wagon. After back-filling the pit, the trappers burned a large fire on top of the pit to disguise the site. They feared the supplies would be taken by the native Arapaho and Cheyenne Indians. Included in the buried supplies were several hundred pounds of gunpowder. The French-speaking trappers called this place, "cache la poudre" ("the hiding place of the powder"). Some months later, the party returned to the Poudre Canyon and recovered all of their supplies. The name stuck.

Typical of the mountain biking trails of Colorado's Front Range, Hewlett Gulch delivers smooth, fast-riding singletrack; rocky, non-negotiable climbs and descents; and a dizzying array of creek crossings. The trail begins as an overgrown doubletrack, which soon turns to singletrack within half a mile. There are four creek crossings within the first mile of the trail. Waterbars lie across the trail for the first 2 to 3 miles, making for some steep drop-offs and tough, taco-bending hill hops. The erosion logs have effectively made Hewlett Gulch more technical than ever before.

Within the first mile, you encounter the remnants of Horace Huleatt's old homestead. Huleatt settled the gulch in 1870 on land he later found out was sacred

Ute Indian land. When word passed to Horace that his claim rested on ancient ground, he quickly moved on, leaving his homestead as a parting gift. Today a stone chimney and a concrete foundation are all we have of old Horace Huleatt, but his name lives on, though slightly corrupted, in Hewlett Gulch. Legions of wild lilac and what looks like poppy surround the old homestead—evidence that Huleatt appreciated a landscaped homestead. After the homestead the trail leads into a lush pine-covered sanctuary awash with thousands of wildflowers. This is a great place to string a hammock and blow the soul out of your saxophone.

The trail continues through intermittent fields and groves of cedar and pine. The canyon narrows here. Sheer granite walls climb the sides of the canyon in a vain attempt to pierce the sky. The surroundings become more rugged, save the yellow flowering cacti—a bittersweet reminder of the agony and ecstasy through which we mountain bikers put ourselves.

After about 2 miles into the ride, the trail comes to a T before a big gully, offering the opportunity for sick air. Bear left and climb the side of the hill. The hit is on the right side of the trail as you scream up the other side of the gully. From there the trail meanders through alternating stands of lodgepole pine and spruce, offering occasional short, rocky, and steep climbs. After one such climb the trail lets out onto a broad grassy hill completely devoid of trees. A half mile to the north of this hill stands a beautiful house boasting an even better southerly view. Turn around and enjoy an inspiring view of the canyon through which you've just ridden.

The 2-mile climb to the top of this hill is deceiving, as there is a false summit at 4.8 miles. This false summit does, however, offer a great opportunity to dismount and take in the views. Although Hewlett Gulch does have its challenging short, steep climbs, it rewards the persistent rider with incredible rocky singletrack descents. After arriving at the second gully, the trail once again comes to a T. Here you have the option to bear right for a rugged 4-mile out-and-back, or simply bear left and continue on the main trail.

The descent from this point is famed for its technical riding. Complete with steep grades and loose, football-sized rocks, all sidelined with thorny cacti and thistle, this descent has some of the sickest singletrack descents on Colorado's Front Range. Once you arrive at the bottom, bear right and backtrack for the remaining 2.3 miles.

The author splashes down after managing the rocky drop behind him.

Miles and Directions

0.0 START from CO 14. Cross the gated, wooden-planked bridge. The Cache la Poudre River is below you. Ride up the road.

0.1 Bear left onto a rough doubletrack, and enter Roosevelt National Forest. (A right will take you to private homes.)

0.4 The singletrack begins.

1.1 Here the trail crosses its fourth creek and leads into a lush pine forest carpeted with what looks like wild poppies. This is a great place for a picnic or resting spot.

2.3 Sick air. The trail comes to a T. Bear right.

3.3 An extremely difficult and rocky descent delivers you to a broad and grassy 2-mile hill climb.

4.2 Don't be fooled. This is a false summit, albeit an ideal resting spot for those in need.

4.3 A short but fast stretch of singletrack, highlighted by a couple of rocky sections, rewards the patient hill climber.

5.3 The trail leads into a deep gully. You'll need your speed getting out of it. The trail continues up a steep but short ascent. At the top of this short climb, come to a T in the trail. Bearing right offers a 4-mile out-and-back option, while bearing left continues on the main trail. Bear left here, toward your eventual descent.

5.4 Begin a rugged, sick descent.

6.2 Arrive at the bottom where you caught the sick air. Bear right and backtrack the remaining 2.3 miles of the first and last part of Hewlett Gulch.

8.5 Arrive at your vehicle.

Ride Information

Local Information

Forest to Grassland Information Center, Fort Collins; (970) 498-2770.
Fortnet, 213 Linden Street, Suite 230, Fort Collins, 80524; (970) 224-8524; www.fort-net.org.

Local Events and Attractions

Mishawaka Amphitheater, Fort Collins; (970) 482-4420; As a point of reference for anyone traveling the Poudre Canyon, the first digit of a four-digit address (or the first two digits of a five-digit address) marks the distance from the start of the canyon to the residence. For instance, Mishawaka Amphitheater, at 13714 Poudre Canyon is 13 miles up the canyon.

Restaurants

Rio Grande, Fort Collins; (970) 224-5428 (best margaritas you'll ever drink).
CooperSmith's Pub & Brewing, Fort Collins; (970) 498-0483.

Organizations

Friends of the Poudre, Fort Collins; (970) 221-2957.

35 Young Gulch

Young Gulch is a great ride for those who like to get wet. During the spring thaw, the trail crosses a number of larger creeks. Since this ride travels through mixed conifer forests and under thick canopies, the trail remains quite cool, so don't expect to be warm and dry too quickly. In fact, it's best that you bring a towel and an extra pair of shoes and socks. There are a few rocky and steep technical sections, but for the most part, this out-and-back is well suited for the beginner and intermediate rider. The advanced rider will find some of the steeper, rockier sections a challenge and the descent back to his or her vehicle an absolute thrill.

Start: Young Gulch Trailhead. From the south side of Colorado Highway 14, at milepost 109, 3.2 miles from Poudre Park.
Length: 10.3-mile out-and-back.
Approximate riding time: Advanced riders, 1.5 hours; intermediate riders, 2.5 hours.
Technical difficulty: Technically moderate to challenging due to its rocky, but short climbs and descents.
Physical difficulty: Physically moderate due to its mellower elevation gain: from 5,800 to 7,040 feet.
Terrain: Singletrack, traveling through a gulch. As such, there are many creek crossings under forest cover.

Trail contacts: Diamond Peaks Mountain Bike Patrol, Timnath; (970) 482-6006, ext. 22; DPMBP@aol.com.
Arapaho and Roosevelt National Forests, Supervisor's Office, 240 West Prospect, Fort Collins, 80526; (970) 498-1375.
Schedule: April to November.
Maps: USGS maps: Poudre Park; *Trails Illustrated* map 101, Cache La Poudre and Big Thompson; Arapaho and Roosevelt National Forests map.
Nearest town: Poudre Park.
Other trail users: Campers, hikers, and equestrians.
Canine compatibility: Dog friendly.

Getting There

From Fort Collins: Head north on U.S. Highway 287. Turn left onto Colorado Highway 14, following signs for the Poudre Canyon. Drive on CO 14 for 13 miles. The dirt road turnoff to Young Gulch is 3.2 miles past the tiny town of Poudre Park and will be on the left, at milepost 109. Drive up the dirt road to the parking area and trailhead. A wooden and wired gate marks the beginning of the trail. After entering the gate, please be sure to close it behind you. *DeLorme: Colorado Atlas & Gazetteer:* Page 19, C-7.

The Ride

Young Gulch trail is located in Roosevelt National Forest's beautiful Poudre Canyon. In 1918 the Forest Service granted the town of Fort Collins permission to develop Young Gulch as a place where people could picnic, camp, and hike. Three years later Young Gulch was opened. Today it stands as a reminder of Colorado's early commitment to mountain recreation.

Convict labor built the original road leading to Young Gulch, now Colorado Highway 14. The Poudre Valley Good Roads Association constructed a masonry fireplace to celebrate the completion of the road to that point. Located just beyond the turnoff for Young Gulch, the fireplace was left for others to use in the future.

Just before coming to the old fireplace, one notices the Forest Service's sign marking the Cache la Poudre River as a "Wild and Scenic River System." Seventy-five miles of the Poudre, from Poudre Park to Rocky Mountain National Park, have been preserved for future generations. The Poudre is the only river in Colorado to receive protection under the National Wild and Scenic River Act. Covering an estimated 150 miles, the Poudre River originates from Poudre Lake (an alpine lake located high in the mountains of Rocky Mountain National Park) and extends to the South Platte River, just east of the town of Greeley.

The Poudre Canyon is dedicated to a variety of outdoor activities: mountain biking, hiking, camping, rock climbing, four-wheeling, kayaking, and rafting. Local citizen groups, like Friends of the Poudre, are currently working together to develop boat chutes at diversion structures on the river so kayakers and rafters can run the entire river in the lower canyon without having to portage their crafts. These chutes are estimated to cost between $200,000 and $300,000 each—further evidence of Colorado's commitment to recreation and healthy living.

Just 3 miles up CO 14 from the Young Gulch Trailhead stands the Mishawaka Inn, a laid back, riverside amphitheater serving locally brewed beer. The Inn is a summer venue for the likes of Merle Saunders, The Radiators, Arlo Guthrie, The Ugly Americans, Robert Bradley's Blackwater Surprise, Bella Fleck and the Flecktones, and the David Grisman Quintet—to name but a few. In February 1916, Walter S.

Thompson, a musician from Fort Collins, purchased the surrounding land with the intent of operating a self-supporting home. Within three years, Thompson had built himself a very comfortable house, several cabins, a general store, and a dance hall. More than eighty years later, the music continues to play throughout the Poudre Canyon, keeping time with the rocking and rolling of our bikes through Young Gulch.

Rocking and rolling do well to describe this trail. Young Gulch offers a vast array of terrain for any level mountain biker. Its steep-sided, narrow, and rocky terrain offers challenges for even the best riders, while its many creek crossings allow the novice mountain biker many chilling thrills. The creek crossings, along with dense forests, make this trail ideal for those hot summer days. Unfortunately the heavy forest cover causes the snow at Young Gulch to melt late, creating a potentially cold and wet environment late into spring. These spring conditions can be tricky to ride in. Deep creek crossings, wet rocks, and slippery roots are all factors of significant braking power loss.

At 1.4 miles, the trail will lead to a rocky impasse, over which you'll have to portage your bike. The remaining 3 miles of Young Gulch are smoother and wider, making for a fast descent on your way back. Take care on your return, as rocky approaches into creeks come up on you fast. The rocky downhills can be hairy if not approached carefully—but oh the fun.

Miles and Directions

As a point of reference for anyone traveling the Poudre Canyon, the first digit of a four-digit address (or the first two digits of a five-digit address) marks the distance from the residence to the start of the canyon. For instance, the Mishawaka Inn Amphitheater, at 13714 Poudre Canyon, is 13 miles up the canyon.

0.0 START from the gate at the trailhead. Begin riding through the thickly forested gulch.

0.6 Arrive at a sweet, shaded spot, just to your right—ideal for a quick rest or snack. Blooming cacti abound, creekside.

1.3 Reach one of two short, but technical climbs. Climb this section with thoughts of your returning descent. Picking the line to your right on your return is probably best.

Splashing through one of the many creeks.

3.5 Pick up the trail by walking up creek for approximately 50 feet. From here the gulch widens, letting up on some of the rocks and roots.

5.0 The trail merges with a four-wheel-drive road heading up the hillside to your left. Climb for another 0.2 mile to reach the turnaround point. As the top of this climb levels out, bear an immediate right for a short grind to the top of a knob of stone. From here, there is a good view of the gulch and Stove Prairie Road. Private property begins beyond the gate. Do not cross without permission. After resting, backtrack and enjoy the fast and rocky descent.

10.3 Arrive back at your vehicle.

Ride Information

Local Information
Forest to Grassland Information Center, Fort Collins; (970) 498-2770.
Fort Collins Web site: www.fortnet.org.

Local Events and Attractions
Mishawaka Inn Amphitheater, Fort Collins; (970) 482-4420.

Restaurants
Rio Grande, Fort Collins; (970) 224-5428 (great margaritas).

Cooper Smith's Pub & Brewing, Fort Collins; (970) 498-0483.

Organizations
Diamond Peaks Mountain Bike Patrol, Timnath; (970) 482-6006 ext. 22; DPMBP@aol.com.
Friends of the Poudre, Fort Collins; (970) 221-2957.

36 Mill Creek Trail

Lory State Park and Horsetooth Mountain Park are prime real estate for some of the area's best mountain biking. Mill Creek Trail is one of the most technically and physically challenging rides in all of Fort Collins. Riders climb into the semi-arid woodlands of Colorado's Front Range, the first step into the Rocky Mountains. Aside from gorgeous views of Colorado's Eastern Plains, this route offers rolling terrain alongside Horsetooth Reservoir, a burly climb to Horsetooth Mountain, and a steep and rocky descent down Mill Creek Trail.

Start: From the entrance to Lory State Park, at the guard station, just beyond the stop sign
Length: 13.3-mile loop.
Approximate riding time: Advanced riders; 1.5 to 2 hours; intermediate riders; 2.5 to 3 hours.
Technical difficulty: Technically moderate to challenging due to its rocky and steep singletrack descents.
Physical difficulty: Physically moderate to challenging due to 3 miles of steep and arduous hill climbing.
Terrain: Rocky and rolling terrain on both singletrack and dirt road surfaces.
Trail contacts: Diamond Peaks Mountain Bike Patrol, Timnath; (970) 482-6006 ext. 22; DPMBP@aol.com.
Friends of Lory Trails, Lory State Park, Bellvue; (970) 493-1623.
Lory State Park, 708 Lodgepole Drive, Bellvue, 80512; (970) 493-1623; parks.state.co.us/lory.

Larimer County Parks and Open Lands Department, 1800 South County Road 31, Loveland, 80537; (970) 679-4570; www.co.larimer.co.us/parks.
Schedule: April to November.
Fees and permits: $2.00 individual park pass must be purchased before entering the park. Prices are subject to change.
Maps: USGS maps: Horsetooth Reservoir; *Trails Illustrated* map 101; Lory State Park: Colorado State Parks maps; Larimer County Parks Department map: Horsetooth Mountain Park.
Nearest town: Fort Collins.
Other trail users: Hikers, campers, equestrians, and water recreationalists.
Canine compatibility: Dog friendly (but beware the equestrians).

Getting There

From downtown Fort Collins: Drive north on College Avenue (from the junction of College Avenue and Mountain Road) for 6.3 miles, heading toward Laporte and Lory State Park. After you pass Laporte, veer left onto County Road 52E. Drive on CR 52E for approximately 1 mile before making a left on CR 23, by the red, flagstone Bellvue Senior Center. At 8.7 miles, turn right onto CR 25G and follow signs to Lory State Park. Drive another 1.6 miles to the entrance of Charles A. Lory State Park. Leave your vehicle outside of the park, as you will begin your ride by the guard station. *DeLorme: Colorado Atlas & Gazetteer: Page 20, D-1.*

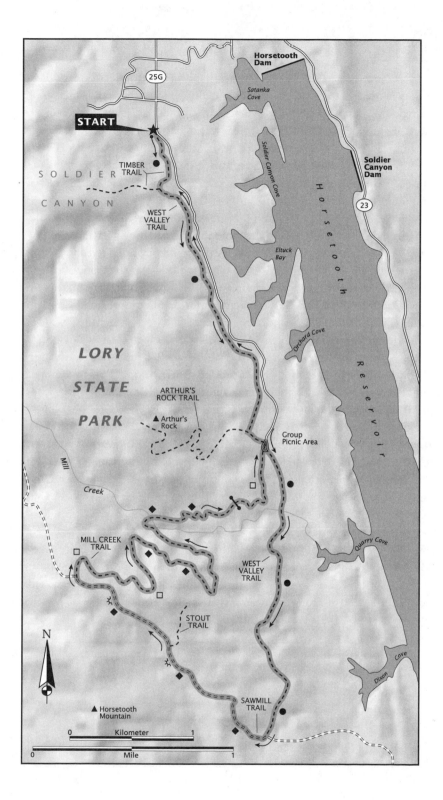

START

25G

Horsetooth
Dam

Satanka
Cove

TIMBER
TRAIL

SOLDIER

Soldier Canyon Cove

CANYON

Soldier
Canyon
Dam

23

WEST
VALLEY
TRAIL

Eltuck
Bay

Horsetooth

LORY

STATE

Orchard Cove

PARK

ARTHUR'S
ROCK TRAIL

Reservoir

▲ Arthur's
Rock

Group
Picnic Area

Mill

Creek

Quarry Cove

MILL CREEK
TRAIL

WEST
VALLEY
TRAIL

STOUT
TRAIL

Dixon

Cove

N

SAWMILL
TRAIL

▲ Horsetooth
Mountain

0   Kilometer   1

0   Mile   1

The Ride

The 4,500 acres that make up Lory State Park and Horsetooth Mountain Park boast a venous network of trails. This network, running along the transitional ecology of the Rocky Mountain foothills, weaves its way through a variety of terrain and vegetation: unique rock outcroppings, sandstone hogbacks, grassy open meadows, cacti-laden hillsides, and ponderosa pine forests. To the northwest, Arthur's Rock (6,780 feet) marks the high point in Lory State Park and overlooks the city of Fort Collins. Its jutting granite foundation stands as a memorial to the strength of will and the indomitable character of the people of Fort Collins.

On July 29, 1997, Fort Collins's local newspaper, the *Coloradoan,* ran the headline: "Torrential rain floods city." That same morning, City Manager John Fischbach declared Fort Collins under a state of local emergency. In a five-hour span, Fort Collins received 8.41 inches of rain. The ensuing flood washed trains off their tracks. Ninety-two mobile homes were destroyed, 145 houses and 116 apartments were damaged, and five lives were lost. The city suffered millions of dollars in damage. It was Fort Collins's worst natural disaster to date.

The deluge dropped in excess of 10 inches of rain on nearby Lory State Park, wreaking havoc on the park's trails. By September 1997 a massive reconstruction effort was underway, involving the efforts of the Diamond Peaks Mountain Bike Patrol, trail design professionals from the International Mountain Biking Association (IMBA), and local residents and riders. Reconstruction efforts are ongoing.

Prior to becoming a state park in 1967, Lory State Park was primarily ranch land. The trails in the park most likely started as game trails. Over the years, and after much use, they've evolved into mountain bike trails. Unfortunately, the trails had never received proper attention, not in the way of erosion-proofing or trail system design. And so, when the flood of '97 hit, Lory State Park's trail system sustained incredible damage. Since the flood, a concerted effort has been made to redesign and preserve these natural trails.

Through a great deal of hard work, the Diamond Peaks Mountain Bike Patrol, IMBA, and local residents and riders have rectified much of the damage brought on by the flood of '97. The lower stretches of trail—those hardest hit by the flood—which lie just west of Horsetooth Reservoir in Lory State Park's valley, offer ideal

Original trapper's lodge in Laporte, Colorado.

riding conditions for beginners practicing their techniques. New area trails have been built in recent years. Advanced riders wanting to increase their heart rates will enjoy it as well. The first 4.7 miles of West Valley Trail meander through rolling, open meadows and past a number of Horsetooth Reservoir's coves and bays. There's Santanka Cove, named for the red sedimentary formations in the area; and Soldier Cove, located at the base of Soldier Canyon—so called because a skeleton and three U.S. Army buttons were found there. Eltuck Bay was named after Elton Collins, who with the help of Tuck (J. Morris) Howell helped build the reservoir, as part of the Colorado–Big Thompson Irrigation Project in the late 1940s. Before the waters of the reservoir swept in to cover them, Quarry Cove was a sandstone quarry and Orchard Cove a cherry orchard.

Once you arrive at the service road in Horsetooth Mountain Park (a.k.a. Sawmill Trail), you begin your 2.4-mile climb to the top of Horsetooth Mountain—the Front Range's answer to those lung-busting climbs of the Colorado high-country interior. While climbing, you pass beneath Horsetooth Rock, from which the mountain receives its name. According to an Arapaho Indian legend, Horsetooth Rock is the heart of the Great Red Warrior who was killed by the Great Black Warrior in a long and bitter struggle in the heavens. The blood shed in the battle is said to have stained the rock red. So how did it get its name? A not so careful inspection will reveal its striking resemblance to a horse's molar.

With the grind of capping this tooth accomplished, it's time for a sick ride down the singletrack of Mill Creek Trail. The trail begins through a dense ponderosa pine forest. Heading south, as you hug the east face of Horsetooth Mountain, you'll have to negotiate your line through some steep and rocky sections, all within the first mile of starting Mill Creek Trail. Remember, the straightest line is always your strongest line. At 9.6 miles, you cross Mill Creek—so-called because the Latham Mill once operated on it, behind Horsetooth Reservoir. The mill provided lumber for bridges in the early history of Larimer County. Nothing of the mill remains.

As you cross the creek and begin your climb out, notice the cool little wading pond to your left. If you don't cool off here, the next leg of the trail may toss you. Just 0.2 mile ahead is the tight switchback section of the trail. Although the approaches to each switchback can be ridden quickly, check your speed, as the switchbacks come up quickly. The remaining descent through Lory State Park to your vehicle comes complete with short, rocky sections and smooth-running singletrack.

Miles and Directions

0.0 START on the singletrack by the visitor center, just beyond the stop sign. Drinking water is available here. Follow the singletrack to the group picnic area.

0.3 Ride right into the Timber Trail group area and pick up the singletrack of Timber Trail to the left of the sign. Follow it as it climbs. Within 0.2 mile from where Timber Trail started, the singletrack comes to a Y. Bear left onto West Valley Trail. (Timber Trail continues to the right—where bikes are not allowed.) West Valley Trail crosses a number of other trails that lead into the hills. Be sure not to veer right on any offshoots.

2.3 Reach a group picnic area. From here, there are a number of routes that branch left to coves at Horsetooth Reservoir. Following the rolling terrain of West Valley Trail, continue through the meadow, parallel to the sandstone hogbacks of Horsetooth Reservoir to your left.

4.7 Reach the junction of West Valley Trail and Sawmill Trail. Look for a frog pond to your right. Head right and climb up Sawmill Trail. Sawmill Trail is a rough service road and marks your entrance into Horsetooth Mountain Park.

7.1 Having climbed 2.4 miles, and having passed the tempting singletrack of Stout, Loggers, and East Ridge Trails, find the trailhead to Mill Creek Trail to your right. (Note: There are a number of offshoots to your left, which lead down the west side of Horsetooth Mountain. Reserve taking any of these trails for another day.)

9.1 Reach the junction of Loggers Trail and Mill Creek Trail. Veer left and continue on Mill Creek Trail.

10.2 Arrive at a red gate, which marks your reentrance into Lory State Park. Close the gate behind you and enjoy the views of Fort Collins and Horsetooth Reservoir to the east. Ride for 0.1 mile to the sign for ARTHUR'S ROCK, HORSETOOTH MOUNTAIN, and PARKING AREA. Ride straight ahead, past the sign.

10.8 Arrive at the sign that marks the trailheads for Bridal and Arthur's Rock Trails. From here, return via either the road or the singletrack to your vehicle.

13.3 Reach the entrance of Lory State Park and ranger station.

Ride Information

Local Information

Fort Collins Web site: www.fortnet.org.

Local Events and Attractions

Horsetooth Reservoir, contact Larimer County Parks and Open Lands Department, Loveland; (970) 679-4570.

Horsetooth Mountain Park, contact Larimer County Parks and Open Lands Department, Loveland; (970) 679-4570.

Lory State Park, Bellvue; (970) 493-1623.

Restaurants

Rio Grande Rio Grande, Fort Collins; (970) 224-5428 (the best margaritas you'll ever drink).

CooperSmith's Pub & Brewing, Fort Collins; (970) 498-0483.

Organizations

Diamond Peaks Mountain Bike Patrol, Timnath; (970) 482-6006 ext. 22; DPMBP@ aol.com.

Friends of Lory Trails, Lory State Park, Bellvue; (970) 493-1623.

37 House Rock to Pierson Park

House Rock to Pierson Park follows a primitive jeep road. There are a number of steep switchbacks, both up and down, which will test your bike-handling skills. The ride also offers a good amount of fast, flat tracking, particularly around House Rock. The descent into Pierson Park is fast and under dense forest cover. Although close to popular Estes Park, this ride sees little traffic, therefore offering riders a generally undisturbed experience. Although the riding is not particularly technical, the fast and rocky descent to Pierson Park may try to throw you, so beware.

Start: From the first gate after turning onto Forest Road 119 off Cabin Creek Road.
Length: 8.4-mile point-to-point (with options to explore the Homestead Meadows area via Lion Gulch Trail from Pierson Park Trailhead).
Approximate riding time: Advanced riders, 2 hours; intermediate riders, 2.5 to 3 hours.
Technical difficulty: Technically easy to moderate. Some rocky sections test your mountain biking skills.
Physical difficulty: Physically moderate to challenging due to sustained climbs at higher elevations.
Terrain: Forest Service fire roads with rocky and sandy patches. Most of the route leads through thick ponderosa pine and aspen forests.

Trail contacts: Arapaho and Roosevelt National Forests, Canyon Lakes Ranger District, 1311 South College, Fort Collins, 80524; (970) 498-1375.
Schedule: June to October.
Maps: USGS maps: Allens Park, Panorama Peak, Raymond; *Trails Illustrated* map 101, Cache La Poudre and Big Thompson, and map 200, Rocky Mountain National Park; Boulder County Mountain Bike Map by ZIA Maps.
Nearest town: Estes Park.
Other trail users: Hikers, campers, motorcyclists, and equestrians.
Canine compatibility: Dog friendly.

Getting There

To the start: Drive south on Colorado Highway 7 (Peak-to-Peak Highway) from Estes Park for 11.5 miles. Turn left onto Cabin Creek Road (County Road 82). After a mile, Cabin Creek Road comes to a T. Bear right following signs for Larimer CR 82 east. Cross a gate. After roughly 1 mile turn left onto Forest Road 119 and follow signs for Pierson Park. Park your vehicle at the first gate you come to and begin your ride ascending FR 119. *DeLorme: Colorado Atlas & Gazetteer:* Page 29, C-6.
To shuttle point: Drive east on U.S. Highway 36 from Estes Park to Fishcreek Road (just past Lake Estes). Turn right and drive 2.8 miles to Little Valley Road (dirt road) on the left. Take Little Valley Road and follow the forest access signs for 1.5 miles up a number of switchbacks before parking your vehicle at Pierson Park. The ride will end here. *DeLorme: Colorado Atlas & Gazetteer:* Page 29, B-7.

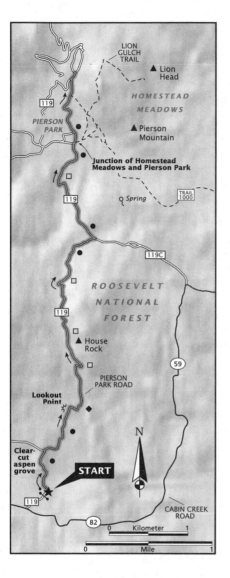

The Ride

House Rock to Pierson Park is a scenic ride that winds its way along dirt roads originally used by the area's first home-steaders. With views of Mount Meeker and Long's Peak, this route offers much climbing and descending around the 11,428-foot Twin Sisters Peaks. The area is a veritable web of primitive jeep roads. For those wanting to extend their day's outing, there's plenty of camping on the south side of House Rock, so bring a tent if you like.

The route begins as you ascend FR 119. The climbing here is not as techni-cally difficult as it is physically challeng-ing. At 8,160 feet even the widest of dirt roads becomes a struggle. At the 0.5-mile mark you may notice a stand of very young aspen trees surrounded by much larger and more mature ponderosa pines—a sight demanding investigation. In place of nature's regenerative method (that is to say, fire), aspen stands are often clearcut to preserve the forest habitat. Over-mature aspen trees are removed to allow young, healthier trees to grow and add more diversity to the forest. This thin-ning process also encourages the growth of low-lying shrubs, which are a food source for livestock and wildlife.

The trail climbs gradually for the next 4 miles. Although this trail is not highly technical, it does offer a sense of serenity that can be found only in the deepest of covers. All too often, that serenity is broken when one is beleaguered with choices of which line to take and at what speed to take it. After 4 miles of gradual climbing and descending, the trail begins to descend very rapidly. This section of trail is per-haps the fastest mile you'll ride.

Standing stone cold in the middle of an idyllic meadow, House Rock stands monumental, a tribute to the area's earliest homesteaders who struggled to survive in some of the most rugged yet remarkably beautiful country known to anyone. "We used what we had for medicines," remembered Nina Boren in a 1992 interview at the age of ninety-nine. "If someone had a cough, we'd put drops of coal oil on a tea-spoon of sugar. It cut the phlegm in your throat; 'course it just about killed you too."

All of the homes in the Homestead Meadows area have stories to tell about early pioneer life. Names of past inhabitants are carved into the log walls of the Brown Homestead of 1918, and some of its original furniture remains inside. The Irvin Homestead of 1917 is still in good condition and boasts a barn, springhouse, and bunkhouse. The Walker Homestead of 1914 sleeps in an ocean of tall grass. Because of what it can teach us, and has taught us, about the settling of the American West, Homestead Meadows was placed on the National Register of Historic Places on October 4, 1990. Since none of the surviving structures have been properly but-tressed, take care when exploring in and around them.

Over one hundred years ago, the promise of abundant game, rich pastures, and crystal clear waters lured hearty homesteaders to the lush, albeit isolated, meadows of this valley. These pioneers made their livelihood primarily in cattle ranching and timber harvesting. As a result of the depression of the 1930s and the declining price of cattle and timber in the 1950s, many of those early pioneers were forced to sell their homesteads. Some just picked up and left. The result: Individual homesteads were consolidated and sold. The Holnholz family bought what is today Homestead Meadows. In 1978 the U.S. Forest Service purchased the land and made it available for public use.

From the junction of FR 119 and Homestead Meadows, take the left fork and begin your last 1.6 miles to your vehicle at Pierson Park. Having traveled along roads that once felt the weight of a "wagon load" and whose dusty sands tasted the fears and dreams in a cattle farmer's sweat, we mountain bikers may begin to appreciate the tougher climbs, welcome the narrower descents, and relish the harrowing escapes that make up a day in the saddle.

Miles and Directions

0.0 START at the first gate of FR 119, off Cabin Creek Road.

0.5 Reach the aspen clearcut. FR 119 ascends for 4 miles through thick forest cover. There are a number of offshoots from FR 119—don't take any of them.

4.0 Reach the view of Mount Meeker to the west and its neighbor, Longs Peak.

5.0 FR 119 intersects FR 119C. Veer left, continuing on FR 119.

House Rock framed by ponderosa pines.

6.0 The route begins to climb again as it wraps its way around House Rock, named for its houselike appearance.

6.8 Reach the junction of Pierson Park, Homestead Meadows, and Lion Gulch. Forest Road 119 forks at this point. To reach your vehicle parked at Pierson Park, take the left fork. Another option is to head toward the Homestead Meadows Area and Lion Gulch Trail. These sections begin as singletrack. However, unless you have prearranged for a vehicle to be at the Lion Gulch Trailhead, continue on FR 119.

8.4 Arrive at the Pierson Park parking lot after descending a fast section of FR 119.

Ride Information

Local Information
Estes Park Resort Chamber Association, Estes Park; (800) 44-ESTES.

Local Events and Attractions
Rocky Mountain National Park: (970) 586-1333 (prerecorded message); (970) 586-1206 (general information). For additional information or correspondence, please write to Superintendent, Rocky Mountain National Park, Estes Park, 80517. Backcountry permit information: During the summer months, permits cost $10.00. Reservations are recommended. For reservations or bivouac permits call (970) 586-1242.

Tours
Colorado Bicycling Adventures, Estes Park; (970) 586-4241; www.coloradobicycling.com.

THE HOMESTEAD ACT OF 1862

Much of America's expansion relied on the willingness of pioneers to pick up their lives and their meager belongings and resettle in the rugged, unfenced, and unbroken lands leading west. The incentive to draw these people west had to be either money or land. Under the Homestead Act of 1862, Congress encouraged expansion by opening its public lands to agricultural settlement. Contrary to what you might imagine, homesteads were not just given to any Joe with a traveling bone. There were qualifications to meet—albeit rather inclusive qualifications.

An individual had to be a United States citizen—or at least intend to become one. He or she had to be older than twenty-one and own no more than 159 acres of land—not a great problem for most Americans. That's it. You're qualified! But here's the rub. To acquire title to the property, you had to build a house within five years, occupy the land for at least six months of the year, make an income related to the property, and cultivate a portion of the land. Then yours . . . to buy. Yes, after six months you held the option to buy the land for $1.25 an acre—not a bad deal. After you homesteaded the land for five years, the title would be granted in full for the mere filing fee of $15.00; not quite the deal you had in mind, but still pretty darn cheap.

Under the Homestead Act of 1862, homesteaders could acquire as much as 320 acres. This program ended in 1976 in all states except Alaska, which continued its program until 1986.

38 Sourdough Trail

Sourdough Trail skirts the fringes of the beautiful Indian Peaks Wilderness Area. The drive from Boulder to the trailhead is reason enough to head for Sourdough Trail. While travelling up Boulder Canyon, multisport adventurers can stop to enjoy great climbing and hiking opportunities before continuing on Colorado's famed Peak-to-Peak Highway. Once on the trail, however, the fun really starts. Sourdough Trail is almost entirely covered by a thick forest canopy, providing cool, shaded relief the whole ride through. Although the climb to Brainard Lake is challenging (but enjoyable), the descent is what you ride it for. A fast and smooth descent through a thick emerald forest will have you screaming: "There's no place like here and now."

Start: Sourdough Trailhead off County Road 116 (the road to the University of Colorado Research Station).
Length: 12.2-mile out-and-back (with an optional 13.2-mile loop).
Approximate riding time: Advanced riders, 2 to 2.5 hours; intermediate riders, 3 to 3.5 hours.
Technical difficulty: Technically moderate due to a relatively smooth trail with little in the way of rocks. There are, however, a few switchbacks that make the riding moderately technical.
Physical difficulty: Physically moderate to challenging due to the extended climbing to Brainard Lake Road.
Terrain: Singletrack, plus some paved and dirt road if optional loop is taken.
Trail contacts: Happy Trails & Cool Beans Espresso, Nederland; (303) 258-3435.

Boulder Area Trails Coalition (BATCO), Boulder; (303) 441-5262.
Boulder Off-road Alliance (BOA), Boulder; (303) 441-5262.
Front Range Mountain Bike Association, Boulder; (303) 674-4862.
Trail Mix-Nederland Area, Nederland; (303) 258-3435.
Roosevelt National Forest, Boulder Ranger District, 2140 Yarmouth Avenue, Boulder, 80301; (303) 541-2500.
Schedule: May to October.
Maps: USGS maps: Ward · Trails Illustrated map 102, Boulder; Boulder County Mountain Bike Map by Mary Morrison and Jim Robb, ZIA Maps.
Nearest town: Ward.
Other trail users: Hikers, campers, skiers, and snowshoers.
Canine compatibility: Dog friendly.

Getting There

From Boulder: Drive west on Canyon Boulevard to the town of Nederland. Canyon Boulevard will eventually become a two-lane highway (Colorado Highway 119), winding its way through steep-walled Boulder Canyon. Before reaching Nederland, you'll drive alongside Barker Reservoir and be offered stunning views of Eldora Mountain Resort. From Nederland, take CO 72 east (a.k.a. the Peak-to-Peak Highway) toward Ward for 7.5 miles until seeing the sign for the University of Colorado Research Station on the right side of the road. Turn left immediately after the sign onto County Road 116 and drive another 0.5 mile. The trailhead is on the right. *DeLorme: Colorado Atlas & Gazetteer:* Page 29, D-6.

The Ride

Sourdough Trail is one of Boulder County's most popular singletrack routes. It's located just half a mile west of the majestic Peak-to-Peak Highway, between the historic tungsten- and gold-mining towns of Nederland and Ward. The trail brings together rolling climbs with a number of narrowly negotiable switchbacks through densely mixed forests of lodgepole pine, Douglas fir, and aspen. The forest opens occasionally to reveal outstanding views of the Continental Divide above, the foothills of the Front Range below, and the Great Plains to the east. As you near the Peace Memorial Bridge, the canopy of the forest flatters its Northwestern cousins by mimicking the lush woodland of Oregon and Washington. When many of the other trails in the foothills area turn sandy as the summer nears its end, Sourdough

Trail, owing to its superb tree coverage and high altitude, remains ideal with smooth-running, hard-packed singletrack.

Sourdough Trail begins at 9,220 feet and stretches to a dizzying 10,280 feet. The trail provides some of the highest alpine mountain biking you'll find near Boulder and Denver. With elevations such as these, it's hard to believe that Sourdough's sinewy path skirts only the base of the Indian Peaks—a congeries of jagged mountain summits, ragged arêtes, windswept tundra uplands, and cirque glaciers. The range stretches southward for 27 miles and constitutes the crest of the Continental Divide in this part of Colorado.

For years Ellsworth Bethel (1863–1925), a Denver high school botany teacher, enjoyed a view of the peaks from his classroom. Moved by them, Bethel and his students went about naming each of them after various Native American tribes from Colorado's history. Although Bethel didn't succeed with all of his suggestions, he did secure approval from the United States Board on Geographic Names for seven tribe names on seven Front Range peaks: the Indian Peaks.

South and North Arapaho Peaks (13,397 and 13,502 feet, respectively) are so called for the tribe whose name means "our people" and who are part of the Algonquin family of Native Americans. Mount Neva (12,814 feet) is the principal summit on the western skyline and is named in honor of an Arapaho Indian who once hunted in the area. Arikaree Peak (13,150 feet) recalls the story of the tribe who migrated to this area of Colorado from North Dakota after having been exiled by the United States Army in 1823 for attacking a party of fur traders heading up the Missouri River. Shoshoni Peak (12,967 feet) is named after the "Sentinels of the Rockies," a tribe who eventually settled themselves in naturally fortified mountain positions from which they battled their enemies. Pawnee Peak (12,943 feet) honors the Pawnees of eastern Colorado, whose name translates to "horn." The Pawnees would stiffen their hair with berry juices and bear grease, making it stand up like a horn, and would dare their enemies to touch their scalps. North and South Arapaho Peaks mark the southern end of the Indian Peaks and cradle the Arapaho Glacier, the largest snowfield in Colorado and the site of incredible backcountry skiing opportunities. The Arapaho Glacier furnishes about 10 percent of the city of Boulder's water supply.

The general store in Ward.

The snowfields and glaciers of the Indian Peaks are some of the most studied alpine environments in the world. Just north of the Sourdough Trailhead lies the University of Colorado's Institute of Arctic and Alpine Research. Modest and cramped huts—some of them secured to the mountainside with cables as thick as a man's wrists—form the offensive line of this world-renowned field station. Rustic buildings resembling early trapper homesteads are tucked among trees just below timberline, camouflaging modern laboratories housing state-of-the-art meteorological equipment. Studies and classes are conducted on topics such as acid precipitation, climatic patterns, and alpine flora.

Just a few miles from Sourdough Trail, amid the cutting edge technology of the University of Colorado's Institute of Arctic and Alpine Research, are the small, one-time mining communities of Nederland and Ward. Just 12 miles from Boulder, Nederland was originally named Brownsville after its first founder. Its close proximity to Boulder prompted Brownsville to be called Middle Boulder. When a homesick Dutch company bought the tungsten mill, the town was renamed Nederland—an archaic spelling for Netherlands. From 1900 to 1918, Nederland produced $23 million worth of tungsten, making Boulder County the largest tungsten producer in the United States. The town of Ward also boasts a prosperous mining heritage. During Ward's heyday (1860 to 1900), the mining district's population peaked at 5,000 and it was the greatest mining camp in northern Colorado. With five hotels, eight lodges, and seven saloons—not to mention $5 million in gold reserves—Ward achieved a certain Vegas status among Colorado mining towns of the late 1800s and early 1900s.

From state-of-the-art weather tracking devices to tungsten mines, Sourdough Trail hangs in the balance between the new and the old. As such, it is a pleasure to ride and an education to experience.

Miles and Directions

0.0 START at the Sourdough Trailhead.

0.3 Crossing the footbridge begins a short climb through a thick pine forest.

1.4 After negotiating a challenging climb with a number of switchbacks, the forest opens and the trail continues under a stretch of power lines, offering views of the Peak-to-Peak Highway to the east—a good resting spot before attempting a short, technical section of trail.

1.9 Arrive at a sign that reads SOURDOUGH TRAIL and RED ROCK TRAILHEAD. Follow the SOURDOUGH TRAIL.

2.7 Cross the Peace Memorial Bridge.

5.7 Sourdough Trail arrives at a trail intersection. Bearing left will take you to Little Raven Ski Trail and Brainard Lake. Continuing straight will deliver you to Brainard Lake Road via Sourdough Trail.

6.1 Arrive at Brainard Lake Road. At this point, you can either bear right onto Brainard Lake Road and do the loop or simply backtrack to your vehicle, going the way you came. I suggest backtracking and enjoying the Sourdough's fast singletrack descent. **Option:** Turn north onto Brainard Lake Road and follow it to the Peak-to-Peak Highway where you'll ride west along the paved highway for 6.5 miles until once again arriving at CR 116. Turn right onto CR 116 and ride for another 0.5 mile to your parked vehicle.

12.2 Arrive at your vehicle.

Ride Information

Local Information
Nederland Area Chamber of Commerce, P.O. Box 85, Nederland, 80466; (303) 228-3936, (800) 221-0044; www.nederlandchamber.org.

Local Events and Attractions
Eldora Mountain Resort, Nederland; (888) 2-ELDORA or Denver Direct: (303) 440-8700.

Peak-to-Peak Highway, Colorado Highways 7, 72, and 119 offer a beautiful drive, connecting Estes Park and the Black Hawk/Central City gambling district.

Accommodations
Sundance Lodge & Stables, Nederland; (303) 258-3797, (800) 817-3797.

In Addition

The RTD's Bike-n-Ride Program

Part of Colorado's appeal to cyclists is its bicycle-friendly attitude. Even Denver, Colorado's capital, boasts a healthy attitude toward its lycra-wearing residents.

In a city as beautiful as Denver, with its Rocky Mountain backdrop and over 300 days of sunshine a year, it makes sense to commute on your bicycle—which is why Denver has reserved cycling lanes alongside its car lanes. The Greater Colorado Transit Authority goes to great lengths to secure this healthy alternative to commuting.

Commuting via cycle does have its unexpected obstacles: rainy weather, flat tires, and lack of leg power. For this reason, the Regional Transportation District (RTD) developed its Bike-n-Ride program. As a service to commuters and cyclists alike, the Boulder and Longmont local numbered buses provide bicycle mounts, should a commuting cyclist find himself or herself in need of an alternate mode of transportation. Fort Collins's buses are all equipped with bicycle mounts. The Denver local, limited, and express buses also offer bicycle racks for distressed cyclists.

As if this weren't enough, the RTD permits bicycles inside luggage compartments on its regional buses. The cost for such convenience? Nil. Light rail trains also welcome bicycles. Although there's no fee for bringing your bicycle on a light rail train, you are required to obtain a permit.

With Colorado's ever-growing population, many commuters are taking advantage of the many Park-n-Rides throughout the RTD's six-county district. Free bicycle lockers and racks are provided at many Park-n-Ride locations. With a $25.00 refundable deposit, lockers can be leased for up to six months.

For further information on the RTD's Bike-n-Ride program, contact the RTD's telephone information center at (303) 299–6000, and then press 140. For those of you outside the Denver-Boulder metro area, call (800) 388–7433, then press 140.

Bike racks on buses are also available in Aspen/Glenwood Springs (Roaring Fork Transit), Avon/Vail (ECO Transit), Summit County (The Summit Stage), and in Colorado Springs (Springs Transit).

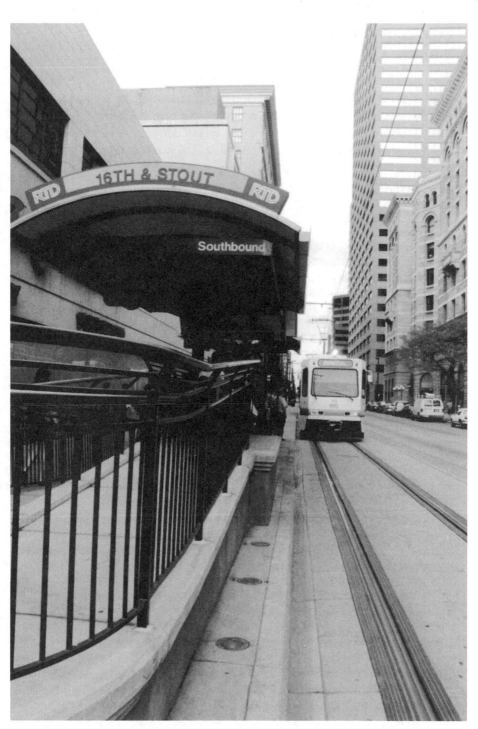

RTD offers a number of ways to tranport your bike.

39 Walker Ranch Loop

Walker Ranch Loop is a popular ride among Boulder mountain bikers. Its initial singletrack descent to South Boulder Creek is amazing. During the spring thaw, South Boulder Creek is an impressive torrent of white water—an exhilarating sound to hear while riding along its banks. This ride weaves in and out of mixed conifer forests and offers a number of rocky singletrack sections. There is one section of the trail that requires you to portage down a steep cliff section, a section some area riders consider the Walker Ranch Loop's best or worst feature. Mountain lions have been spotted in the area, so pay attention to the mountain lion warning signs.

Start: From the parking lot of Walker Ranch Open Space, at the South Boulder Creek Trailhead. Riders can also park and start from the Ethel Harrold Picnic Area and trailhead, where there is more parking and restrooms are available.

Length: 8-mile loop, with other options to ride in Walker Ranch.

Approximate riding time: Advanced riders, 1 hour; intermediate riders, 2 hours.

Technical difficulty: Technically moderate to challenging due to smooth, fast singletrack coupled with tough rocky sections. Note: There is a section of trail called "Cliff Conditions," which requires you to portage your bicycle down steep steps and over rock faces. Take care.

Physical difficulty: Physically challenging due to the variety of climbing involved.

Terrain: Singletrack with patches of rocks and sand; improved dirt road.

Trail contacts: Boulder County Parks and Open Space Department, Boulder; (303) 441-3950; www.co.boulder.co/usopenspace. U.S. Forest Service, Boulder District, 2140 Yarmouth Avenue, Boulder, 80301; (303) 541-2500.

Schedule: May to October.

Maps: USGS maps: Eldorado Springs; Walker Ranch: Boulder County Parks and Open Space map; Boulder County Mountain Bike Map, by ZIA Maps, available at select mountain bike retailers.

Nearest town: Boulder.

Other trail users: Hikers, anglers, picnickers, equestrians, and climbers.

Canine compatibility: Dog friendly, but dogs must be on a leash at all times.

Getting There

From Boulder: Drive west on Baseline Road to Flagstaff Mountain Road. Baseline turns into Flagstaff after Chautauqua Auditorium (on your left). Stay on Flagstaff Mountain Road for about 8 miles, as it winds its way up and over Flagstaff Mountain. The road is crisscrossed heavily by hiking trails, so keep an eye out for pedestrians and cyclists. Following the signs for Walker Ranch, drive past the sign for the Flagstaff Mountain Amphitheater and Green Mountain Lodge, after roughly 4 miles. Flagstaff Mountain Road eventually "tops out" before descending down the other side of Flagstaff Mountain. Pass the Meyers Homestead Picnic Area and trailhead on the right. From there, Walker Ranch is roughly 0.5 mile on the left. Pull into the dirt road and drive up the short distance to the South Boulder Creek Trailhead and parking lot. *DeLorme: Colorado Atlas & Gazetteer:* Page 39, A-7 and Page 40, A-1.

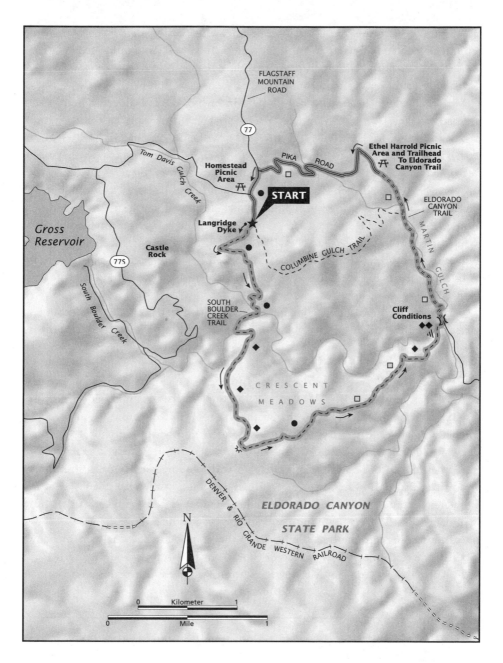

FLAGSTAFF
MOUNTAIN
ROAD

77

Tom Davis Gulch Creek

PIKA ROAD

Ethel Harrold Picnic
Area and Trailhead
To Eldorado
Canyon Trail

Homestead
Picnic
Area

START

ELDORADO
CANYON
TRAIL

Langridge
Dyke

Gross
Reservoir

Castle
Rock

COLUMBINE GULCH TRAIL

MARTIN GULCH

775

South Boulder Creek

SOUTH
BOULDER
CREEK
TRAIL

Cliff
Conditions

C R E S C E N T

M E A D O W S

DENVER & RIO GRANDE WESTERN RAILROAD

ELDORADO CANYON

STATE PARK

N

Kilometer
0   1

Mile
0   1

The Ride

Near Flagstaff Mountain and just west of Boulder is an area that evokes a love/hate
relationship among many mountain bikers. Walker Ranch's clifflike descent from
South Boulder Creek Trail to South Boulder Creek has the reputation of being one

of the more hazardous portages in Colorado. This section of trail—loved for its uniqueness, hated for its vertigo-inducing incline—has summoned many a masochist. The portage notwithstanding, Walker Ranch offers some exciting single-track mountain biking and beautiful scenery, set amid a rich local history.

In 1869 James Walker, with only $12.00 in his pocket and suffering from a life-threatening illness, traveled from Missouri to Boulder on the advice of his physician. Colorado's high, dry climate would prove to be Walker's salvation. His health dramatically improved. Having reclaimed his health, Walker, along with his wife, Phoebe, reclaimed their lives together by filing a homestead claim to 160 acres in 1882.

By 1883 Walker Ranch—consisting of a ranch house, barn, blacksmith shop, root cellar, granary, smokehouse, springhouse, chicken and turkey houses, corn storage house, and pig barn—afforded James and Phoebe the self-sufficient lifestyle with which they both would eventually fall in love. With various corrals, fenced pastures, and 160 acres, Walker Ranch was one of the largest cattle ranches in this region and is listed on the National Register of Historic Places. Not bad for a sick tiger with only $12.00 to his name.

Today, posted signs of "mountain lion" territory greet the would-be mountain biker at South Boulder Creek's trailhead. If you decide to park and begin your ride at the Ethel Harrold Picnic Area and trailhead, you will begin by riding up Pika Road to South Boulder Creek Trail. Otherwise, the route begins on South Boulder Creek Trail, contouring to the south of Langridge Dyke and descending to Tom Davis Gulch and South Boulder Creek at 1.0 mile. There are a number of great fly-fishing holes along this patch of the creek. The route to this point is fast on rock-riddled singletrack with varying patches of sand. A number of switchbacks and dips prevent the rider from going too fast. Once it reaches South Boulder Creek, the trail smoothes to soft forest singletrack blanketed with pine needles. Ride upstream to a footbridge that crosses the creek at 1.5 miles, whereupon the trail divides. Bear left here and continue your ride. For those requiring a bit of a dip, riding straight ahead will deliver you to a cool wading pond about 50 yards up.

After bearing left, the trail climbs out of the drainage to the Crescent Meadows Trailhead at 2.7 miles, offering views of the Denver & Rio Grande Western Railroad. The climb to Crescent Meadows is a grunt but one well worth undertaking. It

On the climb to Crescent Meadows.

climbs to 7,300 feet and offers a beautiful view of Gross Dam and snowcapped peaks to the west. Ride east on Crescent Meadows Trail as it parallels Eldorado Canyon State Park to the right. Mountain bikes are prohibited beyond the county boundary in Eldorado Canyon State Park.

This section of the route begins as a moderate descent through meadows awash with wildflowers and then becomes considerably steeper as it drops to South Boulder Creek. This may be the best section of the entire route. After dropping some big rocky hits, arrive at a sign at 4.8 miles that reads DANGER: CLIFF CONDITIONS. Dismount and carefully climb down the very technical terrain to South Boulder Creek. Once at its shores, scramble over the boulder field directly downstream, and head to the bridge that crosses the creek.

After crossing the bridge, Crescent Meadows Trail connects with Eldorado Canyon Trail. (Note: Mountain bikers are prohibited from entering Eldorado Canyon State Park via Eldorado Canyon Trail from lower Walker Ranch.) Climbing through Martin Gulch, Eldorado Canyon Trail intersects with Columbine Gulch Trail at 6.1 miles. Here you have the option of veering left onto Columbine Gulch Trail and shortcutting over the 1.5-mile trail back to the South Boulder Creek Trailhead and to your vehicle. Or, you can continue straight ahead to Pika Road, past Ethel Harrold Picnic Area.

The Columbine Gulch Trail climbs for 400 feet via a number of steep switchbacks—testimony to this trail's designation as one NOT RECOMMENDED FOR MOUNTAIN BIKES. For those seeking the challenge of tough singletrack climbing, this part of the route, which ascends under thick forest cover, delivers all you'll ever want. For the spinners who prefer constant pedaling over intermittent singletrack, ride straight past Columbine Gulch Trail to the Ethel Harrold Picnic Area. Pass the gate, ride out of the parking lot, and intercept Pika Road to the left. Pika Road offers 1.3 miles of gradual "cool down" climbing before intersecting with Flagstaff Mountain Road. Turn left onto Flagstaff Mountain Road and ride to your vehicle atop the dirt road at the South Boulder Creek Trailhead.

Miles and Directions

0.0 START at the South Boulder Creek Trailhead. As the trail contours south of Langridge Dyke, descend the switchbacks south into Tom Davis Gulch, to South Boulder Creek.

1.0 Descend to South Boulder Creek. Follow the creek upstream.

2.7 Reach Crescent Meadows (7,300 feet). From here you can see Gross Dam due west.

5.0 Reach the "Cliff Conditons" area. Dismount and portage your bike down to South Boulder Creek carefully.

6.1 Meet the junction of Columbine Gulch Trail and Crescent Meadows Trail. Columbine Gulch Trail will return you to your vehicles, but the trail is not recommended for bicycles. Continue straight to the Ethel Harrold Picnic Area and trailhead for the Eldorado Canyon Trail.

6.3 Reach the Ethel Harrold Picnic Area and trailhead for Eldorado Canyon Trail. Ride straight out of the parking lot and turn left onto Pika Road.

7.6 Reach a stop sign and the intersection of Pika Road and Flagstaff Mountain Road. Bear left onto Flagstaff Mountain Road.

8.0 Reach the South Boulder Creek Trailhead and Walker Ranch parking lot. You're at your vehicle.

Ride Information

Local Information

City of Boulder Parks and Recreation, 3198 Broadway, Boulder, 80304; (303) 413-7200; www.ci.boulder.co.us/parks-recreation.
Boulder Convention and Visitors Bureau, 2440 Pearl Street, Boulder, 80302; (303) 442-2911; www.bouldercoloradousa.com.
Boulder Chamber of Commerce, 2440 Pearl Street, P.O. Box 73, Boulder, 80302; (303) 442-1044; www.boulderchamber.com.

Local Events and Attractions

Walker Ranch Tours, contact Boulder County Parks and Open Space Department, Boulder; (303) 441-3950.

Organizations

International Mountain Biking Association (IMBA), Boulder; (303) 545-9011.
Boulder Bicycle Commuters, Boulder; (303) 499-7466.
Boulder Off-Road Alliance, Boulder; (303) 447-9378 or (303) 441-5262.
Boulder Old Wheelers, Boulder; (303) 444-0801.

40 White Ranch

White Ranch offers grueling climbs, steep and narrow descents, and tight switch-backs. The route described here includes all of these features but is still only a small sampling of what White Ranch has to offer. With steep grades, loose rock, and plastic erosion bars strewn across the trail, the initial climb from the parking lot is one of the toughest on the Front Range. From there, riders are offered fast descents along precipitously sloping terrain and through mixed conifer and piñon forests. Though close to Golden, Boulder, and Denver, White Ranch is seldom crowded, largely due to its being viewed as a more advanced area to mountain bike.

Start: From the parking lot off Pine Ridge Road.

Length: 8.4-mile loop, with many options to add and/or subtract from this distance.

Approximate riding time: Advanced riders, 1.5 hours; intermediate riders, 2 to 2.5 hours.

Technical difficulty: Technically moderate to challenging due to its steep and rocky climbs and descents with many tight switchbacks.

Physical difficulty: Physically challenging due to the climbing involved in very exposed and hot terrain.

Terrain: Singletrack and doubletrack that runs over very rocky terrain, as well as very smooth, forested terrain.

Trail contacts: Jefferson County Open Space, 700 Jefferson County Parkway, Suite 100, Golden, 80401; (303) 271-5925, trails hotline (303) 271-5975; openspace.jeffco.us.

Schedule: April to November.

Maps: USGS maps: Golden Ralston Buttes; *Trails Illustrated* map 102; White Ranch Park Map, Jefferson County Open Space.

Nearest town: Golden.

Other trail users: Hikers, equestrians, campers, picnickers.

Canine compatibility: Dog friendly, but bring plenty of water for the pooch, and dogs must be on a leash at all times.

Getting There

From Boulder: Drive south on Colorado Highway 93 (Broadway) for 17.4 miles (from the intersection with Canyon Boulevard) until you see the WHITE RANCH OPEN SPACE sign to your left. Before the sign turn right onto 56th Avenue. Drive approximately 1 mile on 56th Avenue before turning right onto Pine Ridge Road. Pine Ridge Road will lead you to the White Ranch parking lot. *DeLorme: Colorado Atlas & Gazetteer:* Page 40, B-1.

The Ride

Once a cattle operation, today White Ranch is a 3,040-acre Open Space Park. Taking its name from a local homesteader, Paul R. White, the park includes roughly 18 miles of multi-use trails. Only 0.5-mile northwest of Golden, White Ranch offers mountain bikers living in the Denver metro area a great escape from the city grind.

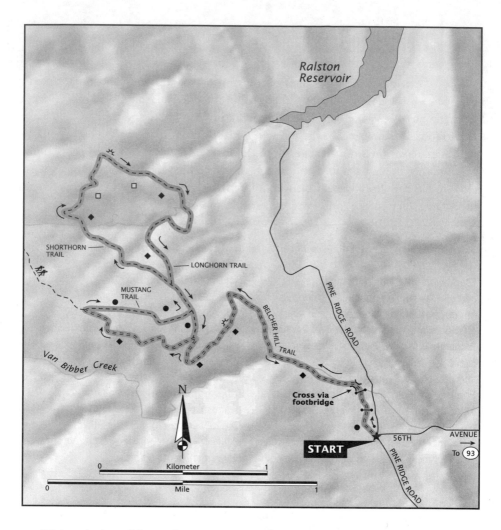

The majority of the park is exposed, particularly the east side, which traverses a steep slope, and so for this reason, White Ranch receives ample amounts of sunlight—making it one of the first mountain bike areas of Colorado's higher foothills region to open for the mountain biking season. Because of the jump on the season, White Ranch tends to get sandy toward the end of summer. Because of the exposure, you'd be well advised to bring plenty of water with you while riding the Ranch.

From advanced riding to novice riding, White Ranch offers it all. Rugged and rocky steep climbs challenge even the best of riders, while smooth and gentle meadow shots tempt weary neophytes to release the death grip on the brakes. From the many vantage points in the park, mountain bikers are offered sweeping views of the Great Plains and the Denver skyline.

The first part of the route ascends a steep, sandy, and rocky doubletrack. Even the best riders will feel the burn after 2.4 miles of this kind of climbing. Luckily, the singletrack descent of Mustang Trail to Longhorn Trail offers a brief respite. After passing the continuation of Longhorn Trail and continuing to climb up Shorthorn Trail, the route winds its way through a dense pine forest. The terrain of the singletrack here is narrow and smooth. The trail eventually exits the forest and winds its way north along an east-facing slope.

Along the slope you'll find patches of what is more commonly referred to as Indian T.P. (toilet paper). Botanists would probably rather you call the plant by its proper name, mullein (also spelled "mullen"). The plant's wide leaves account for the nickname. Tea made from brewing mullein leaves is said to relieve respiratory problems—a great thing to know when riding at higher altitudes.

At 4.3 miles, the northern junction of Shorthorn and Longhorn Trails marks the beginning of your return. The most challenging part of this entire route begins once you turn onto Longhorn Trail. At 5.0 miles, the route hits a steep and rocky descent, followed by tight switchbacks and big drop-offs, eventually delivering you to the bottom of a steep-walled drainage. What follows is a steep and rocky ascent up the other side, with tight switchbacks. From here, it's a fast race back to Belcher Hill Trail and an even faster race back to the parking lot.

With elevations ranging from 6,150 feet to 8,000 feet (atop Belcher Hill), White Ranch offers some tough climbing but rewards you with bombing singletrack. One note of caution: Because of the many narrow trails leading around blind curves, it's likely that you may run into someone. Control your speed while descending. Mountain bikers are responsible for yielding to all other trail users, and downhill trail users yield to uphill trail users.

Miles and Directions

0.0 START from the parking lot at the trailhead of Belcher Hill Trail. Pass through two gates and cross Van Bibber Creek via a footbridge within the first 0.5 mile. Please close both gates behind you and begin climbing up Belcher Hill Trail after crossing the creek.

1.8 Arrive at the junction of Longhorn (to your right) and Belcher Hill Trails. You will eventually return via Longhorn Trail, but for now, forgo turning right onto Longhorn Trail and continue

Racing man's best friend down Belcher Hill Trail.

pedaling west up Belcher Hill Trail. To your east, views of the Denver skyline sprawl out before you.

2.4 Belcher Hill Trail intersects Mustang Trail. Here is a good place to rest, as your initial climb has ended—not to mention there's a bench seat to sit on. Hang a right, now descending on the singletrack of Mustang Trail.

3.0 Arrive at the junction of Mustang and Longhorn Trails. Veer left onto Longhorn Trail, which within a quarter of a mile will Y: Longhorn to your right, Shorthorn to your left. Continue left and begin climbing, now on Shorthorn Trail.

4.3 Arrive at the northern junction of Shorthorn and Longhorn Trails. Bear right onto Longhorn Trail.

6.0 Arrive at the southern junction of Shorthorn and Longhorn Trails. Bear left, continuing your ride on Longhorn. Within 0.3 mile you will once again arrive at the junction of Mustang and Longhorn. Continue on Longhorn for another 0.1 mile before arriving at the junction of Longhorn and Belcher Hill Trails. Veer left onto Belcher Hill Trail and descend—along what previously you had climbed—back to the parking lot.

8.4 Arrive at the parking lot.

Ride Information

Local Information

Greater Golden Chamber of Commerce, 1010 Washington Avenue, P.O. Box 1035, Golden, 80402; (303) 279-3113; www.goldenchamber.org.

Local Events and Attractions

Coors Brewing Company Tours, Monday through Saturday, 10:00 A.M. to 4:00 P.M., Golden; (303) 279-6565.

Hakushika Sake Tours, Monday through Friday, 10:00 A.M. to 3:00 P.M., Golden; (303) 278-0161.

In Addition

Mountain Lions

The mountain lion (felis concolor)—sometimes called cougar, panther, or puma—is one of North America's biggest cats and inhabits much of Colorado, including the Front Range, residing in areas of piñon pine, juniper, mountain mahogany, ponderosa pine, and oak brush. For this reason, it's not uncommon to see mountain lion warning signs at many mountain bike trailheads. Although encounters are rare, due to the big cat's calm, quiet, and elusive nature, they are on the rise as a consequence, in part, of increased mountain biking in lion habitat. In fact, a standoff involving a mountain lion and a mountain biker occurred on October 22, 1997, at one of Boulder County's most popular mountain biking areas, Walker Ranch.

Varying from 7 to 8 feet in length and 90 to 150 pounds, the mountain lion is much larger than other wild cat species in Colorado. According to wildlife experts, a mountain biker may run a higher-than-normal risk of being attacked. A mountain biker's lowered head posture may spark a lion's curiosity. Also, to a lion, a mountain biker riding through the forest may look like fleeing prey, stimulating its predatory attack response. When bicycling in mountain lion habitat, keep the following suggestions in mind:

- Ride in groups
- Make noise during times of prime mountain lion activity—dawn and dusk.

If you should encounter a mountain lion:

- Never approach a lion, but keep your bicycle between yourself and the lion.
- Stay calm. Speak calmly but firmly to the animal.
- Back away from the lion slowly, facing the lion and standing upright. Do not turn and run and chance stimulating the lion's predatory instincts.
- Make yourself larger in appearance: raise your arms, open your jacket if you're wearing one.
- If the lion becomes aggressive, throw stones or branches, trying not to crouch down too often or turn your back.
- If the lion attacks, fight back and avoid falling to the ground.

To report mountain lion sightings or encounters, immediately contact the Colorado Division of Wildlife. Their hours are Monday to Friday, 8:00 A.M. to 5:00 P.M. Here are the regional offices:

Northeast Region and Denver
Service Center
6060 Broadway
Denver, CO 80216
(303) 291–7230

West Region and Grand Junction
Service Center
711 Independent Avenue
Grand Junction, CO 81505
(970) 248–7175

Southeast Region and Colorado Springs Service Center
2126 North Weber Street
Colorado Springs, CO 80907
(719) 473–2945

For more information on mountain lions, refer to Harley G. Shaw's excellent book
Soul Among Lions: The Cougar as Peaceful Adversary, 1989, Johnson Books, Boulder CO; or Sandra Chisholm Robinson's *The Wonder Series: Mountain Lion, a Story and Activities,* Denver Museum of Natural History.

41 The Hogback: Dakota Ridge and Red Rocks Trail

The Hogback is a popular mountain bike ride within easy reach of Denver or Golden. From its highest points, you can see stunning views of Red Rocks Amphitheater. The ride demands sound legs and technical skills. With some of the most technically challenging terrain in the Front Range, the Hogback is not for the faint of heart. Its rocky drop-offs and narrow singletrack, tightening atop a steep ridge of tilted strata, have left many cyclists crying "mommy." Once you descend from the hogback, the ride continues within Red Rocks Park and among its beautiful sanguine rocks.

Start: From the Village Walk parking lot in Matthews/Winters Park.
Length: 6.5-mile loop.
Approximate riding time: Advanced riders, 1 hour; intermediate riders, 2 hours.
Technical difficulty: Technically moderate to challenging due to steep, sandy drop-offs and climbs.
Physical difficulty: Physically moderate to challenging due to some short but steep climbs.
Terrain: Singletrack, dirt road, and paved highway. The terrain is very rocky and sandy in spots. This is a good early season ride, as it tends to get too sandy after long dry spells. Not recommended as an autumn ride.

Trail contacts: Jefferson County Open Space, 700 Jefferson County Parkway, Suite 100, Golden, 80401; (303) 271-5925, trails hotline (303) 271-5975; openspace.jeffco.us.
Schedule: April to November.
Maps: USGS maps: Morrison; Matthews/Winters Park Map, Jefferson County Open Space.
Nearest town: Golden.
Other trail users: Hikers, concert-goers, and picnickers.
Canine compatibility: Dog friendly, but watch out for the rattlesnakes, and dogs must be on a leash at all times.

Getting There

From Denver: Head west on I-70 to exit 259, following signs to Morrison. Exit at 259 and turn left, driving under I-70. Now on Colorado Highway 26, turn right into Matthews/Winters Park, marked by a brown sign on the right side of the road. Park in the Village Walk parking lot. *DeLorme: Colorado Atlas & Gazetteer:* Page 40, C-1.

The Ride

Dakota Ridge is part of the Dakota Group, a 14-mile-long ridge of steeply sloping, tilted strata—otherwise known as a "hogback." The ridge extends from Golden to Roxborough Park and is composed of Lower Cretaceous rock units. Formed roughly sixty-six million years ago, the Hogback is the result of the upward thrust of the Rocky Mountains' Front Range. Due to the abundance of Jurassic dinosaur

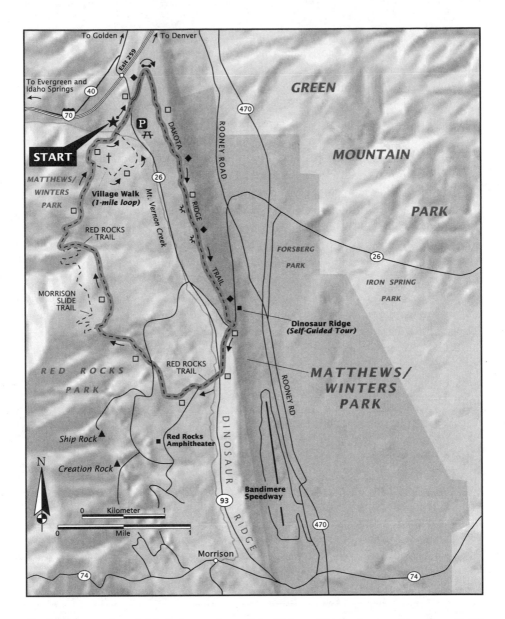

fossils this area has yielded, the section of the Dakota Hogback stretching from I–70 to the town of Morrison has been renamed "Dinosaur Ridge" and is a geologically famous national landmark.

Dinosaur discoveries near Morrison date back to as early as 1877 when Arthur Lakes, a part-time professor at what later became the Colorado School of Mines, found a stegosaurus vertebra with a 33-inch circumference. Aside from offering up the first dinosaur fossils found in the western United States, many of the discoveries near Morrison were the first of their kind.

With fossilized remains of Jurassic dinosaurs, millions of years old, tucked in its geological folds, the Hogback invites the mountain biker not with the terrors of a Jurassic Park but with a subtlety that whispers the secrets of the ages. Riders begin their journey with an instant lung-buster to the top of the Hogback and onto Dakota Ridge Trail. From this knifelike ridge, sweeping views of the High Plains lie to the east, marked distinctly by Green Mountain and Denver. The Rocky Mountains lie to the west, with Mount Morrison and Red Rocks Park in plain view. The crest is marked by plentiful patches of sand and rock, remnants of a 135-million-year-old sea moving westward across Colorado.

The trail snakes atop the Hogback for roughly 2 miles. Rattlesnakes are occasionally spotted here, though they typically stick to the rock piles and tall grasses that dot Dakota Ridge. It's recommended that riders carry—and know how to use—a snake-bite kit. If you stick to the trails, it's unlikely you'll have an encounter, but better safe than sorry. The southern end of Dakota Ridge Trail delivers some of the trickiest rocky sections found along the entire route. At 2.1 miles there's a rock face embedded in the ground. The line to the left requires deft technical skills, particularly since it cuts sharply to the right along the edge of a big drop-off. The center line is attractive but delivers a strong blow to your front tire, not to mention your ego.

Ride for another mile before entering Red Rocks Park, en route to Red Rocks Trail. The town of Morrison opened the park as "The Garden of the Titans" in 1906. Students studying mythology at nearby Episcopal College imagined the park to be the Titans' playground and attached fitting names to each rock formation.

To the north of the stage of the Red Rocks Amphitheater stands the 400-foot monolith Creation Rock. Facing Creation Rock is Shiprock, so named because it looks like a sinking ship. The formation behind the stage is the Rock of Mnemosyne, named for the Greek goddess of song and memory. Iron oxide deposits, left over from the vast inland sea that once engulfed Red Rocks Park, hardened as the ancient waters receded and are responsible for the many shades of red.

Today, Red Rocks Park is best known for its naturally formed amphitheater. Nestled between two 400-foot-high red sandstone formations, the amphitheater provides near perfect acoustics. The 9,200-seat theater provides concert-goers with

Descending the technically challenging singletrack along the southern end of the Dakota Ridge Trail.

an intimate listening experience—complete with a 30-mile panoramic view of hued plains and the stunning Denver city lights.

Once on Red Rocks Trail, be sure to keep bearing right (north) at all trail crossings. Red Rocks Trail offers rolling hills and mild climbs, mixed with some smooth descents. At 5.8 miles Red Rocks Trail once again intersects with Morrison Slide Trail at Cherry Gulch. Taking Morrison Slide Trail on your left for 1.2 miles adds about 0.5 mile and some more climbing to your route. Continue on Red Rocks Trail until you reach the intersection of the Village Walk. This is a 1-mile loop that will lead you back to your vehicle, whichever way you decide to turn.

Miles and Directions

0.0 START at the Village Walk parking lot in Matthews/Winters Park. Ride back out of the parking lot and cross Colorado Highway 26. Begin ascending the rock- and sand-laden dirt road to the top of Hogback Park.

0.3 Bear right at the gate onto the Dakota Ridge Trail.

0.7 Reach the top of the hogback. I–70 is behind you leading west into the mountains. There are some big drop-offs from here until you reach a killer but short climb.

1.0 Reach the killer but short climb. What makes this climb difficult is its steep pitch coupled with large waterbars strewn across the trail.

2.2 The trail comes to a Y intersection. Hang a left. (By continuing straight, you end up having to duck under a gate to get back onto the main trail.) Ride down the trail with caution. Arrive at a staircase and bear right onto the paved road (Dinosaur Ridge). Ride to where the road curves to the right and cross over the cement barricade to rejoin the trail on your left. Climb briefly and then descend sharply.

3.0 After riding down a fast singletrack, the trail once again lets out onto a paved road (CR 93). Be cautious here and stay in control, as the trail leads you right onto the road. Bear right here again and follow signs for Red Rocks Trail. Cross the paved road and hang an immediate left onto an access road into Red Rocks Park. Pedal for 0.2 mile and bear right onto the singletrack Red Rocks Trail.

4.2 Reach the junction of Morrison Slide Trail and Red Rocks Trail. Bear right here, continuing on Red Rocks Trail.

6.5 Arrive back at the Village Walk parking lot in Matthews/Winters Park.

Ride Information

Local Information
Evergreen Area Chamber of Commerce, P.O. Box 97, Evergreen, 80437; (303) 674-3412; www.evergreenchamber.org.

Local Events and Attractions
Dinosaur Ridge, Morrison; (303) 697-3466; www.dinoridge.org.
Red Rocks Park and Amphitheater; (303) 697-6486; www.red-rocks.com.

Bandimere Speedway, Morrison; (303) 697-6001.

Restaurants
The Fort, Morrison; (303) 697-4771 (specializes in big-game entrees).

Organizations
Friends of Dinosaur Ridge, Morrison; (303) 697-3466 or www.dinoridge.org.

42 Waterton Canyon

Waterton Canyon is a favorite trail among Denver-area residents. Therefore it may be crowded during the weekends. The trail begins on a wide, dirt service road, as it travels through the canyon. Following the South Platte River, this section of the trail offers a mellow cruise, a great family ride. The trail, however, becomes increasingly more difficult, with steeper climbs and moderate switchbacks, as one nears the trailhead and beginning of the 470-mile Colorado Trail. Reaching this junction of the Colorado Trail and the Roxborough Connection, riders continue on the Roxborough Connection. Note: The beginning of the Roxborough Connection is very thick and overgrown, so control your speed. This section of trail offers a screaming singletrack descent, complete with steeps and creek crossings, before letting out into Waterton Canyon.

Start: From the trailhead of the Colorado Trail in Waterton Canyon.

Length: 17.5-mile loop, with options to continue on the Colorado Trail. (Note: If you do decide to continue on the Colorado Trail, special arrangements for your return must be considered, as these routes will not lead you back to your vehicle at the mouth of Waterton Canyon.)

Approximate riding time: Advanced riders, 1.5 hours; intermediate riders, 2 to 2.5 hours.

Technical difficulty: Technically moderate. The first 6 miles offer an easy, scenic ride along the South Platte River on an improved dirt road. The singletrack of the Roxborough Connection offers some tight ascending switchbacks, with sudden tight twists along the trail on the descent.

Physical difficulty: Physically moderate. Although there is no significant elevation gain, there are a number of tough steep climbs.

Terrain: Singletrack, doubletrack, and improved dirt road. The singletrack and doubletrack offer a variety of terrain: sand, rocks, and softened forest growth.

Trail contacts: Pike National Forest, South Platte Ranger District, 19316 Goddard Ranch Court, Morrison, 80465; (303) 275-5610. The Colorado Trail Foundation, American Mountaineering Center, 710 Tenth Street, Golden, 80401; (303) 384-3729, ext. 113.

Schedule: Although Waterton Canyon is open daily from 4:00 A.M. to 9:00 P.M. year-round, riding the Roxborough Connection may only be reasonable between the months of May and October.

Maps: USGS maps: Kassler, Platte Canyon; *Trails Illustrated* map 135, Deckers and Rampart Range; Waterton Canyon Map, Denver Water Department, available at the trailhead or through the U.S. Army Corps of Engineers; (303) 979-4120.

Nearest town: Littleton.

Other trail users: Hikers, equestrians, anglers, campers, and picnickers.

Canine compatibility: Not dog friendly. Dogs are not allowed in the canyon because they may contaminate drinking water, as well as disturb the resident herd of bighorn sheep.

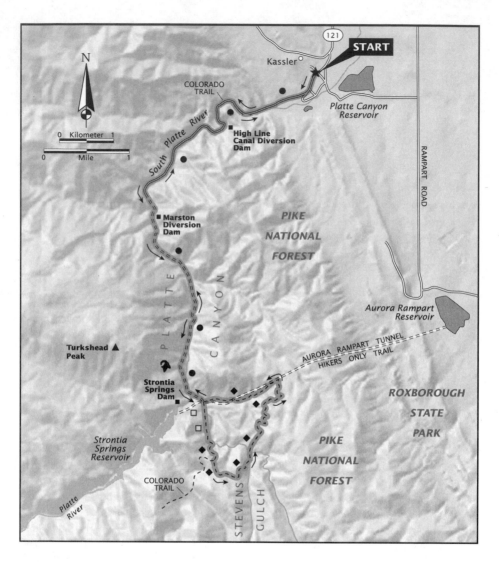

Getting There

From Denver: Take I-25 south to exit 207B. Exit and drive south on U.S. Highway 85, which will Y shortly after exiting I-25; stay to your left. Take US 85 south for 10 miles until you reach C-470. Veer right onto C-470, and head west. Drive west on C-470 for a few miles before exiting at Wadsworth Boulevard, following signs for Waterton Canyon. After exiting at Wadsworth, bear left, driving under C-470 and pick up Colorado Highway 121 south. Drive south on CO 121 for roughly 4.5 miles before turning left into Waterton Canyon State Park. The parking lot will be on your left. *DeLorme: Colorado Atlas & Gazetteer:* Page 50, A-1 to A-2.

The Ride

If you're looking for testament to Denver's metropolis status, you need only look to the Denver Broncos, the Colorado Rockies, the Denver Nuggets, and the Colorado Avalanche, but that wouldn't present the whole picture. Consider the $4.3 billion Denver International Airport, the $76 million refurbished Central Library, and the yearly loss of 90,000 acres of farmland to development, and you've got one hell of a megalopolis. But what distinguishes Denver from other large U.S. cities isn't its sports teams, or even the fact that its airport rests on a site larger than Manhattan, but rather that it's only minutes away from some of the sweetest stretches of single-track in all of Colorado.

The easternmost trailhead of the 470-mile Colorado Trail begins on an improved dirt road in Waterton Canyon. Following the former railroad bed of the Denver, South Park, and Pacific Railroads through Waterton Canyon, the first 6 miles of this route are a mellow cruise along the South Platte River—admittedly, not the most excitingly technical. What the first 6 miles through Waterton Canyon lack in technical challenge, they delivers in natural beauty and historical significance.

On July 6, 1820, Stephen H. Long (remembered in the naming of Longs Peak) led an expedition to the mouth of what is now Waterton Canyon. As a member of the U.S. Engineering Corps, Long was instructed to find the headwaters of the Platte, Arkansas, and Red Rivers. His expedition camped at the site where the South Platte River emerges from the mountains. His camp would become the town of Waterton, and even later the location of the Denver Union Water Company, forbear of the Denver Water Department—the largest water district on the entire Front Range.

The initial 6 miles through Waterton Canyon are a hydrologist's dream. In 1912 the Kassler Treatment Plant, located at the mouth of Waterton Canyon, became the first English slow-sand water filtration plant west of the Mississippi. At the time, the English slow-sand water filtration system was the newest technological advancement in the area of water filtration. Only two other towns could boast being equipped with this latest filtration process: Albany, New York, and Ashland, Wisconsin (on Lake Superior).

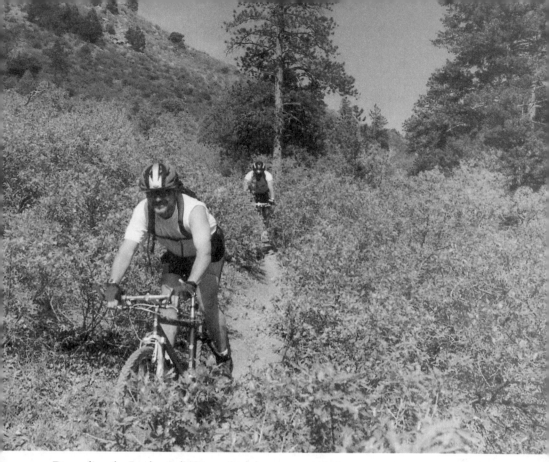

Descending the Roxborough Connection.

The process at the Kassler Treatment Plant involved diverting water from the South Platte River into large beds of sand. These beds can still be seen today. Underneath these sand beds were perforated pipes. The English slow-sand water filtration process allowed for water to flow through the sand and into the pipes. As the water sifted through the sand, debris and sediment would collect on the sand's top layer. Once the filtered water reached the perforated pipes, chlorine would be added, and the water was delivered to Denver as drinking water. From time to time, the top layer of these sand beds would have to be skimmed to keep them clean, a very labor-intensive process. In 1979 the plant became a national Waterworks Landmark. One hundred years earlier, the High Line Canal (just over a mile into the canyon), constructed by an English-Scottish land development company, was supplying irrigation water to plains settlements east of Denver. Marking the start of the High Line Canal, the original rock and timber diversion dam is visible from the trail.

About 3 miles from the trailhead and the mouth of the canyon, the Platte Canyon Intake Dam and the Marston Diversion routes South Platte and Blue River water to Marston Reservoir. At 6.1 miles the Strontia Springs Dam skies 243 feet above the South Platte streambed and diverts water into a 3.4-mile-long tunnel under the mountains to the Foothills Water Treatment Plant. This massive tunnel project, and others like it in Colorado, are necessary because the state only receives 14 inches of annual precipitation. An even larger tunnel (23 miles long and 10 feet wide) connects the South Platte River with a Dillon reservoir. This particular conduit, bored through the Front Range, is one of the world's longest such tunnels.

As you head west from the Strontia Springs Dam, the road begins to climb. Within a mile, the Colorado Trail's singletrack will begin to your left. From here the trail rises out of the canyon to Russell Ridge (6,560 feet). The singletrack to this point offers a moderately challenging climb to the top. Among this section's highlights are smooth singletrack, thick ponderosa pine forests, and switchbacks (which deserve special attention). Intermediate riders can manage the switchbacks with careful balance and control, while advanced riders can spin their way to the top with minimal effort. The last switchback, which breaks right before summiting Russell Ridge, is beset with rocks. Keep spinning, don't forget to smile, and you'll make it with relative ease.

Atop the ridge, the Colorado Trail will continue southwest to Durango. To begin your return on the Waterton Canyon route, you'll have to turn off the Colorado Trail at this point and follow the sign marking Roxborough State Park.

The singletrack of this section of trail is sweet. Thick overgrowth at the section's beginning makes for very narrow and tight paths. The trail weaves its way through cool forests and offers riders a number of screams. One such scream comes at mile 8.2. The singletrack descent is steep and narrow as it hugs the slope of the ridge. For an added element of fear, a tree at this section's bottom welcomes any would-be tree-hugger. The trail winds through forests, over creeks, and through one meadow before delivering another tight spot at 10.8 miles. A rocky and big drop-off invites you to take it down the center.

From here, ride for another mile using "The Force" as you go. The forest once again struggles to engulf the trail and impede visibility. Having finished the Roxborough Loop, the feeling with which one is left is a kind of pleasant amazement: How can such sweet singletrack be so close to a city? Arrive at the road where you started your ride. Bear right and top-ring it back to your vehicle.

Miles and Directions

0.0 START at the parking lot of Waterton Canyon State Park. Ride back out of the parking lot and cross the road. The Colorado Trail sign marks the beginning of the ride into Waterton Canyon. Follow the trail around as it weaves itself onto the improved dirt road and into Waterton Canyon.

2.2 Pass an abandoned mine to your left.

3.3 Reach Marston Diversion Dam.

4.3 Cross Mill Gulch Bridge.

6.1 Reach Strontia Springs Dam and Reservoir. Beware of the bighorn sheep that descend from the tall canyon walls, making their way to the Colorado Trail. A herd of twenty to thirty-five bighorn sheep lives in the canyon, remaining at low elevation all year.

6.3 Reach the junction of the Roxborough Connection and the Colorado Trail. Here is where the loop ends. For now, keep heading west, ascending straight.

6.6 Reach the start of the Colorado Trail singletrack, on the left side of the road. From this point, the maintained dirt road is closed to public use.

8.0 Reach the top of Russell Ridge, the route's high point. At this point, the Colorado Trail continues heading southwest all the way to Durango. Bear left (east) onto the singletrack marked by the Roxborough State Park sign.

10.3 Here the singletrack will T. Bear left and head toward Waterton Canyon. This way will lead you back to the improved dirt road on which you began your ride, just above the Strontia Springs Dam in Waterton Canyon. (Bearing right will lead you to the Roxborough State Park and Visitor Center; however, this section of trail is off limits to bikes.)

11.2 You're back on the improved dirt road of the Colorado Trail in Waterton Canyon. From here, bear right and follow the road back toward the trailhead.

17.5 Return to your vehicle.

Ride Information

Local Information
Colorado Division of Wildlife, Denver; (303) 297-1192.

U.S. Army Corps of Engineers, Omaha District, Tri-Lakes Project Office, Littleton; (303) 979-4120; www.nwo.usace.army.mil.

Town of Morrison, 321 Highway 8, Morrison; town.morrison.co.us.

Local Events and Attractions
Roxborough State Park, Littleton; (303) 973-3959.

Chatfield State Park, Littleton; (303) 791-7275.

Organizations
Chatfield Environmental Education Resource System (CHEERS), a group of agencies within Chatfield Basin that share educational opportunities and deliver recreational resources for residents; contact the Chatfield State Park, Littleton; (303) 791-7275.

43 Kenosha Pass to Georgia Pass

The Kenosha Pass to Georgia Pass ride is mack-daddy. On top of plush terrain and the rich groves of aspen, the trail includes awe-inspiring descents through hillside meadows and dense forests, as well as technical rocky and rooty climbs. Views from the top of Georgia Pass and the Continental Divide are breathtaking, including the entire South Park Valley below. South Park, incidentally, was the inspiration for the quirky fictional town in Comedy Central's popular cartoon series South Park. South Park City, a restored mining town located in South Park, also offers a glimpse into the life of a nineteenth-century Colorado mining town.

Start: From the trailhead for the Colorado Trail atop Kenosha Pass.
Length: 23.8-mile out-and-back.
Approximate riding time: Advanced riders, 3 hours; intermediate riders, 4 hours.
Technical difficulty: Technically moderate to challenging due to the abundance of exposed roots and rocks.
Physical difficulty: Physically moderate to challenging due to the higher elevations at which you're riding.
Terrain: Singletrack and doubletrack. Most of this route rolls over smooth, soft forest earth. There are, however, a few rougher sections of roots and rocks. Aspen and evergreen forests, high-alpine valleys, and mountain passes form the backdrop to this incredible ride.

Trail contacts: Pike National Forest, South Park Ranger District, 320 U.S. Highway 285, P.O. Box 219, Fairplay, 80440; (719) 836-2031.
Colorado Trail Foundation, 710 Tenth Street, Golden, 80401; (303) 384-3729, ext. 113.
Schedule: July to September.
Maps: USGS maps: Jefferson, Boreas Pass; *Trails Illustrated* map 105, Bailey and 109, Breckenridge; Pike National Forest Map.
Nearest town: Fairplay.
Other trail users: Hikers, bikepackers, equestrians, and backpackers.
Canine compatibility: Dog friendly.

Getting There

From Denver: Drive west on U.S. Highway 285, passing through the town of Bailey at approximately 43 miles. Continue for another 19 miles to Kenosha Pass (10,001 feet). Once atop Kenosha Pass, turn right (west) into the Kenosha Pass Campground lot. Park in the designated area marked by Colorado Trail parking signs. Bike into the campground. Drinking water and toilet facilities are available. The Colorado Trail begins just to the left of these facilities. *DeLorme: Colorado Atlas & Gazetteer:* Page 49, A-4.

The Ride

Situated at the western end of the Pike National Forest, the trail begins atop 10,001-foot Kenosha Pass and continues to 11,585-foot Georgia Pass, on the Continental

Divide. Green and gold Q-tipped aspens crowd the trail along its westerly route like bristles in a mountainous brush, lending a special quality found only in Colorado's highest places.

As home to this kind of Colorado quality, it's fitting that the Pike National Forest should enjoy the respectable history it does. After the private Front Range timber stores were savagely depleted for the mining and railroad industries in the late 1800s, cutters turned to scouring public lands to obtain their valuable timber. As a result, large tracts of public forestland were rubbed out along the Front Range. In response to growing concerns for Colorado's depleting natural resources, Congress passed an act in 1891 delegating President Benjamin Harrison the authority to create timber reserves. These reserves, forebears to our national forests, were large tracts of forestland that were set aside and protected from further depletion.

In 1892 the Plum Creek, South Platte, and Pikes Peak reserves southwest of Denver were among Colorado's earliest timber reserves. In August 1898, William Kreutzer was appointed ranger for the Plum Creek Reserve, making him the first U.S. Forest Ranger. As one might expect, the early years of Kreutzer's appointment were beset by timber bootleggers, scalpers, and poachers—often calling for dangerous confrontations with Kreutzer himself. Overcoming these corrupting pressures, Kreutzer stayed true to his duties as Forest Ranger and eventually moved on to become supervisor for all of Colorado's national forests.

Comprising the Plum Creek, South Platte, and Pikes Peak Reserves, the Pikes Peak Forest Reserve was created in 1905. Later that year, the Department of Agriculture and the newly formed Forest Service took over as managers of the reserve. As part of President Theodore Roosevelt's conservation program, Pikes Peak Forest Reserve was designated the Pike National Forest in 1907. Now under management of the Forest Service, the Pike National Forest expanded its services to include the preservation of all natural resources, not just timber. Today, the Pike National Forest contains a whopping 1,106,604 acres.

The first mile of the trail climbs moderately over very smooth terrain. Riders are caught between a feeling of peaceful quietude descending from the thick canopy above and the snap, crackle, and pop of a tire's first meeting with a fallen pine needle below. The first technical section arrives within the first 2 miles. After descending very rapidly through a meadow and into an aspen grove, the trail switches back sharply to the left and over a group of large rocks, adding a nice wake-up call to the drowsily smooth singletrack. After roughly 2.4 miles, the singletrack exits the forest and opens up onto a hillside meadow awash with wildflowers. In view are the Continental Divide and Mount Guyot (13,370 feet), both straight ahead. Georgia Pass (11,585 feet) lies to the northwest, while the entire South Park Valley opens to the south.

South Park is an expansive 900-square-mile flat and open valley surrounded by rolling mountains. After gold was discovered here in 1859, eager prospectors flocked to South Park in droves. Within months, the unblemished valley floor became freckled with the mining camps of Tarryall, Leavick, Eureka, and Buckskin Joe. With increased development and trade, these rough-and-tumble mining camps metamorphosed into flourishing communities until all the gold was gone. With no gold to dig, miners found little reason to stay, and the mining camps, in turn, crumbled. These camps and the spirit that fueled their development had all but been forgotten until 1957 when a remarkable restoration of these early buildings took shape in what was to become South Park City.

Completed in 1959 and including thirty-four original buildings housing over 60,000 artifacts collected from historic area mining camps, South Park City stands as an accurate representation of a late 1880s South Park mining camp. The year also marked the centennial anniversary of Colorado's first gold rush. The restored mining camp of South Park City features the industries that made life in nineteenth-century Colorado livable. This re-creation of a Colorado boomtown invites you to take a step back in time and listen for the slightly out-of-tune piano heard from Rache's Place. Farther up the street you'll notice the Simpkins General Store, the

Returning from lightning strikes on Georgia Pass.

Garo School, and Merriam's City Drug Store. Complete with all the early-day tinctures, remedies, and poultices, Merriam's may provide temporary relief from the pains of climbing to Georgia Pass.

After crossing Deadman Creek, the trail becomes very narrow as it runs its course over large exposed roots. As you begin the last 6-mile push to Georgia Pass, the route climbs steadily. Upon reaching Forest Road 400, bear left and pedal to Georgia Pass. The descent from Georgia Pass to Jefferson Creek Road is fast and rocky. After crossing Deadman Creek for the second time, begin a tough climb through the meadow to the gate. From the gate, it's a fast and smooth descent through clustered aspens to the floor of South Park.

The final 1.5 miles to Kenosha Pass and your vehicle are perhaps the most exhilarating. Smooth-running singletrack through quiet stands of aspen and pine offers the weary rider a certain peace-in-motion. The trail's narrow width, its smooth-running course, and the close-standing trunks of pine and aspen offer the rider inclusion in the forest's high society. Riders silently track their tires into the soft belly of the earth, revealing unto no one but themselves and the surrounding forest the simple pleasures shared by two.

Miles and Directions

0.0 START at the Trail 1776 (the Colorado Trail) Trailhead atop Kenosha Pass. Begin riding through serene groves of aspen and pine on smooth and hard-packed singletrack.

2.5 Cross Guernsey Creek and continue riding on the singletrack into a turnpiked section of the trail.

4.3 Cross Deadman Creek and continue riding in a westerly direction, negotiating through a tough root singletrack section, as it winds its way up a hillside marked by a miniature forest of pine saplings.

5.1 Pass through a gate, closing it behind you, and continue riding through a moderately technical rocky singletrack section.

5.8 After closing the gate behind you, descend through lush forests of pine and aspen before arriving at Forest Road 401 (Jefferson Creek Road). Cross FR 401 and Jefferson Creek, continuing on the Colorado Trail to Georgia Pass. Just after crossing Jefferson Creek, ride to where the singletrack intersects with a doubletrack. Bear right onto this doubletrack, following signs for the Colorado Trail and Georgia Pass. Roughly 0.1 mile from where you picked up this doubletrack, notice the continuation of the Colorado Trail singletrack bearing left into the pine forest. Another sign on the right reads WEST JEFFERSON TRAIL 643, JEFFERSON CREEK CAMPGROUND, and GEORGIA PASS VIA TRAIL 643. Following signs for the Colorado Trail and Georgia Pass, veering left onto the singletrack. At this point, you're about 6 miles from Georgia Pass.

7.7 The Colorado Trail intersects with Michigan Creek Road Trail. Continue on the Colorado Trail in a northerly direction, passing Michigan Creek Road Trail on your left (west).

10.5 Near the timberline, with views of Mount Guyot and Bald Mountain immediately to your left. Continue climbing over tundralike terrain to Georgia Pass. Since the area is treeless, cairns mark the way of travel.

11.9 Arrive at FR 400. Bear left and ride to the top of Georgia Pass. Turn around here and retrace your tracks back to your vehicle.

23.8 Arrive back at your vehicle.

Ride Information

Local Information

Park County Tourism Office, Fairplay; (719) 836-4279 or www.idirect.com/~showcase.

Local Events and Attractions

South Park City Museum, Fairplay; (719) 836-2387.

Forest Service Mountain Bike Trails, Fairplay; (719) 836-4279.

Fairplay Beach Recreation Area, Fairplay; (719) 836-4279.

44 Baldy Trail to Gashouse Gulch Trail

The Buffalo Creek Mountain Bike Area includes a network of outstanding single-track within an hour's drive of Denver. Most of the riding rolls through thick forests over smooth and tacky singletrack. Some sandy sections appear along the way, but they don't last long. Charred trees mark the path of a forest fire that devastated much of this area. Despite the burn scars, the Buffalo Creek Mountain Bike Area remains a mountain biker's playground. A variety of campsites dot the region in case you want to turn your day ride into an overnighter.

Start: From the junction of Forest Road 550 and FR 543.
Length: 7.7-mile loop, with options to connect to a host of other singletrack trails.
Approximate riding time: Advanced riders, 45 to 60 minutes; intermediate riders, 1.5 hours.
Technical difficulty: Technically easy to moderate due to occasional sandy and rocky sections.
Physical difficulty: Physically easy to moderate due to short mileage and some moderate climbing.
Terrain: Improved dirt roads, doubletrack, and singletrack. Consists of mostly smooth-running singletrack, but there are a number of sandy patches, particularly at the route's onset. Two small rocky sections along the Gashouse Gulch Trail offer a challenge.
Trail contacts: Pike National Forest, South Platte Ranger District, Morrison; (303) 275-5610.
Colorado Trail Foundation, 710 Tenth Street, Golden, 80401; (303) 384-3729 ext. 113.
Schedule: May to October.
Maps: USGS maps: Green Mountain; *Trails Illustrated:* map 135, Deckers and Rampart Range.
Nearest town: Buffalo Creek.
Other trail users: Hikers, campers, anglers, and picnickers.
Canine compatibility: Dog friendly.

Getting There

From Denver: Take U.S. Highway 285 west to Pine Junction. At the light in Pine Junction make a left onto Pine Valley Road and go 13.9 miles. Turn right onto Forest Road 550, roughly 4 miles past the town of Buffalo Creek, and travel another 5 miles before parking your vehicle at the junction of FR 550 and FR 543. Park your vehicle on the right side, alongside Buffalo Creek. There is additional parking at the nearby Meadows Group Campground. The route begins on FR 543 after crossing Buffalo Creek. *DeLorme: Colorado Atlas & Gazetteer:* Page 49, B-7.

The Ride

Just 30 miles southwest of Denver lies a mini metro–mountain biking mecca. Commonly referred to as the "Buffalo Creek Mountain Bike Area," this part of the Pike National Forest provides a vast network of fine singletrack. Along with being one of several put-ins for the 470-mile Colorado Trail, the Buffalo Creek Mountain Bike

Area is also home to Baldy and Gashouse Gulch Trails. Acclaimed for its smooth and negotiable singletrack, the 7.7-mile Baldy to Gashouse Gulch route provides as much satisfying sweetness as a short stack of flapjacks on a breezy camper's morning.

The route begins with a fast and cool descent on FR 543, following Buffalo Creek downstream. After a mile, you come upon the chilling remains of a once thriving forest. Thrown from your mountain biking reverie, the bitter reality of nature's destructive and regenerative forces is brought immediately to bear. Before you lie the charred remains of the 1996 Buffalo Creek forest fire.

On Saturday, May 18, 1996, a campfire left for dead atop Gashouse Gulch turned itself into a wind-whipped wildfire. Within hours, the flames had grown from the confines of a rock-lined fire pit to a 10,000-acre furnace. Ten miles long and 2 miles wide, the fire raged for five days and destroyed 12,000 acres at a cost of $2.8 million. The effects of such an inferno take on a whole new reality after one enters into its devastating path. Beginning at 1.5 miles, Baldy Trail weaves its singletrack course in between the standing corpses of ponderosa pine. As Baldy Trail scratches its sandy way to higher ground, staccato islands of roundleaf bluebell (campanula rotundifo-lia) and mullein (verbascum thapsus) reaffirm nature's recuperative powers.

Portions of this route's 7.7 miles remain remarkably unscathed by fire and are full of life. About 2 miles into the ride, the trail enters into a wonderful ponderosa pine forest and climbs gradually. The singletrack narrows, and the forest through which you're riding widens a bit. The trees here seem taller and less crowded—a welcomed contrast to the soot-caked skeletons that introduced your ride.

As you near the summit and the junction of Baldy and Gashouse Gulch Trails, the singletrack exits the forest and enters onto a huge rock face. Pushing its way into overlying metamorphic rocks, this granite batholith remains as a tremendous intru-sion of molten magma. Continue your fire-ride by scaling this formerly molten magma and then veer to the left. By 3.7 miles the forest has been overtaken by boul-ders. A natural grotto to your left provides a dry respite from the area's sudden and regular thunderstorms.

From this point, the trail takes you over grassy knolls and through meadows and flat-surfaced forests before exiting to Gashouse Gulch Trail. Beginning as a dirt road, Gashouse Gulch Trail eventually disintegrates into a rough-looking doubletrack before connecting to a singletrack trail leading off to the left. The Gashouse Gulch singletrack offers fast descents, tight switchbacks, creek crossings, and one very tech-nical rocky section at 5.8 miles. Riders can choose to complete the loop where the Baldy Trail singletrack begins, but this description foregoes part of that connection because of the many non-negotiable blowdowns that litter the trail. Instead, proceed to the Gashouse Gulch Trailhead, pass through its wooden gate, and enjoy a fast ride on the road to FR 550, hitting as many jumps as possible. From there, FR 550 takes you back to your vehicle.

Miles and Directions

0.0 START from the gate at Forest Road 543. Go under the gate and begin your ride, with Buf-falo Creek to your right. A beautiful alpine log home sits to your left. Fashioned after the Euro-style log homes of old, this private residence backs up to a collection of enormous rocks.

0.4 Go around another gate and cross Buffalo Creek a second time.

Riding through the remains of the Buffalo Creek fire.

1.3 Arrive at the sandy bottom. A revegetation project along the banks of Buffalo Creek is to your left. Approximately 50 yards past this project, still following FR 543 downstream, is a large sandy area to your left. Strewn across this area are four large rocks imbedded in the sand. Veer left off FR 543, riding between these rocks. Continue through the sand and head into the burned forest. The singletrack begins to your left shortly thereafter, marked by the Gashouse Gulch Trail sign.

1.5 Reach the junction of Gashouse Gulch and Baldy Trails. Veer right onto Baldy Trail.

2.3 A fallen pine tree obstructs the trail. Carefully walk your bike under it and continue your ride. Be aware of blowdowns.

3.7 Cross a wire gate. The area here is distinct for its large rock formations—a great place to mix bouldering with your day of riding. If you scurry to the tops of the boulders to your right, you'll be treated to a killer view of Baldy Peak.

4.5 Reach the junction of Gashouse Gulch and Baldy Trails. Gashouse Gulch leads both to the right and to the left. Take the left route. At this point the trail becomes a rough-looking dirt road.

5.1 The rough doubletrack/dirt road intersects with a singletrack veering off to the left. Veer left onto this singletrack.

6.1 Cross another wire fence.

6.8 Arrive at FR 550, veer left, and cross the cattle guard at 6.9 miles.

7.2 Forest Road 550 intersects with FR 543 to your right. Bear left and continue on FR 550.

7.7 Arrive at your vehicle.

Ride Information

Local Information

Conifer Area Chamber of Commerce, 26437 Conifer Road, P.O. Box 127, Conifer, 80433; (303) 838-0178; www.coniferchamber.com.

Local Events and Attractions

Colorado Trail, 470-mile trail from Denver to Durango.

Restaurants

Coney Dog Stand, Conifer; (303) 838-4210.

45 Jackson Creek Loop

Jackson Creek Loop is a mellow ride through some of metro Denver's most remote woodlands and mountains. Combining relatively easy road ascents, ridge rides of touring ease, fast and furious descents, and steady climbs through mountain-flanked canyons, this route offers the most bang for your buck. The descent toward Watson Park and Jackson Creek is a blast, delivering sandy sections, rooty sections, and a number of dips, while the climb from Jackson Creek to your car will have you churning your pedals. For those packing a lunch, the optional out-and-back spur will lead you to Watson Park, a great place for a picnic. Should your visit to Jackson Creek include camping, this ride passes Jackson Creek Campground at 11.2 miles.

Start: From the junction of Rampart Range Road (Forest Road 300) and Jackson Creek Road (Forest Road 502). Begin your ride from the PIKE NATIONAL FOREST: JACKSON CREEK CAMP-GROUND sign and ascend Rampart Range Road.
Length: 12.8-mile loop (with many options to explore a vast network of fire roads).
Approximate riding time: Advanced riders, 1 hour; intermediate riders, 1.5 to 2 hours.
Technical difficulty: Technically easy, due to the well-maintained forest road. There are some sandy and rooty sections, but none that are overly technical.
Physical difficulty: Physically easy to moderate. Although there is little elevation gain, the last half-mile climb to your vehicle is relatively tough.

Terrain: Forest Service and jeep roads, which are typically smooth; however, some sections include sand, roots, and larger rocks, along with a variety of dips and washouts.
Trail contacts: Pike National Forest, South Platte Ranger District, 19316 Goddard Ranch Court, Morrison; (303) 275-5610.
Schedule: April to November.
Maps: USGS maps: Devil's Head, Dakan Mountain; *Trails Illustrated* map 135, Deckers, and Rampart Range.
Nearest town: Sedalia.
Other trail users: Hikers, campers, motorcyclists, and equestrians.
Canine compatibility: Dog friendly.

Getting There

From Denver: Drive south on I-25 to exit 183 and connect with U.S. Highway 85. Drive north on U.S. Highway 85 for roughly 7 miles before turning left onto Colorado Highway 67 west in Sedalia. After about a mile, turn left onto CO 105 south. Colorado Highway 105 turns into Perry Park Road. At 28.5 miles, turn right onto Jackson Creek Road (County Road 38). After 2 miles, Jackson Creek Road will turn to dirt. At 33 miles the road forks. Head right, continuing on Jackson Creek Road. Drive 4.5 miles from the fork and come to a stop sign, where Jackson Creek Road merges with Rampart Range Road. Veer left, continuing on Rampart Range Road. At 40.3 miles, come to a three-sided wooden sign in the middle of the road. Bear right, following signs to Woodland Park. At 45.1 miles, arrive at the junction of Rampart Range Road (FR 300) and Jackson Creek Road (FR 502). Park your vehicle behind the PIKE NATIONAL FOREST: JACKSON CREEK CAMPGROUND sign. *DeLorme: Colorado Atlas & Gazetteer:* Page 50, C-2.

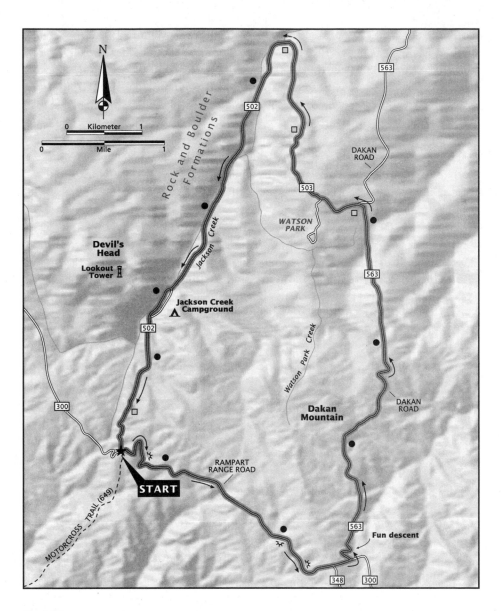

The Ride

You'll want to ride Jackson Creek Loop more for what it is not than for what it actually is. What it is not is overpopulated or technically frustrating or physically demanding—making it a purely enjoyable ride for those who simply want to spend the day spinning in one of Colorado's hidden treasures. A ride the whole family can enjoy, Jackson Creek Loop offers the perfect mellow, out-of-town ride. Bear in mind, however, that this area is also popular with motorized vehicles during the weekend, particularly motorcycles.

From the trailhead parking, you begin the route by climbing the moderately pitched Rampart Range Road. This road was built by the now defunct Civil Conservation Corps (CCC) in the 1930s, during America's Great Depression. Part of President Franklin Roosevelt's New Deal project to jumpstart the American economy, the CCC provided employment for out-of-work, physically fit, unmarried men between the ages of eighteen and twenty-five. The bivouacking workers each received a weekly salary of $30.00, $25.00 of which had to be sent home to family members. All told, the corps constructed 41,000 bridges, 3,982,000 dams, and 44,475 buildings in thirty-one states. By building shelter beds, fire lanes, trails, and rural roads, the CCC enabled three times the number of visitors to visit the state parks in 1936.

Much like the Appalachian Trail and the Pacific Crest Trail, Rampart Range Road remains a symbol of the old "pull-yourself-up-by-the-bootstraps" work ethic. A monument to its builders who camped along its 60 miles and braved the mountain elements, Rampart Range Road is still in use today and invites mountain bikers to choose the road less traveled. Dotting much of the road are the CCC's original handmade rail fences. The route along Rampart Range Road continues for 2.7 miles before intersecting Forest Road 563 (Dakan Road).

Veer left onto FR 563 and begin a fast 0.5-mile descent. The route eventually climbs through a densely populated lodgepole pine forest. If you're looking for a brief respite from the thick forest travel, the route passes areas with views of Castle Rock and the Front Range high plains to the east. From this point (about 4 to 4.5 miles) the trail descends again. Here you're offered a chance to practice your bunny-hop, as a number of "whoop-di-doos" cross your path.

After 6.5 miles, FR 563 intersects FR 503. Veer left onto FR 503. This section of the Jackson Creek Loop is the steepest part of the entire route. Luckily, it's all downhill. Forest Road 503 does have some thick, sandy sections, so take care at warp speeds. At 7.0 miles, FR 503 comes to a Y. (Veering left here and riding for 0.5 mile will deliver you to Watson Park, an idyllic picnicking point.) Jackson Creek Loop, however, continues to the right as it drops to Jackson Creek. After you cross Jackson Creek, veer left onto Jackson Creek Road (FR 502) and follow the creek upstream.

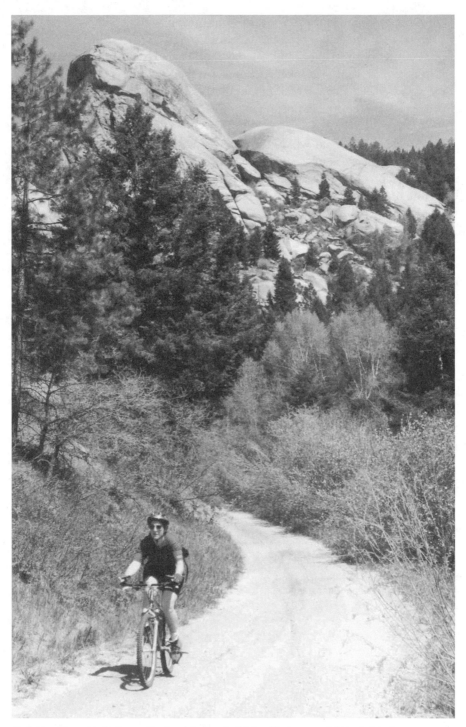

Pedaling alongside Jackson Creek with wonderful bouldering possibilities behind.

This section of the loop follows through a canyon with ghoulish-looking rock formations to your right, the most prominent of which takes its name and its image from the master of the netherworld. The hike to Devil's Head Mountain via Devil's Head Trail is a great one, but bikes are not allowed on the trail. The 1.25-mile hike is moderately challenging. Once at the summit, scale the steps to the top of the fire lookout tower and breathe in one of Colorado's best panoramic views of the Front Range.

Devil's Head Mountain will be to your right after passing the Jackson Creek Campground. Since a number of motorcycle trails run through this area, it offers campers a wide selection of trails and roads on which to mountain bike. From the campground, FR 502 begins to gradually ascend, with the last 0.5 mile being a bit of a grunt. While the most physically challenging section of this ride arrives toward the very end, it won't leave you regretting having ridden the otherwise mellow Jackson Creek Loop.

Miles and Directions

0.0 START at the junction of Jackson Creek Road (FR 502) and Rampart Range Road (FR 300). The route begins as a gradual ascent along Rampart Range Road.

2.5 Forest Road 300 meets with FR 348. Ride straight ahead on FR 300, climbing the short hill in front of you.

2.7 Reach the junction of FR 300 and FR 563. Turn left onto FR 563.

6.5 Reach the junction of FR 563 and FR 503. Turn left onto FR 503.

8.6 Reach the junction of FR 503 and FR 502 (Jackson Creek Road). Veer left onto FR 502.

11.2 Jackson Creek Campground is to your left. Continue riding upstream.

12.8 Arrive at your vehicle.

Ride Information

Local Events and Attractions

Devil's Head Tower and Trail—Backtrack 4.8 miles on Rampart Range Road from where you parked your car. Bear right at the three-sided wooden sign in the middle of the road and head toward Devil's Head Campground and Trailhead.

46 Rampart Reservoir Shoreline Loop

The Rampart Reservoir Shoreline Loop offers mountain bikers of any ability the chance to test their skills on a variety of terrain. From sand to gravel to rocks and soft forest earth, the loop delivers it all. Within a stone's throw of the reservoir and under the watchful eye of Pikes Peak, this trail follows the shoreline all the way around, providing opportunities for fishing access and picnicking. A favorite among locals, the Rampart Reservoir Shoreline Loop can get crowded on the weekends. It's best that mountain bikers ride the trail in a clockwise direction, so as not to come upon riders unexpectedly around the many tight and rocky curves.

Start: From the Rampart Reservoir Shoreline Loop Trailhead.
Length: 15.3-mile loop.
Approximate riding time: Advanced riders, 1.5 hours; intermediate riders, 2 to 2.5 hours.
Technical difficulty: Technically moderate to difficult due to a few tight rocky sections.
Physical difficulty: Physically moderate, due to a modest elevation gain.
Terrain: Improved dirt road and singletrack. The singletrack is covered in Pikes Peak granite (pebble-like rocks that absorb water), which keeps the trails in good shape during wet weather. These rocks are like ball bearings under your tires, making it tough to get out of steeper climbs.

Trail contacts: Pikes Peak Ranger District, 601 South Weber Street, Colorado Springs, 80903; (719) 636-1602.
Schedule: April to November.
Maps: USGS maps: Woodland Park, Cascade; *Trails Illustrated* map 137, Pikes Peak and Canon City; Team Telecycle map; Selected Colorado Hiking Trails: Pikes Peak Series.
Nearest town: Woodland Park.
Other trail users: Hikers, anglers, picnickers, boaters, equestrians, campers, and ski-tour groups.
Canine compatibility: Dog friendly.

Getting There

From Colorado Springs: Take I-25 to exit 141. After exiting, head west on U.S. Highway 24 to Woodland Park. Drive west on US 24 for 17.8 miles before reaching the WELCOME TO WOODLAND PARK sign on your right. Turn right onto Baldwin Road, which takes you behind McDonald's. Passing the Woodland Park High School on your right, Baldwin Road becomes Rampart Range Road. After 2.9 miles from when you turned onto Baldwin Road, Rampart Range Road forks. Take the right fork and then turn right again onto the dirt road and the continuation of Rampart Range Road at 4.4 miles, following signs to the reservoir. After 6.8 miles (from when you turned onto Baldwin Road), the trailhead appears on your left side. Pull into the lot for the Rampart Reservoir Shoreline Loop and begin your ride beyond the wooden gate. *DeLorme: Colorado Atlas & Gazetteer:* Page 62, A-3.

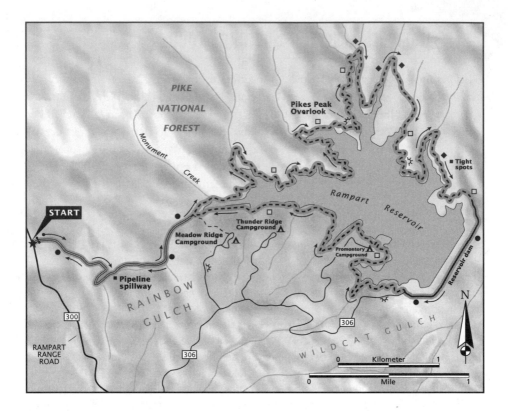

The Ride

Due in large part to the eye-catching pink granite pebbles blanketing this trail's 12-mile stretch of singletrack, the Rampart Reservoir Shoreline Loop is a popular mountain biking ride among Colorado Springs riders. This trail's singletrack is made of the same stuff as Pikes Peak—namely, Pikes Peak granite. The rock consists of interlocking crystals of glasslike quartz, flat-surfaced white and pink feldspar, and a dash of black flaky mica. For those mountain bikers with a less than roadside knowledge of geology, the presence of these cute pink pebbles on the trail requires a more practical interpretation.

Pikes Peak granite absorbs a great deal of water. For this reason, the Rampart Reservoir Loop sheds water easily, keeping the trail dry and in good shape, even after the wettest of weather. This feature allows the loop to remain active nearly twice the measly three-month, prime-time window Colorado typically affords mountain bikers. But Pikes Peak granite isn't necessarily always working in the mountain biker's best interest.

Its pebbly form acts as a kind of geological ball bearing. A collection of these pesky pink pebbles can throw even sequoia-like limbs into a tizzy. With the Rampart Reservoir's many roller coaster dips, up and around protruding boulders, and in and out of a variety of creek beds, the Pikes Peak granite singletrack does make for a physically challenging ride.

The ride begins at the Rampart Reservoir Shoreline Loop Trailhead. As you cross the wooden gate, the trail begins with a fast, easterly 1.5-mile run through stands of quaking aspen to the pipeline spillway and the bridge. Bear left and continue on the north side of the spillway. Now on your right side, the spillway brings water from mountain runoff to Rampart Reservoir.

After 4 miles, you cross a creek and confront huge granite formations along the banks of the reservoir. For all you lounge lizards, here's a great place to take your rest and bask in pleasant warmth. Just beyond these rocks is a thick evergreen forest, complete with coiling roots and moist earth. This section quickly fades as the trail dries and leads into a tricky rocky section before offering a beautiful view of Pikes Peak. Part of the Rampart Reservoir Loop's appeal is its flirtatious skirting around huge boulders and through tight rocky sections. Pick your lines carefully and watch the noggin.

At 8.4 miles the trail leads to what local riders call "The Dip." Large boulders lie in front of you as the trail descends to meet the banks of the reservoir. When the water is high, you'll have to take the left spur of the singletrack, traversing up and over these rocks. If the water level is low, after carefully negotiating the tight rocky section just before these boulders, lift your bicycle and scramble over the rocks to rejoin the trail above. Just beyond this section is the Triple Squeeze: three tight rocky sections that are very technical but can be done. These tight rocky sections keep you honest on a trail as user-friendly as this. Once you reach the dam, absorbing views of Pikes Peak await. Be careful here, as vehicles readily use this road.

As a holding tank, Rampart Reservoir supplies Colorado Springs with water via a 12-foot-wide tunnel. A Swedish engineering firm bored Rampart Reservoir's shaft and its connecting tunnel. They bet city planners that the shaft and the tunnel would connect within one inch of spec. The Swedes hit it right on the nose, an impressive display of engineering acuity if you consider the 20 miles the tunnel had to travel.

After rejoining the Rampart Reservoir singletrack just beyond the Wildcat Wayside Pike National Forest sign, continue through the ponderosa pine forest. Cross a stone culvert before arriving at Picnic Peninsula, a picnic area offering tables, water spigots, and shoreline views. Continue on the singletrack, veering right as it passes in front of the picnic table with the large boulder backdrop. This area contains many offshoots from the main trail. Know that the shoreline loop generally runs the course of the land contour through here. Passing through Picnic Peninsula, you're rewarded with a fast and smooth singletrack descent to the bridge. Veer left by the bridge and return to your vehicle.

Miles and Directions

0.0 START at the trailhead located to the left of the parking lot. Go through the wooden gate and begin riding on the fast-descending Rampart Reservoir Shoreline Road to the spillway.

0.7 Reach the spillway and bear left over it. The trail continues after crossing the pipeline spillway. Continue riding downstream, now with the spillway on your right.

1.5 Reach a footbridge. This footbridge also marks the end of the loop. Pass the bridge and keep heading straight—we're going clockwise. **Option:** You have the option of riding the trail in a clockwise or counterclockwise direction. But there are three good reasons to ride the trail clockwise. 1. Logic and courtesy dictate that you travel in a clockwise direction, so as to avoid colliding with other trail users around the many blind curves. 2. It's more ridable in a clockwise direction. 3. Your drive train will usually be hanging downhill if ridden in a clockwise direction, minimizing the chances of damaging it.

1.7 The singletrack begins.

2.3 Reach a marshy area. Cross this marshy area via footbridge.

5.4 Encounter a technical, rocky section. The middle line offers the best results. Since this trail does have some tight rocky sections, pick your lines carefully.

6.3 Beautiful place to take your rest and take in the view of Pikes Peak.

6.8 The trail divides here, leading into another marshy, forested area. The tendency is to follow the trail to the left, which will soon thereafter lead into a meadow, ultimately coming to a dead end. Instead, bear right, scouting out the trail and cross the creek.

8.4 Reach The Dip. Here a rock wall blocks immediate passage. You'll have to portage your bicycle up and around this wall.

9.7 Reach the dam. Cross the dam and pick up the singletrack on the other side.

10.4 Come to the Wildcat Wayside sign (Pike National Forest). The singletrack trail continues 10 yards past the sign, on the right, just beyond the parked cars. **Option:** At this point, you can take the road back to your vehicle. Although far less technical, this option does add some mileage to your ride, as well as a significant amount of climbing. Bear right onto the singletrack. Note that this section of the trail has a higher level of foot traffic, so be cautious.

11.6 Reach a sweet picnic spot, offering picnic tables and water spigots. Here the trail will Y. A hiking trail will veer to the left and split the two picnic tables, as the Rampart Reservoir Loop veers to the right, passing the picnic table with the large boulder behind it.

13.8 Reach the bridge. Veer left and climb back up the road the way you came to your vehicle.

15.3 Arrive back at your vehicle.

Ride Information

Local Information

The Greater Woodland Park Chamber of Commerce, P.O. Box 9022, Woodland Park, 80866; (719) 687-9885, (800) 551-7886; www.woodlandparkchamber.com.

Local Events and Attractions

Florissant Fossil Beds National Monument, Florissant; (719) 748-3252 ($2.00 to $4.00 admission fee).

Garden of the Gods, Colorado Springs; (719) 634-6666 (admission is free).

Restaurants

Grandmother's Kitchen, Woodland Park; (719) 687-3118.

The Donut Mill, Woodland Park; (719) 687-9793.

Tres Hombres, Woodland Park; (719) 687-0625.

Mountain Bike Tours

Challenge Unlimited, Colorado Springs; (800) 798-5954, (719) 633-6399; www.pikespeak.com/challenge.

Organizations

Friends of the Peak, Colorado Springs; (719) 570-8958.

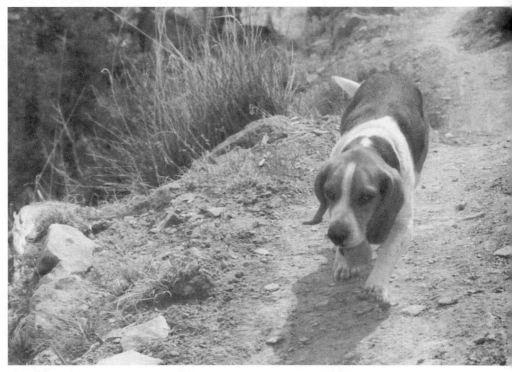

Otis, our fearless leader.

In Addition

Huckleberry Bread Pudding

Wild huckleberries thrive in upper montane and subalpine forests, often growing for miles as a solid carpet under spruce and fir trees. The berries have an almost nutlike flavor and are extremely juicy—perfect pie potential. The leaves can be stewed to make a kind of backcountry tea. Just imagine.

American Indians valued the berry highly, combining huckleberries boiled in bear grease with dog flesh for their feast meal. Cherokee women would encase huckleberries in corn-meal dough and deep-fry them in bear fat. These dishes are still showcased at the annual feast of Cherokee foods held in Cherokee, North Carolina.

Huckleberries were so much a part of early American life that they were adopted into the vernacular. Since huckleberries are tiny, plentiful, and common, a "huckleberry" became early nineteenth-century slang for a person of little consequence—undoubtedly inspiring Mark Twain to dub his most memorable literary character Huckleberry Finn.

When you do come across a patch of wild huckleberries, be sure to pick a shirt-full, as you can travel for miles and never see any. I should also add: BE SURE YOU'RE PICKING HUCKLEBERRIES!

The following recipe has the charm of an old railway carriage and the staying power of a great American classic.

8 thin slices of white bread
4 cups of huckleberries
butter
½ to ¾ cup sugar
⅓ cup water
bourbon

Butter each slice of bread lightly and line a round four- to five-cup bowl with the slices. Fill in the small spaces with bread so that the bowl is completely covered, sparing one slice for the crown. Cook the huckleberries with the sugar and ⅓ cup of water for 10 minutes. Add bourbon to taste. Then, pour the mixture into the bread-lined bowl. Place a slice on top and fold the edges over to meet. Place a saucer on top and press down. Chill for five hours and then serve with heavy cream. Serve excess liquid with pudding. Enjoy.

47 Waldo Canyon

Waldo Canyon Trail, although primarily a hikers' trail, does invite gonzo-minded mountain bikers to strut their stuff. What makes this trail particularly appealing to tough riders is its steep climbs out of creek beds and its fast and rocky descent—added to this is the variety of terrain Waldo Canyon delivers. Views from its highest point include Pikes Peak, Colorado Springs, and NORAD. Its location right beside U.S. Highway 24 makes for a speedy assault on the trail for those in transit. For those of you whose riding mentality is one fry short of a happy meal, try tackling the stairs on your return.

Start: From the trailhead to Waldo Canyon.
Length: 7-mile loop.
Approximate riding time: Advanced riders, 1 hour; intermediate riders, 1.5 to 2 hours.
Technical difficulty: Technically moderate to challenging due to the many rocky sections and big drop-offs.
Physical difficulty: Physically challenging due to the variety of climbing and having to portage your bicycle over rocky creeks.
Terrain: Singletrack. Although this trail is all singletrack, it covers a variety of different terrain: various kinds of rock surfaces, hard-packed dirt, wet forest earth, large roots, and Pikes Peak granite.

Trail contacts: Pike National Forest, Pikes Peak Ranger District, 601 South Weber Street, Colorado Springs, 80903; (719) 636-1602.
Schedule: May to October.
Maps: USGS maps: Woodland Park, Cascade; *Trails Illustrated* map 137, Pikes Peak and Canon City.
Nearest town: Colorado Springs.
Other trail users: Primarily day-hikers, a good reason not to mountain bike in this area on the weekends.
Canine compatibility: Dog friendly.

Getting There

From Colorado Springs: Take I-25 to exit 141 and U.S. Highway 24 west. Drive west on US 24 for 7.8 miles before reaching the turnoff for Waldo Canyon on your right. Park your vehicle here. You'll have to portage your bicycle up two sets of stairs to the registration box and the trailhead before beginning your ride.
From Woodland Park: Head east on US 24 toward Colorado Springs, starting from the intersection of US 24 and Baldwin Road. At 9.9 miles, arrive at the turnoff for the Waldo Canyon Trailhead, which is on your left. The trailhead is on the north side of US 24, so you'll have to cross US 24's westbound traffic. (Should you miss this opportunity to cross the westbound traffic, another turnoff will be to your left. Stay in the left lane. Turn left at 11.0 miles and backtrack westbound on US 24. Drive for 1.1 miles from where you joined westbound traffic and bear right into the Waldo Canyon parking lot.) *DeLorme: Colorado Atlas & Gazetteer:* Page 62, A-3 to B-3.

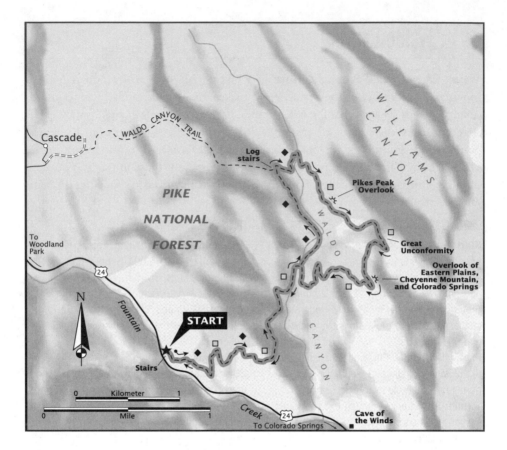

The Ride

At its worst, Waldo Canyon is a crowded thoroughfare for weekend hikers. At its best, it's a grunt of a climb to some of the area's best unobstructed views of Pikes Peak. The tireless mountain biker is rewarded with a singletrack descent of titillating switchbacks, past a veritable smorgasbord of geological timetables and drop-offs.

To help maintain and operate the district system trails, a donation of $1.00 is asked of every user and is collected at the bottom of the wooden stairs leading to the trail's registration box and the start of your ride. If not paralyzed with quizzical angst, wondering why you just carried yourself and your bike up these steep wooden steps, begin riding up the switchbacks. The trail parallels U.S. Highway 24 for roughly a mile and then climbs steadily, your tires relentlessly spinning through the ball-bearing-like Pikes Peak granite that blankets the trail. On a softer note, patches of lavender mullein (Verbascum thapsus) and roundleaf bluebell (Campanula rotundifolia) stand alongside of these unrelenting granite pebbles. They're called to arms each spring and summer to passively assert Waldo Canyon's soft beauty among the harshness of semi-arid sand and rock. As the trail turns away from the highway, you're given your last look at civilization for awhile. Views of the city of Colorado Springs vanish as you descend farther into this sun-splashed foothill oasis.

Riding through tall stands of leafy greens, surrounded by the smell of summer camp, you descend into a cool meadow area, complete with campfire rings. If you plan to camp and need a campfire, it's best that you use these campfire rings, so as not to scorch the earth any further than necessary. Once you arrive at the WALDO CANYON LOOP, 3½ MILES sign, bear left. In so doing, you'll be riding the loop in a clockwise direction, choosing to climb in the shade rather than in the more exposed areas of Waldo Canyon. From here the work begins.

A mile of steep climbing awaits you. The large rocks, knotty tree roots, and creek crossings make it a grunt by anyone's standards—a true

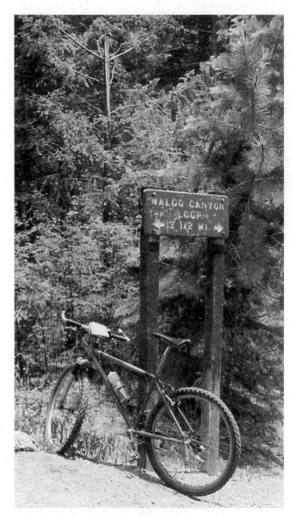

The beginning of Waldo Canyon Loop.

trial rider's dream. At 2.5 miles, the trail will Y before sending you up another set of wooden stairs. This time, the stairs are a bit more manageable, as long as you hug the left side—anyone less than advanced might find this difficult to ride. Bear right at the Waldo Canyon sign and continue ascending through the ponderosa and fir forest. Areas of this trail are severely loaded with rocks, so be aware on the approach. By the third mile the trail levels out and offers incredible views of 14,110-foot Pikes Peak along the east rim of Waldo Canyon.

At 3.4 miles you come upon an example of the "Great Unconformity"—a term coined by the "Father of Geology" James Hutton. The Great Unconformity refers to a break in the geologic record in which two kinds of rock are found in abnormal succession. In this case, Precambrian metamorphic rock (granite) sits directly beneath Pennsylvanian red sandstone, with no sign between of the Ordovician, Silurian, Devonian, or Mississippian periods. With 500 million years of time apparently lost, a crucial piece in Earth's geological jigsaw puzzle remains missing. Possible explanations for this mysterious absence are severe erosion and folding and faulting.

From the site of the Great Unconformity, the trail traverses the sun-exposed hills above Williams Canyon before snaking its way back down into Waldo Canyon. Williams Canyon cuts through the hillside in which the Cave of the Winds is located. The only limestone cavern in Colorado developed as a tourist attraction, Cave of the Winds deposits its dissolved limestone along the roadside leading through Williams Canyon. Cave of the Winds is a dazzling network of rooms and passageways encrusted with limestone stalactites, stalagmites, and flowstone curtains. The cave is one of the nation's oldest show caves. In 1881 two young brothers, picnicking with their church, decided to explore the area. What they discovered was a 200-million-year-old geological phenomenon. Today, Cave of the Winds is one of Colorado's leading attractions. Open year-round (10:00 A.M. to 5:00 P.M. in the winter and 9:00 A.M. to 9:00 P.M. in the summer), the cave offers a variety of tours, from the casual walker to the hard-core spelunker, and puts on an outstanding laser-light show.

▶ **In 1929 Bill Williams rolled a peanut to the top of Pikes Peak using his nose. His performance lasted twenty days.**

Riding high above Williams Canyon, the trail passes gorgeous views of the Eastern Plains, Colorado Springs, and the hollowed-out Cheyenne Mountain—home to NORAD (North American Aerospace Defense). The underground city housing NORAD monitors foreign aircraft, missiles, and space systems that could threaten U.S. security. Aside from the vast array of antennae protruding from its scalp, Cheyenne Mountain is virtually indistinguishable from any other mountain in Colorado. The trail from this point is packed with dirt and thick with overgrowth as it begins its descent back into Waldo Canyon.

This descent is fast and fun, as it travels over a variety of terrain, keeping you on your toes if not putting you on your noggin. Manitou limestone–sprinkled switchbacks, precipitously sloping Sawatch sandstone, crowded Peerless (better known as "Fearless") dolomite sections, and carvable Pikes Peak granite turns—all question

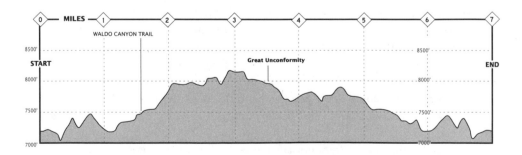

the standards of your ANSI and SNELL head. Riders are afforded a crash course in geology as a host of interpretive signs explain the geology of each of these sections.

At 5.3 miles you arrive at a tributary of Fountain Creek and the WALDO CANYON LOOP, 3½ MILES sign. Bear left and return to your vehicle. After a short climb out of this valley, the descent to your vehicle is sweet and fast, offering blind corners and a number of rocks. You'll arrive at the trail register at 7.0 miles. If you're feeling lucky, try doing the stairs down to the parking lot.

Miles and Directions

- **0.0** START at the registration tower and box at the top of the stairs.
- **0.1** Waldo Canyon Trail will bear left. To the right is an overlook of US 24 and a description of the composition of Pikes Peak granite.
- **0.8** Cross the ridge and begin descending into a clearing.
- **1.6** Arrive at a brown sign reading WALDO CANYON LOOP, 3½ MILES. Bear left here. You'll eventually return to this spot after completing the loop.
- **2.5** Reach the set of log stairs leading to the trail's intersection. Veer right, as the left route will lead you out of Waldo Canyon and to the town of Cascade.
- **3.4** Here's a good example of the Great Unconformity.
- **4.9** Begin your switchback descent.
- **5.3** Arrive at the creek and the Waldo Canyon sign.
- **7.0** Arrive back at the trail register box and tower.

Ride Information

Local Information
The Greater Woodland Park Chamber of Commerce, P.O. Box 9022, Woodland Park, 80866; (719) 687-9885, (800) 551-7886; www. woodlandparkchamber.com.

Local Events and Attractions
Cave of the Winds, Manitou Springs; (719) 685-5444.
Florissant Fossil Beds National Monument, Florissant; (719) 748-3252.
Garden of the Gods, Manitou Springs; (719) 634-6666. (It's free!).

Restaurants
Grandmother's Kitchen, Woodland Park; (719) 687-3118.

The Donut Mill, Woodland Park; (719) 687-9793.
Tres Hombres, Woodland Park; (719) 687-0625.

Mountain Bike Tours
Challenge Unlimited, Colorado Springs; (800) 798-5954, (719) 633-6399; www.pikespeak.com/challenge.

Organizations
Friends of the Peak (FOTP), Colorado Springs; (719) 570-8958.

In Addition

Composition of "America the Beautiful"

"We stood at last on that gait-of-heaven summit [Pikes Peak] . . . and gazed in wordless rapture over the far expanse of mountain ranges and sea-like sweep of plain. It was then and there that the opening lines of 'America the Beautiful' sprang into being."

Katherine Lee Bates

In the summer of 1893, Katherine Lee Bates braved the wild, open prairies of the United States' interior on her way to Colorado. A renowned professor of English literature at Wellesley College in Massachusetts, Bates was invited by her cross-continent colleagues to spend the summer as a visiting professor at Colorado College in Colorado Springs.

No sooner had she arrived than friends urged Bates to summit the 14,110-foot Pikes Peak—a must-see for first-time visitors to Colorado Springs. Just thirty-five years prior, Pikes Peak had been the focus of one of Colorado's most famous gold

Katherine Lee Bates's inspiration, Pikes Peak.

rushes. Although gold was never found, the magnificent mountain still drew visitors. Since 1891 the Pikes Peak Cog Railway had been ferrying visitors to the summit, so Bates's trip to the top wasn't of the lung-busting and scree-scrambling order.

Once Bates reached the summit of Colorado's most famous mountain, she found herself in the middle of a lover's kiss, overcome with poetic inspiration. There lay glittering Denver 70 miles to the north, a vast ocean of green prairies to the east, the towering jagged peaks of the Sangre de Cristo Mountains and the Spanish Peaks to the south, and the imposing granite mammoths of the Sawatch and Mosquito ranges due west. The dramatic contrast of the flat prairie oceans crashing against the towering peaks of the Rockies seemed a striking metaphor not just for the West but for the nation as a whole. Inspired, she penned these inspirational words:

> Oh beautiful for spacious skies,
> For amber waves of grain:
> For purple mountain majesties
> Above the fruited plain—
> America, America, God shed his grace on thee,
> And crown thy good with brotherhood
> From sea to shining sea . . .

The poem "America the Beautiful" did not appear in print until 1911, when Bates featured it in one of her many books of poetry. But as soon as the poem reached the public, it was set to music. The rest, as they say, is history. Today, many a patriot considers "America the Beautiful" (the song) America's real national anthem.

48 Shelf Road

Shelf Road is a historic stagecoach toll road that connects Cañon City with the gold-mining camps of Cripple Creek and Victor. The Shelf travels precipitously along the limestone cliffs of Helena Canyon and then descends into the canyon, revealing incredibly tall red rock walls. Here is a mellow ride that offers a lot of spinning. It's a cool ride to combine with a day of gambling in Cripple Creek. The Banks–Shelf Road area is also world-renowned for its rock climbing. For those who want something a little more laid-back than Cripple Creek, make tracks to Victor, a traditional turn-of-the-century mining town that doesn't allow gambling. Bighorn sheep abound within Helena Canyon and most often can be spotted drinking from Four-mile Creek at dusk. Helena Canyon is a "hard hat" zone, meaning that loose rock will occasionally give in to gravity. The return from Cripple Creek or Victor is fast, offering a number of blind curves and washboard sections of road, with the last push to the Banks–Shelf Road parking area one burley climb.

Start: From the Banks-Shelf Road parking area. Take the right fork (Shelf Road).
Length: 27.2-mile out-and-back.
Approximate riding time: Advanced riders, 3.5 hours; intermediate riders, 4.5 to 5 hours.
Technical difficulty: Technically easy; there are no major obstacles.
Physical difficulty: Physically easy to moderate due to some degree of climbing.
Terrain: Shelf Road Trail follows an old wagon and stagecoach toll road; aside from the occasional washboard effect, the road is relatively smooth; at times it is very exposed.

Trail contacts: Bureau of Land Management, Royal Gorge Field Office, 3170 East Main Street, Cañon City, 81212; (719) 269–8500.
Schedule: April to October.
Maps: USGS maps: Cooper Mountain, Cripple Creek South; *Trails Illustrated* map 137, Pikes Peak and Cañon City.
Nearest town: Cripple Creek.
Other trail users: Equestrians, hikers, four-wheelers, bighorn sheep viewers, climbers, and gamblers.
Canine compatibility: Not dog friendly, as there is vehicular traffic on Shelf Road.

Getting There

From Cañon City: Drive east on U.S. Highway 50. Make a left onto Dozier Avenue, near the Wal-Mart. In 0.5 mile, Dozier turns west and becomes Central. Continuing on Central (Dozier), drive west for 1.6 miles before turning right onto Fields Avenue. Fields Avenue turns into a dirt road at 11.6 miles. Continue on Fields for another 2.3 miles before arriving at the Banks, a limestone cliff area located near the beginning of Shelf Road and known internationally for its incredible sport climbing. Park here and begin your ride, taking the right fork (Shelf Road). *DeLorme: Colorado Atlas & Gazetteer:* Page 62, D-1 to B-1.

The Ride

As part of the National Scenic Byway of Colorado's Gold Belt Tour and the Bureau of Land Management's designated National Backcountry Byway system, Shelf Road recalls much of the Old West. Originally built in 1892 as a wagon and stagecoach toll road, Shelf Road connected the Arkansas River Valley community of Cañon City with the turn-of-the-century gold camps of Cripple Creek and Victor. Today the road offers the relaxed mountain biker a chance to experience Colorado history from the seat of his or her mountain bike.

Colorado in the 1890s was home to America's last great gold rush. Towns like Cripple Creek, Victor, Florence, McCourt, Adelaide, and Wilbur (towns included within the Cripple Creek Mining District) all shared in the spoils that gold could afford. Gold offered these towns a chance to make a name for themselves—or as in the case of Cripple Creek, a new name. When Bob Womack discovered gold in October 1890 in a high-country cow pasture west of Pikes Peak, the town of Poverty Gulch officially changed its name to Cripple Creek.

Throughout its gold-mining days, Cripple Creek enjoyed a standard of living never before seen in Colorado. By 1893 Cripple Creek had unearthed $3 million in gold ore. That figure grew to $59 million by 1899, and by the end of the gold rush (circa 1903), area gold mines within the Cripple Creek Mining District had produced $432 million—making it the fourth largest gold-producing camp in the world.

Cripple Creek established itself as a social center as well. Grand opera houses were built. A variety of musicians performed for area residents. Jack Dempsey drew huge crowds to his boxing bouts in town. Even President Teddy Roosevelt visited Cripple Creek and, while squatting and rubbing elbows with fellow miners, panned for gold.

Today Cripple Creek continues to grow by offering limited-stakes gambling. Other than housing an estimated 2,200 new jobs, many of Cripple Creek's original brick buildings now merely serve as vintage facades to the glittering casinos within. Though meant to maintain the city's National Historic District designation, Cripple Creek casinos can't help but lend an element of gross excess. Its buzzing bells, neon lights, and reeling pace all but erase any semblance of Cripple Creek's Old West charm.

Six miles from Cripple Creek lies the gold-mining town of Victor. Known as the City of Mines, Victor is the heart of the great Cripple Creek Mining District, and as a point of pride, still remains true to its roots. Its century-old streets offer a quiet, non-gambling relief from Cripple Creek, while retaining much of the area's 1890s authenticity. The original brick buildings, built by residents after a fire destroyed their town in 1898, still stand. Even the hillsides are dotted with original miners' homes, visual echoes recalling the town's illustrious past.

Connecting Colorado's past with its present is Shelf Road. Six hundred feet above Fourmile Creek, Shelf Road cuts through Helena Canyon's limestone cliff walls. The initial 4 miles is perhaps the most dramatic section of the entire route. If you fear heights or are prone to vertigo, this section could be difficult. Shelf Road skirts dangerously above Helena Canyon, often offering only a car width's margin of error.

As you descend to the canyon floor and the banks of Fourmile Creek, a feeling of peace overcomes you as the exposed road gives way to hosts of juniper, legions of scrub oak, and a smattering of lush cottonwoods. Behind you are the limestone crags, whose allure has attracted many a rock climber. From here, one begins the extended 10-mile push to Cripple Creek. Shelf Road gradually climbs as it winds its way across and back over Fourmile Creek.

At 6.0 miles, the steeper part of the climbing begins, leading you through forests of lodgepole pine by 8 miles. These elegant and slender tree trunks were used by American Indians as poles for their teepees, hence the name. Like smoke from a fire ring, your eyes are drawn upward to the tips of these trees and onward toward the tops of the canyon walls.

After passing a number of abandoned mines between 10.0 and 11.4 miles, Shelf Road eventually forks at 11.8 miles. Victor is to the right, and Cripple Creek to the left. Here remnants of the El Paso Mine remain. After veering left, your solitary bicycle ride quickly fades as you become absorbed in the bustle of Cripple Creek.

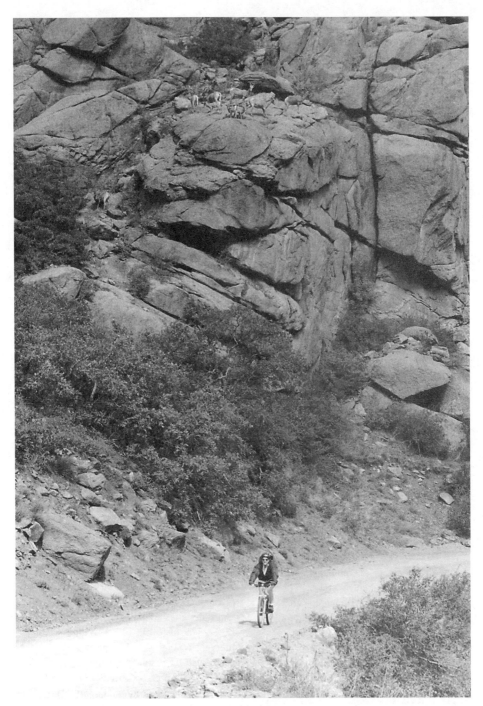

Bighorn sheep abound in Helena Canyon. Notice the family of sheep at the top of the photo.

Veer left once again onto CO 67 at 13.3 miles and you come to downtown Cripple Creek, home to the largest population of free-roving donkeys—some the direct descendants of those used during Cripple Creek's gold-mining glory.

Your return trip is fast and bumpy. Be cautious of your speed, as the descent on Shelf Road offers many tight turns. The many washboards are sure to test your shocks and, for those without shocks, your patience. Enjoy the ride.

Miles and Directions

0.0 START at the Banks–Shelf Road parking area. Take the right fork and begin climbing up Shelf Road.

2.0 Riding along the steep limestone walls of Helena Canyon, you'll notice an old abandoned cabin from the late 1800s on the canyon floor.

4.0 Shelf Road eventually widens and leads into the floor of Helena Canyon, affording additional parking for climbers and those who would like to forgo the initial, narrow descent to the canyon bottom. (The crags behind you offer great climbing opportunities and can be accessed via a variety of foot trails.)

5.0 The remains of an old stone home are on your right.

8.1 Come to an abandoned mine shaft to your right.

10.0 Take in the beautiful vista of the Sangre de Cristo Mountains off to the west.

11.4 Cross Cripple Creek.

11.8 Shelf Road forks. Here signs for Cripple Creek point to the left fork, while signs for Victor point to the right fork. Take the left fork and ride toward Cripple Creek. Pass the Scenic Byway sign, marked by a Colorado columbine.

13.3 Shelf Road connects to CO 67. At the stop sign, bear left onto CO 67 and ride into Cripple Creek.

13.6 Reach the corner of Second Street and Bennett Avenue, downtown Cripple Creek. Turn around here and return the way you came.

27.2 Arrive at your vehicle.

Ride Information

Local Information

Cañon City Chamber of Commerce, 403 Royal Gorge Boulevard, Cañon City, 81212; (719) 275-2331; www.canoncitychamber.com.

City of Cripple Creek, P.O. Box 430, Cripple Creek, 80813; (877) 858-GOLD (4653); www.cripple-creek.co.us.

Cañon City District Office, Cañon City, 81212; (719) 269-8500.

Local Events and Attractions

Donkey Derby Days, last full weekend of June, Cripple Creek; (719) 689-2169, (800) 526-8777 (donkey races, greased pigs, and lots of fun).

Fiddlers on the Arkansas, July, Cañon City; (719) 276-3225.

Limited-stakes gambling, Cripple Creek; (719) 689-2169 or (800) 526-8777 (slot machines, poker, and blackjack tables).

Gold Rush Days, third weekend of July, Victor; (719) 689-3553, (719) 689-3211.

Gold Belt Tour, year-round, Cañon City; (719) 275-2331.

Honorable Mentions

Front Range

Described here are great rides in the Front Range region that didn't make the A-list this time around but deserve recognition. Check them out and let us know what you think. You may decide that one or more of these rides deserves higher status in future editions or, perhaps, you may have a ride of your own that merits some attention.

H Crosier Mountain Loop

Located just outside of the gateway town for Rocky Mountain National Park, the Crosier Mountain Loop is quite possibly Estes Park's best kept secret. This trail's layout is almost entirely all singletrack. Complete with rocks, water, and switchbacks, the trail winds around the northeastern slope of Crosier Mountain before briefly intersecting with Devil's Gulch Road, and then it's back to your vehicle. The trail is roughly 10 miles long and reaches above 9,000 feet, which accounts for its physically and technically challenging rating.

Estes Park, set before the towering peaks of Rocky Mountain National Park, offers its own brand of alpine entertainment. Resident elk herds continually descend upon area lawns and gardens, unabashed by staring visitors. It's no surprise to see and hear a herd of elk bugling in someone's backyard. While in town, check out the Stanley Hotel. Built in 1909, the hotel served as an inspirational setting for Stephen King's *The Shining*.

To reach the Crosier Mountain Loop, drive north on Devil's Gulch Road from downtown Estes Park. The road winds around the Stanley Hotel before bearing northeast to Glen Haven. Park your vehicle in Glen Haven and begin riding here.

For more information, contact Colorado Bicycling Adventures at Estes Park, 184 East Elkhorn, Estes Park, 80517; (800) 607–8765; www.coloradobicycling.com. Or contact the Estes Park Chamber of Commerce, 500 Big Thompson Highway Avenue, Estes Park, 80517; (970) 586–4431, (800) 44–ESTES. *DeLorme: Colorado Atlas & Gazetteer:* Page 29, A-7.

I Deer Haven Ranch

Offering stunning views of the Sangre de Cristo Mountains and set in the semi-arid region of Cañon City, Deer Haven Ranch is a diamond in the rough. Although limited to a minimal amount of rideable miles—5 to 7 miles of mostly doubletrack and dirt roads—Deer Haven Ranch is an isolated and relatively unknown mountain biking destination.

Located about 25 miles northwest of Cañon City, Deer Haven Ranch is a relatively new acquisition of the Bureau of Land Management. In 1992 a private foundation purchased the 4,840-acre ranch for $650,000 and presented it to the Bureau of Land Management as a gift. Since that time, the BLM, in conjunction with Medicine Wheel (a mountain bike advocacy group from Manitou Springs) and a local equestrian group, has worked on developing a trail system for Deer Haven Ranch.

With grassy rolling meadows, an abundance of wildlife, an isolation factor of ten, and the BLM's continued commitment to developing a trail system, Deer Haven Ranch remains a diamond in the rough, but one whose edges are increasingly becoming smoother. Look to Deer Haven Ranch as an up-and-coming success story for the mountain biking community.

To reach Deer Haven Ranch, travel west on U.S. Highway 50 from the First National Bank in downtown Cañon City, on the corner of 9th Street and Royal Gorge Boulevard (US 50 west). Drive west on US 50 for 9.7 miles. Turn right onto Colorado Highway 9 north and drive for 9 miles before turning right onto County Road 11 (a.k.a. Scenic Byway: Gold Belt Tour). Cross the creek after the red ranch house and barn. Drive on CR 11 for 5.3 miles. After a long and gentle descent, make a right into Deer Haven Ranch (marked by the DEER HAVEN RANCH sign) and drive on CR 69 (dirt road) for just under a mile before turning right onto a rough-looking doubletrack. Marked by the THOMPSON MOUNTAIN and DEAD END signs, drive on this doubletrack for roughly 1 mile. After 0.3 a mile, you'll need to go through a fenced gate. Be sure to close it behind you. After passing through this first gate, continue driving for 0.5 mile to the Deer Haven Ranch Trailhead, marked by another gate and a bulletin board.

For more information, contact the Bureau of Land Management, Royal Gorge Field Office, 3170 E. Main Street, Cañon City, 81212; (719) 269–8538. *DeLorme: Colorado Atlas & Gazetteer:* Page 61, D-7.

Eastern Plains

The eastern plains provide a stark contrast to the mountainous terrain typically thought of when referring to Colorado's landscape. Although the rocky mountains do cast an ominous shadow over these amber waves of grain, these behemoths still cannot darken all of the eastern plains, an area covering nearly half of Colorado's acreage.

Commonly referred to as "Colorado's Outback," the plains mark the western terminus of the high plains of the midwest. Across these plains came droves of pioneers during America's great expansion out west. Peppered by old forts, wagon trails, and former farm settlements, Colorado's Outback is a treasure trove of the pioneering spirit. Roughly 10 miles east of the town of La Junta, near the southern end of this region, lies Bent's Old Fort National Historic Site.

Although today Bent's Old Fort may seem to lie in the middle of nowhere, it was unquestionably the epicenter of the frontier during America's expansion. Built in 1833, the fort lies on the north bank of the Arkansas River (then the U.S.-Mexican border). As the only trading post between Missouri and Santa Fe, New Mexico, Bent's Old Fort catered to all walks of pioneer: prospectors and fur traders from the mountains, Native Americans and soldiers from the plains, and Mexican and Anglo merchants arriving via the Mountain Branch of the Santa Fe Trail.

The Santa Fe Trail was a major thoroughfare for explorers, pioneers, and homesteaders making their way across the American frontier. Following a direct line along the Arkansas River, the Sante Fe Trail offered frontiersmen like Kit Carson and John C. Fremont passage into the Rockies. Following limestone posts marking the route, history buffs can follow 22 miles of the Santa Fe Trail along U.S. Highways 350 and 160, as it runs its course through the Comanche National Grasslands.

The Comanche National Grasslands occupy 435,707 acres just south of La Junta. Not only were they a major thoroughfare for early pioneers, but these grasslands continue to be a major flyway zone for some 275 different species of birds migrating in the spring and fall. Ranging in topography from deep cut canyons with vertical walls to gently rolling slopes and flatlands, the Comanche National Grasslands offer great recreational opportunities. Picketwire Canyonlands offers a great ride past ancient Native American art, old homesteads, and North America's longest-recorded set of Precambrian dinosaur tracks. Other areas of interest include Vogel Canyon, Picture Canyon, and Carrizo Canyon.

The northern Plains are home to Colorado's other national grassland: Pawnee National Grasslands. Roughly 30 miles east of Fort Collins, near Briggsdale, the Pawnee National Grasslands occupies an area of 193,000 acres. Its flat and gently rolling landscape is predominantly composed of a wide expanse of blue grama and buffalo grass. These grasslands are distinguished, however, by a pair of buttes (Pawnee Buttes). These islands in the sky rise to 5,500 feet, 600 feet above the prairie's surface. The buttes support over 296 species of birds, a bird-watcher's paradise. Although riding to the base of these buttes is prohibited, there is a short hiking trail to the buttes. A scenic and relaxing ride through the grasslands includes traveling the Auto Bird Tour.

Other riding possibilities include traveling the famed Overland Trail. During America's expansion, the Overland Trail became the most heavily used pioneer route to the West. Established in 1862, this route avoided the Native American uprisings that were occuring on the Oregon Trail farther north through central Wyoming. The Overland Trail Museum, located in the town of Sterling, east of the Pawnee National Grasslands, showcases a reproduction of an old fort, provides details on the trail's route, and displays a vast array of historical memorabilia. East of Sterling, in the town of Julesburg, lies the Fort Sedgwick Depot Museum. Here is where the fourteen-year-old Buffalo Bill Cody signed on with the Pony Express, at Colorado's sole Pony Express stop.

49 Picketwire Canyonlands

Picketwire Canyonlands takes you far away from Colorado's high country and delivers you nearly to Kansas. Roughly 80 miles from the state line, Picketwire Canyonlands is often overlooked by many Coloradoans, but remains, most certainly, one of its treasures. The initial 500-foot drop into the canyon is steep and rock-laden—the only technically challenging section of the entire ride. The rest of the ride travels over a worn jeep road that has since been reclaimed by doubletrack. While passing outcroppings of blocky limestone engraved with Native American artwork, the route delivers you to the banks of the Purgatoire River and to North America's longest-recorded set of Precambrian dinosaur tracks.

Start: From the Picketwire Canyon Trailhead, by the pipe gate.

Length: 18.2-mile out-and-back.

Approximate riding time: Advanced riders, 1.5 to 2 hours; intermediate riders, 2 to 2.5 hours.

Technical difficulty: Technically easy to moderate. The first and last 500 feet of this out-and-back trail offer some steep, rock- and sand-laden terrain as you begin by descending and end by climbing this portion of the trail. The route between rolls over relatively flat terrain with some climbs and descents thrown in.

Physical difficulty: Physically easy to moderate. Although the route meanders at a considerably lower elevation (4,660 feet) than most mountain bike trails in Colorado, the heat and dryness of the desert bottom will tax your body's hydration tanks. Bring as much water as you can carry. It'd be a good idea to bring a water filter as well, since filtered water can

be obtained throughout the ride from the Purgatoire River.

Terrain: Doubletrack and dirt road on desert terrain with sand and rocks.

Trail contacts: Comanche National Grassland, 27162 Highway 287, P.O. Box 127, Springfield, 81073; (719) 523-6591.

Schedule: Picketwire Canyonlands stays open from dawn to dusk and is best visited between March and November.

Maps: USGS maps: Riley Canyon, Beaty Canyon, O V Mesa.

Nearest town: La Junta.

Other trail users: Hikers, tour groups, and equestrians. Vault toilets are located at the dinosaur tracks site as well as the Rourke Ranch.

Canine compatibility: Dog friendly; however, you will be riding through a desert, with lots of cacti and exceedingly hot temperatures. Fortunately, there is the Purgatoire River.

Getting There

From La Junta: Drive south on Colorado Highway 109 for 13 miles. Turn right onto County Road 802 (dirt road) and continue for 8 miles. Turn left (south) on CR 25 and drive for 6 miles before turning left (east) again at Forest Road 500.A. Drive on FR 500.A for 1 mile and pass the wire gate. (FR 500.A is not maintained and may be hazardous driving for anyone without a high-clearance four-wheel-drive vehicle, particularly after a strong rain.) Continue following this dirt road for 2 miles until the road forks. Take the left fork. Drive to the parking sign and park your

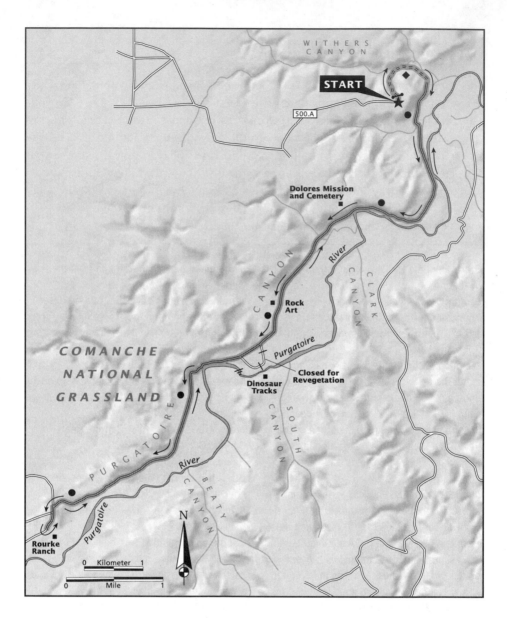

vehicle. For those unable to make it on this road, you may park your vehicle at the start of FR 500.A, at the bulletin board, and start your ride there. *DeLorme: Colorado Atlas & Gazetteer:* Page 100, B-3.

The Ride

Not all of Colorado's open spaces have been overrun by urban sprawl, as many would have you believe. The Canyonlands' 16,000–plus acres, surrounded by the

400,000-acre Comanche National Grassland, offer room to spare in a remarkably beautiful and sun-drenched landscape.

Picketwire Canyonlands may never have received its protected status had it not been for two Colorado legislators, Senator Timothy Wirth and Representative Hank Brown. Their proposal to shift the land's management from the U.S. Army to the Forest Service passed in 1991. The one-time training site became expressly our own. Today it's one of our most treasured inheritances. The Canyonlands' boiling desert sands and scorched canyon walls remain patient attendants to this desert solitaire. The winding Purgatoire River is its only relief—and ours.

Mountain bikers must access Picketwire Canyonlands by descending Withers Canyon via Picketwire Trail. Picketwire Trail leads you on a journey through time. About 150 million years ago, long-necked gentle giants like the Brontosaurus and four-ton carnivores like the Allosaurus walked along the banks of the Purgatoire. Evidence of this is their footprints. Roughly 10,000 years ago, ancient Anasazi Indians passed through the canyon, leaving their mark on its surrounding walls. By the mid–fourteenth century, Picketwire Canyonlands saw the exploration of the Spaniards—most notably Francisco Vasquez de Coronado, whose search for gold led him throughout southeast Colorado, including Picketwire Canyonlands. Today, mountain bikers imbed their own tracks into Picketwire sands, searching also for something within the blazing confines of the canyonlands.

With a pucker-rating of 9-plus, the 500-foot doubletrack descent through Withers Canyon is steep and rocky. Prickly pear, cholla cactus, prairie rattlesnakes, scorpions, tarantulas, badgers, and lizards—the poetry of natural selection—all await your arrival. Since temperatures are ten degrees hotter on the canyon floor than atop the prairie and since summer temperatures range from 90 to 105 degrees, riders ought to bring a gallon of water per person.

Once on the canyon floor, Picketwire Trail becomes a doubletrack, with the semblance of a dirt road, and snakes its way through the Purgatoire Canyon in a south-southwesterly direction. Following along an old telegraph line—one still standing—the first 5 miles of trail lead past historic adobe ruins, probably left over from when migrant Spaniards roamed this area, and through thick and tall stands of

Marveling at the natural arch on the way to the Rourke Ranch.

vegetation. The latter will have you questioning your line of travel, as any semblance of earth beneath you becomes lost in a sea of green.

As you exit these tall grasses, the flat-faced vertical rocks to your right contain a number of prehistoric Anasazi petroglyphs. Although not much is known about these ancients, archeologists speculate that they were a nomadic people who tracked migrating game. Studies of these ancient petroglyphs reveal some to be 4,500 years old. Native Americans left markings of themselves hunting game on the canyon walls. These prehistoric people, along with tribes of Comanche, Kiowa, Cheyenne, and Apache, left images of deer, elk, humans, and other abstract illustrations. It's speculated that these images serve to recall a successful hunt or a year of plentiful food.

The hunger for food wasn't the only driving force behind human exploration of Purgatoire Canyon. In 1540 Coronado, a prospector for the Spanish crown, set out with 340 fellow Spaniards, 300 Native American allies, and 1,000 slaves (both Indian and African) in search of gold in this region. Because they found none, the Purgatoire Canyon remained unsettled for some time. However, as a result of Coronado claiming for Spain all the land through which he traveled, this area has since become steeped in Spanish and Mexican culture. If legend holds true, the name of the Purgatoire River recalls the unfortunate deaths of a few Spanish fortune seekers who ventured into this canyon and eventually died of exposure. Since the deceased died before receiving their last rites—seeing as no priests were present—the Spanish religious faithfuls named the river "El Rio de Las Animas Perdidas en Purgatorio" (The River of Lost Souls in Purgatory). French trappers wandering into the canyon during the eighteenth century later renamed the river Purgatoire.

At 4.0 miles lies the Dolores Mission and Cemetery, built sometime between 1871 and 1889 when Mexican pioneers first began permanent settlement in this valley. Proof that offerings never go out of style, a rusting pot still hangs from a beam in the mission. Decorating the mission's small courtyard are the crumbling headstones of these early pioneers.

Just 1.6 miles from the Dolores Mission and Cemetery lie the 150-million-year-old footprints of Brontosaurus and Allosaurus. Imbedded in the limestone rock along the banks of the Purgatoire River are 1,300 visible dinosaur tracks that extend for 0.25 mile. Imagine two-stepping with a thirty-three-ton, 16-foot-tall, 70-foot-long lizard. Watch the toes! The majority of tracks (about 60 percent) were left by the Allosaurus. The sharp claw prints of the three-toed Allosaurus sink deep into the antediluvian mud of the Purgatoire River.

Having feasted your eyes on these enormous tracks and cooled your caboose in the Purgatoire River's waterfall, continue south along the trail over the relatively easy terrain of rock and sand and past a natural arch. At 9.1 miles your route ends at the Rourke Ranch. Only a fenced-off house and a shed remain. Built in 1871 by Eugene Rourke, the Rourke Ranch remained in the Rourke family for 100 years, three generations. When it was sold in 1971, the Rourke Ranch was known as one of the oldest and most successful operations in southeast Colorado. Its acreage had grown from Eugene's original settlement of forty acres to well over 52,000. With that kind of aged wealth, it's no wonder the Rourke Ranch was known as the "Wineglass Ranch." From the Rourke Ranch, turn your mountain bike around and return back to the future.

Miles and Directions

Since ranching is a primary means of livelihood in this area, please close all gates behind you and do not disturb livestock. Sunscreen, sunglasses, hat, insect repellent, and first aid kit are highly recommended.

0.0 START at the trailhead to Picketwire Canyonlands.

0.1 Reach a pipe gate. Pass beyond the pipe gate and begin your ride by descending 500 feet through Withers Canyon to the canyon floor.

3.0 First views of the Purgatoire River, as the trail rolls over mellow doubletrack through a meadow.

4.0 You come to the remains of the Dolores Mission.

5.6 The trail will Y. Bearing left will take you to the banks of the Purgatoire River and site of the longest-recorded set of dinosaur tracks in North America.

9.1 Reach Rourke Ranch and return the way you came.

18.2 Arrive back at your vehicle.

Ride Information

Local Information

Rocky Ford Chamber of Commerce, 105 North Main Street, Rocky Ford, 81067; (719) 254-7483.

Local Events and Attractions

Annual Arkansas Valley Fair held each August in Rocky Ford, (719) 254-7483.

Restaurants

Café Grandmere, La Junta; (719) 384-2711.

Camping

No overnight camping is allowed in Picketwire Canyonlands.

Honorable Mention

Eastern Plains

Described below is one of the great rides in the Eastern Plains region that didn't make the A-list this time around but deserves recognition nonetheless. Check it out and let us know what you think. You may decide that it deserves higher status in future editions or, perhaps, you may have a ride of your own that merits some attention.

↲ Pawnee National Grasslands

Although Colorado's lowlands tend to get overlooked for more sloping terrain, one of Colorado's flat-landed areas demands attention. Located 90 miles northeast of Denver and 30 miles east of Fort Collins, the 193,000-acre Pawnee National Grasslands is located in the expansive grasslands east of I–25. The most striking feature of these grasslands is the sandstone towers of the Pawnee Buttes. Each of the three buttes stands 0.5 mile apart and rises 350 feet above the plains to an elevation of

Ahh, a smooth dirt road. The joys of mountain biking's gentler side.

5,375 feet. Since cliffs along the buttes are a preferred nesting area for larger birds of prey, riders are restricted to a designated road. Access to these buttes is by foot travel only. Users should know that these birds breed and nest from March through June, so this area is closed during this time.

The Pawnee Buttes have long been noted as a haven for many unique and interesting birds. In fact, the American Bird Conservancy designated the Pawnee Buttes a "Globally Important Bird Area." On a more local level, the Audubon Society of Colorado listed the Pawnee Buttes area as one of roughly fifty important bird areas in Colorado. Bird-watchers from all over the country visit the Pawnee Buttes in hopes of adding the likes of the mountain plover, long-billed curlew, and burrowing owl to their "life lists."

The Pawnee Buttes are also one of the finest sites in the world for vertebrate fossils. A number of horse species (including three-toed and dwarf versions), rhinoceros, ancient swine, and camel (a hippopotamus-like animal) have all been unearthed here. The buttes also have a link to America's westward expansion, as a pioneer trail led straight across the Pawnee National Grasslands.

To reach the Pawnee National Grasslands, drive north from Denver on I–25 for roughly 60 miles. Turn right (east) onto Colorado Highway 14, following signs for Ault. Drive on CO 14 for roughly 30 miles to the grasslands.

For more information, contact Pawnee National Grassland, 660 O Street Greeley, 80631; (970) 353–5004. *DeLorme: Colorado Atlas & Gazetteer:* Page 94, B-2.

Great Escape

Telluride to Moab
Hut to Hut

Day 1: Telluride to Last Dollar Hut

Day 2: Last Dollar Hut to Spring Creek Hut

Day 3: Spring Creek Hut to Columbine Hut

Day 4: Columbine Hut to Big Creek Cabin

Day 5: Big Creek Cabin to Gateway Hut

Day 6: Gateway Hut to La Sal Hut

Day 7: La Sal Hut to Moab

50 Telluride to Moab: Hut to Hut

Trail contacts: San Juan Hut System, P.O. Box 773, Ridgway, 81432; (970) 626-3033; www.sanjuanhuts.com.
Poison Spider Bicycle Shop, 497 North Main Street, Moab, Utah; (435) 259-7882, (800) 635-1792; www.poisonspiderbicycles.com.
Kaibab Mountain Bike Tours, 391 South Main Street, Moab, Utah; (435) 259-7423, (800) 451-1133; www.kaibabtours@aol.com.
Chili Pepper Bike Shop, 702 South Main Street, Moab, Utah; (435) 259-4688, (800) 677-4688.

Schedule: June 1 to October 1.
Fees and Permits: Through the San Juan Hut System, it's $475.00 per person for a seven-day, self-guided hut-to-hut tour from Telluride to Moab.
Maps: *DeLorme Colorado Atlas & Gazetteer:* page 76, A-2 to A-3; page 66, D-1 to B-2; page 65, B-7 to A-4; page 55, D-4; page 54, D-4 to C-1—continued in *DeLorme Utah Atlas & Gazetteer:* page 41, D-6 to D-4; page 31, A-5 to A-3; Uncompahgre National Forest Map and the Manti–La Sal National Forest Map.

The Ride

Riders taking part in the San Juan Hut System's Telluride to Moab bicycle tour are in for an epic adventure. Expect to be treated to the 14,000-foot, snow-capped peaks of the San Juans, the 100-mile-long Uncompahgre Plateau, the awe-inspiring canyons of the Dolores River Valley, the rugged La Sal Mountains rising high above the red plain deserts of Moab, and the surreal red-rocked canyons and mesas of Moab. Save for the few singletrack trails that spur from the main route, the trip from the one-time tent city of Telluride to the outlaw town of Moab is more a test of stamina than of mountain bike handling skills.

Riders travel for seven days (shorter trips are available), mostly along U.S. Forest Service and Bureau of Land Management roads in the Uncompahgre and Manti–La Sal National Forests, staying in a different hut each night. Situated along the route, these huts stand anywhere from 13 to 38 miles apart and include all the comforts of home. The six huts are equipped with eight padded bunks, a propane cook stove, propane lights, a wood-burning stove (except for the Gateway and La Sal huts), firewood (usually), and kitchen facilities. Although there is no running water, all huts include a water supply for drinking and cooking. The hut is stocked with dry and canned goods, some fresh fruit and vegetables, spices, drinking water, and sleeping bags. Note: Riders have occasionally found that huts were lacking certain food and/or cooking items, e.g. jelly, Gatorade, pizza, and propane, so make sure your hut is stocked properly by contacting the San Juan Hut System.

Mike Turrin and Joe Ryan, Telluride locals, started the San Juan Hut System and their Telluride to Moab Hut to Hut trip in 1988. Since then, this trip has amassed classic status among fat tire enthusiasts. Riders receive three meals a day, lodging, and miles of jaw-dropping views. And if that doesn't sell you, try adding a 7,000-foot vertical drop from the Last Dollar Hut, atop Last Dollar Pass, and a cold glass of beer

Packing up for the great escape.

at the Moab Brewery into the mix. All this and more can be yours for just $475.00 per person. That's $67.85 per day.

Although riders are given a minimum-suggested equipment list and route descriptions, this hut tour is designed to be self-guided. Riders are expected to be in good physical shape and have knowledge of backcountry safety, first aid, and bicycle repair. A consideration often overlooked when assessing one's physical ability is the extra weight one may be carrying along this trip. Since this route travels through remote mountain territory, expect the unexpected, particularly weather—which can range from sweltering heat to snowstorms. You'll need to equip yourselves with a bicycle repair kit, first aid kit, hydration system or at least three large bottles of water, rain gear, a full layering system (shirt, hat, gloves, socks, separate pair of shoes), and bug repellent. The added weight of these items, coupled with the length and elevations of some of the day's rides, may greatly reduce an individual's stamina. Please know your limits.

From Telluride, the Victorian mining town tucked deep in the corner of a San Juan box canyon, riders ascend Last Dollar Pass along the western edge of the Sneffels Range. From there, it's a savage descent to Buck Canyon and Howard Flats before connecting with the Uncompahgre Plateau, a massive mesa whose sides are

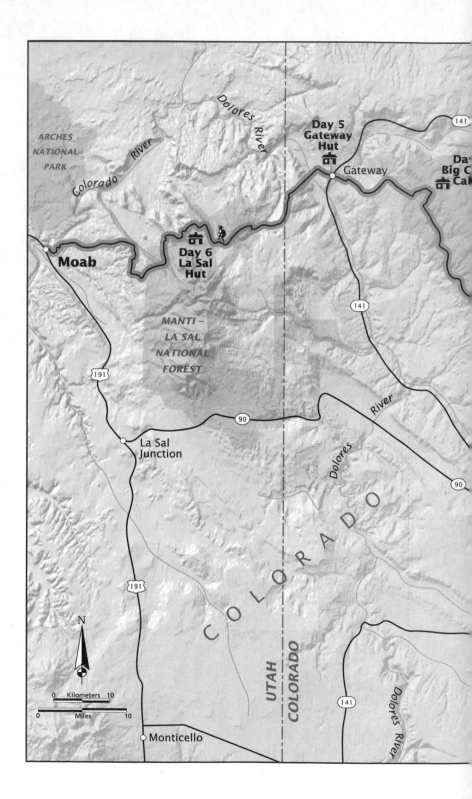

ARCHES
NATIONAL
PARK

Colorado River

Dolores River

Day 5
Gateway
Hut

Gateway

Da
Big C
Ca

Moab

Day 6
La Sal
Hut

MANTI –
LA SAL
NATIONAL
FOREST

141

141

Dolores River

90

191

La Sal
Junction

90

Dolores River

C O L O R A D O

N

0   Kilometers   10

0   Miles   10

191

141

UTAH

COLORADO

Monticello

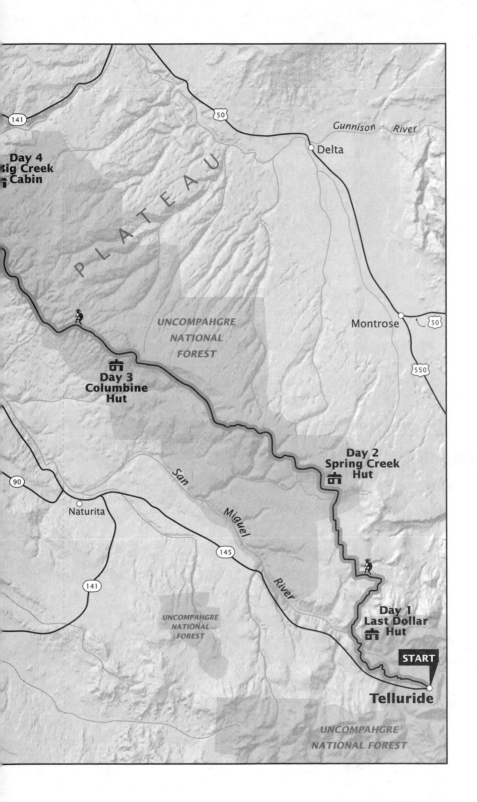

141

50

Gunnison River

Delta

Day 4
Big Creek
Cabin

P L A T E A U

UNCOMPAHGRE
NATIONAL
FOREST

Montrose

50

550

Day 3
Columbine
Hut

Day 2
Spring Creek
Hut

90

San

Naturita

Miguel

145

141

River

UNCOMPAHGRE
NATIONAL
FOREST

Day 1
Last Dollar
Hut

START

Telluride

UNCOMPAHGRE
NATIONAL FOREST

cut by massive gorges. Riding west atop the entire length of the plateau's spine, riders descend via a knuckle-wrenching road into the Dolores River Valley. From deep in the heart of the valley, a long and arduous climb up John Brown Canyon awaits, as riders head toward the Utah border and the La Sal Mountains. From the La Sal Mountains, it's a fast-paced ride down into Moab, where millions of years of wind, water, and erosion have carved some of this country's most startling landscapes.

This kind of mountain bike tour includes some momentous gems one might not otherwise consider. Conversations with riding companions range from the day's sorest bum to the unrivaled benefits of being in Colorado. The days tend to pass quickly as you ride, eat, sleep, and ride again. In between the rhythm of the days, you may find the time to harmonize with friends during a heated wood-chopping competition. Not seeing your own reflection for a week, enduring unexpected rain delays, and meeting the challenge of making a new and exciting meal at the end of each day are just a few of the interesting times shared by all.

Although most of the riding is nontechnical, there are three great singletrack rides you can do: Spring Creek, Ute Creek, and Porcupine Rim. Consult with the San Juan Hut System for more information on these and other available alternatives. With the Telluride-to-Moab mountain bike tour becoming as popular as it is, would-be vacationers should reserve their spaces early, probably three to six months in advance. Reservations are made through the San Juan Hut System at (970) 626–3033.

HUT-TO-HUT BIKING

There are hut-to-hut trips available throughout the country. Most, however, are booked six to twelve months in advance. Here is a short list of other hut-to-hut outfitters you might be interested in contacting.

The Yurts of Never Summer Nordic, P.O. Box 1903, Fort Collins, 80502; (970) 482-9411. May 1 to October 1. Situated on the eastern flank of North Park in the Colorado State Forest, the Never Summer Nordic yurts are canvas, tent-like structures. There are as many as five yurts to which you can ride. Although kitchen facilities are provided, you must bring your own food, water, and sleeping bags. Rates range from $45.00 to $75.00 per person per night.

10th Mountain Hut System, 1280 Ute Avenue, Suite 21, Aspen, 81611; (970) 925-5775; www.aspen.com/huts. Aspen to Vail, Colorado. July 1 to September 30. Surrounding the Holy Cross Wilderness Area, this system includes eleven huts between Aspen and Vail. Most of the huts are $22.00 per person per night and include sleeping bunks and kitchen facilities. Riders must bring their own food. Guided tours are available.

Just desserts on top of Last Dollar Pass.

Ride Information for Telluride

Local Information

Telluride Visitor Center, 666 West Colorado Ave., Telluride; (970) 728–6265, (800) 525–2717.

Ridgway Area Chamber of Commerce, 150 Racecourse Road, Ridgway, 81432; (970) 626–5181, (800) 220–4959.

Outermost Adventures, Telluride; (970) 626–5491.

Visitors Information on Telluride; www.telluride.com.

Local Events and Attractions

Telluride Bluegrass Festival, in June, Telluride (contact Telluride Visitor Center, 970–728–6265, 800–525–2717).

Melee in the Mines Mountain Bike Races, in July (contact Telluride Visitor Center, 970–728–6265, 800–525–2717).

Wild Mushrooms Conference, in August (contact Telluride Visitor Center, 970–728–6265, 800–525–2717).

Film Festival, in September (contact Telluride Visitor Center, 970–728–6265, 800–525–2717).

Blues & Brews Festival, in September (contact Telluride Visitor Center, 970–728–6265, 800–525–2717).

Accommodations

Town Park and Campground, Telluride; (970) 728–2173 ($11.00 per night camping; showers and toilet facilities available May 15 to October 15).

Restaurants

La Cocina De Luz, 123 East Colorado Ave., Telluride; (970) 728–9355 (Mexican take-out and catering company).

Rustico Ristorante, 114 East Colorado, Telluride; (970) 728-4046.
Smuggler's, 101 West San Juan Ave., Telluride; (970) 728-0919 (Telluride's only brewpub).

Tours

Telluride Outside, 1982 West Highway 145, Telluride; (970) 728-3895, (800) 831-6230; www.tellurideoutside.com.
Back Country Biking, Telluride; (970) 728-0861.

Telluride Sports/Adventure Desk, 150 West Colorado Ave., Telluride; (970) 728-4477, (800) 828-7547.
Telski/Mountain Adventures, Telluride; (970) 728-6900.

Shipping Bikes

Easy Rider Mountain Sports, Telluride; (970) 728-4734 (contact Missy Smith).

Ride Information for Moab

Local Information

Moab, Green River Visitors Center, Moab, Utah; (800) 635-6622.
Moab Chamber of Commerce, 805 North Main Street, Moab, Utah, 84532; (435) 259-7814.
Visitors Information on Moab; www.moab utah.com.

Local Events and Attractions

Canyonlands National Park, (435) 259-7164.
Arches National Park, (435) 259-8161.

Accommodations

Free camping along the Colorado River
Slickrock Campground, 1301½ North U.S. Highway 191, (435) 259-7660, (800) 448-8873.

Restaurants

Moab Brewery, 686 South Main (next to McDonald's), Moab, Utah; (435) 259-6333.
Grand Old Ranch House, 1266 North U.S. Highway 191, Moab, Utah; (435) 259-5753.

La Hacienda, 574 North Main, Moab, Utah; (435) 259-6319.
Eddie McStiff's, 57 South Main, Moab, Utah; (435) 259-BEER.
Moab Diner, 189 South Moab, Utah; (435) 259-4006 (great milkshakes).

Tours

Dreamride Tours, Moab, Utah; (888) MOABUTAH; www.dreamride.com.
Never Summer Western Spirit Cycling, Moab, Utah; (800) 845-2453.
Nichols Expedition, 497 North Main, Moab, Utah; (801) 259-3999; www.Nichols Expeditions.com.
O.A.R.S/North American River Expeditions, 543 North Main, Moab, Utah; (800) 342-5938; www.oars.com/moab.
Holiday Expeditions, Inc., 544 East 3900 South, Salt Lake City, Utah; (801) 266-2087, (800) 624-6323; www.bikeraft.com.

Day 1 Telluride to Last Dollar Hut

One of the most scenic and most photographed Colorado back roads, Last Dollar Road leads to the Last Dollar Hut. Last Dollar Hut overlooks the La Sal Mountains and Utah to the west, the Wilson Peaks and the Lizard Head Wilderness Area to the south, and the Silverton West Group of the San Juan Mountains to the east. While the route is not particularly long, it does climb steeply at high elevations, and it delivers challenging switchbacks as you near Last Dollar Pass at 11,000 feet. Once you reach the pass, you're greeted with a 300-vertical-foot hike-a-bike section to the hut itself. You can view this as your final payment for one of Colorado's most exquisite panoramic views.

Start: From downtown Telluride.
Length: 13.7 miles.
Approximate riding time: Advanced riders, 2 to 3 hours; intermediate riders, 3 to 4 hours.
Technical difficulty: Technically easy to moderate. Much of the route travels on well-maintained paved and dirt roads. There are a couple of talus field crossings with which you'll have to contend.
Physical difficulty: Physically moderate to challenging due to the sustained and steep climbs at high elevations. The final approach to the Last Dollar Hut is particularly demanding.
Terrain: Paved bike path, paved road, and dirt road. The terrain encountered includes loose talus-field rock, sand, and dirt.
Nearest town: Telluride.
Other trail users: Hikers, backpackers, sightseers, and photographers.

Getting There

From Telluride: Drive west on Colorado Avenue to Mahoney Drive. Turn left on Mahoney Drive, passing Prospect and Smuggler Streets to your left, and bear right into the Coonskin parking lot at the base of the Coonskin Lift (Lift 7). Park your vehicle here and begin riding.

The Ride

At around 10:00 A.M. on June 24, 1889, Butch Cassidy, Tom McCarty, and Matt Warner robbed the San Miguel National Bank in Telluride, forever labeling this Telluride depository as the first bank Butch Cassidy ever robbed. After their successful gunpoint withdrawal, the "Wild Bunch" took to the hills with the loot. Destination? Moab, Utah. They were headed to Brown's Hole, located in a large valley along the foot of Diamond Mountain, near the Green River of Utah. In his autobiography, Tom McCarty spoke of their first hit. "Our plans were accordingly laid very carefully to go to a certain bank [San Miguel National Bank of Telluride, which handled large mine payrolls] and relieve the cashier of his ready cash." The plan involved following a secret route from Telluride to Moab, with food and supplies

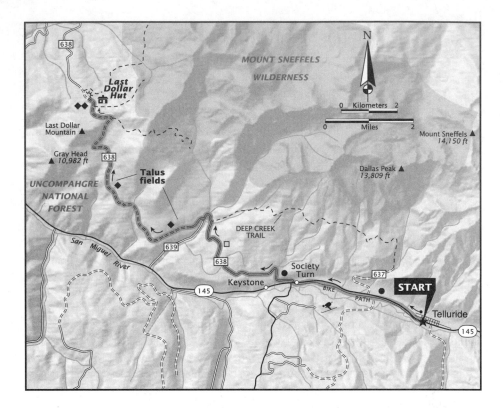

located at key hideouts along the way. The threesome had even taken time to train the horses to stand perfectly still while each man vaulted into the saddle.

To aid in their getaway, Cassidy enlisted the services of his younger brother, Dan Parker. Parker served as supply runner. He'd travel ahead of the outlaws and drop stores of food and supplies at prearranged locations along the route—an important consideration if one hoped to cross the rugged San Juan and La Sal Mountains successfully. No one doubted the Wild Bunch's ability to get away, even with a reputed $30,000 weighing them down—they were all accomplished riders—but Butch's little brother didn't fare so well. Parker was arrested while transporting the supplies. He was brought to Wyoming to answer to these and older charges. His subsequent arrest and imprisonment forced Cassidy, McCarty, and Warner to fend for themselves.

As for Butch and his gang, they were never found, nor was the stolen money. The posse employed to track the outlaws was not as enthusiastic about the chase as might be expected. The Wild Bunch were legendary gunmen whose pistol skills, no doubt, preceded them wherever they went. Telluride Sheriff Beattie, masking his shame for never having captured the gang, resorted to boasting about the one thing he did manage to capture: Butch's horse. For years after the robbery, Sheriff Beattie delighted himself by riding around downtown Telluride on Butch Cassidy's horse, the only one who didn't get away.

Today, riders can travel a similar route on their getaway from Telluride to Moab. By replacing saddlebags with panniers and horses with mountain bikes, riders can relive what it must have been like for Butch and his gang, riding from one food and supply hideout to the other. You begin your escape by riding up Telluride's Last Dollar Road, across the western corner of the Sneffels Range, to your first night's hideout, Last Dollar Hut. Although the 13.7-mile stretch from Telluride to the Last Dollar Hut is the shortest leg (in terms of miles) of the weeklong getaway, it climbs an impressive 2,800 feet to Last Dollar Pass (11,000 feet).

The Last Dollar Hut, the highest hut along the route and one of the first to be built in the San Juan Hut System, sleeps eight and sits atop a wind-beleaguered ledge, above the sheep-grazing meadows below. The Last Dollar Hut offers one of the most dramatic panoramic vistas in Colorado. From the perch you can take in views of the Silverton West Group of the San Juans, the La Sal Mountains in Utah (Day 6), and the Wilson Peaks (Mount Wilson, 14,246 feet, and Wilson Peak, 14,017 feet). The Wilson Peaks are perhaps the most prominent.

Mount Wilson and Wilson Peak were named after one man, the famed topographer of the Hayden Survey Team. To have even one of Colorado's fifty-four Fourteeners named after you would be an incredible honor, but to have two peaks bear your name is almost unimaginable. A. D. Wilson is so honored. Wilson's list of accomplishments includes doing topographic work with Clarence King's 14th Parallel Survey, being the second to ascend Mount Rainier (within weeks of the first), and helping to organize the Hayden Atlas. The Hayden Survey Team was one of the first teams to accurately survey Colorado in the mid-1800s. Their extensive research and study were included in the Hayden Atlas. It was, however, primarily Wilson's work with the Hayden Survey Team that ensured him his place among the highest peaks of the Colorado mountains.

As you rest by a blazing campfire outside the Last Dollar Hut and stare off across the canyon, you can't help but marvel at the grandness of the San Juans. Now nearly eye level with these surrounding 14,000-foot peaks, you also can't help but marvel at the strength it took to reach this point in your own journey. Make sure you return from your reverie before too long, as another day awaits.

The crew setting out on Last Dollar Road.

Miles and Directions

0.0 START from the Coonskin parking lot in downtown Telluride. Bear left onto Mahoney Drive and again on Colorado Avenue, riding west out of town. Intercept the paved Telluride Bicycle Path and ride to Society Turn.

3.0 Reach the intersection of Telluride Bicycle Path and Last Dollar Road by Society Turn. Cross Colorado Highway 145 and bear right on Last Dollar Road (Forest Road 638).

5.1 Reach the intersection of the airport road and Last Dollar Road. Bear right at the top of the airport road (with the runway and hangers in sight to the left) onto the now dirt Last Dollar Road. A National Forest access sign and a stop sign (facing the opposite direction) mark this intersection.

10.7 Enter the Uncompahgre National Forest.

11.2 Cross a talus field and continue riding through the aspen.

11.4 Cross another talus field.

12.8 Pass an old homestead to your left. Before crossing Summit Creek, a spring with water pouring from a black hose will be on your right. Begin climbing switchbacks as you near the final approach to the hut.

13.3 Reach Last Dollar Pass. Bear right at the crest, following the steep and rocky road at the edge of the trees, and hike-a-bike the last 0.25 mile up the ridge to the east. (Don't follow the road that darts left into the forest.) You'll be able to see the hut when you're within 50 feet of it.

13.7 Arrive at the Last Dollar Hut.

Day 2 Last Dollar Hut to Spring Creek Hut

Starting with one massive loss in elevation, this day's ride is perhaps the easiest of the tour. The ruddy complexion of Hastings Mesa offers a bit of insight into the kind of landscape into which you're heading (the lunar-scaped terrain of Moab, Utah), while the grandness of Howard Flats recalls visions of the galloping ponies Ute Indians once raced there. Once arriving at the Spring Creek Hut, riders can include some sideline riding on Spring Creek Trail 116. Spring Creek Trail 116 features some of the Uncompahgre Plateau's best singletrack. The 12-mile (one way) Spring Creek Trail 116 passes through meadows, aspen groves, and creeks. Consult with the San Juan Hut System for more information.

Start: From the Last Dollar Hut.
Length: 27 miles.
Approximate riding time: Advanced riders, 2 to 3 hours; intermediate riders, 3 to 4 hours.
Technical difficulty: Technically easy due to the well-maintained dirt roads.
Physical difficulty: Physically easy to moderate due to the large descent from the Last Dollar Hut. What moderate ascending there is comes at the end of the ride.

Terrain: Paved state road and well-maintained dirt road. Aside from a fast, sometimes loose, rocky descent from the Last Dollar Hut, the route to the Spring Creek Hut travels mostly through flat meadows, large valleys, and expansive plateaus.
Nearest town: Montrose.
Other trail users: Sightseers, hunters, hikers, campers, anglers, and picnickers.

The Ride

The second day of your escape has all the makings of a fast getaway. You drop almost 3,000 feet to the paved Colorado Highway 62 before eventually intersecting with Howard Flats, site of an old Ute horse-racing track. Day two marks the beginning of your two-and-one-half-day tour of the Uncompahgre Plateau, where Ute Indians once thrived. From Last Dollar Hut, continue riding on Last Dollar Road to Divide Pass and CO 62. En route, you'll descend through a forest of mixed aspens and conifers, passing old homesteads and paralleling Hastings Mesa. Once atop Hastings Mesa, you're treated to views of the Mount Sneffels Wilderness, including 14,150-foot Mount Sneffels. After intersecting CO 62 (the road that joins Placerville, in the southwest, with Dallas Divide and Ridgway, in the northeast), bear eft onto CO 62 and speed down the paved road. If you were to bear right onto CO 62, you'd soon reach the top of Dallas Divide and the town of Ridgway, which is perhaps next on Colorado's ever-dwindling list of mountain towns on the brink of massive discovery. Peter R. Decker's *Old Fences, New Neighbors* (University of Arizona Press, Tucson, 1998) eloquently details Ridgway's burgeoning popularity.

After turning right off Highway 62, you ride up Buck Canyon and onto Howard Flats. Howard Flats used to be an old Ute horse-racing track. Aside from its recreational use, the horse proved a formidable addition to the Utes' culture. Before the Spanish brought horses into North America, the Utes had led a primarily leaderless and wandering existence. With the arrival of the horse, the Utes began to redefine themselves. They became individual, chief-led bands of hunters and warriors. They were also among the first tribes to maintain extensive domesticated horse herds. More horses meant more Ute Indians could hunt and raid more quickly and easily. Ute hunters gradually perfected their economy of motion. They would blitz into enemy Comanche-Arapaho territory and kill as many buffalo as they could, and still manage to make it back to their camps within half a moon's time (roughly fifteen days). The efficiency with which Utes could now travel enabled braves standing watch to react to enemy attacks with lightning speed. With their improved response, life inside Ute camps became more relaxed.

Horse racing became one of the Utes' most beloved pastimes. Whenever there was a social occasion, whether it be a wedding or a dance or a powwow, there was horse racing. The race became so much a part of Ute life that no camp was complete without its own racetrack. Before there was a Denver or an INVESCO field at Mile High, there was Howard Flats, home to the original big league broncos. If viewed from above, the Flats show long, straight sections of hoof-trodden earth, pinpointing the precise location where these races were held. Gambling eventually found its way into horse racing, and the scene began to spread, now starting to include white settlers. It was horse-racing that would prove to be the gateway to a life of crime for men such as Butch Cassidy and his gang.

Cassidy first met Matt Warner, already an accomplished cattle rustler and horse racer, while at a horse race in Telluride in 1885. The young Cassidy, who worked as an ore hauler for one of the area mines, took a liking to Warner—despite the fact that Cassidy had lost his savings to Warner in horse racing debts. And Warner, in turn, liked Cassidy, if for no other reason than that Cassidy kept him in business. The two eventually became partners in their own horse-racing business.

With their best horse Betty, and others like her, Butch and Matt managed to beat every horse in southern Colorado and Utah. While racing in Cortez, Matt met up with his brother-in-law Tom McCarty and invited him to join in their racing business. The three of them set out to become the area's most successful horse-racing team. Butch, Matt, and Tom made names for themselves throughout the racing circuit of southern Colorado and Utah, so much so that, in time, only Indians would race against them.

At one such race, an Indian, who had lost his pony and a stack of blankets to the three men, launched a barrage of insults and threats, objecting to their win. Having been so affronted, Tom beat the Indian with a rawhide riding whip. The three quickly bolted from the scene to Tom's cabin. The next morning, Butch, Matt, and Tom awoke to the shrill cries of Indians howling. The Indians approached the cabin and demanded the return of their pony. When one of the Indians pointed a rifle at Tom, Tom quickly returned the idle threat by shooting the Indian off his horse, effectively ending the discussion.

From Howard Flats, you ride silently on, brooding over the possibility of a ghost encounter with an envious Indian. Once beyond the Flats, you begin your two-and-one-half-day journey across the Uncompahgre Plateau, Ute domain.

Miles and Directions

0.0 START from the Last Dollar Hut. Bear left from the front door and walk (reducing further trail damage) your bicycle down the path located to the north side of the hut. This is not the way you came. When the path widens enough to allow a truck's passing, begin riding and descend from the pass on Last Dollar Road.

0.4 Reach the intersection of the path and Last Dollar Road (Forest Road 638). Bear right onto Last Dollar Road and descend the north side of Last Dollar Mountain.

Spring Creek Hut.

1.7 Arrive at a beautiful vista, on your left, with views of Hastings Mesa to the north, Wilson Peak to the south, and the La Sal Mountains to the distant west.

4.4 After crossing two cattle guards, cross Alder Creek. Climb from Alder Creek onto Hastings Mesa and intersect County Road 58P.

6.0 Reach the intersection of Last Dollar Road, Sawpit Road, and CR 58P. Bear right onto CR 58P.

8.4 Near San Juan Vista, pass an old ranch to the left. (This ranch was in the John Wayne movie *True Grit*.)

11.1 County Road 58P intersects with the paved Colorado Highway 62 at a stop sign. Bear left onto CO 62 and descend on pavement to CR 60X, passing CR 62X on the right.

13.8 Reach the intersection of CO 62 and CR 60X. Bear right onto CR 60X, by an old ski cabin on the left. Begin climbing, moderately, up Buck Canyon into Howard Flats, site of an old Ute Indian horse-racing track.

17.2 Pass an old homestead, seen through a wide valley to your left.

18.7 Reach the intersection of roads CR JJ6 and CR 59Z, by the San Juan Ranch gate and sign. Bear left onto CR JJ6.

19.1 County Road JJ6 will turn into CR 58.5 at a right curve. Bear right, continuing on CR 58.5.

20.8 County Road 58.5 connects with CR 11. Bear left onto CR 11.

21.0 County Road 11 intersects with Dave Wood Road. Bear right onto Dave Wood Road, passing under power lines and descending moderately into a large valley.

23.9 Reach the intersection of Sanborn Park Road (marked by a Sanborn Park sign) and Dave Wood Road. Bear right, continuing on Dave Wood Road, past the sign for Montrose. From here, the next and final 3 miles make up one long, steady climb to the Spring Creek Hut.

24.6 Enter into the Uncompahgre National Forest.

25.5 Pass the Johnson Spring on your right. This spring, fenced in by split aspen logs, features potable water pouring from a black hose.

25.6 Reach the intersection of Dave Wood Road and Divide Road. A sign reads COLUMBINE PASS, 31 MILES. Bear left here onto the Divide Road (Forest Road 402).

25.9 Reach the intersection of Divide Road and Spring Creek Rim Road. Bear right onto Spring Creek Rim Road and cross three cattle guards before turning left onto the path leading to the Spring Creek Hut.

26.1 Cross the first cattle guard.

26.4 Cross the second cattle guard.

26.8 Cross the third cattle guard.

27.0 Bear left, after a large water bar ditch, onto a path leading into the woods. An enormous cut section of a Douglas fir trunk lies to the left of the path. Follow this short path to the Spring Creek Hut.

27.0 Arrive at the Spring Creek Hut.

Day 3 Spring Creek Hut to Columbine Hut

Day three offers a pleasurably mellow cruise atop the Uncompahgre Plateau, traveling over gently rolling terrain on Divide Road, the major southwest-to-northeast thoroughfare across the Plateau. Divide Road is thickly lined with old-growth evergreen forests, lending the riding an air of peaceful solitude. Although the trees enclose most of the way, there are three dramatic overlooks, evenly spaced along the route, which demand attention.

Start: From the Spring Creek Hut.
Length: 34.8 miles.
Approximate riding time: Advanced riders, 3 to 3.5 hours; intermediate riders, 4 to 5 hours.
Technical difficulty: Technically easy. The route follows atop the relatively flat Uncompahgre Plateau via the well-maintained Divide Road.

Physical difficulty: Physically easy due to the minimal elevation gain.
Terrain: Improved dirt road. The Uncompahgre Plateau offers a relatively flat, but densely forested ride.
Nearest town: Montrose.
Other trail users: Anglers, hikers, hunters, and campers.

The Ride

The third leg of the journey travels through the heart of the Uncompahgre Plateau, summiting it atop Columbine Pass. From the Spring Creek Hut, the riding on Divide Road features densely forested terrain. The day's riding is marked more by a sense of quiet solitude than by mind-blowing views. That's not to say there are no views; quite the contrary. The first of three incredible overlooks is at 5.7 miles, the Uncompahgre Overlook. To the east lie the peaks of Wetterhorn and Uncompahgre.

Wetterhorn Peak resembles a shark's nose. Named by the Wheeler Survey Team in 1874, the peak undoubtedly takes its name from the Swiss mountain of the same name, but finding a resemblance to the Swiss behemoth might require a bit of imagination. Just to the south of Wetterhorn Peak lies the Henson Creek Valley, a hotbed of mining activity. The chief city in the valley was Capitol City (established in the mid-1870s). Its misleading name was purely intentional. George T. Lee, Capitol City founder and owner of the town's main economic draw, the Lee Mining and Smelting Company, had visions of relocating Colorado's capital to Capitol City. His scheme was so elaborate as to include building a two-story brick house, later dubbed "the Governor's Mansion," with bricks imported from Pueblo. Lee's capital dreams would eventually dissolve after silver prices dropped in 1893.

To the east of Wetterhorn Peak lies Uncompahgre Peak, the largest in the San Juan Range. Towering over the Cimarron River and Big Blue Creek drainage, the

Uncompahgre Peak is one of the San Juan's most prominent landmarks. The word "uncompahgre" (pronounced "oon-cum-pa-gray") comes from the Shoshonean language, a dialect of the Uto-Aztecan language, and means "hot [unca] water [pah] spring [gre]." The Ute Indians found this San Juan precipice an ideal lookout. The name was officially given by the Hayden Survey Team during the latter part of the 1800s.

During a massive study of the San Juans, Hayden Survey members A. D. Wilson and Franklin Rhoda made the first documented ascent of the peak in the summer of 1874. Once atop the peak, the two noticed markings in the ground. The markings turned out to be grizzly paw prints. Evidently, the area surrounding the Uncompahgre Peak was a favorite haunt among grizzlies. Given this, it seems no surprise that the Utes would convene here, as they held the bear in high regard, so much so that they called their most sacred and popular spring dance the Bear Dance. With thoughts of dancing bears aside, riders press on past the Uncompahgre Overlook to the Mount Sneffels Overlook.

The Mount Sneffels Overlook is at 10.3 miles into your ride. Mount Sneffels has been dubbed "Queen of the San Juans." It is one of those hallmark precipices that can hypnotize an observer for hours. Below this royal peak, reflecting its lofty throne, is the Blue Lakes Basin. During the Hayden Survey of 1874, a member of the team remarked that the basin reminded him of the absorbing hole described in Jules Verne's *Journey to the Center of the Earth*. Alluding to the Icelandic mountain located near the "hole" in Verne's novel, survey member Dr. Endlich exclaimed "There's Snaefell," which in Icelandic means "snowfield." Today, we have sufficiently corrupted the spelling and pronunciation enough to give us Mount Sneffels.

Just under a mile from Columbine Pass and the top of the Uncompahgre Plateau, riders are offered their third and most dramatic scenic overlook: the Tabeguache Overlook, with views of the Dolores River Valley to the west. The Tabeguache (meaning "sunny side") were a band of Ute Indians who lived in the valleys of the Gunnison and Uncompahgre Rivers. They lived in harmony with their natural surroundings. Of all the Tabeguache, perhaps no one was more prominent than Chief Shavano. The chief worked closely with Chief Ouray, leader of the Ute Nation, to help establish peaceful relations between the whites and the Utes. Chief Shavano's leadership was such that Chief Ouray, perhaps the greatest of all Ute chiefs, favored him as his successor. In continued respect for his tireless efforts to bring about peace, Chief Shavano is one of only four Indians to have a Colorado Fourteener bear his name: Mount Shavano (14,229 feet). Today, descendants of the Tabeguache, along with members of the Grand, Yampa, and Uintah bands, constitute the Northern Utes. They live on the Uintah-Ouray Reservation, with their headquarters in Fort Duchesne, Utah.

From the Tabeguache Overlook, riders pass over Columbine Pass (where potable water is available) and continue in the direction of Windy Point, before arriving at the Columbine Hut.

Miles and Directions

- **0.0** START from the Spring Creek Hut. Ride up the path back to Spring Creek Road. Bear right on Spring Creek Road, heading back toward Divide Road.
- **0.2** Cross the first cattle guard.
- **0.6** Cross the second cattle guard.
- **0.9** Cross the third cattle guard.

Sitting out a rain and hail storm.

1.0 Reach the intersection of Spring Creek Road and Divide Road (Forest Road 402). Bear right (north) onto Divide Road, toward Columbine Pass.

5.7 Reach the Uncompahgre Overlook, to your left. There are views of Precipice Peak (13,144 feet), Uncompahgre Peak (14,309 feet), and Wetterhorn Peak (14,015 feet).

8.3 Reach the intersection of Divide Road and the Spring Creek Trailhead, the Uncompahgre Plateau's premier singletrack. Continue riding on Divide Road.

10.3 Mount Sneffels Overlook is to your left. There are views of Mount Sneffels (14,150 feet), Lizard Head (13,113 feet), Wilson Peak (14,017 feet), and Mount Wilson (14,246 feet).

15.6 Reach the intersection of Divide Road and Colorado Highway 90 (FR 540). Highway 90 will be to your right. Continue on Divide Road, following signs for Columbine Pass.

16.1 Pass Iron Springs Campground, on your left.

16.6 Pass Transfer East Road, to your right.

17.3 The intersection for Transfer Road and FR 27 will be to your right, as you continue riding on Divide Road.

18.8 Pass West Antone Springs 559, to your left.

19.9 Pass Pool Creek Trail 113, to your right.

20.6 Pass Delta/Nucla Road, to your left.

21.8 Pass Pool Creek Trailhead, to your right.

22.2 Pass West Pool Creek Trail, to your right.

Taking in the views.

23.4 Pass East Bull Creek, to your right.

31.7 Tabeguache Overlook is on your left.

32.5 Reach Columbine Pass and bear right onto FR 503.

33.3 Reach Columbine Campground. Toilet facilities are available. Good drinking water is available from the spring.

33.7 Pass the now-defunct Columbine Ranger Station and arrive at the intersection of FR 402 and FR 503. Bear left (west), following FR 402 (still Divide Road) toward Windy Point.

34.5 Pass a dirt road leading off to the left.

34.7 Bear left onto this second dirt road leading into the woods. Follow this small non-gravel road for roughly 200 yards to the hut.

34.8 Arrive at the Columbine Hut.

Day 4 Columbine Hut to Big Creek Cabin

Day four is perhaps the journey's most spectacular leg. As you near the end of your two-and-a-half-day tour of the Uncompahgre Plateau, you ride down the western edge of the plateau over the rolling Divide Road. En route, vertigo-inducing views of the La Sal Mountains and the high deserts of southeastern Utah mesmerize your visual senses. Fear not the hypnotic trance in which you may find yourself. Let it carry you through to the Big Creek Cabin. A turn-of-the-century rancher's cabin, Big Creek is constructed of notched logs chinked with mortar. Poised among quaking aspens in a far corner of the Craig Ranch, overlooking a horse corral, Big Creek's idyllic setting only serves to enhance the buzz already acquired from the day's viewtiful ride.

Start: From the Columbine Hut.
Length: 36.9 miles.
Approximate riding time: Advanced riders, 2.5 to 3 hours; intermediate riders, 3.5 to 4 hours.
Technical difficulty: Technically easy due to traveling on mildly undulating terrain, along the well-maintained Divide Road.
Physical difficulty: Physically easy due to the little ascending involved, roughly 1,600 feet.

Terrain: Improved dirt road. The route travels atop the densely forested Uncompahgre Plateau, with open views as you near the plateau's western edge.
Nearest town: Gateway.
Other trail users: Hikers, hunters, campers, anglers, and sightseers.

The Ride

For two and one-half days you've been riding on the Uncompahgre Plateau. Day four marks the final leg of your travels on Divide Road and the plateau. But what exactly is this Uncompahgre Plateau, and where does it fit in the grand scheme of

▶ **For further reading:** *Uncompahgre: A Guide to the Uncompahgre Plateau,* by Muriel Marshall, Valley Books, 3rd edition, 1998, 328 East Main Street, Montrose, 81401; (970) 249–1841.

things? Unlike the San Juan Mountains, whose high-alpine peaks were formed ten to forty million years ago by volcanic upheaval and glaciation, the Uncompahgre Plateau was formed by a series of massive uplifts caused by internal disturbances of the Earth's crust. Mysteriously, the Uncompahgre Plateau somehow escaped the geological turmoil that swept across the West to form the Sierra Nevadas, the ranges of Nevada and Utah, and the Rocky Mountains.

The Uncompahgre Plateau is located on the Colorado Plateau Province's eastern border. This province encompasses the vast area of flat-lying sedimentary rock extending into Utah, Arizona, and New Mexico. The Uncompahgre Plateau

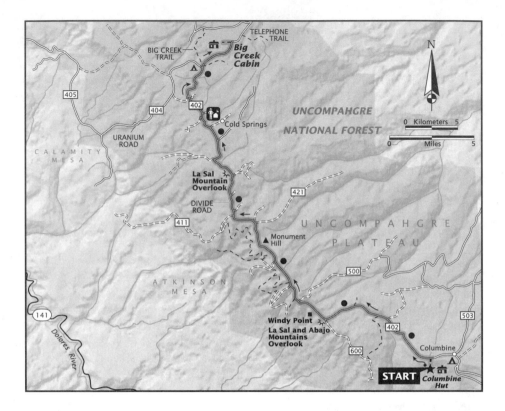

stretches in a southeast-to-northwest direction from the San Juan Mountains to the Utah border southwest of Grand Junction. A virtually flat mesa stretching 25 by 100 miles, the plateau, when viewed from a distance, is far less striking than its neighboring San Juan and West Elk Mountains. This paling-by-comparison situation has allowed the plateau a certain degree of anonymity. Nevertheless, the Uncompahgre Plateau is, indeed, part of the ancestral Rocky Mountains and deserves attention. Its existence stems from the Uncompahgria uplift, the ancient range lifted high by faulting 310 million years ago. A series of lesser uplifts, occurring roughly one million years ago, gave the plateau its present formation.

Although archeological evidence suggests that people have been living on the Uncompahgre Plateau for at least 10,000 years, its recorded history did not start until the late 1770s. In 1776 two Spanish priests, Silvestre Velez de Escalante and Francisco Antanasio Dominguez, accompanied by a Ute guide, led a party from Sante Fe, New Mexico, across the Uncompahgre Plateau in search of safe passage to the missions of California. As winter approached, the two decided to call off their search and head back to Santa Fe.

Fifty-two years later, Antoine Robidoux, who had been operating a fur trapper supply business in St. Louis, built a trading post near the present town of Delta, Colorado. In response to the popularity of the top hat (which was made of beaver pelts), many trappers flocked to the Uncompahgre in search of beaver. Robidoux's Fort Uncompahgre, functioning as a supply station for trappers and Indians alike, became a meeting ground for these two very different peoples. The fort was significant in that it provided an arena where trappers and Indians would meet; these two groups would seldom see each other outside of the trading room. Fort Uncompahgre was also significant in that it was one of only two white settlements in all of Colorado. This would change, however, when in 1850 the U.S. laid claim to all of western Colorado.

In 1853 Congress ordered Captain John Gunnison to explore the new territory and report on its potential. His travels took him from the Great Plains to the San Luis Valley, over Cochetopa Pass, down the Gunnison River, and into the Uncompahgre Valley. Gunnison would happen upon the ruins of Fort Uncompahgre, which had been set ablaze by Ute Indians shortly after it was built. Gunnison wrote of a savage and rugged Colorado, one that did not sound entirely hospitable. But to his credit, he did detail information that proved particularly helpful in future expeditions, like the Wheeler and Hayden surveys.

Wheeler and Hayden discovered the Uncompahgre Plateau to be rife with minerals. Once the news of this got out, countless miners and prospectors flocked to the plateau to set up shop. As the plateau mining increased, resident Utes were pushed farther and farther from their settlements. The mushrooming mining towns became the economic, social, and political lifeline of the Uncompahgre country and paved the way for other industries to move in. By the 1880s it was no surprise when tens of thousands of cattle were grazing on the plateau. The large number of cattle, coupled with loose grazing regulations, eventually tuned many large tracts into barren wastelands. This resulted in the turn-of-the-century establishment of federal land reserves, precursors to our national forests.

As you ride the former chuckwagon trail of the Divide Road, dodging perhaps ten cattle, instead of tens of thousands, you can't help but appreciate our national forest system. That appreciation comes fully to bear when you arrive at Windy Point. Here the dramatic upward arching of the plateau's rock layers is brought into view, as the plateau itself drops precipitously nearly 2,000 feet in a collection of cliffs and slopes to Burro Creek. Looking northwest from Windy Point, you're offered a

Big Creek Cabin and bikes.

unique bird's-eye view of the plateau's abrupt west face. A pair of eagles can often be seen soaring high above the plateau's west face.

But eagles aren't the only birds to take up permanent residence on the plateau. Located just after the turnoff leading to the Big Creek Cabin lies the nearby Telephone Trail, so called for the variety of nesting holes bored in the trail's tree trunks. Telephone Trail makes for a great wind-down hike after you settle in at the cabin. The entire trail courses through a cavity-nesting bird habitat that's noted for its variety of uncommon birds, which nest in holes burrowed into standing dead trees. Northern pygmy-owls (Glancidium gnoma), flammulated owls (Otus flammeolus), hairy woodpeckers (Picoides villosus), nuthatches (Sitta canadensis and Sitta carolinensis), and swallows (Tachycineta thalassina) all may be seen while hiking. If hiking after biking isn't your style, simply chill out at the cabin, a hideout with real character.

Miles and Directions

0.0 START from the Columbine Hut and backtrack to Divide Road.

0.1 Intersect with Divide Road. Bear left (north) onto Divide Road and start riding toward Windy Point.

9.4 Reach Windy Point. A scenic overlook of the La Sal and Abajo (Blue) Mountains faces west.

13.0 You're offered the first view of the Grand Mesa, to your right (northeast), near the town of Grand Junction.

13.9 Leave Montrose County and enter Mesa County.

22.3 Pass the Uncompahgre Butte (9,732 feet) to your right.

23.2 The La Sal Mountains vista is to the west.

25.2 Pass Mesa Creek, to the left.

27.6 To the northeast lies the largest view of the Grand Mesa.

29.1 Pass the ranger station and the Cold Springs Work Center on your right.

33.3 Pass the Divide Forks Campground on your left.

33.5 Reach the junction of Divide Road (FR 402) and Uranium Road (FR 404). Continue straight (right) on Divide Road toward Grand Junction.

33.7 Pass Big Creek Trail 656, on your left.

36.6 Reach the intersection of Divide Road and the doubletrack on the left, which leads to the cabin. Bear left onto this doubletrack (which bears the sign PRIVATE ACCESS ROAD) directly before the cattle guard that crosses Divide Road. Follow the split-rail fence (which eventually turns into a barbed wire fence) to the cabin. Telephone Trail begins to the right, just over the cattle guard.

36.9 Arrive at the Big Creek Cabin.

Day 5 Big Creek Cabin to Gateway Hut

Along with the mostly descending, 9-mile stretch of singletrack of Ute Creek Trail 608, on this section riders are treated to great views of the La Sal Mountains and the canyons of the Dolores River Valley. From the cool forests atop the western flank of the Uncompahgre Plateau, riders also descend along a 6-mile shelf into the sandstone canyons of the Dolores River Valley. In total, the ride drops you 4,900 feet from the Big Creek Cabin to the Gateway Hut. The Gateway Hut is located in the tiny town of Gateway, Colorado. Unless you brought it with you, you've had no access to adult beverages in over four days. The Gateway Tavern can help. But take note: it's closed on Mondays, so plan your trip accordingly.

Start: From the Big Creek Cabin.
Length: 28 miles.
Approximate riding time: Advanced riders, 2.5 to 3 hours; intermediate riders, 3 to 4 hours.
Technical difficulty: Technically easy to challenging. Most of this leg travels over well-maintained dirt road; however, the optional singletrack spur involves steep, rocky descents along sand and dirt-packed trail. Also, there's a pulse-racing descent over rocky road from the top of the Uncompahgre Plateau into the Dolores River Valley.
Physical difficulty: Physically easy to moderate. The intermittent short, but tough, climbs of the singletrack spur, coupled with the more moderate climbs along the road, make this leg of the journey moderately physical.
Terrain: Improved dirt road, paved state highway, doubletrack, and singletrack. Near the western edge of the plateau, the thick, forested terrain gives way to rockier and sandier, semi-arid terrain. Sand and exposed rocks and roots are all to be expected along this route, particularly on the singletrack spur. As you enter into the Dolores River Valley and a flash flood zone, there are large sections of deep sand.
Nearest town: Gateway.
Other trail users: Hikers, campers, four-wheelers, hunters, and sightseers.

The Ride

From the Big Creek Cabin, riders return to Divide Road and backtrack to its intersection with Uranium Road. As its name suggests, Uranium Road was once used to transport uranium from the many plateau mines. Uranium was being shipped to Grand Junction as early as World War I, where it was used to aid in the war effort. Uranium Road follows an old Ute trail that the Indians used frequently. This old Ute trail will eventually connect with one of the day's highlights, the singletrack of the aptly named Ute Creek Trail 608.

Ute Creek Trail is an optional singletrack spur from the main route, but one well worth taking. The trail descends through thick aspens, over big rock drop-offs, into chilling creek beds, across sweeping meadows, and through piñon-juniper forests before letting out onto slickrock and sandstone. At 9.4 miles the views of the La Sal

Mountains and John Brown Canyon are engulfing. Adding to the challenge of the singletrack is the extra weight that bike touring necessitates. Panniers might be the way to go when touring on well-maintained forest roads, but their value is called into question when barreling down tight and rocky singletrack. The extra weight adds a new dimension to singletrack riding. After you intersect with Snowshoe Trail, it's a short grunt of a climb to Pine Mountain Road.

After riding roughly 1.5 miles from this intersection, the route unfolds to an overwhelming view of the Dolores River Valley. From the western flank of the Uncompahgre Plateau, you descend abruptly along a shelf road into the valley—a valley consisting of a maze of mesas and canyons. This is a hair-raising section of the ride. The shelf falls steeply from the plateau with nothing to your right save a 300-foot drop to the canyon floor. This marks the beginning of a fast and furious descent into the Dolores River Valley and the town of Gateway.

The Dolores River received its name from the Spanish missionaries Dominguez and Escalante, who, in 1776, led an expedition across the Uncompahgre Plateau in search of safe passage to the missions of California. To reach Ute Trail (Uranium Road), which crossed over the Uncompahgre Plateau, the expedition had to ford the then unnamed Dolores River. After realizing that they had passed the point where they should have crossed the river, Dominguez and Escalante hastily ordered their expedition to cross where they were. This decision proved costly, since Dominguez, Escalante, and their expedition found themselves entangled in thorny brush and standing before a steep canyon wall. They struggled to scale the wall to the top of the plateau, so much so that their horses' hooves started to bleed. Having endured such great pain and suffering in the crossing, the priests consequently named the river, appropriately enough, "dolores" or "pains."

In the 1880s gold was discovered on Mesa Creek Flats, located upriver, just 4 miles below the junction of the Dolores River and the San Miguel River. Soon thereafter, prospectors were panning for gold in Mesa Creek. However, there was one slight hitch to this endeavor: gold panning was limited to only the spring and early summer, since water flow from Mesa Creek was quite small. By mid-summer, in fact, Mesa Creek would run dry, effectively putting an end to gold panning in Mesa Creek Flats until the winter's snowmelt would again give rise to Mesa Creek. These circumstances inspired the Montrose Placer Mining Company, managed by Colonel N. P. Turner, to construct the San Miguel Flume, one of Colorado's greatest engineering achievements. The mining company believed that if enough water were to rush through Mesa Creek and into the flats, millions of dollars' worth of gold could be recovered from the soil all year through. Construction on the flume began in 1889 and was completed two years later. In 1891 this ambitious project began diverting water from the San Miguel River to Mesa Creek, a distance of roughly 12 miles.

Turner's intent was to mine Mesa Creek hydraulically, using pressurized water to sift the heavier gold particles from the river sediment. The water and sediment mixture would flow through a sluice box and over a riffle board. The sluice, which closely resembles a flume, was angled to allow the mixture to sift through. The riffles were small slats that ran perpendicular to the sides of the sluice box, much like venetian blinds might look if lain open in a shoebox. The riffles would catch the sand containing the heavier gold particles.

Turner's diversion plan called for an 8-mile-long, 4-foot-deep, and 6-foot-wide flume running along the northern wall of the San Miguel Canyon. Workers were literally hung over the canyon wall, 250 to 500 feet below the rim and 100 to 150 feet

Doing a balancing act with the La Sal Mountains beyond.

above the riverbed, all in order to secure the flume into the sandstone walls. Once completed, the flume ran 1.5 miles on the sandstone cliffs above the San Miguel River and 6.5 miles on the canyon wall above the Dolores River. An estimated 1.8 million board-feet of lumber was used to construct the flume, which cost over $100,000 to build. Completed in 1891, the flume was an engineering success. It worked beautifully, delivering over eighty million gallons of water a day. But its true success was yet to be tested. Would it yield gold?

The gold found along the Mesa Creek Flats was known as "leaf gold," or "flour gold," consisting of a very fine powder. Because of the gold's fine consistency, it washed straight through the sluice. Remaining suspended in the water, the gold flushed directly over the riffles in the flume, in effect rendering them useless. It didn't take long for Turner, along with the Montrose Placer Mining Company stockholders, to realize that the entire project was a failure. With the entire investment in the flume lost, Turner became so dejected that he traveled to Chicago, rented a room, and shot himself in the head. After Turner's horrific demise, the flume was soon abandoned, left only to the scavenging ranchers whose cabins and sheds and fences needed mending. Remnants of the flume still cling to sections of the canyon, near Uravan, roughly 25 miles south of Gateway.

Miles and Directions

0.0 START from the Big Creek Cabin and ride back up the doubletrack to Divide Road (FR 402).

0.3 Reach the intersection of the doubletrack and Divide Road (FR 402). Bear right onto Divide Road (FR 402), and return to the intersection of Divide Road (FR 402) and Uranium Road (FR 404).

3.2 Pass Big Creek Trail, on your right.

3.4 Reach the junction of Divide Road (FR 402) and Uranium Road (FR 404). Bear right onto Uranium Road (FR 404) and ride in a northwesterly direction.

4.6 Pass the Big Creek Cutoff Trail, to your right.

6.3 Pass Rim Trail (WOLF HILL—2 and BIG POND—3), to your right.

6.7 Reach the intersection of Uranium Road and Ute Creek Trail 608. Bear right onto Ute Creek Trail. **Option:** For those not interested in riding the singletrack, you can continue on Uranium Road for roughly 14.6 miles to the intersection of Uranium Road and CR 6.30/FR 405. At a sign marking the turnoff to the town of Gateway, bear right onto CR 6.30/FR 405 and descend to Indian Creek. Continue on CR 6.30/FR 405 at all other intersections and ride for roughly 6.5 miles to Calamity Basin. Rejoin the others at the Snowshoe Trailhead. For more information, contact the San Juan Hut System.

7.7 Descend the rocky singletrack and ride straight through an opening in a barbed wire fence.

8.5 The singletrack delivers a short but rocky and sandy climb. Continue straight, through some scrub oak.

9.4 Arrive at an incredible vista of the La Sal Mountains and John Brown Canyon. This is a great lunch spot and photo op.

10.2 Arrive at another fence. Continue straight, passing through an opening in the fence, in a westerly direction between two pine trees. This marks the beginning of a very long and rocky descent.

11.4 The singletrack turns into a doubletrack. Continue riding on the doubletrack, which is marked by iron fence posts, as it snakes its way through sage and scrub oak forests.

14.5 Reach the intersection of Ute Creek Trail 608 and Snowshoe Trail (Trail 607); there are no trail signs at this intersection. Bear left onto Snowshoe Trail, a rough-looking dirt road, and ride back to Pine Road and the main route.

15.6 Reach the intersection of Snowshoe Trail and CR 6.30/FR 405 (Pine Mountain Road). Bear right onto Pine Mountain Road.

17.2 Reach the junction of Pine Mountain Road and CR 10.80. A sign for the town of Gateway will be to your right. Continue straight here, descending along the steep and rocky Pine Mountain Road (CR 6.30) into the Dolores River Valley.

17.9 Descend to a cattle guard with a vista of the Dolores River Valley. Views of Palisade Cliff are offered.

21.3 Enter into a flash flood zone and patches of deep sand.

23.1 Reach the intersection of Pine Mountain Road (CR 6.30) and Colorado Highway 141, by a stop sign. Bear left (west), onto the paved highway, and descend into Gateway.

27.1 Enter into Gateway and ride west through it.

27.6 Bear right onto the dirt road, just before crossing the Dolores River via a steel bridge. Ride on this dirt road to the hut, with the Dolores River to your left.

28.0 Arrive at the Gateway Hut.

Day 6 Gateway Hut to La Sal Hut

The route connecting the Gateway Hut with the La Sal Hut is probably the toughest leg of the entire journey. Riders climb over 4,000 feet and descend only 900 feet. Although the initial climb through John Brown Canyon is the steepest in the day, it also comes at the beginning of the day, so riders get the toughest part of the day over with first. The route crosses the Colorado border and enters Utah near the Keesee Cow Camp. Since summertime temperatures in Gateway may exceed one hundred degrees, it's strongly suggested that you get an early start on the day's riding, taking advantage of the morning's cooler temperatures. The La Sal Hut is the San Juan Hut System's newest hut. It was previously a yurt, until a local black bear clawed through its canvas walls. Gateway sits at 4,600 feet, while the La Sal Hut sits at 8,400 feet. You can do the math; it's a tough climb.

Start: From the Gateway Hut.
Length: 22.3 miles.
Approximate riding time: Advanced riders, 3 to 4 hours; intermediate riders, 5 to 6 hours.
Technical difficulty: Technically easy to moderate due to the route's well-maintained dirt roads. Some areas include washboard and sandy segments.
Physical difficulty: Physically challenging due to the hotter temperatures and the steep and long climb from the Dolores River Valley to the La Sal Mountains via John Brown Canyon.

Terrain: Paved highway and improved dirt road. The route's sandy and rocky in spots, as it makes its way through John Brown Canyon. Once above the canyon, loose gravel roads, along with rutted and sandy sections, make the climb to the La Sal Hut tough.
Nearest town: Moab, Utah.
Other trail users: Sightseers, anglers, campers, and hikers.

The Ride

From the Gateway Hut, you start climbing almost immediately. The route through John Brown Canyon is a sandy—rutted in spots—road that cuts laboriously through the sheer, red sandstone canyon walls on its way to the La Sal Mountains. Only John Brown Creek, its accompanying cottonwoods, and the late-rising canyon sun provide any kind of relief from this torturous climb. Overhead, an old telegraph line suggests that there's a story of men who came long before you.

During America's early push west, these lines of communication proved to be a settlement's only link to the rest of the country. And it wasn't until 1897 that the link came into being. Due to this area's rugged and remote location, it didn't experience the relatively early colonization that Utah's Great Basin experienced. By 1847 Salt Lake City had already been established, but the areas surrounding the La Sal Mountains would not see any kind of settlement until the latter part of the 1870s.

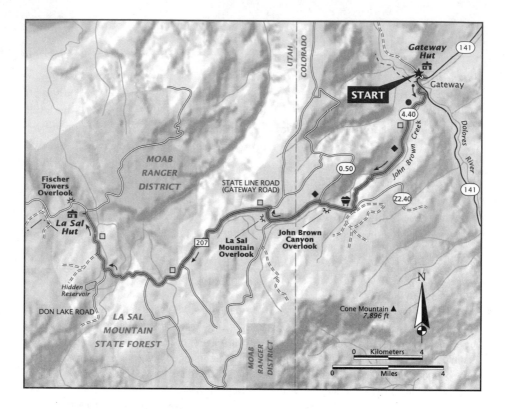

Although Spanish, Mexican, and American expeditions had passed through these parts as early as the 1760s, this area was considered far too remote and rugged to warrant settlement. In fact, the La Sal Mountains were one of the last areas in the continental United States to attract government explorers and survey teams.

For all intents and purposes, it wasn't until 1877, when gritty stockmen and their livestock first arrived in the area, that the La Sal Mountains were given much consideration. The first settlers to stake their claim to the area's large mineral and grazing resources were William Granstaff, an African-American, and a French-Canadian trapper, whose name has escaped historical records. The two prospected, grew vegetables, and raised cattle. The two eagerly claimed substantial portions of a major La Sal Mountain drainage. To the west of these claims lies the Colorado River; to the south, the San Juan River; to the north, the Grand River; and to the east, Mesa Verde country. Granstaff grazed his cattle in the drainage, which later became known as Negro Bill Canyon, the canyon paralleling Porcupine Rim in Moab, Utah. During the next five years, cattle ranchers continued their move into the La Sal region, establishing communities in Little Grand Valley, later to be renamed "Moab," Little Castle Valley, and on the south side of the La Sals. These early communities, remained isolated from one another.

It wasn't until 1897 that J. N. Corbin organized the area's first telephone company, bringing service to Moab. Some of the more remote areas surrounding the La Sal Mountains, however, would remain without telephone service well into the 1920s. Following Corbin's lead, the newly created La Sal National Forest Service played a pivotal role in establishing the lines of communication in southeastern Utah. The La Sal Forest Reserve joined President Roosevelt's forest reserves relatively late—it wasn't created until January 25, 1906, roughly one year before all "reserves" became known as "national forests." As a latecomer, the La Sal National Forest Service was eager to establish itself as a viable institution.

With 128,960 acres in Utah and 29,502 acres in Colorado, it was crucial that the La Sal National Forest have the telephone communications to conduct its business. Most important, the telephone lines would allow for speedy notification in case of fire. By 1910 phone lines ran through most of the La Sal National Forest and phone service, in turn, was made available to area locals. With these phone lines in place, ranches and outlying settlements were now in contact with one another, paving the way for further settlement.

With old telegraph lines looming overhead, you can't help but feel, somehow, in touch with those who have traveled this road before. Heading up John Brown Canyon, you pass into an old uranium-mining area. Take care to stay on the main road and stay out of the dilapidated mines. These mines have a tendency to cave in and contain noxious and highly combustible gasses. Be thankful that your day's climbing is half over, with the steepest part of the climb behind you. Once you cross over into Utah, the La Sal Mountains seemingly pop up from nowhere, looking curiously out of place.

Dubbed by early Spanish explorers the "mountains of salt," the La Sals are, quite visibly, an island range. Though the range never erupted, the core of the range began its life as a volcano. Over the years, erosion crumpled away the softer, volcanic rock on the outside and revealed the cooled volcanic core on the inside. This cooled core subsequently solidified the remaining range. What had at one time been a volcano now remains exposed as the La Sal Mountains. With two prominent passes reaching over 10,000 feet, the La Sal Mountains are, indeed, no mere mounds of salt. The eleven peaks that make up the range have an average combined elevation of 11,930

Crossing the state line into Utah!

feet. They are, from south to north: South Mountain (11,798 feet), Mount Tukuh-nikivatz (12,483 feet), Mount Peale (12,721 feet), Mount Mellenthin (12,646 feet), Haystack Mountain (11,642 feet), Mount Tomasaki (12,230 feet), Manns Peak (12,273 feet), Gold Knob (11,055 feet), Mount Waas (12,331 feet), Horse Mountain (11,150 feet), and Grand View Mountain (10,905 feet). Their enormity only empha-sizes the beauty of the mesas and valleys. The mountains and the mesas and the val-leys all make this one of the country's most striking landscapes.

Miles and Directions

0.0 Start from the Gateway Hut. Return the way you came to Colorado Highway 141.

0.4 Bear right onto CO 141, crossing the Dolores River. The road bends left and leads to a sign for John Brown Canyon.

0.9 Reach the junction of CO 141 and County Road 4.40. Bear right onto CR 4.40, after passing a sign for John Brown Canyon on the left, and cross a cattle guard.

1.4 The pavement ends. Here begins the climb through the steep and narrow-walled John Brown Canyon. The road through the canyon is called alternately State Line Road or Gateway Road.

5.0 Begin to rise steeply out of the canyon.

7.1 Enter into the historic uranium-mining area. A warning sign marks your entrance. At this point you've already completed half of the day's climbing, as you begin to notice taller pine trees along the road.

7.2 Pass a BLM sign and a road to your left. Continue straight.

8.0 Pass great views of John Brown Canyon to your right.

8.6 Arrive at an intersection. Bear left here, by the Gateway sign.

9.8 Pass the Keesee Cow Camp in the valley, to your left, as you cross a cattle guard and the state line. Welcome to Utah.

15.4 Enter into the La Sal Mountain State Forest. Bypass the road on the left and continue heading straight for the mountains.

17.3 Arrive at a sign to your right reading 5 BAR A, KIRK'S BASIN—9, and GATEWAY—16. Continue riding straight—do not bear left—as you continue to climb.

19.3 Pass a sign indicating that you are leaving the La Sal Mountain State Forest. There will be another sign for the Taylor Livestock Company. Continue climbing.

19.7 Reach the Hidden Reservoir intersection by Don Lake Road and State Line Road. Pass Don Lake Road to your left and continue on State Line Road. **Option:** Bear left onto Don Lake Road at the sign for DON LAKE and BEAVER BASIN to enjoy a refreshing dip in Hidden Reservoir. It's only a small diversion from the main route. To get to Hidden Reservoir: Travel along Don Lake Road for approximately 0.5 mile. Bear right, down the four-wheel-drive road, just before the first cattle guard you come to.

20.5 Pass the Manti–La Sal National Forest sign.

22.3 Bear left (west), onto the four-wheel-drive road leading into a dense oak thicket. (If you've reached a T intersection bearing a sign for MOAB—38, and NORTH BEAVER MESA—4.5, you've gone too far. Turn around and backtrack roughly 500 feet south to the four-wheel-drive road, which will now be on your right.) Ride the four-wheel-drive road approximately 400 feet to the La Sal Hut.

Day 7 La Sal Hut to Moab

Your final push to the end, in a way, encapsulates your entire seven-day odyssey. From the high-alpine forests of the La Sal Mountains, through the sage-piñon fields of Moab's higher plateaus and mesas, to the surreal slickrock and sandstone formations of Moab's canyonlands, you descend an eye-popping 5,700 feet through a veritable time capsule of natural history. The entire route overlooks western Colorado and eastern Utah, prominently displaying views of Fischer Valley, Fischer Towers, and Castle Valley. Although the main route of this final leg descends Sand Flats Road into Moab, a worthwhile alternative would be to break from this road at 28.1 miles and connect with Porcupine Rim Trail, one of Moab's most incredible singletrack trails.

Start: From La Sal Hut.
Length: 38.4 miles.
Approximate riding time: Advanced riders, 3.5 to 4 hours; intermediate riders, 4 to 5 hours.
Technical difficulty: Technically moderate due to the variety of loose and exposed rocks, particularly once on Sand Flats Road.
Physical difficulty: Physically moderate due to the hotter temperatures of Moab and the length of climbs.

Terrain: Improved dirt road, four-wheel-drive road, and paved road. Slickrock and large, exposed loose rock make up the majority of the terrain. Sand and roots fill in the gaps. The sand and rock may cause unsteadiness on the more heavily weighted bicycles.
Nearest town: Moab, Utah.
Other trail users: Hikers, sightseers, and four-wheelers.

Getting There

From Moab, Utah: Drive south on Main Street (U.S. Highway 191) to 100 South Street. Turn right (west) onto 100 South Street (by the Arby's) and drive for a block and a half. Bear left into the municipal parking lot behind the police station and park your vehicle here.

The Ride

Moab, Utah, seems a fitting finale to this weeklong getaway. It's been host, holdup, and hideout to a number of western outlaws—none more notable than Tom McCarty. Perhaps more than any other bad boy, Tom McCarty helped solidify Moab's outlaw mystique. The McCarty family rode into town in the late 1870s. The McCarty's were part of the vast migration of cattlemen and cowboys who were moving into southeastern Utah at the time. They were an independent lot, aggressive and adventurous. Of course, they had to be, given the area's unsettled terrain and remoteness. When the McCartys led their large herd of cattle across the Wasatch Mountains to roam in Moab's open ranges, no one thought to ask where they had gotten their cattle from; no one much cared.

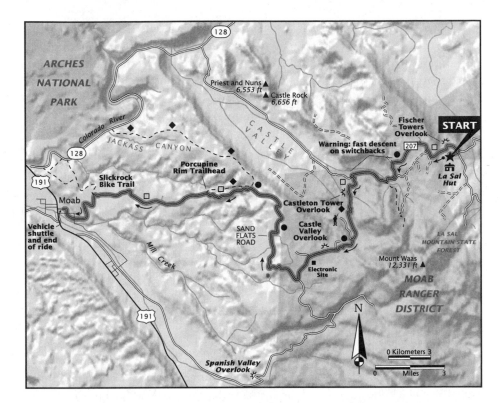

Tom McCarty and his brother Bill operated their ranch near the La Sal Mountains. At the time, the ranch was situated on the best open range in Utah. Nevertheless, the two brothers sold it for $35,000 and turned, instead, to a life of crime. "My downfall commenced by gambling," Tom later wrote. "Horse racing was the first . . ." (see Day 2), followed by cattle rustling soon thereafter. From Moab, Tom took his cattle rustling on the road, traveling to Arizona, New Mexico, and Iowa.

While in Iowa he bought three of the fastest horses he could find. These horses would later provide transport for history's "Wild Bunch" (which included Butch Cassidy, Matt Warner, and, of course, Tom), as they made their getaway with $30,000 of Telluride's money (see Day 1). As leader of another thieving troupe, the "Blue Mountain Gang," Tom would go on robbing in Utah and, indeed, throughout a major part of the American West for another four years. Sometime in the mid- to late 1890s, Tom penned his autobiography and sent the manuscript to Matt Warner's father. Then he simply disappeared. *The History of Tom McCarty* was published in 1898.

With such notorious beginnings, it's curious that Moab acquired its name from the Bible. In 1881 W. A. Pierce, an avid Bible-reader (and minority by association thereof), gave the town its present name. Pierce recalled the stories of the "Far Country," a region distinguished for its remoteness and its flat-topped plateaus. This description of the biblical "Moab" closely resembled what he saw in Moab, Utah. Given what we know of Moab's raucous past, the name seems a fittingly formidable-sounding replacement for what Moab used to be called. "Little Grand Canyon" just doesn't have the punch Moab has; it's too contradictory to stand for that bold and independent town into which we now ride.

We ride into these canyonland badlands following the outlaw trail. High in the La Sal Mountains, we reach the Castle Valley Overlook at 9.3 miles. Here one can view Castleton Tower, Castle Rock, and the entire Castle Valley. From our perch, the valley appears to resemble a large city of rock and sand, a city whose skyscrapers look like giant sandcastles. Situated prominently in the middle of the valley is Castle Rock. When Castle Rock is viewed from Porcupine Rim Trail, one notices the standing profile of a priest and two nuns—hence, Castle Rock is also known as Priest and Nuns.

About 300 million years ago, the Uncompahgre uplift (a range in the ancestral Rocky Mountains) caused thousands of cubic miles of earth to be washed down its western flanks. This earth moved over much of the area that now lies before you, compressing the area's salty bottom left behind by receding seas. As thousands of cubic miles of earth continued to cover this salty bed, the salt was forced to flow through pressure-alleviating fault blocks. Attaching themselves to these blocks, these massive bodies of salt and rock (some of which were 15,000 feet thick) pushed their way upward towards the earth's surface. Nearly 290 million years later, these blocks finally reached the earth's surface in Castle Valley, known in geological circles as a "salt valley."

Located within the Colorado Plateau, the vast area of flat-lying sedimentary rock that extends into almost half of Utah and smaller parts of Colorado, Arizona, and New Mexico, Castle Valley offers an exceptional example of these one-time bodies of salt and rock. Under the pressures of tectonic plate shifting ten million years ago, the Colorado Plateau begun to rise. Rivers and streams, which had followed a relatively flat course across the plateau, were now pouring through over a vertical mile of sedimentary rock. The layers of sedimentary rock, in turn, receded in cliffs, as further erosion carved a path for the valley's formation and exposed the massive bodies

Castleton Tower.

of salt and rock that had been forming since the Uncompahgre uplift. Once these bodies were exposed to the elements, wind and water dissolved the salt, leaving behind the castles in the valley. Today, these formations are made up of mostly calcite, silica, gypsum, and iron oxide, the latter of which gives rise to the castles' ruddy hue. This valley continues to undergo drastic erosion, as castles made of sand slip into the "sea," eventually.

Don't let thoughts of cool ocean breezes trick you into thinking it's all down hill to Moab. From your seagull's perch above Castle Valley, descend briefly before climbing two switchback sections, 5 miles in length, to Sand Flats Road and Porcupine Rim Trail. Once you turn onto Sand Flats Road, descend over loose sand and rock for roughly 11 miles, before intersecting with Porcupine Rim Trail. If you're blown out at this point, I suggest finishing your seven-day tour on Sand Flats Road. For those of you who have a bit more spunk left, bear right onto Porcupine Rim Trail. Either way, enjoy—you got away!

Miles and Directions

0.0 START from the La Sal Hut. Backtrack to Forest Road 207.

0.1 Bear left onto FR 207, heading toward the T intersection.

0.2 Arrive at the T intersection, marked by the sign for MOAB—38, and NORTH BEAVER MESA—4.5. Bear left (west), following signs for Moab.

0.8 See incredible views of Fischer Towers off to your right.

7.6 After a speedy descent, you leave Manti–La Sal Forest.

8.1 Arrive at the head of Castle Valley, with a sign reading MOAB—30 and LA SAL MOUNTAIN LOOP ROAD and OOWAH LAKE, WARNER CAMPGROUND, MOAB. Bear left, onto the La Sal Mountain Loop Road, and begin climbing.

9.3 Enjoy a fantastic view of Castleton Tower to your right.

10.1 Reach Harpole Mesa. Here begins a steady switchback climb on pavement.

13.7 Reach the end of the pavement, as the road continues to climb moderately.

14.3 Pavement begins again.

16.6 Cross under the power lines. To your left are the communication towers. A fast descent to Moab awaits.

17.0 Passing an OOWAH LAKE sign to your left, intersect with CR 67 (Sand Flats Road), to your right. Bear right onto Sand Flats Road, a rough four-wheel-drive road. Look to the distant west and see the Blues (or Abajos), the Henrys (the last mountains to be surveyed in the continental United States), and Navajo Mountain.

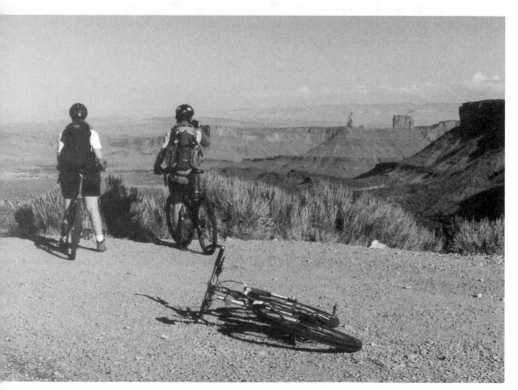

Taking in the view of Castle Valley.

20.6 Leave Manti–La Sal National Forest. Stay on Sand Flats Road, as it parallels a shallow rock canyon to the left, and reenter the national forest.

26.0 Pass the unmarked Porcupine Rim Cutoff Trail to your right.

28.1 Pass the trailhead for Porcupine Rim, to your right, marked by stock troughs with water from a spring, and continue down Sand Flats Road. **Option:** For those wanting to enjoy the great singletrack descent of Porcupine Rim, bear right here. This technically and physically challenging trail will eventually lead to Utah Highway 128 and the Colorado River. From there one may ride in a southwesterly direction to Moab or arrange to be picked up at the trail's terminus on Highway 128. A good place for shuttle vehicles to park would be at the Negro Bill Canyon Trailhead, located off Utah Highway 128, less than a quarter mile southwest of Porcupine Rim Trail's terminus. Arranging to be picked up is highly recommended.]

34.2 Pavement begins.

34.7 Pass the Slickrock Trailhead to your right.

37.2 Sand Flats Road turns into Mill Creek Drive.

37.6 Reach the intersection of Mill Creek Drive and 400 East Street, by Dave's Corner Market. Bear right onto 400 East Street.

37.9 Reach the intersection of 400 East Street and 100 South Street. Bear left onto 100 South Street.

38.4 Reach the intersection of 100 South Street and Main Street. Continue for another 1½ blocks west on 100 South Street to the municipal parking lot and your vehicle, ending your weeklong odyssey.

The Art of Mountain Biking

Within the following pages, you will find everything you need to know about off-road bicycling in Colorado. This section begins by exploring the fascinating history of the mountain bike itself, then goes on to discuss everything from the health benefits of off-road cycling to tips and techniques for bicycling over logs and up hills. Also included are the types of clothing to keep you comfortable and in style, essential equipment ideas to keep your rides smooth and trouble-free, and descriptions of off-road terrain to prepare you for the kinds of bumps and bounces you can expect to encounter.

The mountain bike, with its knobby tread and reinforced frame, takes cyclists to places once unheard of—down rugged mountain trails, through streams of rushing water, across the frozen Alaskan tundra, and even to work in the city. There seem to be few limits on what this fat-tired beast can do and where it can take us. Few obstacles stand in its way, few boundaries slow its progress. Except for one—its own success. If trail closure means little to you now, read on and discover how a trail can be here today and gone tomorrow. With so many new off-road cyclists taking to the trails each year, it's no wonder trail access hinges precariously between universal acceptance and complete termination. But a little work on your part can go a long way to preserving trail access for future use. Nothing is more crucial to the survival of mountain biking itself than to read the examples set forth in the following pages and practice their message.

Without open trails, the maps in this book are virtually useless. Cyclists must learn to be responsible for the trails they use and to share these trails with others. This guidebook addresses such issues as why trail use has become so controversial, what can be done to improve the image of mountain biking, how to have fun and ride responsibly, on-the-spot trail repair techniques, trail maintenance hotlines for each trail, and the worldwide-standard Rules of the Trail.

Mountain Bike Beginnings

It seems the mountain bike, originally designed for lunatic adventurists bored with straight lines, clean clothes, and smooth tires, has become globally popular in as short a time as it would take to race down a mountain trail.

Like many things of a revolutionary nature, the mountain bike was born on the West Coast. But unlike Rollerblades, purple hair, and the peace sign, the concept of the off-road bike cannot be credited solely to the imaginative Californians—they were just the first to make waves.

The design of the first off-road-specific bike was based on the geometry of the old Schwinn Excelsior, a one-speed, camelback cruiser with balloon tires. Joe Breeze was the creator behind it, and in 1977 he built ten of these "Breezers" for himself and his Marin County, California, friends at $750 apiece—a bargain.

Breeze was a serious competitor in bicycle racing, placing thirteenth in the 1977 U.S. Road Racing National Championships. After races, he and friends would scour local bike shops hoping to find old bikes they could then restore.

It was the 1941 Schwinn Excelsior, for which Breeze paid just five dollars, that began to shape and change bicycling history forever. After taking the bike home, removing the fenders, oiling the chain, and pumping up the tires, Breeze hit the dirt. He loved it.

His inspiration, while forerunning, was not altogether unique. On the opposite end of the country, nearly 2,500 miles from Marin County, East Coast bike bums were also growing restless. More and more old, beat-up clunkers were being restored and modified. These behemoths often weighed as much as eighty pounds and were so reinforced they seemed virtually indestructible. But rides that take just forty minutes on today's twenty-five-pound featherweights took the steel-toed-boot-and-blue-jean-clad bikers of the late 1970s and early 1980s nearly four hours to complete.

Not until 1981 was it possible to purchase a production mountain bike, but local retailers found these ungainly bicycles difficult to sell and rarely kept them in stock. By 1983, however, mountain bikes were no longer such a fringe item, and large bike manufacturers quickly jumped into the action, producing their own versions of the off-road bike. By the 1990s the mountain bike had firmly established its place with bicyclists of nearly all ages and abilities, and it now commands nearly 90 percent of the U.S. bike market.

There are many reasons for the mountain bike's success in becoming the hottest two-wheeled vehicle in the nation. They are much friendlier to the cyclist than traditional road bikes because of their comfortable upright position and shock-absorbing fat tires. And because of the health-conscious, environmentalist movement of the late 1980s and 1990s, people are more activity minded and seek nature on a closer front than paved roads can allow. The mountain bike gives you these things and takes you far away from the daily grind—even if you're only minutes from the city.

Mountain Biking into Shape

If your objective is to get in shape and lose weight, then you're on the right track, because mountain biking is one of the best ways to get started.

One way many of us have lost weight in this sport is the crash-and-burn-it-off method. Picture this: You're speeding uncontrollably down a vertical drop that you realize you shouldn't be on—only after it is too late. Your front wheel lodges into a rut and launches you through endless weeds, trees, and pointy rocks before coming to an abrupt halt in a puddle of thick mud. Surveying the damage, you discover, with the layers of skin, body parts, and lost confidence littering the trail above, that those unwanted pounds have been shed—permanently. Instant weight loss.

There is, of course, a more conventional (and quite a bit less painful) approach to losing weight and gaining fitness on a mountain bike. It's called the workout, and bicycles provide an ideal way to get physical. Take a look at some of the benefits associated with cycling.

Cycling helps you shed pounds without gimmicky diet fads or weight-loss programs. You can explore the countryside and burn nearly 10 to 16 calories per minute or close to 600 to 1,000 calories per hour. Moreover, it's a great way to spend an afternoon.

No less significant than the external and cosmetic changes of your body from riding are the internal changes taking place. Over time, cycling regularly will strengthen your heart as your body grows vast networks of new capillaries to carry blood to all those working muscles. This will, in turn, give your skin a healthier glow. The capacity of your lungs may increase up to 20 percent, and your resting heart rate will drop significantly. The Stanford University School of Medicine reports to the American Heart Association that people can reduce their risk of heart attack by nearly 64 percent if they can burn up to 2,000 calories per week. This is only two to three hours of bike riding!

Recommended for insomnia, hypertension, indigestion, anxiety, and even for recuperation from major heart attacks, bicycling can be an excellent cure-all as well as a great preventive. Cycling just a few hours per week can improve your figure and sleeping habits, give you greater resistance to illness, increase your energy levels, and provide feelings of accomplishment and heightened self-esteem.

Be Safe—Know the Law

Occasionally, even the hard-core off-road cyclists will find they have no choice but to ride the pavement. When you are forced to hit the road, it's important for you to know and understand the rules.

Outlined below are a few of the common laws found in Colorado.

- In Colorado, you can pedal on any public road except urban freeways.
- Follow the same driving rules as motorists. Be sure to obey all road signs and traffic lights.
- Wear a helmet and bright clothing so you are more visible to motorists. Bright colors such as orange and lime green are also highly visible at night.
- Equip your bike with lights and wear reflective clothing if you plan on riding at night. When riding at night the bicycle or rider must have a white light visible

at least 500 feet to the front and a red light or reflector visible at least 600 feet to the rear.

- Pass motorists on the left and not the right. Motorists are not expecting you to pass on the right and they may not see you.
- Ride single file on busy roads so motorists can pass you safely.
- Stop off the roadway.
- Use hand signals to alert motorists to what you plan on doing next.
- Ride with the traffic and not against it.
- Follow painted lane markings.
- Make eye contact with drivers. Assume they don't see you until you are sure they do.
- Ride in the middle of the lane at busy intersections and whenever you are moving at the same speed as traffic.
- Don't ride out to the curb between parked cars unless they are far apart. Motorists may not see you when you try to move back into traffic.
- Turn left by looking back, signaling, getting into the left lane, and turning. In urban situations, continue straight to the crosswalk and walk your bike across the crosswalk when the pedestrian walk sign is illuminated.
- Never ride while under the influence of alcohol or drugs. DUI laws apply when you're riding a bicycle.
- Avoid riding in extreme snowy, rainy, or windy conditions.
- Watch out for parallel-slat sewer grates, slippery manhole covers, oily pavement, gravel, wet leaves, and ice.
- Cross railroad tracks as perpendicular as possible. Be especially careful when it's wet out. For better control as you move across bumps and other hazards, stand up on your pedals.
- Don't ride too close to parked cars—a person opening the car door may hit you.
- Avoid riding on sidewalks. Instead, walk your bike. Pedestrians have the right-of-way on walkways. By law, you must give pedestrians audible warning when you pass. Use a bike bell or announce clearly, "On your left/right."
- Slow down at street crossings and driveways.

The Mountain Bike Controversy

Are Off-Road Bicyclists Environmental Outlaws? Do We Have the Right to Use Public Trails?

Mountain bikers have long endured the animosity of folks in the backcountry who complain about the consequences of off-road bicycling. Many people believe that the fat tires and knobby tread do unacceptable environmental damage and that our uncontrollable riding habits are a danger to animals and other trail users. To the contrary, mountain bikes have no more environmental impact than hiking boots or horseshoes. This does not mean, however, that mountain bikes leave no imprint at all. Wherever man treads, there is an impact. By riding responsibly, though, it is possible to leave only a minimal impact—something we all must take care to achieve.

Unfortunately, it is often people of great influence who view the mountain bike as the environment's worst enemy. Consequently, we mountain bike riders and environmentally concerned citizens must be educators, impressing upon others that we also deserve the right to use these trails. Our responsibilities as bicyclists are no more and no less than those of any other trail user. We must all take the soft-cycling approach and show that mountain bicyclists are not environmental outlaws.

Etiquette of Mountain Biking

When discussing mountain biking etiquette, we are in essence discussing the soft-cycling approach. This term, as mentioned previously, describes the art of minimum-impact bicycling and should apply to both the physical and social dimensions of the sport. But make no mistake—it is possible to ride fast and furiously while maintaining the balance of soft-cycling. Here first are a few ways to minimize the physical impact of mountain bike riding.

- **Stay on the trail.** Don't ride around fallen trees or mud holes that block your path. Stop and cross over them. When you come to a vista overlooking a deep valley, don't ride off the trail for a better vantage point. Instead, leave the bike and walk to see the view. Riding off the trail may seem inconsequential when done only once, but soon someone else will follow, then others, and the cumulative results can be catastrophic. Each time you wander from the trail you begin creating a new path, adding one more scar to the earth's surface.

- **Do not disturb the soil.** Follow a line within the trail that will not disturb or damage the soil.

- **Do not ride over soft or wet trails.** After a rain shower or during the thawing season, trails will often resemble muddy, oozing swampland. The best thing to do is stay off the trails altogether. Realistically, however, we're all going to come across some muddy trails we cannot anticipate. Instead of blasting through each section of mud, which may seem both easier and more fun, lift the bike and walk past. Each time a cyclist rides through a soft or muddy section of trail, that part of the trail is permanently damaged. Regardless of the trail's conditions, though, remember always to go over the obstacles across the path, not around them. Stay on the trail.

- **Avoid trails that are considered impassable and impossible.** Don't take a leap of faith down a kamikaze descent on which you will be forced to lock your brakes and skid to the bottom, ripping the ground apart as you go.

Soft cycling should apply to the social dimensions of the sport as well, since mountain bikers are not the only folks who use the trails. Hikers, equestrians, cross-country skiers, and other outdoors people use many of the same trails and can be easily spooked by a marauding mountain biker tearing through the trees. Be friendly in the forest and give ample warning of your approach.

- **Take out what you bring in.** Don't leave broken bike pieces and banana peels scattered along the trail.
- **Be aware of your surroundings.** Don't use popular hiking trails for race training.
- **Slow down! Rocketing** around blind corners is a sure way to ruin an unsuspecting hiker's day. Consider this: If you fly down a quick singletrack descent at 20 miles per hour, then hit the brakes and slow down to only 6 miles per hour to pass someone, you're still moving twice as fast as they are!

Like the trails we ride on, the social dimension of mountain biking is very fragile and must be cared for responsibly. We should not want to destroy another person's enjoyment of the outdoors. By riding in the backcountry with caution, control, and responsibility, our presence should be felt positively by other trail users. By adhering to these rules, trail riding—a privilege that can quickly be taken away—will continue to be ours to share.

Trail Maintenance

Unfortunately, despite all of the preventive measures taken to avoid trail damage, we're still going to run into many trails requiring attention. Simply put, a lot of hikers, equestrians, and cyclists use the same trails—some wear and tear is unavoidable. But like your bike, if you want to use these trails for a long time to come, you must also maintain them.

Trail maintenance and restoration can be accomplished in a variety of ways. One way is for mountain bike clubs to combine efforts with other trail users (i.e., hikers and equestrians) and work closely with land managers to cut new trails or repair existing ones. This not only reinforces to others the commitment cyclists have in caring for and maintaining the land, but also breaks the ice that often separates cyclists from their fellow trail mates. Another good way to help out is to show up, ready to work, on a Saturday morning with a few riding buddies at your favorite off-road domain. With a good attitude, thick gloves, and the local land manager's supervision, trail repair is fun and very rewarding. It's important, of course, that you arrange a trail-repair outing with the local land manager before you start pounding shovels into the dirt. They can lead you to the most needy sections of trail and instruct you on what repairs should be done and how best to accomplish the task. Perhaps the most effective means of trail maintenance, though, can be done by yourself and while you're riding. Read on.

On-the-Spot-Quick Fix

Most of us, when we're riding, have at one time or another come upon muddy trails or fallen trees blocking our path. We notice that over time the mud gets deeper and the trail gets wider as people go through or around the obstacles. We worry that the problem will become so severe and repairs too difficult that the trail's access may be threatened. We also know that our ambition to do anything about it is greatest at that moment, not after a hot shower and a plate of spaghetti. Here are a few on-the-spot quick fixes you can do that will hopefully correct a problem before it gets out of hand and get you back on your bike within minutes.

Muddy trails. What do you do when trails develop huge mud holes destined for the EPA's Superfund status? Corduroy (not the pants) is the term for roads made of logs laid down crosswise. Use small- and medium-size sticks and lay them side by side across the trail until they cover the length of the muddy section (break the sticks to fit the width of the trail). Press them into the mud with your feet, then lay more on top if needed. Keep adding sticks until the trail is firm. Not only will you stay clean as you cross, but the sticks may soak up some of the water and help the puddle dry. This quick fix may last as long as one month before needing to be redone. And as time goes on, with new layers added to the trail, the soil will grow stronger, thicker, and more resistant to erosion. This whole process may take fewer than five minutes, and you can be on your way, knowing the trail behind you is in good repair.

Leaving the trail. What do you do to keep cyclists from cutting corners and leaving the designated trail? The solution is much simpler than you may think. (No, don't hire an off-road police force.) Notice where people are leaving the trail and throw a pile of thick branches or brush along the path, or place logs across the opening to block the way through. There are probably dozens of subtle tricks like these that will manipulate people into staying on the designated trail. If executed well, no one will even notice that the thick branches scattered along the ground in the woods weren't always there. And most folks would probably rather take a moment to hop a log in the trail than get tangled in a web of branches.

Obstacle in the way. If there are large obstacles blocking the trail, try to remove them or push them aside. If you cannot do this by yourself, call the trail maintenance hotline to speak with the land manager of that particular trail and see what can be done.

We must be willing to sweat for our trails in order to sweat on them. Police yourself and point out to others the significance of trail maintenance. "Sweat Equity," the rewards of continued land use won with a fair share of sweat, pays off when the trail is "up for review" by the land manager and he or she remembers the efforts made by trail-conscious mountain bikers.

Rules of the Trail

The International Mountain Bicycling Association (IMBA) has developed these guidelines to trail riding. These "Rules of the Trail" are accepted worldwide and will go a long way in keeping trails open. Please respect and follow these rules for everyone's sake.

1. Ride only on open trails. Respect trail and road closures (if you're not sure, ask a park or state official first), do not trespass on private property, and obtain permits or authorization if required. Federal and state wilderness areas are off-limits to cycling. Parks and state forests may also have certain trails closed to cycling.

2. Zero impact. Be sensitive to the dirt beneath you. Even on open trails, you should not ride under conditions by which you will leave evidence of your passing, such as on certain soils or shortly after a rainfall. Be sure to observe the different types of soils and trails you're riding on, practicing minimum-impact cycling. Never ride off the trail, don't skid your tires, and be sure to bring out at least as much as you bring in.

3. Control your bicycle! Inattention for even one second can cause disaster for yourself or for others. Excessive speed frightens and can injure people, gives mountain biking a bad name, and can result in trail closures.

4. Always yield. Let others know you're coming well in advance (a friendly greeting is always good and often appreciated). Show your respect when passing others by slowing to walking speed or stopping altogether, especially in the presence of horses. Horses can be unpredictable, so be very careful. Anticipate that other trail users may be around corners or in blind spots.

5. Never spook animals. All animals are spooked by sudden movements, unannounced approaches, or loud noises. Give them extra room and time so they can adjust to you. Move slowly or dismount around animals. Running cattle and disturbing wild animals are serious offenses. Leave gates as you find them, or as marked.

6. Plan ahead. Know your equipment, your ability, and the area in which you are riding, and plan your trip accordingly. Be self-sufficient at all times, keep your bike in good repair, and carry necessary supplies for changes in weather or other conditions. You can help keep trails open by setting an example of responsible, courteous, and controlled mountain bike riding.

7. Always wear a helmet when you ride. For your own safety and protection, a helmet should be worn whenever you are riding your bike. You never know when a tree root or small rock will throw you the wrong way and send you tumbling.

Thousands of miles of dirt trails have been closed to mountain bicycling because of the irresponsible riding habits of just a few riders. Don't follow the example of these offending riders. Don't take away trail privileges from thousands of others who work hard each year to keep the backcountry avenues open to us all.

The Necessities of Cycling

When discussing the most important items to have on a bike ride, cyclists generally agree on the following four items:

Helmet. The reasons to wear a helmet should be obvious. Helmets are discussed in more detail in the "Be Safe—Wear Your Armor" section.

Water. Without it, cyclists may face dehydration, which may result in dizziness and fatigue. On a warm day, cyclists should drink at least one full bottle during every hour of riding. Remember, it's always good to drink before you feel thirsty—otherwise, it may be too late.

Cycling shorts. These are necessary if you plan to ride your bike more than 20 to 30 minutes. Padded cycling shorts may be the only thing preventing your derriere from serious saddle soreness by ride's end. There are two types of cycling shorts you can buy. Touring shorts are good for people who don't want to look like they're wearing anatomically correct cellophane. These look like regular athletic shorts with pockets, but they have built-in padding in the crotch area for protection from chafing and saddle sores. The more popular, traditional cycling shorts are made of skintight material, also with a padded crotch. Whichever style you find most comfortable, cycling shorts are a necessity for long rides.

Food. This essential item will keep you rolling. Cycling burns up a lot of calories and is among the few sports in which no one is safe from the "Bonk." Bonking feels like it sounds. Without food in your system, your blood sugar level collapses, and there is no longer any energy in your body. This instantly results in total fatigue and light-headedness. So when you're filling your water bottle, remember to bring along some food. Fruit, energy bars, or some other forms of high-energy food are highly recommended. Candy bars are not, however, because they will deliver a sudden burst of high energy, then let you down soon after, causing you to feel worse than before. Energy bars are available at most bike stores and are similar to candy bars, but they provide complex carbohydrate energy and high nutrition rather than fast-burning simple sugars.

Be Prepared or Die

Do you remember the Boy Scout motto? Be prepared. The following is a list of essential equipment that will keep you from walking out a long trail, being stranded in the woods, or even losing your life.

- Spare tube
- Tire irons
- Patch kit
- Pump
- Money: Spare change for emergency calls.
- Spoke wrench
- Spare spokes: To fit your wheel. Tape these to the chain stay.
- Chain tool
- Allen keys: Bring appropriate sizes to fit your bike.
- Compass/GPS
- Duct tape
- First-Aid kit: See First-Aid Kit sidebar.
- Rain gear: For quick changes in weather.
- Matches
- Guidebook: In case all else fails and you must start a fire to survive, this guidebook will serve as excellent fire starter!
- Food and water
- Jacket

To carry these items, you will need a backpack. There are currently many streamlined backpacks with hydration systems on the market that you can choose from. If you're carrying lots of equipment, you may want to consider a set of panniers. These are much larger and mount on either side of each wheel on a rack.

Be Safe—Wear Your Armor

While on the subject of jerseys, it's crucial to discuss the clothing you must wear to be safe, practical, and—if you prefer—stylish. The following is a list of items that will save you from disaster, outfit you comfortably, and, most important, keep you looking cool.

Helmet. A helmet is an absolute necessity because it protects your head from complete annihilation. It is the only thing that will not disintegrate into a million pieces after a wicked crash on a descent you shouldn't have been on in the first place. A helmet with a solid exterior shell will also protect your head from sharp or protruding objects. Of course, with a hard-shelled helmet, you can paste several stickers of your favorite bicycle manufacturers all over the outer shell, giving companies even more free advertising for your dollar.

Shorts. Padded cycle shorts provide cushioning between your body and the bicycle seat. Cycle shorts also wick moisture away from your body and prevent chafing. Form-fitting shorts are made from synthetic material and have smooth seams to avoid chafing. If you don't feel comfortable wearing form-fitting shorts, baggy-style padded shorts with pockets are available.

Gloves. You may find well-padded cycling gloves invaluable when traveling over rocky trails and gravelly roads for hours on end. When you fall off your bike and land on your palms, gloves are your best friend. Long-fingered gloves may also be useful, as branches, trees, assorted hard objects, and, occasionally small animals will reach out and whack your knuckles. Insulated gloves are essential for winter riding.

Glasses. Not only do sunglasses give you an imposing presence and make you look cool (both are extremely important), they also protect your eyes from harmful ultraviolet rays, invisible branches, creepy bugs, dirt, and may prevent you from being caught sneaking glances at riders of the opposite sex also wearing skintight, revealing Lycra.

Shoes. Mountain bike shoes are constructed with stiff soles in order to transfer more of the power from a pedal stroke to the drive train and to provide a solid platform to stand on, thereby decreasing fatigue in your feet. You can use virtually any good, light, outdoor hiking footwear, but specific mountain bike shoes (especially those with inset cleats) are best. They are lighter, breathe better, and are constructed to work with your pedal strokes instead of the natural walking cadence.

Other Clothing. To prepare for Colorado's weather, it is best to dress in layers that can be added or removed as weather conditions change. In cold weather wear next to your skin a wicking layer made of a modern synthetic fiber. Avoid wearing cotton of any type. It dries slowly and does not wick moisture away from your skin, so it chills you directly as it evaporates. The next layer should be a wool or synthetic insulating layer that helps keep you warm but also is breathable. A fleece jacket or vest works well as an insulating layer. The outer layer should be a jacket and pants that are waterproof, windproof, and breathable. Your ears will also welcome a fleece headband when it's cold out.

First-Aid Kit

- Band-Aids
- mole skin
- various sterile gauze and dressings
- white surgical tape
- an Ace bandage
- an antihistamine
- aspirin
- Betadine solution
- a first-aid book
- Tums
- tweezers
- scissors
- antibacterial wipes
- triple-antibiotic ointment
- plastic gloves
- sterile cotton tip applicators
- syrup of ipecac (to induce vomiting)
- thermometer
- wire splint

Oh, Those Cold Colorado Days

If the weather chooses not to cooperate on the day you've set aside for a bike ride, it's helpful to be prepared.

Tights or leg warmers. These are best in temperatures below 55 degrees Fahrenheit. Knees are sensitive and can develop all kinds of problems if they get cold. Common problems include tendinitis, bursitis, and arthritis.

Plenty of layers on your upper body. When the air has a nip in it, layers of clothing will keep the chill away from your chest and help prevent the development of bronchitis. If the air is cool, a Polypropylene or Capilene long-sleeved shirt is best to wear against the skin beneath other layers of clothing. Polypropylene or Capilene, like wool, wicks away moisture from your skin to keep your body dry. Try to avoid wearing cotton or baggy clothing when the temperature falls. Cotton, as mentioned before, holds moisture like a sponge, and baggy clothing catches cold air and swirls it around your body. Good cold-weather clothing should fit snugly against your body, but not be restrictive.

Wool socks. Don't pack too many layers under those shoes, though. You may stand the chance of restricting circulation, and your feet will get real cold, real fast.

Thinsulate or Gortex gloves. We may all agree that there is nothing worse than frozen feet—unless your hands are frozen. A good pair of Thinsulate or Gortex gloves should keep your hands toasty and warm.

Hat or helmet on cold days. Sometimes, when the weather gets really cold and you still want to hit the trails, it's tough to stay warm. We all know that 130 percent of the body's heat escapes through the head (overactive brains, I imagine), so it's important to keep the cranium warm. Ventilated helmets are designed to keep heads cool in the summer heat, but they do little to help keep heads warm during rides in subzero temperatures. Cyclists should consider wearing a hat on extremely cold days. Capilene Skullcaps are great head and ear warmers that snugly fit over your head beneath the helmet. Head protection is not lost. Another option is a helmet cover that covers those ventilating gaps and helps keep the body heat in. These do not, however, keep your ears warm. Some cyclists will opt for a simple knit cycling cap sans the helmet, but these have never been shown to be very good cranium protectors.

All of this clothing can be found at your local bike store, where the staff should be happy to help fit you into the seasons of the year.

To Have or Not to Have—Other Very Useful Items

There is no shortage of items for you and your bike to make riding better, safer, and easier. We have rummaged through the unending lists and separated the gadgets from the good stuff, coming up with what we believe are items certain to make mountain bike riding easier and more enjoyable.

Tires. Buying a good pair of knobby tires is the quickest way to enhance the off-road handling capabilities of a bike. There are many types of mountain bike tires on the market. Some are made exclusively for very rugged off-road terrain. These big-knobbed, soft rubber tires virtually stick to the ground with magnetlike traction, but they tend to deteriorate quickly on pavement. There are other tires made exclusively for the road. These are called "slicks" and have no tread at all. For the average cyclist, though, a good tire somewhere in the middle of these two extremes should do the trick. Realize, however, that you get what you pay for. Do not skimp and buy cheap tires. As your primary point of contact with the trail, tires may be the most important piece of equipment on a bike. With inexpensive rubber, the tire's beads may unravel or chunks of tread actually rip off the tire. If you're lucky, all you'll suffer is a long walk back to the car. If you're unlucky, your tire could blow out in the middle of a rowdy downhill, causing a wicked crash.

Clipless pedals. Clipless pedals, like ski bindings, attach your shoe directly to the pedal. They allow you to exert pressure on the pedals during the down- and up-strokes. They also help you to maneuver the bike while in the air or climbing various obstacles. Toe clips may be less expensive, but they are also heavier and harder to use. Clipless pedals and toe clips take a little getting used to, but they're definitely worth the trouble.

Bar ends. These clamp-on additions to your original straight bar will provide more leverage, an excellent grip for climbing, and a more natural position for your hands. Be aware, however, of the bar end's propensity for hooking trees on fast descents, sending you, the cyclist, airborne. Opinions are divided on the general usefulness of bar ends these days and, over the last few years, bar ends have fallen out of favor with manufacturers and riders alike.

Back pack. These bags are ideal for carrying keys, extra food and water, guidebooks, foul-weather clothing, tools, spare tubes, and a cellular phone, in case you need to call for help.

Suspension forks. For off-roaders who want nothing to impede their speed on the trails, investing in a pair of suspension forks is a good idea. Like tires, there are plenty of brands to choose from, and they all do the same thing—absorb the brutal beatings of a rough trail. The cost of these forks, however, is sometimes more brutal than the trail itself.

Bike computers. These are fun gadgets to own and are much less expensive than in years past. They have such features as trip distance, speedometer, odometer, time of day, altitude, alarm, average speed, maximum speed, heart rate, global satellite positioning, etc. Bike computers will come in handy when following these maps or to know just how far you've ridden in the wrong direction.

Hydration Pack. This is quickly becoming an essential item for cyclists pedaling for more than a few hours, especially in hot, dry conditions. The most popular brand is, of course, the Camelback, and these water packs can carry in their bladder bags as much as 100 ounces of water. These packs strap on your back with a handy hose running over your shoulder so you can be drinking water while still holding onto the bars with both hands on a rocky descent. These packs are a great way to carry a lot of extra liquid on hot rides in the middle of nowhere, as well as keys, a camera, extra food, guidebooks, tools, spare tubes, and a cellular phone, in case you need to call for help.

Types of Off-Road Terrain

Before roughing it off-road, we may first have to ride the pavement to get to our destination. Please don't be dismayed. Some of the country's best rides are on the road. Once we get past these smooth-surfaced pathways, though, adventures in dirt await us.

Rails-to-Trails. Abandoned rail lines are converted into usable public resources for exercising, commuting, or just enjoying nature. Old rails and ties are torn up and a trail, paved or unpaved, is laid along the existing corridor. This completes the cycle from ancient Indian trading routes to railroad corridors and back again to hiking and cycling trails.

Unpaved roads are typically found in rural areas and are most often public roads. Be careful when exploring, though, not to ride on someone's unpaved private drive.

Forest roads. These dirt and gravel roads are used primarily as access to forestland and are generally kept in good condition. They are almost always open to public use.

Singletrack can be the most fun on a mountain bike. These trails, with only one track to follow, are often narrow, challenging pathways. Remember to make sure these trails are open before zipping into the woods. (At the time of this printing, all trails and roads in this guidebook were open to mountain bikes.)

Open land. Unless there is a marked trail through a field or open space, you should not plan to ride here. Once one person cuts his or her wheels through a field or meadow, many more are sure to follow, causing irreparable damage to the landscape.

Techniques to Sharpen Your Skills

Many of us see ourselves as pure athletes—blessed with power, strength, and endless endurance. However, it may be those with finesse, balance, agility, and grace who get around most quickly on a mountain bike. Although power, strength, and endurance do have their places in mountain biking, these elements don't necessarily form the complete framework for a champion mountain biker.

The bike should become an extension of your body. Slight shifts in your hips or knees can have remarkable results. Experienced bike handlers seem to flash down technical descents, dashing over obstacles in a smooth and graceful effort as if pirouetting in Swan Lake. Here are some tips and techniques to help you connect with your bike and float gracefully over the dirt.

Braking. Using your brakes requires using your head, especially when descending. This doesn't mean using your head as a stopping block, but rather to think intelligently. Use your best judgment in terms of how much or how little to squeeze those brake levers.

The more weight a tire is carrying, the more braking power it has. When you're going downhill, your front wheel carries more weight than the rear. Braking gently with the front brake will help keep you in control without going into a skid. Be careful, though, not to overdo it with the front brakes and accidentally toss yourself over the handlebars. And don't neglect your rear brake! When descending, shift your weight back over the rear wheel, thus increasing your rear braking power as well. This will balance the power of both brakes and give you maximum control.

Good riders learn just how much of their weight to shift over each wheel and how to apply just enough braking power to each brake, so not to "endo" over the handlebars or skid down a trail.

Going Uphill—Climbing Those Treacherous Hills

Shift into a low gear. Before shifting, be sure to ease up on your pedaling so there is not too much pressure on the chain. With that in mind, it's important to shift before you find yourself on a steep slope, where it may too late. Find the best gear for you that matches the terrain and steepness of each climb.

Stay seated. Standing out of the saddle is often helpful when climbing steep hills on a bike, but you may find that on dirt, standing may cause your rear tire to lose its grip and spin out. Climbing is not possible without traction. As you improve, you will likely learn the subtle tricks that make out-of-saddle climbing possible. Until then, have a seat.

Lean forward. On very steep hills, the front end may feel unweighted and suddenly pop up. Slide forward on the saddle and lean over the handlebars. Think about putting your chin down near your stem. This will add more weight to the front wheel and should keep you grounded. It's all about using the weight of your head to your advantage. Most people don't realize how heavy their noggin is.

Relax. As with downhilling, relaxation is a big key to your success when climbing steep, rocky climbs. Smooth pedaling translates into good traction. Tense bodies don't balance well at low speeds. Instead of fixating grimly on the front wheel, look up at the terrain above, and pick a good line.

Keep pedaling. On rocky climbs, be sure to keep the pressure on, and don't let up on those pedals! You'll be surprised at what your bike will just roll over as long as you keep the engine revved up.

Going Downhill—The Real Reason We Get Up in the Morning

Relax. Stay loose on the bike, and don't lock your elbows or clench your grip. Your elbows need to bend with the bumps and absorb the shock, while your hands should have a firm but controlled grip on the bars to keep things steady. Breathing slowly, deeply, and deliberately will help you relax while flying down bumpy singletrack. Maintaining a death-grip on the brakes will be unhelpful. Fear and tension will make you wreck every time.

Use your eyes. Keep your head up and scan the trail as far forward as possible. Choose a line well in advance. *You* decide what line to take—don't let the trail decide for you. Keep the surprises to a minimum. If you have to react quickly to an obstacle, then you've already made a mistake.

Rise above the saddle. When racing down bumpy, technical descents, you should not be sitting on the saddle, but hovering just over it, allowing your bent legs and arms, instead of your rear, to absorb the rocky trail. Think jockey.

Remember your pedals. Be mindful of where your pedals are in relation to upcoming obstacles. Clipping a rock will lead directly to unpleasantness. Most of the time, you'll want to keep your pedals parallel to the ground.

Stay focused. Many descents require your utmost concentration and focus just to reach the bottom. You must notice every groove, every root, every rock, every hole, every bump. You, the bike, and the trail should all become one as you seek singletrack nirvana on your way down the mountain. But if your thoughts wander, however, then so may your bike, and you may instead become one with the trees!

Watch Out!

Back-road Obstacles

Logs. When you want to hop a log, throw your body back, yank up on the handlebars, and pedal forward in one swift motion. This clears the front end of the bike. Then quickly scoot forward and pedal the rear wheel up and over. Keep the forward momentum until you've cleared the log, and by all means, don't hit the brakes, or you may do some interesting acrobatic maneuvers!

Rocks and roots. Worse than highway potholes! Stay relaxed and let your elbows and knees absorb the shock. Staying seated will keep the rear wheel weighted to prevent slipping, and a light front end will help you to respond quickly to each new obstacle.

Water. Before crossing a stream or puddle, be sure to first check the depth and bottom surface. There may be an unseen hole or large rock hidden under the water that could wash you up if you're not careful. You should also consider that riding through a mountain stream can cause great damage to the stream's ecosystem. If you still want to try, hit the water at a good speed, pedal steadily, and allow the bike to steer you through. Once you're across, tap the brakes to squeegee the water off the rims and the guilt off your conscience.

Leaves. Be careful of wet leaves. They may look pretty, but a trail or bridge covered with leaves may cause your wheels to slip out from under you. Leaves are not nearly as unpredictable and dangerous as ice, but they do warrant your attention on a rainy day.

Mud. If you must ride through mud, hit it head on and keep pedaling. You want to part the ooze with your front wheel and get across before it swallows you up. Above all, don't leave the trail to go around the mud. This just widens the path even more and leads to increased trail erosion.

Urban Obstacles

Curbs are fun to jump, but as with logs, be careful.

Curbside drains. Be careful not to get a wheel caught in the grate.

Dogs make great pets, but they seem to have it in for mountain bikers. If you think you can't outrun a dog that's chasing you, stop and walk your bike out of its territory. A loud yell to "Get!" or "Go home!" often works, as does a sharp squirt from your water bottle right between the eyes.

Cars are tremendously convenient when we're in them, but dodging irate motorists in big automobiles becomes a real hazard when riding a bike. As a cyclist, you must realize most drivers aren't expecting you to be there and often wish you weren't. Stay alert and ride carefully, clearly signaling all of your intentions.

Potholes, like grates and back-road canyons, should be avoided. Just because you're on an all-terrain bicycle doesn't mean you're indestructible. Potholes regularly damage rims, pop tires, and sometimes lift unsuspecting cyclists into a spectacular swan dive over the handlebars.

Last-Minute Check

Before a ride, it's a good idea to give your bike a once-over to make sure everything is in working order. Begin by checking the air pressure in your tires before each ride to make sure they are properly inflated. Mountain bikes require about 45 to 55 pounds per square inch of air pressure. If your tires are underinflated, there is greater likelihood that the tubes may get pinched on a rock, causing the tire to go flat.

Looking over your bike to make sure everything is secure and in its place is the next step. Go through the following checklist before each ride.

- **Pinch the tires to feel for proper inflation.** They should give just a little on the sides but feel very hard on the treads. If you have a pressure gauge, use that.
- **Check your brakes.** Squeeze the rear brake and roll your bike forward. The rear tire should skid. Next, squeeze the front brake and roll your bike forward. The rear wheel should lift into the air. If this doesn't happen, then your brakes are

too loose. Make sure the brake levers don't touch the handlebars when squeezed with full force.

- **Check all quick releases on your bike.** Make sure they are all securely tightened.
- **Lube up.** If your chain squeaks, apply some lubricant.
- **Check your nuts and bolts.** Check the handlebars, saddle, cranks, and pedals to make sure that each is tight and securely fastened to your bike.
- **Check your wheels.** Spin each wheel to see that they spin through the frame and between brake pads freely.
- **Have you got everything?** Make sure you have your spare tube, tire irons, patch kit, frame pump, tools, food, water, foul-weather gear, and guidebook.

Need more info on mountain biking? Consider reading *Basic Essentials Mountain Biking*. You'll discover such things as choosing and maintaining a mountain bike; useful bike-handling techniques; preparing for long rides; overcoming obstacles such as rocks, logs, and water; and even preparing for competition.

Repair and Maintenance

Fixing a Flat

TOOLS YOU WILL NEED

- Two tire irons
- Pump (either a floor pump or a frame pump)
- No screwdrivers!!! (This can puncture the tube.)

REMOVING THE WHEEL

The front wheel is easy. Simply disconnect the brake shoes, open the quick release mechanism or undo the bolts with the proper sized wrench, then remove the wheel from the bike.

    The rear wheel is a little more tricky. Before you loosen the wheel from the frame, shift the chain into the smallest gear on the freewheel (the cluster of gears in the back). Once you've done this, removing and installing the wheel, like the front, is much easier.

REMOVING THE TIRE

Step one: Insert a tire iron under the bead of the tire and pry the tire over the lip of the rim. Be careful not to pinch the tube when you do this.

Step two: Hold the first tire iron in place. With the second tire iron, repeat step one, 3 or 4 inches down the rim. Alternate tire irons, pulling the bead of the tire over the rim, section by section, until one side of the tire bead is completely off the rim.

Step three: Remove the rest of the tire and tube from the rim. This can be done by hand. It's easiest to remove the valve stem last. Once the tire is off the rim, pull the tube out of the tire.

CLEAN AND SAFETY CHECK

Step four: Using a rag, wipe the inside of the tire to clean out any dirt, sand, glass, thorns, etc. These may cause the tube to puncture. The inside of a tire should feel smooth. Any pricks or bumps could mean that you have found the culprit responsible for your flat tire.

Step five: Wipe the rim clean, then check the rim strip, making sure it covers the spoke nipples properly on the inside of the rim. If a spoke is poking through the rim strip, it could cause a puncture.

Step six: At this point, you can do one of two things: replace the punctured tube with a new one, or patch the hole. It's easiest to just replace the tube with a new tube when you're out on the trails. Roll up the old tube and take it home to repair later that night in front of the TV. Directions on patching a tube are usually included with the patch kit itself.

INSTALLING THE TIRE AND TUBE

(This can be done entirely by hand.)

Step seven: Inflate the new or repaired tube with enough air to give it shape, then tuck it back into the tire.

Step eight: To put the tire and tube back on the rim, begin by putting the valve in the valve hole. The valve must be straight. Then use your hands to push the beaded edge of the tire onto the rim all the way around so that one side of your tire is on the rim.

Step nine: Let most of the air out of the tube to allow room for the rest of the tire.

Step ten: Beginning opposite the valve, use your thumbs to push the other side of the tire onto the rim. Be careful not to pinch the tube in between the tire and the rim. The last few inches may be difficult, and you may need the tire iron to pry the tire onto the rim. If so, just be careful not to puncture the tube.

BEFORE INFLATING COMPLETELY

Step eleven: Check to make sure the tire is seated properly and that the tube is not caught between the tire and the rim. Do this by adding about five to ten pounds of air, and watch closely that the tube does not bulge out of the tire.

Step twelve: Once you're sure the tire and tube are properly seated, put the wheel back on the bike, then fill the tire with air. It's easier squeezing the wheel through the brake shoes if the tire is still flat.

Step thirteen: Now fill the tire with the proper amount of air, and check constantly to make sure the tube doesn't bulge from the rim. If the tube does appear to bulge out, release all the air as quickly as possible, or you could be in for a big bang. Place the wheel back in the dropost and tighten the quick release lever Reconnect the brake shoes.

When installing the rear wheel, place the chain back onto the smallest cog (farthest gear on the right), and pull the derailleur out of the way. Your wheel should slide right on.

Lubrication Prevents Deterioration

Lubrication is crucial to maintaining your bike. Dry spots will be eliminated. Creaks, squeaks, grinding, and binding will be gone. The chain will run quietly, and the gears will shift smoothly. The brakes will grip quicker, and your bike may last longer with fewer repairs. Need I say more? Well, yes. Without knowing where to put the lubrication, what good is it?

THINGS YOU WILL NEED
* One can of bicycle lubricant, found at any bike store
* A clean rag (to wipe excess lubricant away)

WHAT GETS LUBRICATED
* Front derailleur
* Rear derailleur
* Shift levers
* Front brake
* Rear brake
* Both brake levers
* Chain

WHERE TO LUBRICATE

To make it easy, simply spray a little lubricant on all the pivot points of your bike. If you're using a squeeze bottle, use just a drop or two. Put a few drops on each point wherever metal moves against metal, for instance, at the center of the brake calipers. Then let the lube sink in.

Once you have applied the lubricant to the derailleurs, shift the gears a few times, working the derailleurs back and forth. This allows the lubricant to work itself into the tiny cracks and spaces it must occupy to do its job. Work the brakes a few times as well.

LUBING THE CHAIN

Lubricating the chain should be done after the chain has been wiped clean of most road grime. Do this by spinning the pedals counterclockwise while gripping the chain with a clean rag. As you add the lubricant, be sure to get some in between each link. With an aerosol spray, just spray the chain while pedaling backwards (counterclockwise) until the chain is fully lubricated. Let the lubricant soak in for a few seconds before wiping the excess away. Chains will collect dirt much faster if they're loaded with too much lubrication.

Appendix

Bicycle Clubs and Organizations

Bicycle Camps, Clinics and Museums

Barnett Bicycle Institution, 2755 Ore Mill Drive, Suite 14, Colorado Springs, CO 80904; (719) 632-5173

Carpenter/Phinney Mountain Bike Camp, 2626 Baseline Road, P.O. Box 252, Boulder, CO 80302; (303) 442-2371

Dirt Camp
3131 Endicott, Boulder, CO 80303; (303) 499-3178 or (800) 711-DIRT

Durango Mountain Bike Camp
621 Columbine Road, Durango, CO 81301; (970) 259-0238

Mountain Bike Hall of Fame & Museum
P.O. Box 845, Crested Butte, CO 81224; (970) 349-7382

Local Cycling Clubs

Aspen Cycling Club, P.O. Box 4945, Aspen, CO 81612; (970) 925-7334

Bicycle Colorado
P.O. Box 698, Salida, CO 81201; (719) 530-0051

Bicycle Racing Association of Colorado (BRAC), 4615 East 23rd Street, Denver, CO 80207; (303) 440-5366, (303) 820-2453. A statewide bicycling road-racing association.

Boulder Bicycle Commuters
4820 Thunderbird Circle, #108, Boulder, CO 80303; (303) 499-7466

Boulder Off-Road Alliance
1420 Alpine Avenue, P.O. Box 4954, Boulder, CO 80306; (303) 447-9378, (303) 441-5262

Boulder Old Wheelers
1740 Sunset Boulevard, Boulder, CO 80304; (303) 444-0801

Boulder Women's Cycling Team
Goes on road and mountain bike rides for women only. Boulder, CO; (303) 497-8427

Breckenridge Fat Tire Society
P.O. Box 2845, Breckenridge, CO 80424; (970) 453-5548; recorded info (970) 453-INFO, then push #FATT

Cañon City Cycling Club
1248 North Reynolds, Cañon City, CO 81212; (719) 275-1963

City & County of Denver Bicycle Program
200 West 14th Avenue, Room 302, Denver, CO 80204; (303) 649-BIKE

Colorado Bicycling Program
4201 East Arkansas Avenue, Room 225, Denver, CO 80222; (303) 757-9982

Colorado Heart Cycle Association
P.O. Box 100743, Denver, CO 80210; (303) 267-1112

Colorado Off-Road Point Series
222 North Main Street, Gunnison, CO 81230; (970) 641-1137

Colorado Plateau Mountain Bike Trail Association (COPMOBA) P.O. Box 4602, Grand Junction, CO 81502; (970) 241-9561

Colorado Springs Cycling Club
P.O. Box 49602, Colorado Springs, CO 80949-9602; (719) 594-6354; CSCC@bikesprings.com

Colorado Velodrome Association
4940 Meredith Way, #305, Boulder, CO 80303; (303) 938-8679

Crested Butte Mountain Bicycling Association
P.O. Box 845, Crested Butte, CO 81224; (970) 349-6817

Custer County Bicycle Club
P.O. Box 352, Westcliffe, CO 81252; (719) 783-9231

Denver Bicycle Touring Club
P.O. Box 101301, Denver, CO 80250; (303) 756-7240

Diamond Peaks Mountain Bike Patrol
P.O. Box 251, Timnath, CO 80547; (970) 482-6006, ext. 22; DPMBP@aol.com

Durango Wheel Club
340 South Camino Del Rio, P.O. Box 1389, Durango, CO 81301; (970) 259-4621

Fat Tire Week
P.O. Box 782, Crested Butte, CO 81224; (970) 349-6817

Fort Collins Cycling Club
Puts on social group rides. Fort Collins, CO; (970) 482-6006

Front Range Mountain Biking Association
P.O. Box 1003, Englewood, CO 80150; (303) 674-4862

Mountain Road Biking Association of Rocky Flats, 8566 Cody Court, Westminster, CO 80005; (970) 422-2792, (303) 966-5135

Peak to Pub
Fort Collins, CO; (970) 226-6519, (970) 266-1212

Pikes Peak Area Trails Coalition
P.O. Box 34, Colorado Springs, CO 80901; (719) 633-6884

Ridefinders
8 South Nevada Avenue, Suite 401, Colorado Springs, CO 80903; (719) 471-7665, (800) 719-RIDE

Rocky Mountain Cycling Club
P.O. Box 101473, Denver, CO 80250-1473

Rocky Mountain Cycling Club
Weekend road and training rides throughout the year. Denver, CO. www.rmccrides.com. No contact phone number available

Routt County Riders Bicycle Club
P.O. Box 770094, Steamboat Springs, CO 80477-0094; President: Pete Wither (970) 978-1735

San Juan National Forest Association
P.O. Box 2261, Durango, CO 81302; (970) 385-1210

San Luis Valley Cycling Club
Kristi Mountain Sports, Villa Mall, 7565 West Highway 160, Alamosa, CO 81101; (719) 589-9759

Summit County Mountain Bike Hotline
Free 24-hour information source. Summit County, CO; (970) 453-INFO, ext. #FATT

Summit Fat Tire Society
P.O. Box 5533, Breckenridge, CO 80424; (970) 949-8057

Team Evergreen Bicycle Club
P.O. Box 3804, Evergreen, CO 80439; (970) 674-6048

The Medicine Wheel
P.O. Box 685, Manitou Springs, CO 80829

Trails 2000
1025 East 5th Avenue, Durango, CO 81301;
(970) 259-4682

Tune-Up Ski & Bike Club
222 North Main Street, Gunnison, CO 81230;
(970) 641-0285

Vail Velo Club
Social road or mountain bike rides. Vail, CO;
(970) 845-7928

National Organizations

Alpine Snow Bicycle Association
620 South Knox Court, Denver, CO 80218;
(303) 935-8494

American Alpine Club
Deals with mountain related activities and
interests. Golden, CO; (303) 384-0110

American Trails
P.O. Box 200787, Denver, CO 80220; (303)
321-6606, national trails advocacy organization

International Christian Cycling Club
7972 South Vincennes Way, Englewood, CO
80112; (303) 290-9182

**International Mountain Bicycling Associa-
tion (IMBA)** P.O. Box 7578, Boulder, CO
80306; (303) 545-9011, works to keep public lands accessible to bikers and provides
information on design and maintenance

**National Off-Road Bicycling Association
(NORBA),** One Olympic Plaza, Colorado
Springs, CO 80909; (719) 578-4717, national
governing body of U.S. mountain bike racing

Outdoor Recreation Coalition of America
Oversees and examines issues for outdoor
recreation. (ORCA), Boulder, CO; (303)
444-3353; www.orca.org, info@orca.org

Rails-to-Trails Conservancy
Organized to promote conversion of abandoned
rail corridors to trails for public use. Washington, D.C.; (202) 331-9696; www.railtrails.org

Trail Conservation Services
11694 West Marlowe Place, Morrison, CO
80465; (303) 932-1627

United States Cycling Federation
Governing body for amateur cycling. Colorado
Springs, CO; (719) 578-4581

**United States Professional Cycling Federa-
tion** Governing body for professional cycling.
Colorado Springs, CO; (719) 578-4581

USA Cycling
One Olympic Plaza, Colorado Springs, CO
80909; (719) 578-4581

World Bicycle Polo Federation
P.O. Box 1039, Bailey, CO 80421; (303)
838-4878, manufactures and distributes
equipment for official bicycle polo

Bicycle Advocacy Groups
Colorado Trail Foundation, P.O. Box 260876,
Lakewood, CO 80226; (970) 526-0809

Greenway Foundation
1666 South University Boulevard, Suite B,
Denver, CO 80210; (303) 698-1322

Trail Action Group
A trails advocacy group. Contact Dawes Wilson
of Pedal Power, Vail, CO; (970) 845-0931

**Peoples' Effort to De-emphasize Autos in
Loveland (P.E.D.A.L.)**
Loveland, CO; (970) 669-8858

Colorado Department of Transportation
Colorado Department of Transportation, Bicy-
cle/Pedestrian Program, 4201 East Arkansas
Avenue, Room 212, Denver, CO 80222; (303)
757-9982

Colorado Festivals

April

Fruita Fat Tire Festival, Fruita, CO, Call Over the Edge Sports at (800) 873-3068. (Chapters 2 and 3).
Peach Blossom Home Tour, Palisade, CO; (970) 464-7458. (Chapters 2 and 3).
Southwest Festival, Grand Junction, CO; (970) 256-4060. (Chapters 2 and 3).

May

Annual Blossom Festival, Cañon City, CO; (719) 275-7234. (Chapter 49).
Buena Vista Bicycle Festival, Buena Vista, CO; (719) 594-6354. (Chapters 27 and 44).
Capital Hill People's Fair, Denver, CO; (303) 830-1651. (Chapters 41, 42, 43, 44, 45, and 46).
Cinco de Mayo, Grand Junction, CO; (970) 256-4060 (Chapters 2, 3 and 4).
Colorado State Cowboy Championship, Montrose, CO; (970) 249-5000. (Chapters 4 and 5).
Iron Horse Bicycle Classic, Durango, CO; (970) 259-4621. (Chapters 9 and 10).
Jazz Festival and Art Walk, Estes Park, CO; (970) 586-6104. (Chapters 38 and 39).
Territory Days Celebration, Colorado Springs, CO; (719) 471-0545. (Chapters 46, 47, and 48).
Taste of Creede, Creede, CO; (800) 327-658-2717. (Chapters 31 and 32).

June

Animas Music Festival, Durango, CO; (970) 259-2606. (Chapters 9 and 10).
Annual Yampa River Festival, Steamboat Springs, CO; (970) 879-6249. (Chapters 12, 13, 15, 16, 17, 18, and 19).

Backcountry Mountain Bike Festival, Montrose, CO; (970) 249-5000 or (800) 923-5515. (Chapters 2, 3, 4, and 5).
Breckenridge Music Festival, Breckenridge, CO; (970) 453-2120. (Chapters 22 and 23).
Bluegrass Festival, Telluride, CO; (800) 525-3455. (Chapters 6 and 7).
Colorado Brewers Festival, Fort Collins, CO, (800) 274-FORT. (Chapters 14, 35, 36 and 37).
Crested Butte Fat Tire Festival, Crested Butte, CO; (802) 226-7411. (Chapters 24, 25, 26, and 29).
Downtown Denver International Buskerfest, Denver, CO; (303) 478-7878. (Chapters 41, 42, 43, 44, 45, and 46).
Festival of Nations, Avon, CO; (970) 476-9090. (Chapter 21).
Fibark Boat Races and Festival, Salida, CO; (719) 539-2068. (Chapters 28 and 30).
Mardi Gras Conga, Cañon City, CO; (888) 333-5597. (Chapter 49).
Norwest Art & Jazz Festival, Grand Junction, CO; (970) 256-4060. (Chapters 2, 3 and 4).
Rage in the Sage, Gunnison, CO; (970) 641-0285. (Chapters 24, 25, 26, and 29).
Strawberry Days, Glenwood Springs, CO; (970) 945-6589. (Chapter 1).
Sunshine Festival, Alamosa, CO; (719) 589-6077. (Chapters 33 and 34).
Taste of the Summit, Dillon, CO; (970) 468-2403. (Chapters 22 and 23).
Ute Mountain Rodeo Roundup, Cortez, CO; (970) 565-4485. (Chapter 11).
Western Heritage Days, Estes Park, CO; (970) 586-6104. (Chapters 38 and 39).

July

American Music Festival, Winter Park, CO; (800) 903-PARK. (Chapter 20).

Annual Burro Days, Fairplay, CO; (719) 836-4279. (Chapters 44 and 27).

Annual New Old Fashioned Chaffee County Fair, Poncha Springs, CO; (719) 539-2068 or (719) 395-6612. (Chapters 28 and 30).

AT&T LODO Fest, Denver, CO; (303) 892-1112. (Chapters 41, 42, 43, 44, 45, and 46.)

Big Water Brew Fest, Salida, CO; (719) 539-2068. (Chapters 27, 28, and 30).

Breckenridge Music Festival, Breckenridge, CO; (970) 453-2120. (Chapters 22 and 23).

Cattleman's Days, Gunnison, CO; (800) 274-7580. (Chapters 24, 25, 26, and 29).

Cherry Creek Arts Festival, Denver, CO; (303) 355-ARTS. (Chapters 42, 43, 44, 45, and 46).

Crested Butte Wildflower Festival, Crested Butte, CO; (970) 349-2571. (Chapters 24, 25, 26, and 29).

Deltarado Days, Delta, CO; (800) 874-1741. (Chapters 2, 3, and 4).

Downtown Boulder Art Fair, Boulder, CO; (303) 449-3774. (Chapters 39, 40, and 41).

Fairplay Burro Days, Fairplay, CO; (719) 836-3155. (Chapters 27 and 44).

Logger Days, South Fork, CO; (719) 873-5512 or (800) 571-0881. (Chapters 31 and 32).

Melee in the Mines, Telluride, CO; (970) 728-8666. (Chapters 6 and 7).

Rainbow Weekend, Steamboat Springs, CO; (970) 879-0880. (Chapters 12, 13, 15, 16, 17, 18, and 19).

Ski-Hi Stampede, Monte Vista, CO; (719) 852-2731. (Chapters 33 and 34).

Vail Arts Festival, Vail, CO; (800) 525-3875. (Chapter 21).

Winter Park Jazz Festival, Winter Park, CO; (800) 903-PARK. (Chapter 20).

Wood Carvers Rendezvous, Creede, CO; (800) 327-2102. (Chapter 31 and 32).

August

Arkansas Valley Fair, La Junta, CO; (719) 254-7483. (Chapter 50).

Avon Summer Fest. Avon, CO; (800) 525-3875. (Chapter 21).

Baily Day, Baily, CO; (719) 836-4279. (Chapters 44 and 45).

Breckenridge Music Festival, Breckenridge, CO; (970) 453-9142 or (970) 453-2120. (Chapters 22 and 23).

Downtown Boulder Fall Festival, Boulder, CO; (303) 449-3774. (Chapters 39, 40, and 41).

Garfield County Fair, Rifle, CO; (970) 625-2085 or (800) 842-2085. (Chapter 1).

Gold Rush Days, Buena Vista, CO; (719) 395-6612. (Chapters 27, 28, and 30).

New West Fest, Fort Collins, CO; (970) 484-6500. (Chapters 14, 35, 36, and 37).

Olathe Sweet Corn Festival, Olathe, CO; (970) 323-6006. (Chapters 4 and 5).

Palisade Peach Festival, Palisade, CO; (970) 464-7458. (Chapters 2, 3, and 4).

San Luis Valley Fair, Monte Vista, CO; (719) 852-2731. (Chapters 33 and 34).

Telluride Airmen's Rendezvous, Telluride, CO; (970) 728-9525. (Chapters 6 and 7).

Winter Park King of the Rockies, Winter Park, CO; (970) 726-1590. (Chapter 20).

Wild Mushrooms Festival, Telluride, CO; (970) 728-6265 or (800) 525-2717. (Chapters 6 and 7).

September

100 Years of the American Bicycle (1999), Fort Collins, CO; (970) 221-6738, (970) 221-6735, and (970) 221-6243. (Chapters 14, 35, 36, and 37).

Annual Colorfest Arts & Crafts, Cortez, CO; (970) 565-3414. (Chapter 11).

Banana Belt Mountain Bike Loop Race, Salida, CO; (719) 539-2068. (Chapters 27, 28 and 30).

Coloradofest, Colorado Springs, CO; (719) 275-7507. (Chapters 46, 47, and 48).

Colorado Mountain Winefest, Palisade, CO; (800) 704-3667 (Chapters 2, 3, and 4).

Council Tree Pow Wow, Delta, CO; (800) 874-1741. (Chapters 2, 3, 4, and 5).

Early Settlers' Day, La Junta, CO; (719) 384-7411. (Chapter 50).

Middle Park Fair & Rodeo, Kremmling, CO; (970) 724-3472. (Chapter 17).

North Park Fair, Walden, CO; (970) 723-4600. (Chapter 14).

One World Festival, Crested Butte, CO; (970) 349-6438 or (800) 545-4505. (Chapters 24, 25, 26, and 29).

Telluride Blues & Brews Festival, Telluride CO; (800) 525-3455. (Chapters 6 and 7).

Telluride Film Festival, Telluride, CO; (970) 728-6265 or (800) 525-2717. (Chapters 6, 7, and 8).

Celtic Festival & Highland Games, Clifton, CO; (970) 256-4060. (Chapters 2, 3, and 4).

Rocky Mountain Colorado Campgrounds

While campgrounds marked with a "Y" take reservations, those campgrounds marked with an "N" are on a first come, first served basis. The term "GROUP" designates an area that limits the number of people allowed in a site. Group areas are usually larger recreational areas, providing boating, picnicking, and camping. Daily fees for these group areas vary widely, depending upon the number of people in your group, so individual fees are generally unlisted. Terms, conditions, and fees are subject to change. Contact the respective ranger district for information on current terms, conditions, and fees for individual campsites. Most of these campgrounds are open from Memorial Day through Labor Day. These campgrounds are listed by national forest and ranger district. For specific locations of any of these campgrounds, consult the corresponding national forest visitors map available at its respective national forest office. Reservations may be made by calling the National Recreation Reservation Service at (877) 444-6777 or online at reserveusa.com. Reservations are accepted up to 240 days in advance of your stay but must be made prior to five days in advance. For further information, contact the U.S. Forest Service Rocky Mountain Region Headquarters, Lakewood, CO, at (303) 275-5350 or check its Web site at www.fs.fed.us/r2. All of the information below was provided by the USDA Forest Service in Colorado. Prices and fees are subject to change.

Arapaho and Roosevelt National Forest
240 West Prospect, Fort Collins, 80526; (970) 498-2770

Boulder Ranger District
2140 Yarmouth Avenue, Boulder, 80301; (303) 541-2500
Camp Dick, 8,650 feet, 41 Units, Y, $12.00 daily.
Kelly Dahl, 8,600 feet, 46 Units, Y, $12.00 daily.
Olive Ridge, 8,350 feet, 56 Units, Y, $12.00 daily.
Pawnee, 10,400 feet, 55 Units, Y, $12.00 daily.
Peaceful Valley, 8,500 feet, 17 Units, Y, $12.00 daily.
Rainbow Lakes, 10,000 feet, 16 Units, N, $6.00 daily.

Canyon Lakes Ranger District
1311 South College, Fort Collins, 80524; (970) 498-1375
Ansel Watrous, 5,800 feet, 19 Units, N, $9.00 daily.
Aspen Glen, 8,660 feet, 8 Units, N, $8.00 daily.
Bellaire Lake, 8,600 feet, 26 Units, N, $12.00 daily.
Big Bend, 7,700 feet, 6 Units, N, $9.00 daily.
Big South, 8,440 feet, 4 Units, N, $7.00 daily.
Browns Park, 8,400 feet, 28 Units, N, $8.00 daily.

Chambers Lake, 9,200 feet, 52 Units, Y, $12.00 daily.
Dowdy Lake, 8,100 feet, 62 Units, Y, $10.00 daily.
Dutch George, 6,500 feet, 20 Units, N, $10.00 daily.
Grandview, 10,220 feet, 8 Units, N, $8.00 daily.
Jack's Gulch, 8,100 feet, 70 Units, N, $12.00 daily.
Kelly Flats, 6,600 feet, 23 Units, N, $9.00 daily.
Long Draw, 10,030 feet, 25 Units, N, $8.00 daily.
Mountain Park, 6,500 feet, 55 Units, Y, $12.00 daily.
Narrows, 6,400 feet, 9 Units, N, $7.00 daily.
North Fork Poudre, 9,200 feet, 9 Units, N, $8.00 daily.
Sleeping Elephant, 7,800 feet, 15 Units, N, $9.00 daily.
Stove Prairie, 6,000 feet, 9 Units, N, $10.00 daily.
Tom Bennett, 9,000 feet, 12 Units, N, $8.00 daily.
Tunnel, 8,600 feet, 49 Units, N, $10.00 daily.
West Lake, 8,200 feet, 29 Units, Y, $10.00 daily.
Jack's Gulch Group, 8,100 feet, GROUP, Y.
Mountain Park Group, 6,500 feet, GROUP, Y.

Clear Creek Ranger District
101 Chicago Creek, Idaho Springs, 80452; (303) 567-2901

Clear Lake, 10,000 feet, 8 Units, N, $9.00 daily.
Cold Springs, 9,200 feet, 38 Units, Y, $11.00 daily.
Columbine, 9,200 feet, 47 Units, N, $10.00 daily.
Echo Lake, 10,600 feet, 18 Units, Y, $10.00 daily.
Guanella Pass, 10,900 feet, 18 Units, Y, $11.00 daily.
Mizpah, 9,200 feet, 10 Units, N, $10.00 daily.
West Chicago Creek, 9,600 feet, 16 Units, Y, $9.00 daily.
Pickle Gulch, 9,100 feet, GROUP, Y.

Pawnee Ranger District
660 O Street, Greeley, 80631; (970) 353-5004
Crow Valley, 4,800 feet, 7 Units, N, $8.00 daily.
Crow Valley Overflow, 4,800 feet, GROUP.
Stewart J. Adams, 4,800 feet, GROUP.

Sulphur Ranger District
9 Ten Mile Drive, Granby, 80446; (970) 887-4100
Arapaho Bay, 8,320 feet, 84 Units, Y, $12.00 daily.
Byers Creek, 9,360 feet, 6 Units, N, $8.00 daily.
Denver Creek, 8,800 feet, 25 Units, N, $10.00 daily.
Green Ridge, 8,360 feet, 81 Units, Y, $12.00 daily.
Horseshoe, 8,540 feet, 7 Units, N, $9.00 daily.
Idlewild, 9,000 feet, 26 Units, N, $8.00 daily.
Robbers Roost, 9,826 feet, 11 Units, N, $8.00 daily.
Sawmill Gulch, 8,780 feet, 5 Units, N, $10.00 daily.
South Fork, 8,940 feet, 21 Units, N, $10.00 daily.
Stillwater, 8,300 feet, 128 Units, Y, $12.00 daily.
St. Louis Creek, 8,900 feet, 18 Units, N, $8.00 daily.
Sugarloaf, 8,970 feet, 11 Units, N, $10.00 daily.
Willow Creek, 8,130 feet, 35 Units, N, $10.00 daily.
Cutthroat Bay, 8,400 feet, GROUP.

Grand Mesa Umcompahgre and Gunnison National Forests
2250 U.S. Highway 50, Delta, 80416; (970) 874-6600

Grand Valley Ranger District
218 High Street, P.O. Box 330, 81624; (970) 487-3534
Big Creek, 10,000 feet, 26 Units, N, $6.00 daily.
Cottonwood Lake, 10,000 feet, 42 Units, N, $8.00 daily.
Jumbo, 9,800 feet, 26 Units, N, $10.00 daily.
Spruce Grove, 9,900 feet, 16 Units, N, $8.00 daily.

Grand Valley Ranger District
2777 Crossroads Boulevard, Grand Junction, 81506; (970) 242-8211
Carp Lake, 10,000 feet, 20 Units, N, $7.50 daily.
Crag Crest, 10,100 feet, 11 Units, N, $7.50 daily.
Divide Fork, 9,200 feet, 11 Units, N, FREE.
Eggleston, 10,100 feet, 6 Units, N, $7.50 daily.
Fish Hawk, 10,000 feet, 5 Units, N, FREE.
Hay Press, 9,300 feet, 11 Units, N, FREE.
Island Lake, 10,300 feet, 41 Units, N, $7.50 daily.
Kiser Creek, 10,100 feet, 12 Units, N, FREE.
Little Bear, 10,200 feet, 36 Units, N, $8.75 daily.
Trickle Park, 10,000 feet, 5 Units, N, FREE.
Twin Lake, 10,300 feet, 13 Units, N, FREE.
Ward Lake, 10,200 feet, 27 Units, N, $8.75 daily.
Weir & Johnson, 10,500 feet, 12 Units, N, FREE.
Eggleston Group, 10,100 feet, GROUP, Y.

Gunnison Ranger District
216 North Colorado, Gunnison, 81230; (970) 641-0471
Almont, 8,000 feet, 10 Units, N, $6.00 daily.
Avery Peak, 9,600 feet, 10 Units, N, FREE.
Big Blue, 9,600 feet, 11 Units, N, $4.00 daily.
Cebolla, 9,200 feet, 5 Units, N, $6.00 daily.
Cement Creek, 9,000 feet, 13 Units, $6.00 daily.
Cold Spring, 9,000 feet, 6 Units, N, $6.00 daily.
Comanche, 8,900 feet, 4 Units, N, FREE.
Deer Lakes, 10,400 feet, 12 Units, N, $8.00 daily.
Dinner Station, 9,600 feet, 22 Units, Y, $8.00 daily.
Dorchester, 9,800 feet, 10 Units, N, $8.00 daily.
Emerald Lake, 10,000 feet, 2 Units, N, FREE.
Gold Creek, 10,000 feet, 6 Units, N, $4.00 daily.
Gothic, 9,600 feet, 4 Units, N, FREE.
Hidden Valley, 9,700 feet, 3 Units, N, $6.00 daily.
Lake Irwin, 10,200 feet, 32 Units, Y, $8.00 daily.
Lakeview, 9,400 feet, 46 Units, Y, $10.00 daily.

Lodgepole, 8,800 feet, 16 Units, Y, $8.00 daily.
Lottis Creek, 9,000 feet, 27 Units, N, $10.00 daily.
Middle Quartz, 10,200 feet, 7 Units, N, $4.00 daily.
Mirror Lake, 11,000 feet, 10 Units, N, $6.00 daily.
Mosca, 10,000 feet, 16 Units, N, $8.00 daily.
North Bank, 8,600 feet, 17 Units, N, $8.00 daily.
One Mile, 8,600 feet, 25 Units, Y, $12.00 daily.
Pitkin, 9,300 feet, 22 Units, N, $10.00 daily.
Quartz, 9,800 feet, 10 Units, N, $6.00 daily.
Rivers End, 9,400 feet, 15 Units, N, $8.00 daily.
Rosy Lane, 8,600 feet, 20 Units, Y, $10.00 daily.
Slumgullion, 11,200 feet, 21 Units, N, $6.00 daily.
Snowblind, 9,300 feet, 23 Units, N, $6.00 daily.
Soap Creek, 7,700 feet, 21 Units, N, $8.00 daily.
Spring Creek, 10,900 feet, 12 Units, N, $8.00 daily.
Spruce, 9,300 feet, 9 Units, N, $6.00 daily.
Taylor Canyon Tent, 8,600 feet, 7 Units, N, $4.00 daily.
Williams Creek, 9,200 feet, 23 Units, N, $8.00 daily.

Norwood Ranger District

1150 Forest, P.O. Box 388, Norwood, 81423; (970) 327-4261
Matterhorn, 9,500 feet, 26 Units, N, $10.00/14 daily.
Sunshine, 9,500 feet, 15 Units, N, $10.00 daily.

Ouray Ranger District

2505 South Townsend, Montrose, 81401; (970) 240-5300
Amphitheatre, 8,400 feet, 30 Units, Y, $12.00 daily.
Beaver Lake, 8,800 feet, 11 Units, N, $8.00 daily.
Big Cimarron, 8,600 feet, 10 Units, N, $4.00 daily.
Silver Jack, 8,900 feet, 60 Units, N, $8.00 daily.

Paonia Ranger District

North Rio Grande Avenue, P.O. Box 1030, Paonia, 81428; (970) 527-4131
Erickson Springs, 6,800 feet, 18 Units, N, $8.00 daily.
Lost Lake, 9,600 feet, 11 Units, N, FREE.
McClure, 8,200 feet, 19 Units, N, $8.00 daily.

Pike, San Isabel National Forests

2840 Kachina Drive, Pueblo, 81008; (719) 553-1400

Leadville Ranger District

2015 North Poplar, Leadville, 80461; (719) 486-0749
Baby Doe, 9,900 feet, 50 Units, Y, $12.00 daily.
Belle of Colorado, 9,900 feet, 19 Units, N, $11.00 daily.
Dexter, 9,300 feet, 24 Units, N, $8.00 daily.
Elbert Creek, 10,000 feet, 17 Units, N, $8.00 daily.
Father Dyer, 9,900 feet, 25 Units, Y, $12.00 daily.
Halfmoon, 9,900 feet, 22 Units, N, $8.00 daily.
Lakeview, 9,500 feet, 59 Units, Y, $9.00 daily.
May Queen, 9,900 feet, 27 Units, N, $11.00 daily.
Molly Brown, 9,900 feet, 49 Units, Y, $12.00 daily.
Parry Peak, 9,500 feet, 26 Units, N, $9.00 daily.
Silver Dollar, 9,900 feet, 43 Units, Y, $12.00 daily.
Tabor, 9,900 feet, 44 Units, N, $10.00 daily.
Twin Peaks, 9,600 feet, 39 Units, N, $9.00 daily.
Whitestar, 9,300 feet, 68 Units, Y, $10.00 daily.
Lakeview Group, 9,500 feet, GROUP, Y.
Printer Boy, 9,900 feet, GROUP, Y.

Pikes Peak Ranger District

601 South Weber Street, Colorado Springs, 80903; (719) 636-1602
Colorado, 7,800 feet, 81 Units, Y, $12.00 daily.
Meadow Ridge, 9,200 feet, 19 Units, $10.00 daily.
Painted Rocks, 7,900 feet, 18 Units, Y, $10.00 daily.
South Meadows, 8,000 feet, 64 Units, Y, $12.00 daily.
Springdale, 9,100 feet, 14 Units, N, $9.00 daily.
The Crags, 10,100 feet, 17 Units, N, $9.00 daily.
Thunder Ridge, 9,200 feet, 21 Units, Y, $10.00 daily.
Trail Creek, 7,800 feet, 7 Units, N, FREE.
Wildhorn, 9,100 feet, 9 Units, N, $9.00 daily.
Wye, 10,300 feet, 21 Units, N, $9.00 daily.
Pike Community, 7,700 feet, GROUP (800) 416-6992
Red Rocks, 8,200 feet, GROUP, Y.

Salida Ranger District

325 West Rainbow Boulevard, Salida, 81201; (719) 539-3591

Angel of Shavano, 9,200 feet, 20 Units, N, $10.00 daily.

Bootleg, 8,400 feet, 6 Units, N, $2 daily.

Cascade, 9,000 feet, 23 Units, Y, $10.00 daily.

Chalk Lake, 8,700 feet, 21 Units, Y, $10.00 daily.

Coaldale, 8,500 feet, 11 Units, N, $6.00 daily.

Collegiate Peaks, 9,800 feet, 56 Units, Y, $10.00 daily.

Cottonwood Lake, 9,600 feet, 28 Units, N, $10.00 daily.

Garfield, 10,000 feet, 11 Units, N, $9.00 daily.

Hayden Creek, 8,000 feet, 11 Units, N, $8.00 daily.

Iron City, 9,900 feet, 15 Units, N, $9.00 daily.

Monarch Park, 10,500 feet, 38 Units, Y, $10.00 daily.

Mt. Princeton, 8,000 feet, 17 Units, Y, $10.00 daily.

North Fork Reservoir, 11,000 feet, 8 Units, N, $5.00 daily.

O'Haver Lake, 9,200 feet, 29 Units, Y, $10.00 daily.

Angel of Shavano, 9,200 feet, GROUP, Y.

San Carlos Ranger District

3170 East Main Street, Cañon City, 81212; (719) 269-8500

Alvarado, 9,000 feet, 47 Units, N, $9.00 daily.

Bear Lake, 10,500 feet, 14 Units, N, $9.00 daily.

Blue Lake, 10,500 feet, 15 Units, N, $9.00 daily.

Davenport, 8,500 feet, 12 Units, N, $9.00 daily.

Lake Creek, 8,200 feet, 12 Units, N, $9.00 daily.

Lake Isabel South Side, 8,800 feet, 8 Units, Y, $9.00 daily.

Lake Isabel La Vista, 8,600 feet, 29 Units, Y, $9.00/$14.00 daily.

Lake Isabel St. Charles, 8,800 feet, 15 Units, Y, $9.00 daily.

Oak Creek, 7,600 feet, 15 Units, N, FREE.

Ophir Creek, 8,900 feet, 31 Units, N, $9.00 daily.

Purgatoire, 9,800 feet, 23 Units, N, $9.00 daily.

Ponderosa, 8,800 feet, GROUP, Y.

Spruce, 8,800 feet, GROUP, Y.

South Park Ranger District

320 U.S. Highway 285, P.O. Box 219, Fairplay, 80440; (719) 836-2031; (+) = $3.00 Parking Fee

Aspen (+), 9,900 feet, 12 Units, N, $9.00 daily.

Blue Mountain, 8,200 feet, CLOSED.

Buffalo Springs, 9,000 feet, 17 Units, N, $9.00 daily.

Cove (+), 8,400 feet, 4 Units, N, $9.00 daily.

Fourmile, 10,800 feet, 14 Units, N, $9.00 daily.

Happy Meadows, 7,900 feet, 7 Units, N, $9.00 daily.

Horseshoe, 10,600 feet, 19 units, N, $9.00 daily.

Jefferson Creek (+), 10,100 feet, 17 Units, N, $9.00 daily.

Kite Lake (+), 12,000 feet, 7 Units, N, $5.00 daily.

Lodgepole (+), 9,900 feet, 35 units, N, $9.00 daily.

Lost Park, 10,000 feet, 13 Units, N, $7.00 daily.

Michigan Creek, 10,000 feet, 13 Units, N, $7.00 daily.

Riverside (+), 8,000 feet, 19 Units, N, $9.00 daily.

Round Mountain, 8,500 feet, 17 Units, N, $9.00 daily.

Selkirk, 10,500 feet, 15 Units, N, $7.00 daily.

Spillway (+), 8,500 feet, 24 Units, N, $9.00 daily.

Springer Gulch (+), 8,300 feet, 15 Units, N, $9.00 daily.

Spruce Grove, 8,600 feet, 26 Units, N, $9.00 daily.

Twin Eagles Trailhead, 8,550 feet, 9 Units, N, $5.00 daily.

Weston Pass, 10,200 feet, 14 Units, N, $9.00 daily.

South Platte Ranger District

19316 Goddard Ranch Court, Morrison, 80465; (303) 275-5610

Baldy, 7,800 feet, CLOSED.

Big Turkey, 8,00 feet, 10 Units, N, $9.00 daily.

Buffalo, 7,400 feet, 21 Units, Y, $10.00 daily.

Burning Bear, 9,500 feet, 13 Units, N, $10.00 daily.

Deer Creek, 9,000 feet, 13 Units, N, $10.00 daily.

Devils Head, 8,800 feet, 21 Units, N, $10.00 daily.

Flat Rocks, 8,200 feet, 19 Units, N, $10.00 daily.

Geneva Park, 9,800 feet, 26 Units, N, $10.00 daily.

Goose Creek, 8,100 feet, 10 Units, N, $10.00 daily.
Green Mountain, 7,600 feet, 6 Units, N, $10.00 daily.
Hall Valley, 9,900 feet, 9 Units, N, $10.00 daily.
Handcraft, 9,800 feet, 10 Units, N, $10.00 daily.
Indian Creek, 7,500 feet, 11 Units, N, $10.00 daily.
Jackson Creek, 8,100 feet, 9 Units, N, $10.00 daily.
Kelsey, 8,000 feet, 17 Units, Y, $10.00 daily.
Kenosha Pass, 10,000 feet, 25 Units, N, $10.00 daily.
Lone Rock, 6,400 feet, 19 Units, Y, $10.00 daily.
Meridian, 9,000 feet, 18 Units, N, $10.00 daily.
Molly Gulch, 7,500 feet, 15 Units, N, $10.00 daily.
Osprey, 8,000 feet, 10 Units, N, $10.00 daily.
Ouzel, 8,000 feet, 13 Units, N, $10.00 daily.
Platte River, 6,300 feet, 10 Units, N, $10.00 daily.
Tramway, 7,200 feet, CLOSED.
Whiteside, 8,900 feet, 5 Units, N, $10.00 daily.
Wigwam, 6,600 feet, 10 Units, N, $10.00 daily.
Meadows, 7,000 feet GROUP, Y.

Rio Grande National Forest
1803 West Highway 160, Monte Vista, 81144;
(719) 852-5941

Conejos Peak Ranger District
15571 County Road T.5, La Jara, 81140;
(719) 274-8971
Alamosa, 8,700 feet, 10 Units, N, FREE.
Aspen Glade, 8,500 feet, 34 Units, Y, $10.00 daily.
Conejos, 8,700 feet, 16 Units, N, $8.00 daily.
Elk Creek, 8,500 feet, 34 Units, Y, $10.00 daily.
Elk Creek Overflow, 8,500 feet, 10 Units, N, $5.00 daily.
Lake Fork, 9,500 feet, 18 Units, Y, $8.00 daily.
Mix Lake, 10,000 feet, 22 Units, N, $8.00 daily.
Mogote, 8,400 feet, 41 Units, Y, $10.00 daily.
Spectacle Lake, 8,700 feet, 24 Units, N, $8.00 daily.
Stunner, 9,700 feet, 10 Units, N, FREE.
Trujillo Meadows, 10,000 feet, CLOSED - Summer 1998.
Mogote Group, 8,400 feet, GROUP.

Divide Ranger District
Third and Creede Avenue, Creede, 81130;
(719) 658-2556
Bristol Head, 9,500 feet, 16 Units, N, $9.00 daily.
Marshall Park, 8,800 feet, 15 Units, Y, $10.00 daily.
North Clear Creek, 9,900 feet, 25 Units, N, $9.00 daily.
Palisade, 8,300 feet, 12 Units, N, $10.00 daily.
River Hill, 9,200 feet, 20 Units, Y, 410 daily.
Silver Thread, 9,500 feet, 11 Units, N, $9.00 daily.
Thirty Miles, 9,300 feet, 35 Units, Y, $10.00 daily.

Divide Ranger District
13308 West Highway, Del Norte, 81132;
(719) 657-3321
Big Meadows, 9,500 feet, 52 Units, Y, $11.00 daily.
Cathedral, 9,400 feet, 33 Units, N, FREE.
Comstock, 9,700 feet, 8 Units, N, FREE.
Cross Creek, 8,800 feet, 12 Units, N, $9.00 daily.
Highway Springs, 8,400 feet, 11 Units, N, $5.00 daily.
Lower Beaver Creek, 8,400 feet, 19 Units, N, $10.00 daily.
Park Creek, 8,500 feet, 16 Units, N, $10.00 daily.
Rock Creek, 9,200 feet, 23 Units, N, FREE.
Tucker Ponds, 9,600 feet, 16 Units, N, $8.00 daily.
Upper Beaver Creek, 8,500 feet, 15 Units, N, $10.00 daily.

Saguache Ranger District
46525 State Highway 114, Saguache, 81149;
(719) 655-2547
Buffalo Pass, 9,000 feet, 26 Units, N, $5.00 daily.
Luders, 9,900 feet, 6 Units, N, FREE.
North Crestone, 8,800 feet, 13 Units, N, $7.00 daily.
Poso, 9,100 feet, 11 Units, N, $5.00 daily.
Stone Cellar, 9,500 feet, 4 Units, N, FREE.
Stormking, 9,400 feet, 11 Units, N, $5.00 daily.

Medicine Bow–Routt National Forest
2468 Jackson Street, Laramie, WY 82070;
(970) 879-1870

Hahns Peak/Bears Ears Ranger District

925 Weiss Drive, Steamboat Springs, 80487; (970) 879-1870

Dry Lake, 8,000 feet, 8 Units, N, $10.00 daily.
Dumont Lake, 9,500 feet, 22 Units, N, $10.00 daily.
Freeman Reservoir, 8,800 feet, 17 Units, N, $8.00 daily.
Granite, 9,900 feet, 8 Units, N, $5.00 daily.
Hahns Peak Lake, 8,500 feet, 26 Units, Y, $10.00 daily.
Hinman Park, 7,600 feet, 13 Units, N, $10.00 daily.
Meadows, 9,300 feet, 30 units, N, $10.00 daily.
Sawmill Creek, 9,000 feet, 6 Units, N, $5.00 daily.
Seedhouse, 8,000 feet, CLOSED 1998.
Summit Lake, 10,300 feet, 16 Units, N, $10.00 daily.
Walton Creek, 9,400 feet, 16 Units, N, $10.00 daily.

The Parks Ranger District

100 Main Street, P.O. Box 158, Walden, 80480; (970) 723-8204

Aspen, 8,900 feet, 7 Units, N, $10.00 daily.
Big Creek Lakes, 9,000 feet, 54 Units, Y, $10.00 daily.
Grizzly Creek, 8,500 feet, 12 Units, N, $10.00 daily.
Hidden Lakes, 8,900 feet, 9 Units, N, $10.00 daily.
Pines, 9,200 feet, 11 Units, N, $10.00 daily.
Teal Lake, 9,000 feet, 17 Units, N, $10.00 daily.

Yampa Ranger District

300 Roselawn Avenue, P.O. Box 7, Yampa, 80483; (970) 638-4516

Bear Lake, 9,600 feet, 29 Units, N, $10.00 daily.
Bear River Dispersed, 9,800 feet, 32 Units, N, $3 daily.
Blacktail Creek, 9,100 feet, 8 Units, N, $10.00 daily.
Chapman Reservoir, 9,400 feet, 12 Units, N, $5.00 daily.
Cold Springs, 10,400 feet, 5 Units, N, $10.00 daily.
Gore Pass, 9,500 feet, 12 Units, N, $10.00 daily.

Horseshoe, 10,000 feet, 7 Units, N, $10.00 daily.
Lynx Pass, 8,900 feet, 11 Units, N, $10.00 daily.
Sheriff's Reservoir, 9,800 feet, 5 Units, N, $5.00 daily.
Vaughn Lake, 9,500 feet, 6 Units, N, $7.00 daily.

San Juan National Forest

15 Burnett Court; Durango, 81301; (970) 247-4874

Columbine Ranger District

367 South Pearl Street, Bayfield, 81122; (970) 884-2512

Florida, 8,500 feet, 20 Units, N, $10.00 daily.
Graham Creek, 7,900 feet, 25 Units, N, $10.00 daily.
Middle Mountain, 7,900 feet, 24 Units, N, $10.00 daily.
Miller Creek, 8,000 feet, 12 Units, N, $10.00 daily.
North Canyon, 7,900 feet, 21 Units, N, $10.00 daily.
Old Timers, 7,900 feet, 10 Units, N, $10.00 daily.
Pine Point, 7,900 feet, 30 Units, N, $10.00 daily.
Pine River, 8,100 feet, 6 Units, N, $6.00 daily.
Transfer Park, 8,600 feet, 25 Units, N, $10.00 daily.
Florida Group, 8,500 feet, GROUP, Y.

Columbine West Ranger District

110 West Eleventh, Durango, 81301; (970) 884-2512

Haviland Lake, 8,000 feet, CLOSED - Summer 1998.
Junction Creek, 7,500 feet, 34 Units, N, $10.00 daily.
Kroeger, 9,000 feet, 11 Units, N, $8.00 daily.
Purgatory, 8,800 feet, 14 Units, N, $8.00 daily.
Sig Creek, 9,000 feet, 9 Units, N, $8.00 daily.
Snowslide, 13 Units, N, $8.00 daily.
South Mineral, 10,000 feet, 26 Units, N, $10.00 daily.
Chris Park, 8,000 feet, GROUP, Y.

Mancos–Dolores Ranger District

100 North Sixth, P.O. Box 210, Dolores, 81323; (970) 882-7296

Burro Bridge, 9,000 feet, 15 Units, N, $10.00 daily.

Cabin Canyon, 6,500 feet, 11 Units, N, $8.00 daily.

Cayton, 9,400 feet, 27 Units, N, $10.00 daily.

Ferris Canyon, 6,500 feet, 6 Units, N, $8.00 daily.

House Creek, 6,900 feet, 72 Units, Y, $12.00 daily.

Mavreeso, 7,600 feet, 14 Units, N, $10.00 daily.

McPhee, 7,100 feet, 73 Units, Y, $12.00 daily.

Target Tree, 7,800 feet, 25 Units, N, $10.00 daily.

Transfer, 8,500 feet, 12 Units, N, $10.00 daily.

West Dolores, 7,800 feet, 13 Units, N, $10.00 daily.

House Creek Group, 6,900 feet, GROUP, Y.

McPhee Group, 7,100 feet, GROUP, Y.

Pagosa Ranger District

180 Second Street, P.O. Box 310, Pagosa Springs, 81147; (970) 264-2268

Blanco River, 7,200 feet, 6 Units, N, $8.00 daily.

Bridge, 7,800 feet, 19 Units, N, $8.00 daily.

Cimarrona, 8,400 feet, 21 Units, N, $8.00 daily.

East Fork, 7,600 feet, 26 Units, N, $8.00 daily.

Lower Piedra, 7,200 feet, 17 Units, N, $6.00 daily.

Teal, 8,300 feet, 16 Units, N, $9.00 daily.

West Fork, 8,000 feet, 28 Units, N, $8.00 daily.

Williams Creek, 8,300 feet, 67 Units, N, $9.00 daily.

Wolf Creek, 8,000 feet, 26 Units, N, $8.00 daily.

Ute, 7,200 feet, 24 Units, N, $8.00 daily.

White River National Forest

900 Grand Avenue, P.O. Box 948, Glenwood Springs, 81602; (970) 945-2521

Aspen Ranger District

806 West Hallam, Aspen, 81611; (970) 925-3445

Difficult, 8,200 feet, 47 Units, Y, $12.00 daily.

Lincoln Gulch, 9,600 feet, 7 Units, N, $9.00 daily.

Lost Man, 10,700 feet, 10 Units, N, $9.00 daily.

Portal, 10,500 feet, 7 Units, N, $7.00 daily.

Silver Bar, 8,460 feet, 4 Units, Y, $12.00 daily.

Silver Bell, 8,490 feet, 5 Units, Y, $12.00 daily.

Silver Queen, 8,680 feet, 6 Units, Y, $12.00 daily.

Weller, 9,400 feet, 11 Units, N, $9.00 daily.

Difficult Group, 8,200 feet, GROUP, Y.

Blanco Ranger District

317 Market Street, Meeker, 81641; (970) 878-4039

East Marvine, 8,500 feet, 7 Units, N, $10.00 daily.

Himes Peak, 9,000 feet, 11 Units, N, $10.00 daily.

Marvine, 8,500 feet, 18 Units, N, $10.00 daily.

North Fork, 8,000 feet, 40 Units, Y, $11.00 daily.

South Fork, 8,000 feet, 16 Units, N, $10.00 daily.

Trappers Lake Bucks, 9,900 feet, 10 Units, N, $11.00 daily.

Trappers Lake Cutthroat, 9,900 feet, 14 Units, N, $11.00 daily.

Trappers Lake Shepherds Rim, 9,900 feet, 20 Units, N, $11.00 daily.

Trappers Lake Trapline, 9,900 feet, 13 Units, N, $11.00 daily.

North Fork Group, 8,000 feet, GROUP, Y.

Dillon Ranger District

680 River Parkway, P.O. Box 620, Silverthorne, 80498; (970) 468-5400

Blue River, 8,400 feet, 24 Units, N, $9.00 daily.

Cataract Creek, 8,600 feet, 4 Units, N, $4.00 daily.

Davis Springs, 8,000 feet, 7 Units, N, FREE.

Eliot Creek, 8,000 feet, 64 Units, N, FREE.

Heaton Bay, 9,100 feet, 72 Units, Y, $11.00 daily.

Lowry, 9,300 feet, 29 Units, Y, $10.00 daily.

McDonald Flats, 8,000 feet, 13 Units, N, $7.00 daily.

Peak One, 9,100 feet, 79 Units, Y, $11.00 daily.

Pine Cove, 9,100 feet, 55 Units, N, $8.00 daily.

Prairie Point, 8,000 feet, 44 Units, N, $7.00 daily.

Prospector, 9,100 feet, 108 Units, Y, $10.00 daily.

Willows, 7,950 feet, 35 Units, N, FREE.

Windy Point, 9,100 feet, GROUP, Y.

Eagle Ranger District

125 West Fifth Street, P.O. Box 720, Eagle, 81631; (970) 328-6388

Coffee Pot Spring, 10,160 feet, 15 Units, N, $6.00 daily.

Deep Lake, 10,460 feet, 45 Units, N, $6.00 daily.
Fulford Cave, 7,000 feet, 7 Units, N, $8.00 daily.
Klines Folly, 10,750 feet, 4 Units, N, $6.00 daily.
Supply Basin, 10,750 feet, 6 Units, N, $6.00 daily.
Sweetwater Lake, 7,700 feet, 10 Units, N, $8.00 daily.
White Owl, 9,500 feet, 5 Units, N, FREE.
Yeomen Park, 9,000 feet, 24 Units, N, $8.00 daily.

Holy Cross Ranger District
24747 U.S. Highway 24, P.O. Box 190, Minturn, 81645; (970) 827-5715
Blodgett, 8,900 feet, 6 Units, N, $8.00 daily.
Camp Hale Memorial, 9,200 feet, 21 Units, Y, $9.00 daily.
Gold Park, 9,300 feet, 14 Units, N, $8.00 daily.
Gore Creek, 8,700 feet, 24 Units, N, $10.00 daily.
Hornsilver, 8,800 feet, 12 Units, N, $8.00 daily.
Tigiwon, 9,900 feet, 9 Units, N, $6.00 daily.
Tigiwon Community House, 9,900 feet, GROUP, Y.

Rifle Ranger District
0094 County Road 244, Rifle, 81650; (970) 625-2371

Meadow Lake, 9,600 feet, 10 Units, N, $9.00 daily.
Three Forks, 7,600 feet, 4 Units, N, $10.00 daily.

Sopris Ranger District
620 Main Street, P.O. Box 309, Carbondale, 81623; (970) 963-2266
Avalanche, 7,400 feet, 13 Units, N, $10.00 daily.
Bogan Flats, 7,600 feet, 37 Units, Y, $11.00 daily.
Chapman, 8,800 feet, 84 Units, Y, $11.00 daily.
Dearhamer, 7,800 feet, 13 Units, N, $11.00 daily.
Elk Wallow, 8,800 feet, 7 Units, N, FREE.
Little Mattie, 7,800 feet, 20 Units, N, $10.00 daily.
Little Maud, 7,800 feet, 22 Units, N, FREE.
Mollie B, 7,800 feet, 26 Units, Y, $12.00 daily.
Redstone, 7,200 feet, 20 Units, Y, $15.00/$17.00/$22.00 daily.
Ruedi Marina, 7,800 feet, 5 Units, N, $8.00 daily.
Bogan Flats Group, 7,600 feet, GROUP, Y.
Chapman Group, 8,800 feet, GROUP, Y.

Further Reading

Boody, Carol. *A Mountain Bike Guide for Cañon City, Colorado.*

Bridges, Lee. *Mountain Biking Moab.* 2nd ed. Guilford, Conn.: The Globe Pequot Press, 2003.

Colorado Trail Foundation. *The Colorado Trail: The Official Guidebook.* Golden, Colo.: Colorado Mountain Club Press, 2002.

Feitz, Leland. *A Quick History of Creede: Colorado Boomtown.* Colorado Springs: Little London Press, 1969.

About the Author

Stephen Hlawaty lives with his family in Livermore, Colorado, where he enjoys year-round outdoor bliss: from skiing Cameron Pass in the winter, to mountain biking and camping in Roosevelt National Forest in the spring and summer, to chopping wood alongside his home in the fall. When not offering his blood, sweat, and tears in these outdoor pursuits, he can often be found on his back porch pickin' and slidin' on his Regal Reso.